FORENSICS III

Books by Harry A. Milman, PhD
A Death at Camp David
Soyuz: The Final Flight
Forensics: The Science Behind the Deaths of Famous People
*Forensics II: The Science Behind the Deaths
of Famous and Infamous People*

FORENSICS III

They Got Fifteen Minutes of
Fame from the Way They Died

HARRY A. MILMAN, PHD

Copyright © 2024 by Harry A. Milman, PhD.

Library of Congress Control Number:		2020919977
ISBN:	Hardcover	979-8-3694-1955-7
	Softcover	979-8-3694-1954-0
	eBook	979-8-3694-1953-3

All rights reserved. No part of this book may be reproduced or transmitted in any form or by any means, electronic or mechanical, including photocopying, recording, or by any information storage and retrieval system, without permission in writing from the copyright owner.

Any people depicted in stock imagery provided by Getty Images are models, and such images are being used for illustrative purposes only.
Certain stock imagery © Getty Images.

Print information available on the last page.

Rev. date: 04/11/2024

To order additional copies of this book, contact:
Xlibris
844-714-8691
www.Xlibris.com
Orders@Xlibris.com

857954

CONTENTS

Introduction vii

Chapter 1   Marilyn Sheppard 1
Homicide due to Blunt Force Trauma

Chapter 2   Joseph Zarelli 19
Homicide due to Blunt Force Trauma

Chapter 3   Azaria Chamberlain 27
Accident due to a Dingo

Chapter 4   Sherri Rasmussen 44
Homicide by Gunshot

Chapter 5   Ron Goldman and Nicole Brown Simpson 58
Homicide by Stabbing

Chapter 6   Admiral Mike Boorda 81
Suicide by Gunshot

Chapter 7   Kathleen Savio 98
Homicide by Drowning

Chapter 8   Carlos Sousa 107
Blunt Force Trauma due to a Mauling by a Tiger

Chapter 9   Eve Carson 117
Homicide by Gunshot

Chapter 10   Sahel Kazemi and Steve McNair 127
Murder-Suicide by Gunshot

Chapter 11   Carol Daniels 143
Homicide by Stabbing

Chapter 12   Jayne and Corinne Peters 150
Filicide-Suicide by Gunshot

Chapter 13   Antonio Pettigrew 166
Suicide by a Drug Overdose

Chapter 14	Adrienne Martin	174
	Accident due to a Drug Overdose	
Chapter 15	Michael Faherty	186
	Spontaneous Human Combustion	
Chapter 16	Ellen Greenberg	194
	Undetermined due to Self-Stabbing	
Chapter 17	Russell Armstrong	206
	Suicide by Hanging	
Chapter 18	Katherine Morris	216
	Undetermined due to Carbon Monoxide Poisoning	
Chapter 19	Elisa Lam	231
	Accident due to Drowning	
Chapter 20	Marco McMillian	242
	Homicide by Asphyxiation	
Chapter 21	George Floyd	255
	Homicide due to Police Brutality	
Chapter 22	Thomas Mansfield	274
	Accident due to Caffeine Intoxication	
Chapter 23	Lori McClintock	281
	Accident due to Dietary Supplements	
Chapter 24	Mary Jane Thomas	290
	Accident due to Cosmetic Surgery	
Chapter 25	Angela Craig	298
	Suspected Homicide by Cyanide Poisoning	
Chapter 26	Conclusions	310

Notes 317

INTRODUCTION

THE DICTIONARY DEFINES fame as "a widespread reputation, especially of a favorable character." Edward D. Ramirez and Stephen J. Hagen expanded on the definition, claiming, "Fame is an individual's degree of renown or a state of being well-known.... In contrast, celebrity is the close media attention that is provided to the most famous individuals."[1] While fame and celebrity correlate, they are not the same.

When a person is afforded fame while still alive, it usually accrues because of a special talent or a recognized and appreciated significant accomplishment. For example, during his lifetime, Leonardo da Vinci gained fame in the arts when he painted the *Mona Lisa* and *The Last Supper*. Bill Russell of the Boston Celtics and Wilt Chamberlain of the Philadelphia Warriors achieved fame in sports due to their talent on the basketball court. Andrew Carnegie and John D. Rockefeller earned fame in business through their financial acumen. Walter Lippmann and Walter Cronkite became famous in media through their journalistic talents. Bill Gates and Steve Jobs became very well known for inventing computers and computer software. And Mohandas Gandhi and Franklin Delano Roosevelt earned worldwide attention for their political astuteness.

Often, fame is bestowed for noteworthy achievements long after the recipient has already died. Fame evaded the Dutch postimpressionist painter Vincent van Gogh during his lifetime; he sold just one of his paintings despite producing more than nine hundred. Nonetheless, van Gogh became famous many years after his death. Similarly, Johannes Vermeer, the Dutch baroque-period painter of *Girl with a Pearl Earring,* died leaving his family in debt and only earned fame centuries later. Herman Melville, the author of the classic novel *Moby Dick,* barely sold copies of his book while alive, yet became famous after he died. Gregor Mendel was largely dismissed by scientists while living, but today is revered as the "father of modern genetics." Galileo Galilei spent most of his final decade under house arrest, but in modern times, he is referred to as the "father of modern physics."

One of the most iconic achievers whose fame was realized only after death was Anne Frank, a fifteen-year-old German girl who died in 1945 in the Bergen-Belsen concentration camp. Frank's diary, chronicling her time in hiding between 1942 and 1944 before being captured along with her family and sent to Auschwitz, became one of the most famous nonfiction books of all time.

Occasionally, fame is achieved unexpectedly, for once-in-a-lifetime event. On January 15, 2009, pilot Chesley "Sully" Sullenberger landed American Airlines flight 1549 in the Hudson River in New York after his plane lost power when it was struck by a flock of birds shortly after takeoff from LaGuardia airport. Sullenberger had been a professional pilot for nearly thirty years, but it was this singular event that catapulted him to fame, resulting in a published memoir, numerous media interviews, and a feature film directed by Clint Eastwood and starring Tom Hanks as Sullenberger.

When all else fails, fame is sometimes obtained through inherited wealth, a title of nobility, or by marrying someone who is already famous. Paris Hilton is one such example.

Today, fame is more toxic than ever. So why do people, especially young people, pursue fame? "It's a distinct type, people who expect to get meaning out of fame, who believe the only way to have their lives make sense is to be famous," said Tim Kasser, a psychologist at Knox College in Illinois.[2] "We all need to make meaning out of our lives, and this is one way people attempt to do it."

John Maltby of the University of Leicester in the United Kingdom investigated the fame-seeking phenomenon by comparing six distinct dimensions of fame interest—perceived suitability, intensity, celebrity lifestyle, vulnerability, altruism, and drive—with five personality traits: narcissism, self-esteem, curiosity, attachment style, and perceived family, peer, and media influence.[3] Maltby found that interest in fame can be categorized into four distinct groups. When interest in fame is (1) typified by a perceived suitability and intensity for a celebrity lifestyle, it is associated with perceived family, peer, and media influence; (2) due to a vulnerability, it is a reflection of neuroticism, low self-esteem, and problematic attachments; (3) for altruistic reasons, it is associated with agreeableness; and (4) a result of an overall drive, it is associated with conscientiousness.

Legend has it that Andy Warhol, a leading figure in the pop art movement of the 1960s whose work explored the relationship between artistic expression, advertising, and celebrity culture, once said, "In the future, everyone will be world famous for fifteen minutes."[4] There is some disagreement whether Warhol actually said these exact words; however, the implication is clear. In the current age of reality TV, YouTube, and the internet, where talent or a significant accomplishment is no longer required to obtain fame, a person can become famous simply for being famous; just ask Kim Kardashian. Said Kaysar Ridha of Irvine California, a former fan of the reality TV show *Big Brother*, "To be noticed, to be wanted, to be loved, to walk into a place and have others care about what you're doing, even what you had for lunch that day, that's what people want. It's strange and twisted because when that attention does come, the irony is, you want more privacy."

In this book, I describe how twenty-eight "ordinary" people achieved at least fifteen minutes of fame, sometimes longer, not for their talents, accomplishments, or life experiences, but for the way they died. Deaths were due to blunt force trauma, a dingo at Ayers Rock in Australia, police brutality, multiple self-stabbings, drowning, spontaneous human combustion in Ireland, carbon monoxide poisoning, mauling by a tiger, hanging, dietary supplements, cosmetic surgery, caffeine intoxication, murder-suicide, and filicide-suicide (the killing of a child by a parent), among others.

In determining cause of death, I followed the guidelines published in the *Physicians' Handbook on Medical Certification of Death* by the US Centers for Disease Control and Prevention (CDC), which state, "The reported underlying cause of death ... [is] defined as (a) the disease or injury that initiated the train of morbid events leading directly to death, or (b) the circumstances of the accident or violence that produced the fatal injury."[5] Manner of death was categorized either as natural, accident, homicide, suicide, or undetermined. Information on the history of forensics and the use of forensic toxicology in crime investigation can be found in my first book in this series, *Forensics: The Science Behind the Deaths of Famous People*.[6]

Forensics III: They Got Fifteen Minutes of Fame from the Way They Died reads like a mystery novel, presenting biographical and scientific information that helps readers understand how medical examiners and coroners utilized forensic analysis to determine the causes and manners of death of twenty-eight "not-so-famous" people.

CHAPTER 1
Marilyn Sheppard
Died July 4, 1954
Homicide due to Blunt Force Trauma

IN 1954, THE Fourth of July, a day that commemorates the establishment of the United States of America, fell on a Sunday. On the previous night, Marilyn and her husband, Dr. Sam Sheppard, a thirty-year-old osteopathic physician, invited neighbors Don and Nancy Ahern and their two children for a casual dinner and to watch a movie at their two-story Dutch colonial lakeshore home in Bay Village, an affluent suburb of Cleveland, Ohio.[1] Needless to say, *Strange Holiday*, a 1945 low-budget film starring Claude Rains about a man who returned from a fishing vacation only to find America controlled by fascists, was an unusual selection for the night before America celebrated its day of independence.

When he finished eating dinner, Don took his two children home, put them to bed, and then drove back to join the others in the Sheppards' living room while Chip, the Sheppards' seven-year-old son, went to sleep in his upstairs bedroom, adjacent to his parents' master bedroom.

As can sometimes happen when watching a film on television, Sheppard became drowsy, so he lay down on the living room sofa and soon fell asleep.[2] Shortly after midnight, when the movie was finally over, the Aherns went home, and Marilyn went upstairs to her second-floor bedroom. What happened next remains a mystery.

As he later recounted, Sheppard was awakened by Marilyn screaming "Sam, Sam."[3] Immediately, he rushed up the stairs

1

and in the dim light, he saw a bushy-haired, dark-complexioned figure about six feet three wearing a light-colored shirt standing next to Marilyn's twin bed. Sheppard claimed that on entering the bedroom, he was hit on the back of the head, rendering him unconscious. Once he regained his senses, however, he checked Marilyn for a pulse, but he couldn't find one. Stunned and dazed, he checked on his son, Chip, and found him sound asleep.

Sheppard said that he next heard a noise downstairs and that he ran back down to the first floor of the house. As he reached the landing, he saw a figure running out the back door toward Lake Erie.[4] After catching up with the unidentified person, the two wrestled on the beach. "[I] had a feeling of twisting or choking," Sheppard said, before losing consciousness for a second time.

According to Sheppard, he revived at approximately five-thirty in the morning. Lying face down on the beach, his feet were in the water and the waves were breaking over him. Wet and missing his T-shirt and watch, he staggered back inside the house and went upstairs to again check on Marilyn. Still unable to find a pulse, he covered her lower body with a sheet and went back down to his first-floor office to call his friend, Spencer Houk. "My God, Spence, get over here quick. I think they killed Marilyn," Sheppard told Houk.

Patrolman Fred Drenkhan of the Bay Village Police Department arrived at the Sheppard residence at approximately six o'clock that morning. In an upstairs bedroom, he found Marilyn lying on her back on the four-poster bed, her face turned toward the door. Her white, short-sleeve pajama top was pulled all the way up, exposing her breasts; one of her legs was outside her pajama bottoms. Both of Marilyn's legs were bent at the knees and hanging over the lower end of the bed, underneath the wooden crossbar.

Deeply cut into Marilyn's face and scalp were twenty-seven curved gashes, the blood staining the blanket and pillow; dozens of blood spots were on the walls and the closet door. Under the body, in the area where the small of the back rested, were two broken tooth facings that came from Marilyn's mouth.[5]

Marilyn was pronounced deceased at 8:00 a.m. She was thirty-one years old.

The Autopsy[6]

The autopsy was conducted by Samuel R. Gerber, coroner of Cuyahoga County, at 12:30 p.m. on July 4. It began with the external examination.

"The body is that of a well-developed and well-nourished white female who appears to be the stated age of thirty years," Gerber wrote in the autopsy report. The body weighed 125 pounds and measured sixty-seven inches in length.

The hair on the scalp was brown and normally distributed. The eyes were hazel with swelling; dark purple-brown discoloration was present on both upper and lower eyelids. The pupils were round, regular and equal. The ears, nose, and mouth were unremarkable; the teeth were natural and in good condition, with the exception of a chip defect of the upper left medial incisor and a complete fracture of the upper left and right medial incisors. The lips and nail beds showed pale cyanosis, a bluish discoloration of the skin resulting from inadequate oxygenation of blood. The abdomen revealed a well-healed scar, measuring five inches in length, most likely due to a caesarian delivery.

When pressure was applied on the breasts, a clear watery fluid exuded from the nipples.

Numerous injuries, mostly to the head and face, included multiple abrasions (scrapes), contusions (bruises), lacerations (deep cuts), and a partial avulsion (tearing away) of the fingernail of the left fourth finger. Comminuted fractures (in at least two places) were apparent in the frontal bone, as well as a fracture of the nasal bone.

An abundant amount of dried blood covered the entire face, neck, upper chest, and hand; bloody crusts were present in the nostrils and mouth.

For the internal examination, the body was opened with the usual Y-shaped incision. All the body cavities were smooth and glistening; none contained an excessive amount of fluid.

The cardiovascular system was unremarkable, with the heart surfaces smooth and glistening and the heart weight of 225 grams in the normal range. The heart valves and leaflets were thin and delicate; the major cardiac vessels had no atheromatous changes due to a buildup of plaque.

The right and left lung weights of 550 and 470 grams, respectively, were in the normal range. When under pressure, a moderate amount of bloody, frothy fluid exuded from the lungs, an indication that Marilyn was alive through part of the horrific attack and that she had aspirated blood. The trachea and major bronchi contained a large quantity of blood-stained mucoid froth, consistent with congestion and edema (fluid).

The thyroid had a uniform reddish-brown color throughout and contained a two-centimeter benign nodule described as a follicular adenoma. The adrenals were within normal limits; the pituitary gland was unremarkable.

As for the gastrointestinal tract, the stomach had a half ounce of orange-brown mucoid fluid. The small intestine had yellowish brown chyme (digested food), and the colon had a green-brown stool. The appendix was absent as it had been surgically removed. The liver was smooth and glistening, its weight of 1,480 grams in the normal range; the pancreas was without abnormalities; and the spleen was soft, its weight in the normal range.

The right and left kidney weights of 135 and 130 grams, respectively, were within normal limits; the urinary bladder was empty.

The uterus was enlarged and showed evidence of a pregnancy. Within the amniotic sac was a male fetus measuring fourteen centimeters from crown to rump. The placenta had no gross abnormalities. The cervix was within normal limits, the vagina contained a moderate amount of creamy white exudate, and the ovaries had no gross abnormalities.

None of the lymph nodes was significantly enlarged. The abdominal aorta had minimal atheromatous changes.

Extensive hemorrhaging was seen throughout the scalp when the scalp was incised (cut) from ear to ear and the flaps relocated. The calvarium, the convexity of the skull that encases the brain, revealed severe comminution and splintering of the entire frontal bone, with complete separation of the coronal suture, a dense and fibrous association of connection tissue located in between the frontal and parietal bones of the skull. The brain had a substantial amount of bloody fluid, as well as contusions, splintering, and fragmentation of the cranium and roofs of both orbits.

Aside from the blunt force injuries Marilyn sustained from a severe and horrific beating, the autopsy failed to reveal any other anatomical abnormalities that might have contributed to her death.

Cause and Manner of Death

The time of death was estimated at between three and five o'clock on the morning of July 4, 1954.

Toxicology testing failed to detect barbiturates (sedatives) and alcohol in the blood; similar testing was not done with urine since the urinary bladder was empty.[7]

After reviewing the circumstances surrounding the death, the autopsy and toxicology reports, as well as several lay articles and numerous court documents, I concluded that Marilyn died from multiple impacts to the head and face resulting in comminuted fractures of the skull, separation of the frontal suture, substantial subdural hemorrhaging, and contusions of the brain. The manner of death was homicide.

Life and Career

Marilyn was born in Cleveland, Ohio. When she was a small child, her mother died, and she was raised by her father.[8]

Marilyn met Sheppard at Roosevelt Junior High School; she was in the ninth grade and he in the eighth. Their friendship blossomed when they attended Cleveland Heights High School.

In high school, Sheppard had exceptional grades and he was class president for three years. In his senior year, he was voted "most likely to succeed" and was the school's "Outstanding Athlete of the Year" for his performance in football, basketball, and track.[9] Upon his graduation, Sheppard decided to attend Hanover College in Indiana despite having been offered several athletic scholarships by small Ohio colleges. He subsequently enrolled at the Osteopathic School of Physicians in Los Angeles, California, and completed his internship and residency in neurosurgery at Los Angeles County General Hospital.

Marilyn graduated from high school a year before Sheppard and enrolled at Skidmore College in Saratoga Springs, New York. She followed Sheppard to California after her college graduation.

Marilyn and Sheppard were married at the First Hollywood Methodist Church in Hollywood, California, on February 21, 1945. A few years later, they returned to Cleveland, settling in the upscale community of Bay Village where Sheppard joined the staff of Bay View Hospital, which was founded by his father and two brothers, all physicians. Marilyn taught Bible classes at the Methodist Church.

In 1947, Marilyn gave birth to their first and only child.

Conclusions

When Patrolman Drenkhan arrived at the Sheppard home, he found Sheppard shirtless, sitting in a large red leather chair in the living room, his brown slacks stained with blood on both knees. Complaining of severe pain at the back of his neck, Sheppard's right cheek was discolored and swollen near the corner of his mouth and there was swelling near his right eye.[10]

On the pillow, at the head of Marilyn's twin bed, Drenkhan saw a large spot of blood; an even larger spot was under Marilyn's head.[11] Several blood spots were also present on the bedroom walls, the curtains, the closet doors, and the entrance to the bedroom.

A search of the Sheppard residence revealed a woman's yellow gold watch with a yellow gold stretch band lying on the floor of Sheppard's office, in front of a desk whose drawers were pulled out. On the floor outside the office was an overturned doctor's bag full of surgical instruments; in the living room, three drawers were pulled out from a desk. After examining the "disarray," detectives of the Cleveland Police Department (CPD) concluded that the Sheppard home had been staged to look as if a burglary had taken place.

Sheppard's brother, Dr. Stephen Sheppard, came at about 6:15 a.m. and transported Sheppard to Bay View Hospital where he was treated with sedatives and held for further observation. Charles Elkins, Sheppard's attending physician, later told investigators that Sheppard's neck injury caused him to lose sensation in his left arm and that there was some damage to his teeth.

Drenkhan found no footprints or evidence of a struggle outside of the Sheppard home. A search of the dense underbrush uncovered a green felt bag containing Sheppard's self-winding gold watch with water inside and blood stains on the band, as well as a college fraternity ring and a key chain with a football, keys, knife, and a gold metal tag. When he returned to the house, Drenkhan noticed several water blotches on one of the steps, more toward the porch, and a small pool of water on the threshold between the porch and the living room.

Police found no evidence of forced entry. In addition, the murder weapon and the T-shirt that Sheppard had worn when he fell asleep on the living room couch were nowhere to be found.[12]

On July 8, Sheppard was interviewed by police as he lay in his hospital bed, wearing a neck brace. He told the detectives that he saw a figure whose upper body was white, standing by Marilyn's bed, but that the person he chased to the beach was much bigger and wore dark clothing, thereby suggesting that there were two people involved in his wife's death. When the detectives examined the clothing that Sheppard had worn when he was admitted to the hospital, they found it wet, as were Sheppard's white sweat socks and brown leather loafers.

Almost from the start, the Sheppard murder investigation made headline news. Leading the media charge was the *Cleveland Press*. In a July 9 editorial, the newspaper criticized the pace of the investigation, claiming, "For whatever reason, the investigative authorities were slow in getting started, fumbling when they did, awkward in breaking through the protective barriers of the [Sheppard] family, and far less aggressive than they should have been." Due, in part, to the pressure exerted by the headline printed in bold, capital letters: "WHY NO INQUEST? DO IT NOW, DR. GERBER" that appeared in the July 21 morning edition of the newspaper, Gerber decided to hold an inquest, an infrequently used procedure in the United States, to obtain additional information. "Well, it is evident the doctor did this, so let's go get the confession out of him," Gerber told his colleagues.

The inquest began on July 22 and lasted for three days. It was held in the Normandy School gym in Bay Village, which was packed with several hundred spectators and included seventeen witnesses.[13] A long table was strategically placed at the front of the room to accommodate broadcasting equipment, reporters, and television and radio commentators who transmitted the spectacle live.

Sheppard testified for over five hours without the benefit of his attorney, William J. Corrigan. When Gerber asked Sheppard whether he had an affair with Susan Hayes, a laboratory technician at Bay View Hospital where he worked, Sheppard denied the affair, saying that they were just "good friends." It was a lie that would turn around to bite him at the later trial.

At the conclusion of the inquest, Gerber proclaimed that it was "impossible to believe the explanation in regard to the death of Marilyn Sheppard as told by her husband, Dr. Samuel H. Sheppard." Gerber further declared that "the injuries that caused

[Marilyn's] death were inflicted by her husband, Dr. Samuel H. Sheppard, and that death in this case was homicidal in nature."

The front-page editorial of the July 30 edition of the *Cleveland Press* asked, "Why isn't Sam Sheppard in jail?" As if on cue, Sheppard was arrested at ten o'clock that night and charged with murder in the first degree; he was released on bail seventeen days later.

A grand jury met on August 16; the following day, it returned with a first-degree murder indictment, at which time Sheppard was rearrested. "I am not guilty of the murder of my wife, Marilyn," Sheppard wrote in an op-ed two days after his second arrest. "How could I, who have been trained to help people and devoted my life to saving life, commit such a terrible and revolting crime?"

The Sheppard trial began on October 18, two weeks before an election in which the trial judge, Edward Blythin, was up for reelection, and the chief prosecutor, John J. Mahon, was a candidate for judgeship. Seated at a long table at the front of the courtroom were approximately twenty journalists. Television and radio commentators, as well as reporters from out-of-town newspapers and magazines, were provided additional seating near the jury box and the defense table. Media interest was so intense that three Cleveland newspapers published the names and addresses of prospective jurors even before the trial began. "The fact that at this stage, it is equally possible for the rational mind to find him innocent or guilty is what may make the Sheppard trial a celebrated cause to rank with ... the classic puzzle of Lizzie Borden," wrote Dorothy Kilgallen, a syndicated columnist and popular panelist of the television show *What's My Line?*

In his opening statement, Mahon told the jury, "This defendant and Marilyn were quarreling about the activities of Dr. Sam Sheppard with other women" and that was "the reason she was killed." Corrigan, Sheppard's defense attorney, responded by saying that Sheppard and Marilyn had just "enjoyed the best four months of their marriage," referring to Marilyn's pregnancy.

The prosecution's witnesses included Lester Adelson, a physician, who declared that Marilyn died because she had been bludgeoned to death, since "hemorrhages found in her brain could not otherwise have developed." Patrolman Drenkhan reported that he found no signs of a struggle inside the home or any indication of forced entry, and Gerber, who testified about a blood stain on Marilyn's pillow, said, "In this bloodstain, I could make out the impression of a surgical instrument," thereby suggesting that Sheppard, who was a neurosurgeon, was implicated in his wife's murder.

Celebrity journalists who had flocked to the Sheppard trial on the promise that there would be mystery and intrigue were now anxiously waiting to hear about the salacious nature of the case. They were richly rewarded on December 1 when Hayes, an attractive twenty-four-year old who until then, had only been referred to as "Miss X," was led to the witness box. After preliminary questioning by Assistant Prosecutor Tom Parrino, Hayes was asked about a night in March when Sheppard took her to a party at the home of Dr. Arthur Miller.

"And where did you remain that night?" Parrino asked.

"At the Millers'," as did Sheppard, Hayes replied.

Parrino pressed on. "Did you occupy the same bed?"

"Yes," Hayes responded.

Hayes admitted that she and Sheppard had sexual relations for the first time in December 1952, and that they continued their sexual liaisons for approximately two years.[14] It was damning testimony that highlighted Sheppard's lie and provided a motive for the murder.

Corrigan had his work cut out for him. He aimed to convince the jury that Sheppard's neck injury was so severe that it couldn't possibly have been self-inflicted. Toward that goal, Dr. Steven Sheppard testified that on the morning of July 4, Sheppard exhibited muscle spasms and involuntary movements whenever his neck was touched. Elkins, Sheppard's attending physician, noted that the neck spasms couldn't possibly be faked. Radiologist Gervase Flick proclaimed that an X-ray revealed that Sheppard had a probable fracture of the second cervical vertebra.

It was now up to Sheppard to gain the jury's sympathy. Working against him was his lie about his sexual relations with Hayes and his tendency to be vague and arrogant. Wearing a blue suit, a white shirt, and a knitted tie, Sheppard took the stand on December 9. It was the first of three days of testimony in which he described in somewhat unusual terms the events leading up to Marilyn's death, claiming that he was "stimulated" to run upstairs when Marilyn called out his name. He had "visualized" a "form," instead of "saw an intruder," and had a "vague sensation" of being in the water while at the beach. His testimony was not well received by the jurors.

On December 21, a verdict was reached in the Sheppard trial—guilty of murder in the second degree. In sentencing Sheppard to life in a maximum-security prison, Blythin left open the possibility for parole after ten years. Nonetheless, despite the verdict, Sheppard continued to insist that he was innocent.

The American poet Carl Sandberg once said, "If the facts are against you, argue the law. If the law is against you, argue the facts. If the law and the facts are against you, pound the table and yell like hell." Bearing that in mind, Corrigan filed a motion for a new trial based on the court's failure to shield the jurors from prejudicial pretrial publicity, denial of a change of venue, the presence of the press in the courtroom, replacement of a juror, errors in jury instructions, and denial of a motion for continuance. His motion was denied on January 3, 1955. Corrigan next filed a motion for a new trial based on newly discovered evidence provided by Paul Kirk, a professor of criminalistics and a well-regarded forensic expert. On May 9, Blythin overruled this motion as well. A subsequent appeal to the Ohio Eighth District Court of Appeals did not fare any better.

In July 1961, Corrigan suffered a stroke and died. In his place, Sheppard retained F. Lee Bailey, an up-and-coming defense attorney. Bailey filed a federal habeas corpus petition on April 11, 1963, in the U.S. District Court for the Southern District of Ohio, alleging that Sheppard's fundamental rights had been denied due to various conflicts and prejudicial publicity. In granting the petition on July 15, 1964, Chief Judge Carl A. Weinman called the 1954 trial a "mockery of justice" that violated Sheppard's Fourteenth Amendment rights to due process. The state of Ohio appealed Weinman's ruling to the Sixth Circuit Court of Appeals; it sided with Ohio and reinstated Sheppard's conviction on March 4, 1965. Undeterred, Bailey took the case to the U.S. Supreme Court.

On June 6, 1966, in an eight to one decision, the U.S. Supreme Court concluded that Sheppard had not received a fair trial by an impartial jury consistent with the Due Process Clause of the Fourteenth Amendment. Specifically, the court noted that Sheppard had not been granted a change of venue to a locale far from where the publicity originated; the jurors had been subjected to newspaper, radio, and television coverage of the trial throughout the proceedings, and the jury had not been sequestered. The court also said that Sheppard had been deprived of "judicial serenity and calm to which [he] was entitled" and had been subjected to "bedlam" in the courtroom due to the presence of news reporters and radio and television commentators. In reversing the previous judgment against Sheppard and ordering the murder verdict invalid, the U.S. Supreme Court concluded, "The state trial judge did not fulfill his duty to protect Sheppard from the inherently prejudicial publicity which saturated the community and to control disruptive influences in the courtroom." Days later, the Cuyahoga County prosecutor's office decided to retry the case.

The second Sheppard trial began on October 24. It was presided over by Judge Francis Talt. Talt made sure to avoid the carnival atmosphere of the first trial. Rather than emphasizing the sexual nature of the case, prosecutor Leo Spellacy decided to focus on the blood spots on the watch belonging to Sheppard that was found inside the green felt bag.

One of the early prosecution witnesses was Mary Cowan, a medical technologist at the Cuyahoga County Coroner's office. Cowan testified that a couple of blood spots on the rim of Sheppard's watch were small "blood spatter" stains caused by "flying drops of blood" coming off the murder weapon. The spatter couldn't have been on Sheppard's watch, Cowan claimed, unless Sheppard was the murderer.[15] Bailey countered by bringing in his own forensics expert, Paul Kirk. "For the most part, [the blood on the watch] looks like contact transfer," Kirk told the jury.[16] As for the blood spots on the rim of the watch, "it appears that it is not a symmetrical tail on the blood spot, and flying blood invariably leaves a totally symmetrical tail ... leaving the issue [of blood spatter] somewhat in doubt," Kirk said.

Based on injuries to Marilyn's teeth, Kirk claimed that Marilyn bit her assailant on the hand, leaving him with a significant injury, which accounted for the blood stain on the closet door; Sheppard had no such bite wounds or other bleeding injuries. In addition, because of differences in agglutination times (the "jelling" of blood), Kirk concluded that the blood stain on the closet door was neither Marilyn's nor Sheppard's. In disputing Kirk's opinion, Roger W. Marsters, the prosecution's bloodstain expert, testified that postulating the presence of different qualities of type O blood characteristics to prove the existence of a third person in the murder room was scientifically unjustified.[17]

Kirk further stated that due to the size of the blood spatter and the direction and distance it traveled, the murder weapon was a cylindrical object, such as a flashlight. Moreover, "it was definitely swung with the left hand." Sheppard was right-handed.

Other experts testifying at the trial included Dr. Richard Koch and an osteopathic physician. Both showed that Sheppard's fracture of his vertebra and the bruise on his spinal cord, as well as his two broken teeth, could not have been self-inflicted.[18]

At the first trial, Gerber had testified that the impression on Marilyn's pillow looked like it was made by a surgical instrument. Bailey got him to admit that he had never seen a surgical instrument in any hospital or medical supply catalog that resembled the bloody impression on the pillow. Moreover, Gerber told the jury that despite having looked "all over the United States," he never found such an instrument.[19]

Since Sheppard's demeanor and style had failed to make a positive impression on the jury in the first trial, Bailey took a calculated risk and did not have Sheppard testify in the second trial. It was a wise decision. On November 16, 1966, after deliberating most of the day, the jury found Sheppard not guilty of murdering Marilyn.

Sheppard continued to maintain his innocence until he died on April 6, 1970 from liver failure and Wernicke encephalopathy, a neurological disorder caused by the lack of vitamin B1, often due to alcoholism. He was forty-six years old and had been known to drink as much as two fifths of liquor every day. Nonetheless, there are at least four troubling aspects of the case that potentially implicate Sheppard in his wife's murder. These include the missing T-shirt Sheppard had worn the night Marilyn died, which may have had blood stains; the lack of forced entry to the Sheppard residence the night of the murder; the signs of a staged robbery; and the missing murder weapon, possibly a flashlight.

Police theorized that Sheppard washed his T-shirt in the lake behind his house and then tossed the T-shirt away. By coincidence, a torn T-shirt without blood stains was found a few yards from Sheppard's house; it matched Sheppard's size.[20] In another apparent coincidence, a person swimming in Lake Erie in July 1955 found a dented flashlight in the lake near the Sheppard home. Since I don't believe in coincidences, especially when they occur twice, the finding of a T-shirt and possibly the murder weapon in the vicinity of the Sheppard residence is at the least, very suspicious.

With respect to the lack of forced entry and the staging of a robbery, a report prepared by a scientific investigation unit detailed finding a damaged basement doorway, thereby suggesting that an intruder may have entered the Sheppard home through the cellar.[21] As for the staging of a robbery, it has never been established when the drawers were pulled out of the various cabinets in the Sheppard home—the night of the murder or sometime earlier.

Nearly sixty years after Sheppard was acquitted of murdering his wife, people still wonder whether justice had been served. Several questions remain, the most important of which is if Sheppard didn't kill Marilyn, then who did? Many believe that the more likely suspect is Richard Eberling, a twenty-five-year-old window washer who was arrested for larceny in November 1959. When police searched Eberling's house, they discovered a cocktail ring belonging to Marilyn; however, Eberling claimed that he stole the ring from the home of Sheppard's brother, Dr. Steven Sheppard, three years after Marilyn had already been murdered.[22] When asked why his blood was found throughout the Sheppard home, a question that was only a ploy, Eberling said that he cut his hand while removing storm windows two days before Marilyn died.

In 1989, Eberling was convicted of murdering Ethel May Durkin, an elderly widow. Nine years later, he died in prison without ever confessing to killing Marilyn Sheppard. And yet, despite his criminal record of burglary and murder, there are reasons to eliminate Eberling as a suspect in Marilyn's murder. To begin with, only Marilyn's blood, type O, was recovered from blood stains in the Sheppard home; Eberling's blood was type A, and results of his DNA tests were inconclusive. Furthermore, Eberling passed a lie detector test that showed "no deception" when he was asked whether he killed Marilyn Sheppard; however, other polygraph experts later claimed that the results were "inconclusive." Finally, Eberling was bald, "not bushy-haired," and there is some indication he may have been right-handed.

In the annals of true crime, the Marilyn Sheppard case has received much more than fifteen minutes of fame. The case was instrumental in setting a precedent for future criminal cases in the United States regarding media involvement in the judicial system. With its ruling, the U.S. Supreme Court recognized the need to balance the rights of freedom of the press under the First Amendment and the Sixth Amendment guarantee of a fair trial. In addition, several books have been written about Marilyn's murder, including *The Sheppard Murder Case* by *Chicago Tribune* reporter Paul Holmes that was on the bestseller list for fourteen weeks; *The Defense Never Rests* by F. Lee Bailey, approximately forty pages of which are devoted to the second Sheppard trial; *Dr. Sam:*

An American Tragedy by Jack Harrison Pollack, an absorbing, tragic biography of Sam Sheppard; *Mockery of Justice* by Sam (Chip) Reese Sheppard and Cynthia L. Cooper, a comprehensive reinvestigation of the case from the point of view of the Sheppard family; and *The Wrong Man* by James Neff, a book many claim is the best one written on the Sheppard murder case.

Perhaps one of the more interesting fame-producing aspects of the Marilyn Sheppard murder was its inspiration for the popular television series *The Fugitive*, which was broadcast from 1963 to 1967; the show was also made into a movie starring Harrison Ford. The plot revolved around Dr. Richard Kimble who was wrongfully convicted of his wife's murder. In the show, Kimble escaped during a train derailment and spent the next four years trying to find the real killer—the "one-armed man"—while avoiding capture by Lieutenant Gerard, who aimed to bring Kimble back to prison. In the last episode, the one-armed man fell to his death from the top of a carnival ride, and Kimble walked out of court, a free man.

Officially, the murder of Marilyn Sheppard remains unsolved; however, many would disagree that is really the case. To date, no one other than Sheppard has been charged with Marilyn's murder.

CHAPTER 2
Joseph Zarelli
Died February 1957
Homicide due to Blunt Force Trauma

IN THE EVENING of February 23, 1957, a college student at La Salle University in Philadelphia, Pennsylvania, parked his car off the 700 block of Susquehanna Road near Pennypack Park, and walked across an overgrown, wooded lot for what he later claimed was to check on muskrat traps. Actually, it was to peep through the windows of female residents at the nearby Good Shepherd Home, a Catholic residence for wayward girls.[1]

Walking across the field in the drizzling rain, the young man came across a cardboard box. When he looked inside, he saw that it contained the body of a small boy.[2] Terrified, he ran back to his car. The next day, he confessed his finding to his priest, who urged him to call police.[3]

When Police Officer Elmer Palmer arrived at the vacant lot, he found the large cardboard carton laying on its side; inside was the naked body of a small boy wrapped in a flannel blanket.[4] Said Palmer, "It's something you don't forget."[5]

A search of the field where the body was found yielded a man's cap made of royal blue corduroy. It had a leather strap and a buckle on the back.

The age of the unidentified boy, forever known as the "Boy in the Box," was estimated at approximately four to six years; he was believed to have been dead for a few days.

The Autopsy

The autopsy and toxicology reports were not available for review; however, according to published lay articles, the autopsy was performed by Philadelphia's chief medical examiner, Joseph Spelman.

The external examination revealed a body that was malnourished, weighing only thirty pounds and measuring forty-one inches in length. The scalp was covered by badly cut light-blond hair, short in some areas and shaved close to the scalp in others. The eyes were blue, and the left eye fluoresced to a bright shade of blue when it was exposed to ultraviolet light. The fingernails were trimmed, and the right palm and soles of both feet were rough and wrinkled. There were no noticeable vaccination marks.

Fresh bruises were evident on the face and trunk. Older marks included an L-shaped scar on the chin; a one-inch surgical scar on the left side of the chest; a round, irregular scar on the left elbow; a well-healed scar on the groin, probably from a hernia operation; and a scar on the left ankle that may have been caused by an incision to expose a vein for a blood transfusion.

Based on the autopsy findings, including round-shaped bruises on the forehead and bleeding inside the skull, Spelman concluded that the boy had been severely beaten.

Cause and Manner of Death

Spelman determined that the cause of death was blunt force trauma to the head, probably inflicted with a dull instrument.[6] The manner of death was homicide.

After I reviewed the available records and published lay articles, I had no reason to dispute Spelman's conclusions.

Life Experiences

In the hope that someone might recognize and identify the dead boy, detectives circulated more than hundred thousand flyers with the child's photograph throughout eastern Pennsylvania and southern New Jersey. In addition, the Philadelphia Gas Works mailed two hundred thousand flyers to its customers, and more than three hundred thousand flyers were distributed by the Philadelphia Electric Company, various grocery stores, insurance companies, and a pharmacy association. And yet, despite all these efforts, as well as several published articles written about the case and visits to orphanages, child-care institutions, local doctors, and hospitals, no one came forward to claim or identify the body of the young boy.

Investigators determined that the cardboard box that held the boy's body had originally contained a bassinet sold at JCPenney, a large department store in Upper Darby, Pennsylvania, between December 3, 1956 and February 16, 1957. Police hoped that learning who had purchased the bassinet might lead them to the identity of the dead child; however, the store where the bassinet had been purchased had failed to keep records of individual sales. In addition, Federal Bureau of Investigation technicians were unable to recover usable fingerprints from the cardboard box.

The blanket with which the body had been wrapped was traced to a manufacturer in Swannanoa, North Carolina, and Granby, Quebec. It, too, was of no help in the police investigation since it was one of thousands of identical blankets that had been produced by this manufacturer.

The last piece of evidence police investigated was the blue cap found in the field where the boy's body was discovered; a label inside the cap led investigators to the Robbins Eagle Hat

& Cap Company in Philadelphia. According to the company's proprietor, Hannah Robbins, the cap had been one of twelve caps manufactured prior to May 1956; it had been purchased by a blond man in his late twenties, but Robbins could not provide the man's name or address.

Further investigation into the identity of the "Boy in the Box" languished until 1998, when DNA technology became available. On November 4 of that year, the dead boy's body was exhumed, and DNA was extracted from the teeth; regrettably, the sample did not provide a satisfactory DNA profile.[7] A second exhumation was performed in April 2019, at which time the femur was removed and a sample sent to the International Commission on Missing Persons in The Hague.[8] Upon receipt of the femur sample, Colleen M. Fitzpatrick of Identifinders International attempted to generate a DNA profile using a standard whole genome sequencing technique, but her efforts failed, in part because she was unable to extract enough DNA from the sample.

Not ready to give up, Fitzpatrick sent a sample of the femur to a laboratory that specialized in "ancient DNA," such as the type taken from mummies. After considerable effort, sufficient DNA was extracted in 2021 from this second femur sample to satisfactorily create a DNA profile of the dead child. As important and as necessary a first step as this was in the identification of the dead boy, it was just the beginning of a long and arduous process. There still was the mind-numbing and meticulous "forensic genetic genealogy" to be done, sometimes referred to as "investigative genetic genealogy."

"It's been very personal to me," said Misty Gillis, an investigator at Identifinders International who compared the DNA profile of the unidentified boy with millions of samples held in the company's databases. "I wanted to have his story told. I wanted to have it out in the world to do him justice," Fitzpatrick explained. "We didn't really have a lot of close matches, [like] a brother or a sister or an aunt or an uncle;" the initial hits were distant cousins. Nonetheless, using these third and fourth cousins on the maternal side, Gillis was able to build a genetic tree that helped her identify the boy's birth mother.

After obtaining a copy of the dead child's birth certificate, the "Boy in the Box" was finally identified in October 2021, but his name and that of his parents could not be publicly revealed until they were verified. "You really want to come out and say this fantastic thing we've done, and we can't, and that was very difficult," Fitzpatrick said.

In a press conference on December 8, 2022, Philadelphia Police Commissioner Danielle Outlaw finally announced that the name of the unidentified body was Joseph Zarelli.[9] "This child's story was always remembered by the community," Outlaw said. "His story was never forgotten."

Intensive genealogical research discovered that Zarelli was born out of wedlock on January 13, 1953.[10] His mother, Betsy Abel, was twenty-one years old when she gave birth; she died in 2014. The boy's father, Gus Zarelli, died in 1991. Some of Zarelli's several siblings were still living when Outlaw made the announcement.

"It's going to be an uphill battle for us to definitively determine who caused this child's death," said Captain Jason Smith, commanding officer of Philadelphia's homicide unit. "We may not make an arrest. We may never make an identification. But we're going to do our darndest to try."

Conclusions

The public's strong interest in learning about their genetic makeup and the relationship of their DNA to possible birth defects and disease has resulted in a treasure trove of human genetic information that is stored in private DNA databases. The presence of these DNA profiles, in turn, has also led people to explore their genetic connection to far-removed ancestors.[11] In 2014, *Time* magazine reported that after gardening, genealogy was the second most popular hobby in the world.[12]

There are three types of genealogical methodologies: (1) forensic non-DNA genealogical methods used in historical investigations to identify living descendants of fallen soldiers and in estate and probate cases to identify heirs; (2) familial DNA searching to obtain partial matches between forensic offender profiles in a criminal DNA database and unidentified forensic profiles; and (3) genealogical research that uses historical and other records to build family trees in order to verify identities and kinship. In 2018, a new and novel subdiscipline of forensic science called "forensic genetic genealogy" or "investigative genetic genealogy" was introduced that combined forensic genetics, genetic genealogy, and genealogical research.

Forensic (investigative) genetic genealogy investigations search DNA databases that are different from those searched for traditional DNA profiling, analyze different DNA markers, utilize different technology, and generate different data. Quickly seizing on this new forensic tool, law enforcement began using it to assist in crime investigations and in the identification of human remains.

Since 1994, the US Department of Justice (DOJ) has maintained a nationwide forensic DNA database known as the Combined DNA Index System (CODIS); the database contains forensic

DNA profiles of over 18.4 million people who have been arrested or convicted for various crimes. However, law enforcement has been unable to tap into private forensic DNA databases, such as GEDmatch, FamilyTreeDNA, and DNASolves, until 2013. It was then that the U.S. Supreme Court ruled that collection of DNA by police is "like fingerprinting and photographing, a legitimate police booking procedure that is reasonable under the Fourth Amendment." With the court's judicial ruling, law enforcement can now search not only CODIS, but private forensic DNA databases as long as it can be demonstrated that the data are relevant to a police investigation.[13] Using genetic genealogy and genealogical research methods based on information obtained from CODIS and from private DNA databases, investigators are now better able to construct family trees with the specific goal of identifying potential candidates for an unidentified DNA profile, thereby helping to solve crimes.

The science of investigative genetic genealogy got a significant boost on April 24, 2018, when Joseph DeAngelo, the "Golden State Killer," was arrested.[14] A former police officer, a serial killer of twelve individuals, and a rapist of more than fifty women, DeAngelo terrorized California from 1974 to 1986.[15] Police apprehended DeAngelo after matching DNA at a crime scene with DNA of one of his distant relatives who had contributed DNA data to the private DNA database GEDmatch.

By some estimates, more than five hundred cases have been solved using forensic genetic genealogy.[16] Among these are the identifications in 1981 of Louis Gattaino of Omaha, Nebraska, after he had been missing for ten years; Carl "Charles" Webb in 2022, the so-called "Somerton man," named after the beach in Adelaide, South Australia, where his body was found in December 1948 dressed in a jacket and tie and with a partly smoked cigarette resting on his collar; Jewell Langford in 2023, nearly fifty years after her body was discovered floating in the Nation River in Ontario, Canada; Gardner Smith in 2023, one of the nation's fastest ski racers whose remains were found in June 1970 on Independence Pass in Colorado; and Oliver Mundy in July 2023, whose remains were found in February 1988 in an elevator shaft in an abandoned building in Charlotte, North Carolina.[17]

As law enforcement began searching DNA databases, privacy concerns quickly became apparent.[18] In 2019, the DOJ issued an *Interim Policy for Forensic Genetic Genealogical DNA Analysis and Searching* to ensure that law enforcement personnel did not exceed their authority or infringe on constitutional rights when conducting forensic genetic genealogy searches.[19] GEDmatch and FamilyTreeDNA have similarly modified their policies by having consumers provide their consent before sharing their data with law enforcement.

An ongoing problem that is of great importance to genetic genealogists is finding the right balance between the interest of law enforcement in finding criminals and the people's interest for genetic testing, said Natalie Ram, a law professor at the University of Baltimore in Maryland. Nevertheless, forensic genetic genealogy has taken law enforcement a major step forward in the identification of previously unidentified remains and murder suspects.

CHAPTER 3

Azaria Chamberlain
Died August 17, 1980
Accident due to a Dingo

IN 1606, THE Dutch explorer Willem Janszoon landed on the western side of Cape York Peninsula in the far north area of the country that British navigator and cartographer Matthew Flinders later named Australia; James Cook surveyed the east coast in 1770. By the time Europeans arrived in Australia, aborigines had already been on the remote island over fifty thousand years.

Uluru, known as "Ayers Rock," a massive red sandstone monolith located 450 kilometers from Alice Springs in the heart of Australia's Northern Territory, has been around for at least 550 million years. Indigenous Australians consider Uluru sacred because they believe it to be a resting place for ancient spirits.

In August 1980, Lindy and Michael Chamberlain decided to take their family on a camping vacation in an area close to Ayers Rock.[1] It was a decision that would forever change their lives.

Lindy and Michael, their sons Aidan and Reagan, six and four years old, respectively, and their nine-week-old daughter, Azaria, arrived at the Uluru campsite late on Saturday evening, August 16, just three days after leaving their home in Mount Isa in Queensland, Australia.[2] Pitching a tent in the top camping area on the east side of Ayers Rock, close to an aborigine camp, a general store, and a clinic, the Chamberlains soon went to sleep, but the next morning, at around ten o'clock, Michael took his two sons climbing while Lindy, with Azaria in her arms, explored an area known as "Fertility Cave."[3] Lurking nearby, eyeing Lindy and Azaria, was a wild dingo, a protected animal that is only found in Australia. They resemble dogs but have a wider head, a longer snout, and measure four feet long and weigh about forty pounds. "Look what's watching us," Lindy exclaimed upon seeing the dingo.

Sometime after sunset, the Chamberlains joined five families at a communal barbecue area.[4] Later in the evening, Lindy, Aiden, and Azaria left the group to put Azaria to sleep. After Lindy placed the infant in a bassinet in the rear of their tent, next to Reagan who was already asleep in his sleeping bag, Aidan mentioned that he was still hungry, so Lindy went to their car to get a can of baked beans.[5] When she returned, she fetched Aidan and they both walked back to the barbecue area, the can of beans securely in her hand; they had been away from the barbecue area for approximately five to ten minutes.

At around eight o'clock, Lindy and Sally Lowe, one of the women at the barbecue, heard a baby's cry that originated from the Chamberlain tent.[6] Immediately, Lindy ran to the tent where she found Azaria missing and a dingo exiting the tent. "My God, my God, the dingo's got my baby!" Lindy cried out with horror.

When police arrived, about three hundred volunteers, including Lindy's husband, Michael, and aborigine trackers, helped to look for Azaria. Inside the Chamberlain tent, police found blood on various articles; it was later determined to have been Azaria's blood.

On August 24, Azaria's torn and bloodied jumpsuit and ripped diaper were discovered among the boulders at the base of Ayers Rock, near a dingo's lair, but the infant's matinee jacket remained missing.[7]

Azaria's body has never been found.

The Autopsy

Without Azaria's body, an autopsy and toxicology testing could not be conducted. According to coroner John Lowndes, "the absence of a body and the consequential absence of a postmortem examination and the results thereof, mean that potentially vital evidence as to the cause and manner of death is not available to the coroner."[8]

Cause and Manner of Death

Constable Frank Morris, the first police investigator to arrive on the scene, shined his flashlight inside the Chamberlain tent and noticed a few spots of blood on a couple of blankets and a sleeping bag. A second investigator, Michael Gilroy, believing the Chamberlain's story that a dingo had taken their baby, reminded Morris and John Lincoln, the third investigator on the scene, that there had been eighteen to twenty-five dingoes known to visit the camping area in the recent past and that several dingo attacks had occurred against children, although none had been fatal.

Unlike Gilroy, Lincoln thought that the Chamberlains were lying. "Not a chance. [It] never happened before. There's a fact you can't beat. [It] never, ever happened," Lincoln said, claiming it would have been impossible for a dingo to carry a ten-pound baby in its mouth more than one hundred yards.[9]

An inquest was held in Alice Springs, Australia, on December 15 to determine the cause and manner of Azaria's disappearance and presumed death; it was presided over by magistrate and coroner Denis Barritt. At the inquest, Les Harris, an expert on dingo behavior, testified that "A [baby] weighing ten pounds ... would offer no hindrance [to a dingo], and it can be reasonably presumed that it could be carried over a long distance with ease."[10] Harris further noted that while difficult, it would not have been impossible for a dingo to remove the baby's clothing. "The manipulative skills and the cognitive abilities of dingoes [are] extremely high. If the baby was taken by a dingo, it is improbable that any trace would be found more than thirty minutes later," Harris said.

Approximately two months after the inquest began, Barritt issued his decision—Azaria "met her death when attacked by a wild dingo while [she was] asleep in her family's tent." Neither of her parents was "in any degree whatsoever responsible for her death." Detective Sergeant Graeme Charlwood, who had taken over the investigation, wasn't so sure.

Sometime after the inquest had ended and Barritt had issued his opinion, James Cameron, a British forensic expert and professor of Medicine at the University of London, claimed that he failed to find evidence on Azaria's clothing that a dingo had been involved in the infant's disappearance. Prompted, in part, by Cameron's conclusion, officers of the Northern Territory police searched the Chamberlain home in Cooranbong, New South Wales, on September 19, 1981. Besides seizing over three hundred assorted items, including infant's clothing and scissors, the officers confiscated the 1977 yellow Holden Torana hatchback automobile the Chamberlains had driven on their vacation to Ayers Rock.

Based on evidence gathered during the search, the Supreme Court of the Northern Territory ordered a second inquest into Azaria's disappearance on December 14; it was presided over by Coroner Gerry P. Galvin. "The first inquest was about dingoes," said Malcolm Brown, a reporter for the *Sydney Morning Herald*. "This one is about blood."

At the second inquest, forensic biologist Joy Kuhl testified that she found blood containing fetal hemoglobin, a substance only present in the blood of infants less than six months old, beneath the passenger's side dashboard of the Chamberlain's Torana, as well as on the door and the front seat, thereby suggesting that Azaria had been killed inside the vehicle.[11] Kuhl further claimed that scissors found in the vehicle were smeared with baby's blood. Cameron noted that tears in Azaria's jumpsuit were "consistent with [being cut] with scissors," potentially giving Kuhl's suggestion that Azaria had been stabbed with scissors some validity. Evidence was also presented that soil found on Azaria's clothing suggested that the infant's body had been buried.

Persuaded by the testimony of the two experts, Galvin announced his decision on February 2, 1982. "The evidence is, to a large degree, circumstantial ... [and] is consistent with an attempt to simulate a dingo attack on a child by person or persons who recovered the buried body, removed the clothing, damaged it by cutting, rubbed it in vegetation, and deposited the clothes for later recovery.... There is no evidence to positively support the involvement of a dingo.... In my view, having considered all the evidence, a jury properly instructed could reach a verdict," Galvin proclaimed.[12]

Lindy and Michael Chamberlain went on trial for the murder of Azaria on September 13, 1982. In his opening statement, prosecuting attorney Ian Barker told the jury that Azaria "died very quickly because somebody had cut her throat." Barker further claimed that Lindy's story of a dingo running off with her baby was "a fanciful lie, calculated to conceal the truth."

Since there was no evidence that Azaria's disappearance and probable death had been caused by a stranger, the minor Chamberlain children, or by anyone else at the Ayers Rock campsite, Barker told the jury that there were only two ways it could have happened—either the Chamberlains' story of a dingo snatching their baby was true or that Lindy had murdered her daughter in the family's automobile. Favoring the murder scenario, Barker weaved a highly speculative and, in my opinion, implausible tale that during the approximately five to ten minutes that she had been away from the barbecue area, Lindy stabbed Azaria in the throat with the scissors in the front seat of the family's car, held her daughter until she died, and then hid the infant's body in the family's camera bag. Barker further claimed that as Lindy walked back to the Chamberlain's tent, she inadvertently transferred Azaria's blood on her person to the tent and that she later buried Azaria's body in a sand dune.

Less than seven weeks after the Chamberlain trial began, and despite the lack of a body, a motive, and eyewitness accounts to the alleged crime, the jury reached a verdict—Lindy, guilty of murder, and Michael, guilty of being an accessory after the fact. "It came down to whether you believed it was a dingo or not," one juror said.

Lindy was sentenced to life in prison, but in suspending Michael's eighteen-month sentence, Justice James Muirhead explained, "I consider it not only appropriate, but in the interest of justice to do so." The case was appealed to the Federal Court and then to Australia's High Court, but both courts upheld the conviction.

In an unexpected turn of events, thirty-one-year-old British tourist David Brett fell off Ayers Rock during an evening climb in January 1986. Eight days later, police discovered his body in an area with many dingo lairs; located nearby was Azaria's missing white matinee jacket.

The finding of Azaria's jacket confirmed that Lindy had been telling the truth when she said that a dingo had taken her daughter. Wrongly incarcerated for more than three years, she was released from Berrimah prison, a maximum-security prison located in Darwin, Northern Territory, Australia, on February 7, 1986.

A Royal Commission of Inquiry into the Chamberlain Convictions was held in May 1986 to examine what led to the unjust conviction of the Chamberlains. A year later, Justice Trevor Morling issued a 379-page report in which he concluded, "I am far from being persuaded that Mrs. Chamberlain's account of having seen a dingo near the tent was false ... If the evidence before the Commission had been given at the trial, the trial judge would have been obliged to direct the jury to acquit the Chamberlains."

All convictions against the Chamberlains were unanimously quashed by the Northern Territory Court of Criminal Appeals on September 15, 1988.

On November 29, 1995, a third inquest was held to correct the official record regarding the cause of Azaria's death. Surprisingly, after reviewing all the evidence in the case, Coroner Lowndes announced, "I was unable to be reasonably satisfied ... that Azaria died at the hands of Alice Lynne Chamberlain or alternatively that Azaria died accidentally as a result of being taken by a dingo." He labeled the cause of death an "open verdict," equivalent in the United States to "undetermined."

The Chamberlains were not satisfied with Lowndes's conclusion because it left the possibility that they were responsible for Azaria's death. What they wanted was a definitive declaration of their innocence. They finally got what they wanted in 2012, thirty-two years after the first inquest was held, during which Barritt had concluded that they had nothing to do with Azaria's disappearance and death.

At the end of yet a fourth inquest, Coroner Elizabeth Morris declared once and for all, "The evidence is sufficiently adequate, clear, cogent, and exact and ... excludes all other reasonable possibilities" other than that a dingo had entered the Chamberlain tent on August 17, 1980, and had carried and dragged Azaria as she lay in her bassinet. "No longer will Australia be able to say that dingoes are not dangerous and will only attack if provoked. We live in a beautiful country, but it is dangerous," Lindy said outside of the courtroom.[13] Michael agreed. "It has taken too long [but] I'm here to tell you, you can get justice even when you think all is lost."

After reviewing the circumstances surrounding the death, as well as several published lay articles and court documents, I concluded that Azaria's death was the result of a dingo attack. The manner of death was accidental.

Life Experiences

Azaria was born at 1:16 p.m. on June 11, 1980, in Mount Isa, Queensland, Australia, the third of four children of Lindy and Michael Chamberlain. Weighing six pounds, five and a half ounces, she was a healthy baby with dark, violet eyes, black hair, and olive skin. Azaria's parents were both born in New Zealand; Lindy in Whakatane and Michael in Christchurch.[14]

Lindy was almost two years old when her family moved from New Zealand to Victoria, Australia, where she was raised and educated. Unlike Lindy, Michael was educated in New Zealand, attending Lincoln and Christchurch Boys' High Schools and the University of Canterbury.[15]

After converting to the Seventh-Day Adventist Church in 1965, the same year that Lindy attended college in Benalla, a small city located northeast of Victoria, Michael migrated to Australia where he enrolled at Avondale College in Cooranbong, part of the Seventh-Day Adventist education system.[16]

Michael and Lindy met in Australia in 1968; a year later, Michael graduated with a Bachelor of Arts in Theology. The two got married and moved to Tasmania, where Michael was a pastor at several different churches.

In 1973, Lindy received her certificate in dressmaking, tailoring, and drafting from Launceston Technical College and began working as a seamstress, specializing in wedding dresses. Four years later, the Chamberlains moved to Queensland, eventually settling in Mount Isa where Azaria was born.

In August 1980, the Chamberlain family, which by now included two sons and a daughter, decided to go on a camping vacation at the foot of Ayers Rock. "I wanted to go to Darwin to catch barramundi (Asian sea bass)," Michael said, "but Lindy had been to Uluru before, at the age of sixteen, and she wanted to go again. We [only] meant to spend three days there [and] then go to Darwin." They arrived at their campsite on August 16; the following night, Azaria went missing.

Conclusions

The trial of Lindy and Michael Chamberlain is a prime example of how preconceived ideas, flawed forensic evidence, unreliable expert opinions, a lack of sufficient resources for a vigorous defense, and the court of public opinion can affect the court of law.

I have little doubt that the media played a large role in bringing the Chamberlain case to trial. Newspaper and magazine editors and television producers saw the disappearance of Azaria not only as a huge story, but as a sensational one. Articles were written suggesting that Azaria's death was a religious sacrifice to atone for sins of the Seventh-Day Adventist Church, inevitably turning public opinion against the Chamberlains. "Everyone in Australia judged this woman before she ever got a trial," said Ita Buttrose, a reporter.[17] And when Lindy failed to display sufficient emotion at her interviews for what was deemed appropriate for a grieving parent, it only fueled speculation that she had killed her daughter.

As for the police, it appears the investigators were under the false impression that dingoes never attacked or harmed humans; they remained closed to the possibility that a dingo had, in fact, taken Azaria.

The unique and unprecedented nature of the baby's disappearance and her presumed death made it more likely that the Chamberlain story would not be believed. Morling, the presiding justice at the royal commission, recognized that misconceptions were a major detriment to the defense and warned that "guilt or innocence ... is not to be determined on the basis of preconceptions as to the likelihood of unusual animal behavior."[18]

In my opinion, the judgment of Charlwood, the lead investigator in the case, was clouded by the dubious suggestion proposed by investigator Gilroy that the Chamberlains practiced witchcraft. Noting that Azaria had been dressed completely in black at one of her medical appointments, Gilroy hinted that the Chamberlains dabbled in sorcery because the name Azaria meant "Sacrifice in the Wilderness." When Lindy responded, "I wouldn't want to do it. God slew Saul for that. Do you know Saul and the Witch of Endor?" to Charlwood's suggestion that she be hypnotized, it only seemed to support Gilroy's suspicion.

Pressured by the court of public opinion, and despite Barritt's decision at the end of the first inquest that the Chamberlains had nothing to do with Azaria's disappearance and death, overzealous prosecutors moved forward with a second inquest and a subsequent trial. It was a travesty of justice for which Lindy and Michael Chamberlain paid dearly.

In retrospect, the prosecution's case had several weaknesses, one of which was its desperate and unsubstantiated theory that

Lindy murdered Azaria in the Torana automobile during the approximately five to ten minutes that she was away from the barbecue area. Nearly all the forensic experts who testified at the royal commission of inquiry that followed the trial noted that the bloodstains on Azaria's jumpsuit were caused by venous blood from severed jugular veins in the infant's neck. Unlike arterial blood, venous blood flows slowly, so it would have taken Azaria up to twenty minutes to die, leaving Lindy little time, if any, to clean up the blood in the vehicle, hide Azaria's body in the camera bag, obtain a can of baked beans for Aidan, go back to the tent to collect her son, and then to join the other families at the barbecue area. The prosecution's inability to meet its own time line was, in my view, more than enough for the jury to find Lindy and Michael innocent of the alleged crime.

Another flaw in the prosecution's case was its claim, based on the characteristics of soil found on Azaria's jumpsuit, that Lindy buried Azaria's body under bushes in a sand dune east of the Chamberlain tent, only to later disinter the body, remove its clothing, cut it to simulate dingo damage, and then to place the clothing where it ultimately was discovered. Testing conducted after the trial ended determined that the soil and plant fragments on Azaria's jumpsuit were present throughout the Ayers Rock region and was not limited to the sand dune east of the Chamberlain tent. Furthermore, the quantity and variety of plant material on the jumpsuit made it more likely that Azaria's body had been dragged through low vegetation areas of Ayers Rock by a dingo than buried in a sand dune.

Weakening the prosecution's case further was its assertion that the absence of saliva on Azaria's jumpsuit was proof that a dingo had not held Azaria in its jaws. According to Harris, the dingo behavior expert, dingoes do not slaver when eating, and saliva would not necessarily have been present in discernible quantities on Azaria's clothing. In addition, when she was wearing it, the matinee jacket would have partially covered Azaria's jumpsuit so that dingo saliva, if any, would not have been deposited on the jumpsuit.

One of the most significant failings in the prosecution's case was its reliance on forensic experts whose testimony fell into the realm of "junk science." While I don't suggest that the experts consciously gave false evidence, several of the experts may have been victims of "theory dependence"—believing that the Chamberlains were guilty and looking for evidence confirming their belief while ignoring evidence that did not.[19]

Overconfident in their ability to form reliable opinions in areas that lay outside of their areas of expertise, some experts based their conclusions on inadequate or invalid forensic evidence. For example, Bernard Sims, a senior lecturer in forensic odontology at the London Medical College and a forensic odonatologist, a person who uses their knowledge of the structure of teeth and gums to help solve crimes, testified that a baby's head wouldn't fit in a dingo's jaws. When shown a photo of a dingo with a human-sized baby doll's head snugly in its mouth, Sims admitted that he was mistaken. Similarly, Malcolm Chaikin, Australia's leading textile expert and head of the School of Textile Technology at the University of New South Wales, demonstrated how cutting the jumpsuit with scissors produced small cotton tufts, much like those discovered by police investigators in the Chamberlain's camera bag. Under questioning by defense attorney John Phillips, Chaikin conceded that dingoes produced similar tufts when they severed fabric with their teeth. Finally, Cameron showed the jury what he claimed was an imprint of a human hand with "bloodied fingers" on the back of Azaria's jumpsuit, thereby suggesting that

Azaria had been held by human hands when she was allegedly murdered. Phillips pointed out that the so-called hand imprint had four phalanges (the bones of the fingers and toes). With the exception of the thumbs and large toes, humans only have three; it was later determined that the imprint was actually red sand and not blood.

Perhaps the most damaging flaw in the prosecution's case was its total dependence on unreliable forensic blood evidence. As Morling said, "Some of the most damaging of that evidence has been shown to be either wrong or highly suspect."

In her trial testimony, Kuhl claimed that she found a large amount of Azaria's blood in the front passenger seat of the Chamberlain's vehicle but less so in their tent. However, several forensic experts who testified at the royal commission cast doubt on the reliability of the blood evidence, including whether it was Azaria's blood at all, noting that only a very small quantity of blood, if any, was found in the automobile. This was corroborated by Senior Constable Graham, who, although not called at the trial, failed to see any sign of blood in the Torana hatchback.

To the extent that there was some blood in the car, it was probably deposited by Keyth Lenehan, a bleeding hitchhiker the Chamberlains had picked up a year prior to Azaria's disappearance, or by Aidan and Reagan, the Chamberlain's sons, who sometimes had minor injuries or nosebleeds while traveling in the front passenger seat of the vehicle.

Kuhl further testified that forensic tests showed that spray spots on the support bracket underneath the dashboard of the Chamberlain's Torana was Azaria's blood, since it contained fetal hemoglobin.[20] Unfortunately, Kuhl destroyed all the test plates and gels, a practice she claimed was "standard procedure" in her laboratory, thereby preventing the defense team from independently confirming her blood-testing results. Nonetheless, discussions with the car's manufacturer, as well as independent testing using infrared spectroscopy, determined that the so-called blood spray on the car's support bracket was not infant's blood, but a sand and bituminous compound sprayed on the metal bracket during the car's manufacturing and production process to deaden road noise.

In a further revelation, dust deposited on the Chamberlain's automobile was found to contain chemicals that gave a false positive reading for blood in Kuhl's forensic test. This, as well as the complexity of the testing methodology and the lack of adequate controls, made Kuhl's blood test results on which the prosecution based its entire case completely unreliable. "Two hundred bad tests are poorer than one good test," said pathologist Richard Nairn in response to Kuhl's false positive test results.

With the prosecution's claim of finding Azaria's blood inside the Chamberlain's Torana debunked, it meant that its theory that Lindy murdered her daughter in the vehicle had no basis in fact. Test results allegedly indicating that Azaria's blood was present on items inside the car, such as a towel, a chamois and its container, the camera bag, and scissors were unsubstantiated; and there was no convincing evidence that Azaria's blood had been transferred from the Torana hatchback to the Chamberlain tent.

In 1988, Justice John Nader similarly discounted the prosecution's claim that Lindy stabbed Azaria with scissors, noting that "Kuhl's tests did not confirm the presence of blood of any kind on the scissors ... [and] ... it would be impossible to find that the scissors were even in the car when it was at Ayers Rock."

As for blood found in the Chamberlain tent, it most likely originated from an injury Azaria sustained while in the tent, since animal hair, which was either dog or dingo, was present in the tent.

Since the Chamberlains had not owned a dog in over a decade, the animal hair must have belonged to a dingo.

A final important discrepancy in the prosecution's case was its inability to show that Lindy had the will or the motive to kill her own daughter. "It is not part of our case that [Lindy] had previously shown any ill will toward the child.... All [we say] is that you should find [that] the murder happened.... How could you possibly convict [the dingo] on this evidence?" Barker said. In response, defense attorney Phillips told the jury, "The prosecution has had two years and three months to think of a reason, but they can't."

I find it surprising that more weight was not given at the second trial to the testimony of people who had been with the Chamberlains at the Ayers Rock campsite. "It is extraordinary that the persons present at the barbecue area ... noticed nothing about [Lindy's] appearance or conduct suggesting that she had suddenly killed her daughter," Morling observed. For example, Sally Lowe had spotted a dingo as she left the barbecue area to dispose of some garbage. Lowe testified that shortly before Lindy went to the tent, she heard a baby cry, "Quite a serious cry [and it] definitely came from the [Chamberlain] tent." Lowe's husband, Gregg, further noted that he had not seen the Chamberlains clean blood from their vehicle, but "There were quite a lot of people around at that time at the tent-site, and I'm sure if anything like that happened it would have been noticed."

Another person who had first-hand knowledge of what happened the night Azaria disappeared was Aidan, the Chamberlain's six-year-old son. Aidan showed Lowe the empty bassinet and cried, "The dingo has our Bubby in its tummy." In addition, Murray Haby, another person at the barbecue, photographed a dingo walking toward the Chamberlain tent the night Azaria disappeared. He later followed the dingo's tracks and noticed a depression in the sand that seemed to indicate that a dingo had laid down something it had been carrying. "[It] had left an imprint in the sand which to me looked like a knitted jumper or woven fabric and then it obviously picked it up because it dragged a bit of sand away from the front and kept moving," Haby said. Ranger Derek Roff and aborigine Nuwe Minyintiri, experienced trackers familiar with dingo behavior, studied the depression and concluded that it suggested a knitted weave of some sort. "It was a shallow drag mark and obviously something had been dragged along, and obviously in that track in areas there was dragging vegetation, leaves and grass material," Roff said.

In the end, Lindy was exonerated not because of the new forensic evidence that was developed after the trial had already ended, but because the white matinee jacket that Azaria had worn the night she disappeared was finally discovered. "All the way through, I'd said there was a matinee jacket, and the [prosecutors] said it was a fanciful lie," Lindy said triumphantly when she was released from prison. "I did not kill my lovely daughter and I refuse to be treated as a criminal any longer."

There have been at least twenty-eight other dingo attacks against children and adults since Lindy and Michael Chamberlain were found guilty of murdering Azaria, the most severe of which occurred in April 2001 when Clinton Gage, a nine-year-old boy, was attacked and killed on Fraser Island off the Queensland coast of Australia.[21] Additional serious, but not lethal, dingo attacks against children occurred as recently as June 2023, when a four-year-old boy was attacked and bitten, and a ten-year-old boy was dragged and nearly drowned. In April 2023, a two-year-old boy was attacked and bitten and a six-year-old girl was bitten multiple times and her head held under water before being rescued.[22]

The Chamberlains earned considerably more than fifteen minutes of fame from Azaria's abduction by a dingo. Their story became the subject of several books, television shows, an opera, and a 1988 film titled *A Cry in the Dark* starring Meryl Streep and Sam Neill. "No other actress would have been able" to play me better than Meryl Streep, Lindy said. Although they received substantial monetary remuneration for the terrible injustice that befell upon them, Lindy and Michael Chamberlain suffered much anguish, public humiliation, and trauma after losing their only daughter on what should have been a happy family vacation at Ayers Rock.

CHAPTER 4

Sherri Rasmussen

Died February 24, 1986
Homicide by Gunshot

ON SUNDAY, FEBRUARY 23, 1986, Sherri Rasmussen suffered a back injury while doing aerobics.[1] Using her back pain as an excuse to avoid presenting a motivational speech, she called in sick the following morning to her job as a nurse at the Glendale Adventist Medical Center in Glendale, California.[2]

Newly married, Rasmussen had tied the knot with John Ruetten three months earlier.[3] The two lived in one of the three-story, mock-Tudor white condominium buildings of the Balboa Townhomes, a gated community in Van Nuys, California.[4]

As was his usual practice on weekdays, Ruetten left for work at an engineering company at 7:20 a.m. that Monday.[5] Approximately two and a half hours later, one of his neighbors, Anastasia Volanitis, saw that the garage door to the Ruetten condo was open and that the silver, two-door BMW that Ruetten had given Rasmussen as an engagement present was gone.[6] The undamaged luxury car was found ten days later, about two and a half miles away from the Ruetten home; the doors were unlocked and the keys were still in the ignition.

Ruetten called home around ten o'clock that morning, but Rasmussen did not answer the phone; the answering machine didn't pick up the call either.[7] This wasn't unusual since Rasmussen often forgot to turn on the machine. Ruetten tried calling Rasmussen several more times during the day, as did her sister, but neither of them could reach Rasmussen. Thinking that his wife had decided to go to work after all, Ruetten phoned the hospital where she worked, but her executive assistant told him that she hadn't seen Rasmussen all day.

At about six o'clock that evening, Ruetten returned home.[8] As he got out of his car, he noticed broken glass scattered all over the driveway. In the garage, the BMW was missing and a door leading from the apartment into the garage that Ruetten had locked before he went to work was now wide open.

Upon entering the unit, Ruetten was shocked to discover Rasmussen's battered and bloody body lying barefoot on the living room floor, clad in the same nightshirt, panties, and red bathrobe that she had worn that very morning. "I was reeling," Ruetten said.[9] "I was in shock."

After covering his wife's face with a blanket, Ruetten dialed 911. Police and paramedics arrived within minutes and declared Rasmussen deceased. She was twenty-nine years old. The time of death was estimated at some time before noon.

The Autopsy[10]

A bullet was recovered when the clothing was removed from Rasmussen's body. It was identified as .38J Plus-P ammunition manufactured by Federal, the type of bullet that Los Angeles Police Department (LAPD) officers used in their department-issued weapon and in their personal weapon when they were off duty.

The autopsy began with an external examination. It revealed numerous points of trauma, including small, faint, fine petechiae (pinpoint, round spots due to capillary bleeding) in the conjunctivae (the mucous membrane that covers the front of the eye and lines the inside of the eyelids) of the left eye, as well as on the skin of the neck and the upper chest. Diffuse petechial hemorrhage also was found along the eyelid of the right eye.

Several lacerations (deep cuts or tears of the skin) and abrasions (scrapes) were identified around the right eye, in the right eyebrow, and on the left side of the throat. Abrasions and scratch marks were also present on both cheeks; a slightly curved, reddish-purple abrasion was on the forehead; and scratch abrasions were on the right side of the mouth, the chest, and on both sides of the chin.

The septum of the upper lip was torn and bruised; the right ear and both arms had several areas of reddish-purple contusions (bruises).

The right index finger had soot, an indication that Rasmussen had fired a gun before she died.

Of special significance was a bite mark on the anterior surface of the left forearm. Based on the amount of hemorrhaging and the absence of inflammation, the injury most likely was inflicted at or about the same time that Rasmussen died.

Three gunshot entrance wounds to the chest were readily apparent, but only two gunshot exit wounds were identified in the back. One of the entrance wounds appeared to be a "contact wound," the type of wound incurred when the muzzle of a firearm is in direct contact with the body at the moment of discharge. The bullet was confirmed to have been delivered at close range when fragments of Rasmussen's bathrobe were found embedded in the wound.

While the complete internal examination was not available for review, the three gunshot wounds were described in great detail in the autopsy report.

The first gunshot wound was an entrance wound in the mid-chest inflicted at close range; it was confirmed by the presence of blackish soot running along the wound track. No "stippling," usually caused by unburned particles of gunpowder striking the skin that, unlike soot, cannot be washed away, was found around the wound. Had there been stippling, it would have meant that the muzzle of the gun was within two feet of Rasmussen's body when it was discharged. In the muscle underlying the entry wound was a cherry-red discoloration.

The path of the trajectory of the gunshot wound was front to back, slightly left to right, and downward. As the bullet entered the chest cavity, it passed just right of the sternum, the elongated bone in the center of the chest that provides support for the collarbone and ribs. The bullet then entered the rib cage, slightly grazing the second rib and passing through the right lung. After grazing the sixth rib, the projectile exited in the right side of the back, eighteen inches from the top of the head.

The second gunshot entrance wound, whose trajectory was front to back, left to right, and slightly downward, was just above the left breast. No discoloration, soot, or stippling was present on the skin surface of the wound or along the wound track, an indication that the bullet was not delivered at close range. The bullet entered the chest cavity without fracturing any of the upper or lower ribs.

After lacerating the descending thoracic aorta, the large artery supplying oxygen-rich blood to the rest of the body, the bullet lacerated the spinal cord and became embedded in the subcutaneous tissues of the back, from which it was recovered. The silvery flattened nose, unmarked nine-millimeter bullet had minimal deformity.

The third and final gunshot entrance wound was in the lower left chest. No soot or stippling was noted on the skin surface of the wound. The path of the projectile was through the chest cavity, slightly grazing the edges of the sixth rib and leaving slight reddish discoloration in the underlying muscle.

The bullet entered the right ventricle of the heart, the chamber that pumps blood low in oxygen to be oxygenated in the lungs, as well as the septum, the muscle that separates the left and right sides of the heart, and the left heart ventricle, before exiting through the lower left side of the back. The exit wound had no soot on the skin surface of the wound.

While the first gunshot entrance wound was delivered at close range, police concluded that at least one of the two remaining gunshot entrance wounds was inflicted when Rasmussen was lying on the floor.

Cause and Manner of Death

It's unclear whether toxicology testing was conducted on Rasmussen's postmortem blood or urine. Nonetheless, the autopsy provided substantial forensic evidence that Rasmussen struggled with her assailant before she died—her body had multiple defensive wounds, including contusions, lacerations, and abrasions on the hands, mouth, face, head, and neck, and the facial injuries were consistent with a blow from a muzzle of a gun, a size and configuration that matched a .38-caliber Smith & Wesson revolver.

The arms and wrists had abrasions that were consistent with injury caused by a cord tied around the wrists. When police searched the Ruetten home, they found a white cord stained with Rasmussen's blood near the front door of the house, as well as two broken fingernails belonging to Rasmussen.

A pink and pale-green quilted blanket with gunshot residue and multiple bullet holes was located near the body. Police theorized that the quilt had been wrapped around the assailant's gun to muffle the sound of the gunshots. This was supported by a statement provided by a maid working next door to the Ruetten condominium who, while not hearing the sound of gunfire, heard loud voices, "like two people fighting, and a slamming sound, as if something had fallen."[11] The blanket was examined by a forensic firearms expert who, based on the location of the bullet holes relative to the gunshot residue deposited on the blanket when the firearm was discharged, concluded that the weapon used was a revolver with a two-inch barrel. While several different types of handguns were capable of firing the bullets found at the crime scene, less than a dozen had a two-inch barrel.

A blow to Rasmussen's head was determined to have been caused by a vase found broken near Rasmussen's body.

After reviewing the circumstances surrounding the death, as well as the autopsy report, published lay articles, and the scientific literature, I concluded that the cause of death was three gunshot wounds to the chest. The manner of death was homicide.

Life and Career

Rasmussen was born on February 7, 1957. When she was sixteen years old, she attended Loma Linda University, studying to be a nurse.

In 1984, twenty-seven-year-old Rasmussen was promoted to director of the Critical Care Unit at the Glendale Adventist Medical Center. The beautiful, confident, and according to some, brilliant, six-foot-tall Rasmussen met Ruetten, a handsome, talkative young man, at a spring party in June of that year. Two years younger than Rasmussen, Ruetten had been attending the University of California at Los Angeles (UCLA) to become an engineer.

Rasmussen and Ruetten became engaged in May 1985; they were married in November of the same year. By all outward appearances, their short marriage was a happy one, with Ruetten starting a new job at an engineering company and Rasmussen lecturing internationally on critical-care nursing while at the same time working as a nurse and director at the Glendale Adventist Medical Center. Tragically, that all changed on February 24, 1986.

Conclusions

Los Angeles Police Department (LAPD) detective Lyle Mayer suspected that Rasmussen was murdered in the course of a botched burglary—a VCR and a CD player had been stacked by the door leading to the garage and a drawer in a living room table had been pulled out from a cabinet, its contents strewn all over the floor.[12] In addition, one of the tall stereo speakers had been knocked over and was lying next to Rasmussen's body, and a gray ceramic vase with a heavy base lay shattered on the floor.

Mayer theorized that one or two would-be robbers had entered the Ruetten home through an unlocked front door and were surprised by Rasmussen while they were burglarizing the house. Tragically, Rasmussen was shot during a struggle over a gun. Subsequent break-ins in Ruetten's neighborhood committed by two men described as Latino seemed to reinforce Mayer's theory. In one such incident, the men held a woman at gunpoint after she surprised them during a burglary attempt of her home. Neither of the men was ever identified or apprehended.

There were some facts about the Rasmussen crime scene that were inconsistent with Mayer's theory. For example, there was no evidence of forced entry. Also, several rooms in the Ruetten home had valuables in plain view, including a jewelry box and more stereo equipment, but none of these objects had been taken or disturbed. Oddly enough, besides the BMW, the only other item taken from the Ruetten home was Rasmussen's and Ruetten's marriage certificate. Nonetheless, none of this seemed to matter to Mayer.

"I believe your house was burglarized today, sometime before ten o'clock," Mayer told Ruetten hours after Rasmussen's body was discovered. "I believe they got in your front door. I don't think it was locked.... Once those persons or that person or whoever was inside, I believe they were trying to steal your stereo and probably some other items."

"Why would they do anything to her?" Ruetten asked the detective, crying. "Why wouldn't they just run?"

"I don't know, John," Mayer replied. "John, things happen, OK? Here's what I think happened. I think Sherri came down the stairs. And I think she surprised them. And she was hurt, OK? She was shot."

No physical evidence of the assailant—hair, fiber, or blood—was ever found at the Ruetten home to connect to a possible suspect. Also, police interviews with Ruetten, Rasmussen's family, neighbors, and friends failed to turn up any potential suspects.

"Have you been having any marital problems?" Mayer asked Ruetten.

"We were having the best time," Ruetten replied. "We just got married."

Mayer pressed further. "No financial problems? She's not having problems with an ex-boyfriend, or you with an ex-girlfriend?"

"No," Ruetten responded. Twenty-three years later, Ruetten admitted, "It never crossed my mind that ... [Stephanie Lazarus] ... could be involved," referring to his ex-girlfriend.

Ruetten met Lazarus when they were both at UCLA. The two had dated in college and into the late 1970s and early 1980s. "[We were] necking and fooling around," Ruetten said.[13] After graduating, Ruetten and Lazarus became sexually intimate, but Ruetten never considered Lazarus his girlfriend. "We were good friends," he said. "We saw each other on and off, and on some of those occasions we had sexual intercourse."[14]

For Lazarus, a dark-haired, athletic, and brazen female who became a police officer, it was unrequited love. She did not take it well when Ruetten announced his engagement to Rasmussen in 1984. Upset and crying, Lazarus begged Ruetten to come over to her apartment to discuss the situation further. When he arrived, she "was emotionally distraught" and repeatedly asked Ruetten to have sex with her. He finally agreed, Ruetten said, "to give her closure." He later admitted it was a stupid move.

Vindictive and unwilling to give up her quest to reunite with Ruetten, Lazarus visited Rasmussen at work two days after her sexual encounter with Ruetten and told Rasmussen that she had sex with her fiancé. That evening, Ruetten confessed the incident to Rasmussen and begged her, "Don't let this mess us up. I want nothing more in the world than to be married to you." He promised to end all further contact with Lazarus.

In August 1985, Lazarus sent Ruetten's mother a letter in which she wrote, "I'm truly in love with John and this past year has really torn me up. I wish it didn't end the way it did, and I don't think I'll ever understand his decision."[15] According to an entry in Lazarus's journal, she received a reply that made her "very, very, very sad."

Lazarus did not give up easily, even after Ruetten married Rasmussen. On one occasion, she invited herself to the Ruetten home to ask Ruetten to wax her skis. At another time, she startled

Rasmussen when she unexpectedly appeared dressed in her LAPD police uniform with a gun in her holster on the pretext that she was waiting for Ruetten.

Rasmussen's parents had long suspected that Lazarus was involved in their daughter's death. She had been stalking Rasmussen for quite a while and at one point, had even visited Rasmussen at work, telling her, "If I can't have John, no one else will." Peggy Crabtree, one of Rasmussen's friends, recalled that "John's ex-girlfriend kept appearing in places that Sherri would go. She couldn't go out to the store or go to the gym without having this woman show up. Sherri was clearly fearful and unhappy that she just couldn't get this person out of her life." The Rasmussens felt that the police should consider Lazarus a prime suspect, but Mayer was adamant that Rasmussen's death was the unfortunate result of a burglary gone tragically wrong. "You watch too much television," he allegedly told the Rasmussens.

That Lazarus was an LAPD police officer may have had something to do with Mayer's reluctance to investigate her further. Although a brief entry in the case file on November 19, 1987, read, "John Ruetten called. Verified Stephanie Lazarus, PO (police officer), was former girlfriend," it wasn't enough to dissuade LAPD detectives from being fixated on the theory that one or two male Latino intruders were responsible for Rasmussen's death.

With the police unwilling to investigate Lazarus, a policewoman on the fast track in the department, and with no new leads, Rasmussen's murder investigation languished for the next fifteen years. During that time, Lazarus married an LAPD detective, adopted a daughter, survived thyroid cancer, was promoted to detective, and became a decorated police officer, winning numerous citations, awards, and honors for her work in the art theft unit. She even raised money to start a day-care program for members of the LAPD, became a training officer with the Drug Abuse Resistance Education program, and served as treasurer for the Los Angeles Women Police Officer's Association.

Things began to change in November 2001 after Los Angeles police chief Bernard C. Parks created the Cold Case Homicide Unit. "We were just getting into DNA, so our focus was sexual assault-type crimes or crimes where DNA evidence had been left behind," said LAPD detective Clifford Shephard.

In 2004, LAPD criminalist Jennifer Francis obtained the two saliva-containing swabs of the bite mark collected eighteen years earlier from the wound on Rasmussen's forearm.[14] DNA testing of one of the samples revealed the presence of two separate DNA profiles—a minor, incomplete profile consistent with Rasmussen's DNA, and a major, complete profile of a yet unidentified woman who was not Rasmussen. This seemed to debunk Mayer's theory that Rasmussen's death was caused by two Latino men during a bungled burglary. Subsequent attempts to match the major DNA profile to DNA profiles in the Combined DNA Index System (CODIS), a national law enforcement database, however, were unsuccessful.

Armed with the knowledge that one of the DNA profiles obtained from Rasmussen's bite mark was of a woman who was not Rasmussen, Jim Nuttall, a detective in the Van Nuys Division of the Cold Case Homicide Unit, was convinced that the original theory of the case developed by Mayer was incorrect. "That jumps off the page at you, because when you have that, and you're aware that the case is based on two male burglars—well, that alters the entire course of the investigation," Nuttall said. "You have to go back to square one."

Aware that the Rasmussen family had been urging the LAPD to focus its investigation on Lazarus, Nuttall contacted Ruetten, who informed him that Lazarus was an LAPD police officer. "It was extremely difficult initially to process ... [the] possibility" that one of our own police officers might have killed Rasmussen and that she had been getting away with it for so long, Nuttall said.

On May 19, 2009, undercover police detectives devised a plan to surreptitiously obtain a DNA sample from Lazarus. Following Lazarus on a trip to Costco, a large wholesale retail store, the detectives retrieved a discarded straw and a Styrofoam cup that Lazarus had tossed into a trash bin. Testing the saliva on the discarded straw, LAPD criminalist Michael Mastrocovo developed a partial DNA profile that surprisingly matched the major DNA profile developed from saliva obtained from Rasmussen's bite mark. "[The DNA profile] came back and it was exactly who I'd been pointing to for twenty-three years," Rasmussen's father said. "I never felt so good in my life." Later testing revealed that a complete DNA profile obtained from a sample taken from Lazarus's mouth matched the complete major DNA profile developed from saliva obtained from Rasmussen's bite mark.

Based on the newly developed DNA results, Lazarus was arrested and charged with Rasmussen's murder on June 5, 2009. "The idea of arresting a cop for murder is a pretty dramatic event and doesn't happen very often," said Joel Rubin, a news reporter for the *Los Angeles Times*.

"Never in my wildest imagination would I ever think she could do something like this," said one veteran LAPD police officer. Lazarus was the type of person who made chocolate-covered cherries and handed them to neighbors at Christmas. "We drank beers. She was always quick to give you a hug or tell a joke."

In 2010, Thomas Fedor, a serologist at the Serological Research Institute, independently tested the second swab of the bite mark obtained from Rasmussen's forearm. After identifying amylase in the sample to confirm that the sample was saliva, Fedor detected two distinct DNA profiles—a minor DNA profile consistent with Rasmussen's DNA and a second, major DNA profile that matched Lazarus's DNA profile. The chance that a woman unrelated to Lazarus had the same DNA profile as the major DNA profile from Rasmussen's bite mark was approximately one in 1.7 sextillion. DNA profiles later developed from tissue samples obtained from Rasmussen's fingernails were also consistent with Lazarus's DNA profile.

It was now clear that the "burglary" at the Ruetten home had been staged. Lazarus was very experienced at picking locks, which explained why there was no sign that the front door of Ruetten's condo had been forced open. Police theorized that with the security alarm turned off, Lazarus entered the Ruetten home without being heard. Once inside, she confronted Rasmussen upstairs and fired two shots, both of which missed their mark and shattered the sliding glass patio door instead. When Rasmussen tried to reach for the panic button on the security panel, Lazarus stopped her before she was able to do so. During the vicious fight that followed, Rasmussen managed to wrestle Lazarus's gun away and to place Lazarus in a headlock, but Lazarus bit Rasmussen on the forearm and broke free. Then, picking up the heavy ceramic vase from the living room shelf, Lazarus crashed it on top of Rasmussen's head, temporarily dazing her. After retrieving the gun, Lazarus fired another shot at Rasmussen, this time hitting her in the chest. Finally, using the quilt to muffle the sound, Lazarus fired two more shots into Rasmussen's chest, killing her.

Police determined that a bloody smudge on top of the CD player was consistent with Rasmussen's blood. Investigators believed it was left by Lazarus who, while wearing gloves, was stacking electronic components against the door and trying to make the murder scene look like an interrupted burglary. Lazarus then entered the garage and drove Ruetten's BMW, leaving it about two and a half miles away with the keys in the ignition.

As for the murder weapon, police concluded that Lazarus had used her personal gun to commit the crime, a .38-caliber Smith and Wesson Model 49 revolver with a two-inch barrel. Most likely, she must have tossed the gun in the Pacific Ocean after murdering Rasmussen.

In closing arguments at Lazarus's trial, Deputy District Attorney Paul Nunez told the jury, "The motive in this case was jealousy—jealousy toward Sherri. The ring on Sherri's finger was supposed to be hers (Lazarus's). It was ripped from her."

In March 2012, after more than four weeks and approximately sixty witnesses, the jury reached a guilty verdict in just slightly more than eight hours. "We never had a chance," Lazarus's defense attorney said.

Lazarus was sentenced to twenty-five years to life for killing Rasmussen and two more years for using a weapon during the commission of a crime. If it had not been for DNA technology, she may have gotten away with murder much longer.

Rasmussen got her fifteen minutes of fame by virtue of DNA technology and a family that doggedly pursued her killer, who remained free for twenty-three years despite having killed her love rival. Nonetheless, no one is above the law, not even a police officer on the fast track in the LAPD.

"The fact that Sherri's death occurred because she met and married me brings me to my knees," Ruetten told Rasmussen's parents at Lazarus's sentencing trial.

Apparently, it's true what they say: "Hell hath no fury like a woman scorned."[16] With that kind of hell, the reward inevitably is a very stiff sentence.

CHAPTER 5

Ron Goldman and Nicole Brown Simpson

Died June 12, 1994

Homicide by Stabbing

TWENTY-FIVE-YEAR-OLD RON GOLDMAN was working as a waiter at Mezzaluna Trattoria, a trendy restaurant in the Brentwood suburb of Los Angeles, California, on June 12, 1994. That evening, Nicole Brown Simpson, ex-wife of O.J. Simpson, one of the greatest running backs of all time (mostly for the Buffalo Bills football team), arrived at the restaurant with her family for dinner after attending her daughter's dance recital at the Paul Revere Middle School.[1] Goldman had befriended Brown about six weeks earlier, so later, when Brown called to say that her mother had left a pair of eyeglasses at the restaurant, he agreed to deliver them to Brown's condominium at the end of his shift.

Goldman arrived at Brown's home on South Bundy Drive sometime after ten o'clock, just as Brown was being knifed to death by an assailant.[2] Trapped against an iron fence in a small, enclosed corner of the yard, Goldman was savagely bludgeoned to death as Brown lay barefoot a few feet away, bleeding, unconscious, or possibly already dead. "All of this could have happened within a few minutes," said Los Angeles County Coroner Lakshmanan Sathyavagiswaran.[3]

Up in their bedrooms, Brown's two children were fast asleep while Goldman and their mother were being murdered on the sidewalk. "I would say [Brown] died within a few minutes, probably less," said Sathyavagiswaran.[4] "These kinds of altercations can take place pretty rapidly."

Later that night, a neighbor saw Brown's white Akita dog, barking and walking with bloody paws alone.[5] Police were alerted, and shortly after midnight, they discovered Goldman's bloodied body in the narrow passageway stretching between the front door steps of Brown's condominium and the front gate; Brown's body lay sprawled on the sidewalk nearby.[6] Next to Goldman's body was a white envelope, a blue knit cap, and a man's leather glove.[7] A trail of bloody shoe prints led up to the back gate; heading south on the sidewalk were bloody canine footprints.

The Autopsy

Goldman's autopsy was conducted on June 14, 1994, by Deputy Medical Examiner Irwin L. Golden.[8] It began with the external examination.

Weighing 171 pounds and measuring sixty-nine inches long, the well-developed, well-nourished body was clothed in a long-sleeved shirt, Levi jeans, sweat socks, and canvas boots. The shirt was extensively bloodied with three slit-like tears—one on the lower right side of the front, another on the lower right sleeve, and a third on the lower right side of the back. The bloodstained jeans had a slit-like tear in the left hip area.

The hair on the scalp was brown and straight. The hazel eyes had no evidence of petechial hemorrhage, pinpoint areas of pericapillary bleeding; the pupils were dilated; the sclerae (the "whites of the eyes") and conjunctivae, the mucous membrane that covers the front of the eye and lines the inside of the eyelids, were unremarkable. The teeth were natural.

A "picture-type" tattoo was identified on the left upper arm.

Multiple sharp force injuries were inflicted to the neck, face, scalp, and hands, including stab wounds, some penetrating and fatal, to the chest, thigh, and abdomen, and several defensive wounds and injuries to the hands and upper extremities.

A fatal sharp force injury to the left side of the neck appeared to be a combination of a stabbing and cutting wound that cut across the left internal jugular vein. The total length of the wound path was approximately four to six inches.

There were three nonfatal sharp force injuries across the neck, one of which was a combination of stabbing and cutting with no penetration or injury of a major artery or vein; the two others were superficial incised (cutting) wounds.

Numerous wounds were present on the face, the most significant of which was a nonfatal stabbing wound involving the right earlobe. Other superficial cutting wounds were on the right side of the face, the right cheek, the back of the neck, and on the left ear.

The scalp had at least three nonfatal stab wounds or abrasions (scrapes) with no underlying fractures of the skull or penetration of the cranium (the skull).

Two fatal stab wounds located on the right side of the chest were associated with perforation of the right lung and a hemothorax, a collection of approximately one hundred to two hundred milliliters of blood in the space between the chest wall and the lungs. Another fatal stab wound located on the left side of the abdomen was associated with perforation of the abdominal aorta with intraabdominal hemorrhage.

Three additional nonfatal wounds were identified, including a superficial stab or cutting wound to the chest, a stab wound to the left thigh, and a superficial cutting wound to the right flank.

There were at least three cutting defensive wounds on the hands, two on the right hand and one on the left, as well as multiple abrasions and bruises on the hands and upper extremities.

For the internal examination, the body was opened with the usual Y-shaped incision. The internal organs were in their usual anatomical locations, but the peritoneal cavity, a space defined by the diaphragm, the walls of the abdominal and pelvic cavities, and the abdominal organs, was full of blood due to the stabbing of the abdomen and chest.

Aside from the injuries and stab wounds to the chest and abdomen, the following observations of the internal organs were noted in the autopsy.

The brain weight of 1,400 grams was in the normal range. There were no fractures of the bones at the base of the skull; the cranial nerves were intact; and the cranial blood vessels were intact, free of blood clots, and with no significant atherosclerosis (plaque buildup). No lesions, cysts, or neoplasms were found when brain tissue was examined under a microscope.

The cardiovascular system was normal, with the heart weight of 290 grams in the normal range. The heart chambers and heart valves were unremarkable; the coronary arteries had no significant atherosclerosis; and the aorta, the large artery that delivers oxygenated blood to the rest of the body, and its branches were normal.

The respiratory system had no lesions or obstructions; the hyoid bone and thyroid cartilage were intact; the lungs had minimal congestion; and the right and left lung weights of 420 and 320 grams, respectively, were in the normal range.

The gastrointestinal system had an esophagus that was without lesions. The stomach contained approximately two hundred milliliters of partially digested, semisolid food with fragments of a green, leafy vegetable material consistent with spinach; it was otherwise free of lesions and pill fragments. The duodenum (the first part of the small intestine immediately beyond the stomach, leading to the jejunum), the ileum (the short part of the small intestine that connects to the large intestine), the jejunum, the colon, and the rectum were all unremarkable. The appendix was present; the liver was normal in size and configuration and with the usual color and appearance. The gallbladder had no lesions, and the pancreas was unremarkable.

As for the hemolytic and endocrine systems, the spleen was intact and without lesions, its weight of 210 grams in the normal range. The thymus was not identified, the adrenal glands were the usual size with no lesions or injuries, and the pituitary gland was not enlarged.

The urinary system was normal with the left and right kidney weights of 150 and 140 grams, respectively, in the normal range; the urinary bladder had no measurable amount of urine.

The autopsy failed to find any anatomical changes that might have explained why Goldman died aside from the numerous stab wounds to the chest and abdomen.

Brown's autopsy was conducted on the same day that Golden performed Goldman's.[9]

The external examination revealed a body that weighed 129 pounds, measured sixty-five inches in length, and was clothed in black panties and a short, blood-stained black dress. It was well-developed, well-nourished, and without tattoos, deformities, or amputations.

The hair on the scalp was brown, as were the eyes. The pupils were fixed and dilated; the sclerae and conjunctivae were unremarkable and without evidence of petechial hemorrhages. The teeth were natural. There was no evidence of injury to the cheeks, lips, or gums.

Two linear surgical scars were identified, one beneath each breast, consistent with the presence of intact bilateral silicone breast implants.

The external auditory canals, eyes, nose, and mouth were unremarkable; no recent traumatic injuries were noted on the chest or abdomen. The lower back and some posterior areas had no evidence of recent injuries.

Of special significance for the determination of cause of death were the multiple sharp force injuries to the neck, head, and scalp. Specifically, a fatal incised (cutting) wound of the neck, measuring five and a half inches in length, caused gaping and exposure of the larynx and cervical vertebral column. The wound was associated with transection (cutting) of the right and left common carotid arteries and both internal jugular veins with hemorrhaging in the surrounding areas. In addition, there were four stab wounds on the left side of the neck that extended three inches below the external auditory canal.

Besides the stab injuries to the neck, there were three superficial, nonfatal stab wounds of the scalp as well as a blunt force injury to the head. Both hands had multiple injuries and incised wounds consistent with defensive wounds.

For the internal examination, the body was opened with the usual Y-shaped incision, revealing the abdominal wall and the internal cavity and organs. No blood was found within the pleural (a space that surrounds the lungs), pericardial (a space surrounding the heart), or peritoneal cavities, and no internal traumatic injuries were identified involving the thorax or abdomen.

No fractures of the bones of the skull were identified. In addition, the brain showed no tears or hemorrhaging and was anatomically normal. The pituitary gland was normally situated and not enlarged; the cranial nerves were intact and symmetrical.

As for the respiratory system, besides the injuries to the upper airways due to the incised wound of the neck, the trachea and major bronchi were unremarkable; the hyoid bone and thyroid cartilages were intact.

The thyroid gland was normal in size and location.

The weights of the right and left lungs of 330 and 300 grams, respectively, were within the normal range; the lungs had minimal congestion and no injuries or lesions. The pulmonary arteries were free of thromboemboli (blood clots).

The cardiovascular system was unremarkable, with the heart weight of 280 grams in the normal range. The heart chambers, heart valves, and myocardium (heart muscle) were as expected with minimal amount of blood in the heart chambers, no lesions or congenital anomalies, and no significant atherosclerosis in the coronary arteries.

The gastrointestinal system was normal in appearance. The esophagus was intact and without injuries or lesions; the stomach had no lesions and was without pill fragments, its contents included approximately five hundred milliliters of chewed semisolid food, such as pieces of pasta, fragments of spinach and unrecognized, partially digested food. The duodenum, the first part of the small intestine immediately beyond the stomach, leading to the jejunum, as well as the jejunum, the ileum (the short part of the small intestine that connects to the large intestine), the colon, and the rectum were all free of lesions and blood. The liver was uniformly brown-red in color and free of nodules, its weight of 1,370 grams in the normal range. The gallbladder was without lesions and free of anomalies, and the pancreas was unremarkable.

The spleen was firm, without lesions, and of the usual color, weight, and consistency. The adrenal glands were of the usual size, location, and appearance.

Each kidney weighed one hundred grams and was of the expected size and configuration. The urinary bladder contained only a few milliliters of clear urine.

The uterus had no lesions; there was no evidence of pregnancy.

Beside the multiple sharp force injuries to the neck, head, and scalp, the autopsy failed to find any anatomical changes that might have explained how Brown died.

Cause and Manner of Death

Routine toxicology studies of Goldman's postmortem blood were ordered, but the toxicology report was not available for review. Toxicology testing of urine was not conducted since the urinary bladder was empty.

It was readily apparent that Goldman died from multiple sharp force injuries and stabbings, and that he sustained several fatal stab wounds to the neck, chest, and abdomen. That he bravely fought off his attacker was evident by the presence of numerous defensive wounds on the hands and upper extremities.

After I reviewed the circumstances surrounding the death, the autopsy report, and published lay articles, and in the absence of other possible causes, I concluded that Goldman died as a result of multiple stab wounds to the neck, chest, and abdomen. The manner of death was homicide.

Brown's toxicology report was not available for review.

Brown's body was inflicted with multiple sharp force injuries and stab wounds, as well as a deep incised wound of the neck.

These sharp force injuries included cutting of both common carotid arteries and incisions of both internal jugular veins, thereby causing substantial hemorrhaging resulting in exsanguination and death.

That Brown bravely fought off her attacker was evident by the many defensive injuries to the hands, including an incised wound of the ring finger of the right hand.

After I reviewed the circumstances surrounding the death, the autopsy report, and published lay articles, and in the absence of other possible causes, I concluded that Brown died from multiple sharp force injuries and incision of both common carotid arteries and internal jugular veins in the neck. The manner of death was homicide.

Life and Career

Goldman was born on July 2, 1968, in Chicago, Illinois, and grew up in the nearby suburb of Buffalo Grove. His parents divorced when he was six years old.[10]

Goldman attended Twin Groves Junior High School and Adlai E. Stevenson High School in Lincolnshire, Illinois, where he played soccer and tennis.[11] After graduating in 1986, he enrolled at Illinois State University for one semester.

When Goldman's father remarried a woman with three children, Goldman and his family moved to Los Angeles, California.[12] While there, he took a few classes at Pierce College and worked as a tennis instructor, headhunter, waiter, and as a model for Barry Zeldes, owner of the men's clothing store Z90094 in Brentwood Gardens.[13]

Goldman had a magnetic personality.[14] "My brother was a larger-than-life personality ... there was something about him that people just connected to," said Kim, Goldman's sister.[15] He was "a free spirit."[16]

Although he obtained a license as an emergency medical technician, Goldman never worked in the medical profession. Instead, he considered a career in hotel management or possibly as the owner of a restaurant, even contemplating becoming an actor. In 1992, he appeared as a contestant in the short-lived television game show *Studs*.

Sometime in early May 1994, Goldman met Brown, a beautiful, blonde thirty-five-year-old.[17] Brown had been divorced from Simpson for nearly two years. According to Mike Pincus, one of Goldman's childhood friends, Goldman's and Brown's relationship was strictly platonic—meeting for coffee, dancing at clubs, and exercising together at a local gym. On occasion, Brown let Goldman drive her white Ferrari.

On June 12, 1994, Goldman went to Brown's home to deliver a pair of eyeglasses. He had planned to meet up with a friend after stopping at Brown's condo, but he never made it there.

Brown was born in Frankfurt, Germany, on May 19, 1959.[18] Her American father, Louis, met Juditha, a German woman who ultimately became his wife, while stationed in Germany as a correspondent for the American armed forces newspaper *Stars and Stripes*.

Brown and her family moved to Garden Grove when she was still a toddler; the family later moved to Monarch Beach in the coastal city of Dana Point, California.[19] At first, Brown enrolled at Rancho Alamitos High School in Garden Grove, but she later transferred to Dana Hills High School, where she was named homecoming princess in her senior year.[20]

"Nicole was bubbly, always happy and smiling," said teacher Bill Prestridge. She seemed eager to start life beyond school "and go on to bigger and better things."

When she was eighteen years old, Brown worked for two weeks at a clothing boutique before starting work as a waitress at The Daisy, an upscale Beverly Hills club. Her interest in modeling and photography led her to enroll at Saddleback Junior College in Mission Viejo, California, but she dropped out when she met Simpson, thirty years old and married, while working at The Daisy. "The two were madly in love and had this obvious chemistry that you could feel when you were in the same room with them.... He was already incredibly possessive of Nicole," said Kris Jenner, who met Brown in 1978.

Simpson divorced his wife in 1979. On February 2, 1985, Brown and Simpson were married; within three years, they had two children together. "It was a very passionate, a very volatile, a very obsessive relationship, on both sides," said Cathy Lee Crosby, a close friend of Brown and Simpson.

In 1992, after seven years of marriage and Simpson's philandering and abusive behavior, Brown filed for divorce.

Conclusions

Philip Vannatter, a senior Los Angeles Police Department (LAPD) detective, arrived at the crime scene on Bundy Drive at approximately 4:00 a.m. on June 13, 1994.[21] After learning that Brown's two children with O.J. Simpson, her ex-husband, had been taken to the police station for protection, Vannatter was instructed to notify Simpson that his former wife had been murdered and that he needed to make arrangements to take custody of the children, five and eight years old.

Simpson's mansion was on Rockingham Avenue, a mere two miles and six minutes from where the two killings had occurred. When Vannatter and several detectives arrived at the estate, Simpson wasn't home; he had flown to Chicago to attend a Hertz Rental Car convention.[22] While on Simpson's property, Vannatter noticed drops of blood on the walkway and on the door of Simpson's white Ford Bronco parked at an awkward angle in front of Simpson's house. Near the air conditioning unit was a bloody leather glove, the mate to the one discovered on Brown's yard; blood-stained socks were also found in Simpson's bedroom.

Later that morning, police called Simpson at the O'Hare Plaza Hotel in Chicago and informed him that Brown had been killed. Simpson immediately boarded a flight back to Los Angeles, arriving sometime after noon.[23] Taken to police headquarters for questioning, Simpson claimed that the deep cut on his hand occurred when he accidentally broke a glass in his Chicago hotel room upon learning that Brown had been murdered. While at the police station, a nurse drew blood from Simpson.[24]

As part of their investigation, detectives discovered Simpson's prior conviction for domestic violence against Brown that had occurred on New Year's Day 1989.[25] It was then that police, summoned to the Simpson estate, found Brown with swelling above her right eye, a cut lip, a bruised forehead, and an imprint of a hand around her neck.[26] "He's going to kill me," Brown told the officers when they arrived.[27] "Who's going to kill you?" they asked.[28] "O.J.... Yes, O.J. Simpson, the football player," Brown replied.[29] Mark Fuhrman, one of the detectives on the scene, charged Simpson with spousal abuse; Simpson pled no contest. There had been at least fifty other similar accusations of spousal abuse against Simpson during their seventeen-year marriage, but this was the only time that Simpson had been charged with domestic violence.[30]

Police believed that they had enough evidence to issue an arrest warrant for Simpson in Goldman's and Brown's murders—bloodstained socks in Simpson's bedroom; a bloody glove on Simpson's property that matched the one found at the crime scene; drops of blood on Simpson's white Ford Bronco; and Simpson's prior conviction of physical abuse against Brown. After consulting with his attorney, Simpson agreed to surrender to authorities at 10:00 a.m. on June 17. However, instead of turning himself in as planned, Simpson hid in the back seat of a white Ford Bronco belonging to his friend, A.C. Cowlings. With Simpson in the back of the Bronco, Cowlings then drove on the Los Angeles freeway, all the while announcing, "Simpson is holding a gun to his head and is threatening to blow his brains out," as police followed the Bronco closely behind.[31]

Cowlings returned to the Simpson estate at 7:00 p.m., at which time police arrested Simpson. When police searched Cowling's automobile, they discovered a loaded gun, a passport, a disguise, and $8,750 in cash.

Dubbed the "Trial of the Century," Simpson's criminal trial began on January 24, 1995, and was presided over by Judge Lance Ito; it lasted more than eight months.[32] The "Dream Team" of defense attorneys included Robert Shapiro, Alan Dershowitz, Johnnie Cochran, Robert Blasier, and F. Lee Bailey, the same attorney who nearly thirty years earlier had successfully defended Dr. Sam Sheppard of murdering his wife, Marilyn. Asked by Ito how he pled, Simpson insisted he was "absolutely 100 percent not guilty."[33]

Prosecutors Christopher Darden and Marcia Clark began by establishing that Simpson had the time and the motive to commit

Goldman's and Brown's murders. To set the timeline, they presented their first witness, Kato Kaelin, who lived in Simpson's guesthouse.

Kaelin testified that the last time he saw Simpson on June 12, the day of the two murders, was at 9:35 p.m. The next witness, Allan Park, a limousine driver from the Town and Country Limousine Company, told the jury that when he arrived at the Rockingham Avenue estate at 10:22 p.m. to drive Simpson to the airport, he noticed that Simpson's white Ford Bronco was gone. Park further stated that at 10:40 p.m., he repeatedly buzzed Simpson's intercom, but he received no reply.[34] Finally, Park said he saw an African American figure whose size and build was similar to Simpson's enter Simpson's house at 10:50 p.m. A minute or two later, Simpson answered the intercom, saying, "Sorry, I overslept. I just got out of the shower. I'll be down in one minute." Simpson finally appeared at the front door at 11:00 p.m., thirty minutes later than originally scheduled, after which Park said he drove Simpson to the airport to catch his flight to Chicago.[35]

Based on Kaelin's and Park's testimony, the prosecution claimed that Simpson had one hour and ten minutes, more than enough time to drive from his Rockingham Avenue estate to Brown's home, commit the two murders, and then to drive back to his house, arriving in time for Park to pick him up for the drive to the airport.[36]

As for Simpson's motive for killing Brown, Darden told the jury that it was jealousy. "He killed her because he couldn't have her. And if he couldn't have her, he didn't want anybody else to have her. He killed her to control her." Darden then added, almost as an aside, "He killed Ron Goldman because he got in the way."[37]

In my opinion, Darden presented the jury a very weak motive for the two murders. Simpson had been jealous of Brown for a long time, especially after they divorced. And yet, despite his abusive behavior toward Brown, his jealous outbursts had never ended in murder. What caused Simpson, then, to be so enraged on June 12 that he allegedly went to Brown's condo armed with a knife?[38] The answer, I believe, was provided at the civil trial, about a year after the Simpson criminal trial had already ended.[39]

At the civil trial, Paula Barbieri, Simpson's former girlfriend, testified that at 7:00 a.m. on June 12, she left Simpson a "Dear John" message on his answering machine.[40] "The relationship as far as she was concerned was over," said Michael Brewer, an attorney for the Goldman family.[41] When Simpson received the message at 2:12 p.m., he tried to reach Barbieri at her Florida and Los Angeles phone numbers, but he was unsuccessful. Six minutes later, he was overheard "yelling … very angry and very upset" during a three-minute, heated phone conversation with Brown.[42] Simpson tried calling Barbieri three more times that day but by 10:03 p.m., he still was unable to reach her.[43]

With Barbieri having "dumped" Simpson on the morning of June 12, and the likelihood that Brown had told Simpson later that afternoon that she, too, was not interested in reconciliation, it probably was just too much for Simpson to bear. In my opinion, the two rejections having occurred on the same day was a much stronger motivating factor than jealousy to enrage Simpson to such an extent that he was willing to commit murder. While this motive was never presented at Simpson's criminal trial, it was offered at the civil trial where Simpson was found liable for Goldman's and Brown's murders. It seems likely that Darden's and Clark's inability to offer the jury a strong motive for Brown's murder may have been sufficient to sway the jurors toward acquittal in the criminal trial.

While there were no eyewitnesses to Goldman's and Brown's murders, Clark was convinced that there was "devastating proof of [Simpson's] guilt;" she planned to show the jury of ten women and two men, including nine Blacks, two Whites, and one Hispanic, that there was a path of "blood where there should be no blood ... [and] ... that [the] trail of blood [led] from Bundy through his [Simpson's] own Ford Bronco and into his house in Rockingham." Toward that goal, Clark provided the jury the following forensic evidence: (1) blood with Simpson's blood type and DNA present on the rear gate of Brown's condominium and on the walkway leading from the crime scene to the gate; (2) hair on Goldman's shirt consistent with Simpson's hair; (3) bloody shoe prints at the Bundy Drive crime scene that were made by size 12 Bruno Magli Lorenzo model shoes, the same shoe size that Simpson wore; (4) a bloody, left Aris Isotoner Light, size XL leather glove found near Goldman's body that matched a bloody right leather glove found on Simpson's property that had Goldman's, Brown's, and Simpson's DNA and hair; (5) drops of blood with Simpson's DNA leading from Simpson's Ford Bronco to the foyer of Simpson's home; (6) fibers similar to fibers present in the carpeting in Simpson's Ford Bronco, and hair similar to Simpson's hair inside the blue knit ski cap discovered at the crime scene; (7) fibers similar to fibers in Goldman's shirt on the blue knit cap found at the crime scene; (8) and blood with Brown's and Simpson's DNA in Simpson's Ford Bronco and on socks found in Simpson's bedroom.[44]

As for the leather gloves found at the crime scene and on Simpson's property, Darden told the jury that the gloves must have belonged to Simpson since Brown had purchased two similar pairs of gloves in 1990 at Bloomingdale's, a department store in New York. She most likely had given Simpson one or both pairs.[45]

Simpson's defense attorneys recognized that there was no evidence to indicate that Simpson wasn't at Brown's condominium the night Goldman and Brown were murdered or that the blood found at the Bundy Drive crime scene and at Simpson's estate wasn't Simpson's. At first, they proposed that Goldman and Brown had been killed by drug dealers; however, when Ito overruled them, saying that their theory was "highly speculative," the attorneys instead decided to cast doubt on the reliability of the forensic evidence by insinuating, speculating, and suggesting that the forensic blood evidence had been improperly collected, mishandled, contaminated, compromised, corrupted, and planted.[46]

Thus, when police department nurse Thano Peratis testified that in retrospect, he believed that he only withdrew six and a half milliliters of blood from Simpson the day he was interrogated and not eight milliliters as he had originally testified, Simpson's defense attorneys ignored his testimony and claimed that Vannatter or other "corrupt police officers" used the one and a half milliliters of "missing blood" to stain the evidence.[47] Similarly, when criminalist Collin Yamauchi suddenly remembered that he had gotten blood on his latex gloves while handling a vial of Simpson's blood, defense attorney Barry Scheck suggested that Yamauchi had transferred the blood onto the leather glove found at Simpson's estate and onto Simpson's Ford Bronco.[48]

Furthermore, in their cross examination of the police criminalist, Simpson's attorneys got Dennis Fung to concede that a blanket taken from Brown's home to cover Brown's body "might" have carried hairs or fibers that could have then been transferred to Goldman and Brown. "I knew there was a danger of cross contamination," Fung testified.[49] Fung further admitted to placing blood samples in plastic bags even though he knew that by doing so, it might lead to bacterial growth, and to storing the blood samples for several hours in a hot van where they "might" have deteriorated.[50] Robin Cotton of Cellmark Diagnostics, the laboratory where some of the DNA testing was done, agreed that placing blood samples in plastic bags in a truck without air conditioning for an extended period of time could degrade DNA so that it could give false readings.[51] However, when the prosecutors asked Cotton whether degradation could make the DNA look like that of another person, she emphatically replied, "No!"[52] Simpson's defense team countered that Cotton's laboratory couldn't be relied upon for the accuracy of its DNA analyses since on two separate occasions in the five to six years prior to the Simpson trial, her laboratory made false matches in DNA testing due to sample handling errors or cross contamination.[53]

Genetic statistician Bruce Weir similarly admitted to making mathematical errors, noting that his values of genetic frequencies in mixed blood stains—stains that contain more than one person's blood—were "consistently wrong" because of a computer programming error.[54] "It was worse than I realized," Weir testified. However, Weir was adamant that the conclusions he reached were accurate. Nonetheless, Simpson's defense team claimed that because of Weir's mathematical errors, his analyses could not be trusted.

Later, when Fuhrman, the police detective who found the matching leather glove on Simpson's estate and coincidentally, who had charged Simpson with spousal abuse in 1989, was called to the stand, he denied ever having used the word "nigger" in the prior ten years.[55] Lead defense attorney Cochran, however, had managed to obtain a tape recording of an interview conducted between 1985 and 1994 in which Fuhrman had used the racial slur numerous times and had discussed how police planted evidence on criminal suspects. Much to the prosecution's dismay, Ito permitted a few excerpts of the recording to be heard in open court.[56]

In his closing argument, Cochran played "the race card," or what he called "the credibility card," describing Fuhrman as a racist detective, even comparing him to Hitler. Without providing any evidence to support his claim, Cochran told the jury that Furman planted the bloody leather glove on Simpson's property after he lifted it from the Bundy Drive crime scene.[57] Fuhrman denied the allegation, saying, "There was never ... a remote, not a million, not a billion-to-one possibility I could have planted anything. Nor would I have a reason to," but the harm had already been done.[58]

More than 150 million television viewers, 57 percent of the population of the United States, tuned in at 10:00 a.m. on October 3, 1995, to watch the jury announce the verdict in the Simpson trial. The response to the not guilty verdict was split along racial lines—according to one CNN poll taken at the time, nearly 90 percent of African Americans thought the jury got it right, while 49 percent of White Americans believed that Simpson got away with murder.

I don't discount the possibility that racial bias or "jury nullification," in which the jurors made a political statement about police-minority relations, may have played a role in the decision to render a not guilty verdict. But it is my opinion that the "Keystone Cops" investigation of Goldman's and Brown's murders, as well as the prosecution's mistakes and lack of adequate preparation, Ito's mismanagement of the trial, and celebrity worship—as evident by the cheering crowds and nearly one hundred and fifty million viewers of the white Bronco chase, an early prelude to reality TV—significantly contributed to the outcome of the trial.[59]

One needs only to compare the proceedings of the televised criminal trial to that of the untelevised civil trial to appreciate the effect that television had on the outcome of the two trials. Under Ito's mismanagement, Simpson's was the longest jury trial in California history.[60] Jurors often showed signs of exhaustion, and Ito had to repeatedly urge the defense attorneys to "move along" and to "listen to the jurors groan."[61] Three months into the trial, Ito was still admonishing the attorneys that "they want to go faster than we are going."

Unlike the criminal trial, which lasted nearly eight months, the civil trial took less than half as long. Furthermore, while Ito allowed the defense to introduce racism and to challenge the laboratory test results, this was prohibited in the civil trial. Finally, the jury in the criminal trial deliberated less than four hours before finding Simpson not guilty while the jurors in the civil trial took approximately sixteen hours to conclude that Simpson wrongly caused the deaths of Goldman and Brown.[62]

Simpson's wasn't the only criminal trial to be televised. In 1982, Claus von Bülow was tried for murdering his wife in the first major televised criminal trial in the United States. Found guilty and sentenced to thirty years in prison, von Bülow hired Harvard law professor Alan Dershowitz for his appeal; von Bülow was exonerated in a second trial. By coincidence, Dershowitz was retained by Simpson's defense team to prepare an appeal if Simpson was convicted.

In my opinion, the prosecution in Simpson's criminal trial made at least two very significant blunders, the first of which occurred during jury selection. Contrary to the advice of her jury consultants, Clark believed that women, regardless of race, would sympathize with Brown because she had been physically abused by Simpson.[63] However, when one of the dismissed women jurors told reporters that the evidence of Simpson's physical abuse toward Brown was "a whole lot of nothing that doesn't mean he is guilty of murder," Clark dropped this argument from the prosecution's case.[64]

The second, and perhaps most glaring mistake was made by Darden when he asked Simpson to don the bloody leather gloves allegedly worn by Goldman's and Brown's killer. By now, the blood had dried and the gloves had shrunk by as much as 15 percent.[65] Based on my experience as an expert witness, attorneys do not want to be blindsided by asking a question at trial for which they don't already know the answer.[66] And yet, notwithstanding this "sacred rule," Darden asked Simpson to put on the gloves. In what was a performance worthy of an Oscar, Simpson struggled to put his hands into the gloves, which had shrunk to "a little bit above ... a large size, but well below an extra-large," according to Richard Rubin, former vice president of the glove maker Aris Isotoner, Inc. The prosecution never fully recovered from the damage caused by this serious debacle. This famously led Cochran to proclaim, "If it doesn't fit, you must acquit!" According to Richard Greene, an attorney and a jury consultant, "There seems to [have been] some very sloppy preparation" by the prosecution.

Other prosecutorial errors in the trial included the filing of the case in downtown Los Angeles instead of in Santa Monica, the district in which the crime had been committed and where the jury would have been largely White and more educated. Furthermore, the prosecutors did not seek the death penalty and have a "death-qualified" jury that would have been more likely to convict. In addition, they took too long to provide too much evidence—eight months, fifty-eight witnesses, and 488 exhibits—thereby losing focus and tiring the jury. They also had Fuhrman testify without properly checking his background and they did not find the Bruno

Magli shoes the killer allegedly wore the night of the murders, whereas photographs taken on September 26, 1993, nearly nine months prior to Goodman's and Brown's murders, showing Simpson wearing Bruno Magli shoes, were located and presented at the civil trial. Finally, they did not find the murder weapon or the murderer's bloody clothes.[67]

The impression I was left with after I reviewed the totality of the publicly available information in the Simpson case was that Darden and Clark treated Goldman's murder almost as an afterthought. For its part, the media described Goldman as "an innocent bystander," someone who was "in the wrong place at the wrong time," a conclusion with which I vehemently disagreed.[68] In my opinion, Goldman was exactly where he was supposed to be, doing a good deed for Brown. "He was always a good kid," said Goldman's father, Fred. "He was fun. He had a good sense of humor, always laughing.... He had a good heart.... He didn't deserve this!" It is quite possible that had Goldman's murder been tried separately from Brown's, the prosecution might have gotten a conviction.

After the jury in Simpson's criminal trial reached its verdict, chief prosecutor Gill Garcetti told reporters, "Don't look at this case as being how most cases are handled. Juries do the right thing, nearly all of the time." Deeply disappointed, Fred Goldman took exception to Garcetti's comments. "I deeply believe that this country lost today. Justice was not served."

Forever linked to the death of Nicole Brown Simpson, Goldman earned fifteen minutes of fame because of the circumstances surrounding his death. In time, his name disappeared from the front pages of newspapers and magazines, but not from the minds and hearts of his family and of regular Americans. While Simpson's criminal trial did not produce the result that the Goldman family had hoped for, Fred Goldman was given another opportunity to make things right for his son a year later. At the civil trial, Simpson was found liable for Goldman's and Brown's murders and was ordered to pay $33.5 million in damages to the two families. Then, on October 3, 2008, thirteen years to the day since the criminal trial ended, Simpson was found guilty of robbery and kidnapping in an unrelated case and was sentenced to thirty-three years in prison. But after serving only nine years, Simpson was released on parole, thereby robbing the Goldman family of their one and only consolation. Justice still has not been fully served!

CHAPTER 6
Admiral Mike Boorda
Died May 16, 1996
Suicide by Gunshot

NEWSWEEK MAGAZINE SCHEDULED a meeting with four-star admiral Mike Boorda, chief of U.S. Naval Operations, at 2:30 p.m. on Thursday, May 16, 1996.[1] The magazine's editors were about to publish an article about Boorda wearing two decorations on his uniform that he had not earned, but they wanted to hear his side of the story before doing so.[2] "We were prepared to give the admiral his say. We wanted to be fair," said Roger Charles, a retired Marine Corps officer and a reporter at the *National Security News Service*.[3]

It all began five days earlier, on May 11, when David H. Hackworth, a highly decorated retired army colonel and a part-time contributing editor to *Newsweek* told Maynard Parker, one of the magazine's editors, that he was working on a story that "called into question the military decorations" Boorda had been displaying on his uniform.[4] The medals in question were two small bronze Combat "V" devices, one pinned to a Navy achievement ribbon that Boorda had been awarded in 1965, and the other attached to a Navy commendation ribbon he had earned in 1973.[5] Hackworth said it was a grave matter of honor in the military and "the worst thing you can do" to wear the Combat "V" device when it is not deserved.[6]

Before the anticipated meeting, *Newsweek* Washington, DC Bureau Chief Evan Thomas and the magazine's national

81

security correspondent, John Barry, conferred with Charles. Besides producing documents he obtained under the Freedom of Information Act, Charles presented the newsmen photographs from the 1970s showing Boorda wearing a uniform without the Combat "V" devices, as well as three pictures from the 1980s and one from January 1996 in which they could clearly be seen on Boorda's chest. Subsequent phone calls to other Pentagon sources confirmed Hackworth's story.

On May 16, shortly before noon, Admiral Kendell Pease, the Navy's spokesperson, called *Newsweek* wanting to know what would be discussed at the interview. Thomas described the allegations against Boorda and noted that "Pease sounded quite friendly and cool about the whole thing."

Pease informed Boorda about the upcoming meeting with the journalists approximately fifteen minutes after his conversation with Thomas had ended. Boorda "obviously was concerned," Pease later said. "He asked me, 'What do we do? [But] then he answered his own question—'We tell 'em the truth.'"

Lunch was brought to Boorda's office at 1:00 p.m., but Boorda declined the meal, telling Pease that he was going home to eat. Dismissing his driver, Boorda got into his car and drove to his government-issued residence at the Washington Navy Yard, the Marine guard saluting him as he passed through the gate.[7] Once home, Boorda went up to his second-floor study and typed two letters on his computer.

A half hour prior to the scheduled meeting with *Newsweek*, people at the Washington Navy Yard heard a single gunshot coming from the direction of Boorda's home. Everyone rushed to the admiral's house, where they saw Boorda lying in the back yard with a single gunshot wound to his chest.[8] Attired in his dress white uniform, Boorda displayed his three highest medals over his left breast—the Defense Distinguished Service Medal, the Navy Distinguished Service Medal, and the Legion of Merit, the latter two with gold stars. Lying near Boorda's body was a .38-caliber Smith & Wesson pistol that his son-in-law had given him six months earlier.

An ambulance arrived at 2:15 p.m. and transported Boorda to District of Columbia General Hospital where he was pronounced deceased. He was fifty-six years old.

The Autopsy

The Navy has not released the autopsy report; however, based on published lay articles, Boorda suffered a single, self-inflicted gunshot wound to the chest, the bullet ripping through the sternum, causing massive damage to the heart and emerging from the back.

Cause and Manner of Death

Foul play was not suspected in Boorda's death.

Two suicide notes written by Boorda were discovered at his residence. One was addressed to Boorda's wife and four children. In the other, addressed to "My Sailors," Boorda wrote, "I am about to be accused of wearing combat devices on two ribbons I earned during sea tours in Vietnam. It turns out I didn't really rate them. When I found out I was wrong, I immediately took them off, but it was really too late. I couldn't bear to bring dishonor to you."[9] Fearing that the Navy's already tarnished reputation would be further damaged by his medal controversy, Boorda claimed that it was "an honest mistake," but one that could easily be misinterpreted. A Pentagon official who reviewed the note said that Boorda "was concerned about what he did and how it would be perceived by the fleet, by the sailors, by the media."

Based on my review of the circumstances surrounding the death and published lay articles, as well as the absence of foul play and the presence of two suicide notes, I concluded that the cause of death was a self-inflicted gunshot wound to the chest. The manner of death was suicide.

Life and Career

Boorda was born on November 26, 1939, in South Bend, Indiana, but he grew up in Momence, Illinois.[10] His father served as a storekeeper second class in the Navy during World War II, giving five-year-old Boorda an opportunity to salute "every sailor on the base" and to dream of one day becoming a sailor himself.

A bit of an outcast, Boorda competed on his high school's varsity football team, drank six-packs of beer, occasionally skipped school, and despite being bright, repeated tenth grade.

When he was seventeen years old, Boorda dropped out of school, lied about his age, and joined the Navy. "I wanted to get away from it," Boorda said, referring to his parents' constant arguing. Their marriage eventually ended in divorce. "The Navy filled in some of the things that had been missing in my life," Boorda declared. "I still wanted to go home, but I wanted to go home wearing a uniform that said I was something special—that said I had done it." Two years later, Boorda married Bettie Moran, a freshman at the University of Oklahoma; soon thereafter, he became a dad.

In 1961, Boorda was selected for Officers' Candidate School.[11] Extremely well organized and disciplined, and with new lieutenant epaulets on his shoulders, Boorda was sent to Vietnam in the spring of 1965 aboard the destroyer Craig. While on the Craig, he was awarded a Navy Achievement Medal that sailors claimed was routinely handed out "just for showing up;" in 1973, as executive officer on the frigate Brooke, Boorda earned a Navy Commendation Medal.

Boorda received a Bachelor of Arts in Political Science from the University of Rhode Island in 1971. A "superb, resourceful and daring officer," especially in war games, he served in a variety of staff and command positions. As Commander in Chief, Allied Forces Southern Europe and Commander in Chief, U.S. Naval Forces in Europe and of NATO forces, Boorda ordered an airstrike in 1994 against four Bosnian Serb aircraft flying in violation of the United Nations ban on fixed-wing flights. In April of that year, he became chief of U.S. Naval Operations.

Despite his admirable political skills, some at the Pentagon accused Boorda of being too willing to appease political correctness. In a 1996 speech at the U.S. Naval Institute in Annapolis, Maryland, former Secretary of the Navy Jim Webb proclaimed that the Navy's top officers had lost their "moral courage" and that "some are guilty of the ultimate disloyalty. To save or advance their careers, they abandoned the very ideals of their profession in order to carry favor with politicians," a clear reference to Boorda.

By 1996, news that Boorda had been wearing unauthorized Combat "V" devices for at least ten years had trickled down to the attention of the editors of *Newsweek* magazine.

Conclusions

Boorda stopped wearing the Combat "V" decorations on July 25, 1995, after Joe Trento, a reporter at the *National Security News Service,* started asking questions and Captain Tom Connelly,

Boorda's attorney, told Boorda that he wasn't authorized to wear the medals. Although the citations accompanying the Navy Achievement Medal and the Commendation Medal referred to Boorda's service "while operating in combat missions" on the destroyer John R. Craig and his involvement in "combat operations" in Vietnam, respectively, they didn't explicitly authorize Boorda to wear the Combat "V." "Apparently, the bureaucratic rule is that you shouldn't wear it unless the citation has a specific sentence saying you are entitled to wear the Combat 'V,'" said Admiral Elmo R. Zumwalt, retired chief of Naval Operations from 1970 to 1975. According to senior Navy officers, Boorda should have known that he wasn't entitled to wear the Combat "V," and that by doing so, he was in violation of the rules.[12]

Charles, who was the source for the *Newsweek* article, noted, "It was not sufficient just to be in a combat theater. Boorda was in a combat theater. There was no question about that. But there is absolutely no evidence that his ship was ever shot at." It would have been unacceptable for any soldier, especially a high-ranking Navy officer, to wear the Combat "V" devices without a specific reference to the decoration in the citations because "Your history is on your chest, and there are very precise regulations about this," Charles said.

According to Trento, Boorda had been wearing the disputed Combat "V" devices at least since the mid-1980s. By then, he had attended the Naval Destroyer School and the Naval War College and had risen through the ranks with ever increasing assignments and military and political responsibilities.

Without additional information, it's impossible to know why Boorda began attaching the two unearned Combat "V" medals to his rectangular ribbons. One possibility is that in 1984, when Boorda was up for promotion to Rear Admiral Lower Half, seeing that he lacked experience for "bravery under fire," he may have thought that by wearing the Combat "V" it would help ensure his promotion to flag rank. If true, then Boorda would have been one of as many as 30 percent of all officers eligible for promotion to flag rank in the mid-1980s to have improperly worn their medals. Another possibility is that in his role as executive assistant to the assistant secretary of the navy, manpower and reserve affairs and his prior assignment as executive assistant to the chief of navy personnel/deputy chief of naval operations for manpower, personnel and training, Boorda wanted to impress politicians with whom he had been interacting almost on a daily basis. "When you're dealing with Congress, if you're a guy who's been in combat, they pay more attention to you because you've been through it," said Admiral Jack Shanahan, a retired vice admiral who had commanded the Second Fleet.[13] A third possibility is that wearing the unearned decorations was unintentional; in his suicide note, Boorda called it "a mistake." Whatever the reason, I find it astonishing that no one had ever noticed that Boorda had been wearing the unearned Combat "V" devices despite having been reviewed by four flag promotion review boards. B.G. Burkett, a Vietnam veteran, was not surprised; Burkett was aware of at least one other case of a Navy lieutenant commander who had fabricated a career and had gone through four promotion review boards while wearing unearned decorations, including a Silver Star and a Purple Heart.

The reaction to the Boorda revelation was mixed. As chief of naval operations during the Vietnam War, Zumwalt said that he had informally permitted Vietnam veterans who had sailed in combat areas to wear the Combat "V" medal even if they had not been fired upon or if their citation had not explicitly said that they could. Speaking of Boorda, Zumwalt explained, "In my judgment, he was entitled to wear them. I think the man was absolutely innocent with regard to any intent to do wrong." Eugene R. Fidell, an attorney specializing in military law, took a legal approach. "Even if it's an inadvertent mistake, he's not entitled to wear the 'V' until it's corrected," Fidell said. Lieutenant General Bernard E. Trainor, a retired Marine Corps commander and director of national security programs at the Kennedy School of Government at Harvard University may have said it best. "It would be easier to understand this if he were a more junior officer. Certainly, as you become more senior, particularly as you sit on awards boards, you are aware of these regulations."

The rules for awarding the Combat "V" decoration during the Vietnam War were "a little fuzzy," Fidell said. Zumwalt claimed that he verbally authorized wearing the Combat "V" device "in over one-hundred visits to ships and shore stations.... When I was C.N.O., I certainly would have told him to wear it." However, Zumwalt conceded that "he did not have the authority to authorize such distinguishing devices. Only the Secretary of the Navy has that authority, and it must be granted in writing on each award citation."[14]

Two years after Boorda died, John Dalton, the outgoing secretary of the Navy, "quietly" placed into Boorda's official file a "revised transcript of service" and a memorandum from Zumwalt stating that it was "appropriate, justified and proper" for Boorda to attach the Combat "V" devices to the two ribbons on his uniform since his service included combat operations. "My interpretation is that retroactively, he has been authorized to wear the 'V,'" Zumwalt said. However, in December 1998, a three-member panel of the Board for Correction of Naval Records reviewed the relevant Navy regulations and Boorda's military record and concluded that

Boorda had not been entitled to wear the Combat "V" devices after all.

While some have acknowledged that Boorda probably committed a minor legal offense by attaching the two unearned "V" devices to his Commendation and Achievement ribbons, the regulations in 1996 regarding the wearing of unauthorized medals were ambiguous. Most likely, Boorda's dishonor and extreme shame for violating the trust sailors had in the integrity of military awards led him to take such a drastic action as suicide. "Even if this was an honest mistake, he would be attacked, vehemently attacked, by people seeking to discredit him or to further discredit the Navy through him. It's possible that in his mind, he had become a liability to the Navy," said one of Boorda's close Navy friends. A former colleague of Boorda's at the Pentagon agreed. "The tragedy for him, for all of us in the Navy, is that he chose not to fight on."

And so, Boorda chose suicide rather than to explain how he unintentionally began wearing the unearned Combat "V" devices. Judging by comments from Zumwalt and others, had Boorda gone through with the *Newsweek* interview and explained his position, he most likely would have been forgiven.

One possible explanation for why Boorda committed suicide was because he was under extreme stress. "I think things truly were accumulating on him," said one Navy officer. These "things" included the 1991 Tailhook scandal and the sexual assault of dozens of women, the resignation of decorated admirals over charges of sexual harassment, drug and cheating scandals at the U.S. Naval Academy, a series of crashes of F-14 fighter jets, and the clashes resulting from the placement of women aboard combat ships and aircraft. "Superimpose all of these problems on the downsizing of the Navy; it's a tough situation; a tough environment. It would take it out of anybody," said Norman Polmar, a Navy historian. In my mind, there's no doubt that stress was one factor in Boorda's decision, but I think there were other reasons as well.

Boorda loved the Navy. It was his whole life. To his supporters, he was the ideal Navy officer—skilled at sea, politically savvy, and according to Marine Lieutenant General James L. Jones, "an intuitive leader." Totally devoted to "his sailors," Boorda sometimes circumvented regulations he felt unfairly penalized sailors, even instituting a mentoring program called "one-on-one leadership" to resolve personal problems before they became overwhelming. "A sailor's sailor," said Defense Secretary William Perry. "At every stage of his career, he put the interests of sailors and their families first." Said Admiral Ronald J. Zlatoper, commander in chief of the Pacific Fleet, "He was the quintessential sailor, warrior, Chief of Operations, and American patriot." Missouri Representative Ike Skelton agreed, calling Boorda "one of the finest human beings I ever knew. He just cared for his sailors." "A wise leader, a man of great integrity and character, and a true patriot," said the Chairman of the Joint Chiefs of Staff, General John M. Shalikashvili. "I've never known one better than Mike Boorda. The men and women of the Navy loved him," said Senator Trent Lott of Mississippi.

Boorda's unbridled dedication to the Navy and its sailors may have left him thin-skinned. When Webb, an ex-Marine, implied in his speech at the Naval Academy that Boorda was too political, what hurt Boorda the most was seeing the midshipmen, the future leaders of "the best damn Navy in the world," excitedly applaud as he was being attacked, when in the past, they had cheered him on. "He took many things more personally than many of us appreciated," said one of Boorda's Navy friends. "Appearances can be very deceiving. Sometimes when an individual is so dynamic, so high energy, so charismatic, it could mask the real pain."

Public attacks on Boorda escalated in the first week of May 1996. An article titled "Missing Leaders" published on May 5 in the *San Diego Union-Tribune* included an illustration of a headless Boorda in dress whites, sinking into the sea. "I figured it would sail right over most folks' heads, but the Navy folks would get it," said Bob Caldwell, the newspaper's editor. "I never wanted to hurt Mike Boorda personally." Then, on May 13, the *Navy Times* published an unsigned "Letter to the Editor" with the headline "CNO SHOULD RESIGN." The letter claimed that "Coverup, deception, character assassination and a lack of integrity are rampant at senior levels.... There is only one way out of this predicament. The Chief of Naval Operations needs to put his stars on the table and resign. Admiral Mike Boorda has not only lost the respect of his admirals, now every officer from four star to the newest midshipman at the academy has no respect for the man at the top of their organization.... CNO, they are not behind you. You are not their leader. Go home immediately—for the sake of the Navy you love." As if that wasn't enough to depress Boorda, the attacks reached a boiling point on May 16 when *Newsweek* threatened to publish a story claiming that Boorda had been wearing medals he had not earned nor had been authorized to wear. Since Boorda had already decided to resign from the Navy that August, by committing suicide, he merely hurried the process along. "Maybe this was a military way to go out," said Bob Livingston, Louisiana representative and chair of the House Appropriations Committee.

On December 20, 2006, ten years after Boorda died, President George W. Bush signed into law the Stolen Valor Act of 2005. The act broadened the provisions of the previous law and made it illegal for unauthorized persons to wear, buy, sell, barter, trade, or manufacture any decoration or medal authorized by Congress for the US armed forces. The Stolen Valor Act of 2005 was challenged after Elven Swisher, a former Marine, was convicted of violating the act by wearing the Navy and Marine Commendation Medal with a Bronze Combat "V" device, the Silver Star, and a Purple Heart, medals that he had not earned.[15] On January 13, 2016, the US Court of Appeals for the Ninth Circuit overturned Swisher's conviction. In its ruling, the court declared that wearing the unearned medals had "no purpose other than to communicate a message," which is a form of free speech protected by the First Amendment of the Constitution.[16]

In another 2007 case, Xavier Alvarez, an elected member of a California municipal water board, was convicted for falsely stating at a public meeting that he was a retired US Marine who had been wounded many times in combat and that he had received the Congressional Medal of Honor in 1987.[17] Alvarez appealed his conviction based on First Amendment rights; a three-judge panel of the US Court of Appeals for the Ninth Circuit ruled in his favor, declaring that the Stolen Valor Act of 2005 was unconstitutional.[18] This time the federal government took the Alvarez case to the US Supreme Court.

In a separate case, the US Court of Appeals for the Tenth Circuit ruled on January 27, 2012, that statements made by Rick Standlof, who posed as a Marine captain and falsely claimed to have received a Silver Star and Purple Heart in the Iraq War, were not protected by the First Amendment of the Constitution. The conflicting decisions by the Ninth and Tenth US Circuit Courts of Appeals were instrumental in persuading the US Supreme Court to agree to hear the Alvarez case.

On June 28, 2012, in a six to three decision, the US Supreme Court struck down the Stolen Valor Act of 2005 as unconstitutional, noting that the law criminalized lying about being awarded military decorations or medals. The justices stated that the law had been written so broadly as to infringe on free speech, which was protected by the First Amendment, and that lying, no matter how reprehensible, was constitutional. A year later, on June 3, 2013, President Barack Obama signed into law the new and revised Stolen Valor Act of 2013. Unlike the 2005 law, the 2013 Act had an "intent clause," making it "a federal crime to fraudulently hold oneself out to be a recipient of a decoration or medal ... with intent to obtain money, property, or other tangible benefit."[19] Clearly, this wasn't Boorda's intent when he wore the Combat "V" devices on his uniform.

As tragic as the suicide was, Boorda's was not the only suicide committed by a high-ranking US military leader. On Sunday, May 22, 1949, James V. Forrestal, a former secretary of the Navy and the first secretary of defense, committed suicide at the US Naval Hospital in Bethesda, Maryland. Admitted for "reactive depression," Forrestal left his room on the sixteenth floor of the hospital at two in the morning and walked across the hall to a small, lab-like kitchen.[20] Once there, he took off the sash from his robe, tied one end to the radiator and the other end around his neck, and then climbed out the window and jumped, only to hang for a few seconds before the sash gave way and he fell thirteen stories to his death, landing on top of the roof of the third floor passageway.

A second suicide of a high-ranking military leader was that of Rear Admiral Chester W. Nimitz Jr. A graduate of the Naval Academy, Nimitz was a decorated naval officer who commanded submarines during World War II and a destroyer during the Korean War.[21] According to his daughter, Nimitz and his wife had "always proclaimed that when they got sick and tired of feeling sick and tired, they would do themselves in."[22] Nimitz, eighty-six years old, had undergone quadruple bypass surgery and had been suffering from frequent bouts of congestive heart failure, gastrointestinal problems, incontinence, chronic back pain, impaired vision, and was falling. His eighty-nine year old wife had her own health problems, including severe osteoporosis, bone fractures, and constant pain from peripheral neuropathy. She was slowly becoming blind with macular degeneration. On January 2, 2002, after writing tax-deductible checks to their children, their spouses, and to their grandchildren, Nimitz and his wife committed suicide by ingesting an overdose of barbiturates; to ensure that they died, they secured a plastic bag over their heads.

One of the most baffling suicides of a military leader is that of Army Major General John Rossi, who was found hanging at his home at Redstone Arsenal in Alabama on July 31, 2016.[23] The highest-ranking soldier ever to have taken his own life and the first Army general to commit suicide while on active duty since recordkeeping began in 2000, Rossi was just two days shy of taking charge of the Army Space and Missile Defense Command (SMDC) and obtaining his third star.[24] An army investigation determined that Rossi had been suffering from sleep deprivation and that he had an "irrational belief that he was intellectually incapable of mastering the technical aspects of the SMDC, particularly those related to space defense."[25] Rossi's medical and career stress "ultimately overwhelmed his psychological defenses and ability to cope with these negative emotions, resulting in his decision to commit suicide during the last period of time in which he was likely to be alone before assuming command of the SMDC," the investigation concluded.

The suicide of Vice Admiral Scott Stearney, which occurred at his home in Janabiya, Bahrain, on December 1, 2018, is the most recent suicide of a high-ranking US military leader.[26] Stearney had planned to retire from the Navy in 2018, but in May of that year, he accepted the posts of commander of US Naval Forces Central

Command and Combined Maritime Forces and commander of the US Fifth Fleet in the Middle East.[27] According to his chief of staff, Stearney seemed to be "operating at a pace that was not sustainable" when he first took command in Bahrain. "He burned the midnight oil," said one staffer. Suicide notes left by Stearney described his struggle with the "significant time away from his family" and "military life;" the Navy never revealed how Stearney died.

There's no doubt that high-level military assignments can cause sleeplessness and a great deal of stress, largely due to the inherent demands and the high-profile nature of the responsibilities. Aside from Nimitz, who died while in retirement, two of the three remaining military leaders—Boorda and Stearney—died while on active duty. They were no longer able to withstand the pressures of their jobs and were eagerly waiting to retire. As for Rossi, he felt inadequate and unprepared for his new role, despite having done a good enough job to be promoted to three stars; Rossi committed suicide only two days before assuming his new command.

Common stressors that can increase the risk of suicide in the military are relationship problems, administrative or legal issues, and workplace difficulties.[28] Other conditions include psychological and behavioral disorders, such as post-traumatic stress disorder (PTSD), depression, chronic pain, sleep disorders, and drug abuse.[29] While exposure to combat can increase the risk of psychological and behavioral disorders and drug abuse, all of which can increase the risk of suicide, less than half of military personnel who commit suicide have ever been deployed or have been in combat.[30] Historically, war does not seem to increase the suicide rate in active-duty US Army personnel.

By his death, Boorda gained fifteen minutes of fame for highlighting that the military has a suicide problem, even in its high ranking officers. In 2021, 89 percent of suicides in the military were among active-duty enlisted troops, 94 percent of whom were male, 73 percent of whom were White, and 74 percent of whom were younger than thirty years old.[31] Of these, 65 to 70 percent were with firearms, 90 percent of which were with personal weapons, compared to approximately 50 percent of suicides with firearms in the general population. The second most common method of suicide among active-duty troops, accounting for 26 percent of all suicide deaths in the military, is hanging or asphyxiation. "What we know about the military that's unique is that they're more likely to own firearms and know how to use them, and that they're more likely to use firearms for the purpose of suicidal behavior as compared with the general population," said Craig Bryan, executive director of the National Center for Veterans Studies at the University of Utah.[32]

The number of suicides among active-duty military personnel increased in the first quarter of 2023 to ninety-four compared to seventy-five suicides in the same quarter of 2022.[33] The Army had the greatest increase—forty-nine in the first quarter of 2023 compared to thirty-seven in the first quarter of the prior year; the Marine Corps had fourteen compared to eight in 2022; the Air Force had a minor increase, seventeen compared to sixteen in 2022; and the Navy and Space Force saw no increase in suicide deaths in the first quarter of 2023 compared to the same period in 2022. As for veterans, about twenty have killed themselves daily since 9/11, a rate that is 21 percent higher than the general population.

The Defense Department's Suicide Prevention Office cautions that while suicide counts are informative, suicide rates "provide a more standardized way to make comparisons over time or across groups." With that in mind, according to the World Health

Organization, the global suicide mortality rate in 2021 was 10.7 per 100,000 compared to fourteen and twenty-four per 100,000 in the US general population and among US active duty military personnel, respectively.[34] Of the four military services, the suicide rate of the Army remained at thirty-six per 100,000 troops in 2021 compared to the previous year, but the suicide rates of the Air Force, Marine Corps and Navy dropped to fifteen, twenty-four, and seventeen per 100,000 troops, respectively.

"Taking care of our people is a top priority of the Secretary of Defense," said Elizabeth Foster, executive director of the Office of Force Resiliency.[35] In an effort to reduce, if not eliminate suicide in the military, the Defense Department spent millions of dollars in recent years with plans to hire approximately two thousand new mental health care workers, increase access to mental health professionals, reduce the stigma associated with mental health issues, and create an independent review committee to study the issue of suicide prevention in the military.

In December 2022, the Suicide Prevention and Response Independent Review Committee presented its report to Secretary of Defense Lloyd Austin. It included "ten recommendations addressing overarching issues within the military that the committee believed will improve service member well-being by improving operations and infrastructure" and a multifactorial approach to effectively prevent suicides in the military.[36] Despite recommendations that have yet to be fully implemented, the number of suicides among active duty military personnel increased in the first quarter of 2023 compared to the same period in the prior year.

CHAPTER 7
Kathleen Savio
Died March 1, 2004
Homicide by Drowning

BY THE TIME Drew Peterson, an undercover police officer in the narcotics unit of the Bolingbrook Police Department near Chicago, Illinois, and winner of the 1979 "Police Officer of the Year" award married twenty-nine-year-old Kathleen Savio, an accountant, he had been married twice before.[1] For Savio, it was the first time.[2]

Peterson's first marriage was in 1974 to Carol Brown, his high school sweetheart.[3] But after six years, two sons, and his several infidelities, they divorced.[4] Soon after the marriage dissolved, Peterson became engaged to twenty-year-old Kyle Piry. Piry ended their engagement claiming that Peterson was too controlling—always wanting to know where she was going, who she was seeing, and sometimes even following her. "I decided there were too many things that just made me really uncomfortable," Piry said.

In 1982, Peterson married Vicki Connolly.[5] According to Connolly, Peterson had been violent toward her and her daughter during their nearly ten years together. "[Once,] he put me up against the wall in the garage and grabbed me by the throat," Connolly said. At another time, "He told me he would kill me and make it look like an accident." True to form, Peterson had several extramarital affairs while married to Connolly, the last of which was with Savio, whom he met on a blind date.

Peterson's divorce from Connolly was finalized on May 3, 1992; two months later, he married Savio.[6] Over the course of Peterson's and Savio's marriage, police were called to the Peterson home eighteen times to investigate claims of domestic disturbances.[7] By 2001, despite having fathered two children with Savio, Peterson was having sex in his basement with his latest conquest—sixteen-year-old Stacy Cales. When Savio found out about her husband's infidelities, she filed for divorce.

On March 11, 2002, Savio filed an emergency protection order against her estranged husband.[8] In July of the same year, she alleged that Peterson had threatened her. And in November, Savio wrote to the state's assistant attorney. "He knows how to manipulate the system, and his next step is to take my children away. Or kill me instead."

Savio's and Peterson's divorce was granted in October 2003; that same month, Peterson married Cales, now nineteen years old and pregnant. Heated arguments between Peterson and Savio over the divorce settlement and the custody agreement continued to drag on past the divorce decree. "He's gonna kill me and it's gonna look like an accident," Savio confided to her sister, Susan Doman.[9]

On Sunday, February 29, 2004, Savio did not answer her phone all day.[10] Her lifeless body was discovered two days later lying in a whirlpool bathtub in her master bathroom.[11] Savio's hair was wet and soaked with blood from a wound at the back of the head despite there not being water in the bathtub.[12]

The detective investigating the crime scene happened to know Peterson well. He concluded that Savio's death was an accident. When Cales was questioned by police about Peterson's whereabouts the night Savio's body was discovered, she provided Peterson the perfect alibi—he had been home with her and the children all night.

Harry A. Milman, PhD

The Autopsy[13]

Savio's autopsy was conducted by Bryan Mitchell, a forensic pathologist, at 2:20 in the afternoon of March 2. It began with an external examination.

"The decedent appears to be of normal development, an adequately nourished and hydrated, adult, white female weighing 154 pounds and measuring sixty-five inches in length," Mitchell wrote in the autopsy report.

The long, straight brown hair was soaked in blood. The eyes were brown; the corneae were cloudy; and the sclera, the outer layer of the eyeball, was white. Foam emanated from the nostrils, a sign consistent with drowning.

The lips were purple, and the tongue was partially clenched between the teeth. "Typically you don't die with your tongue clenched between your teeth," said William Walsh, a researcher in biochemistry and medicine who reviewed the autopsy findings. "That might indicate there was a struggle at the end."

The breasts were of normal development and without palpable masses or nipple discharge. Fingerprint blanching was evident over the middle of the right breast, as well as the areola of the left breast, the central portion of the breast, and on the left thigh and calf.

It was clear from the autopsy that Savio had been injured prior to her death. Evidence included a one-inch blunt laceration, a deep cut or tear in the skin on the left parieto-occipital scalp, the region at the back of the head that lies in front and behind the ears. In addition, there were several other external injuries, including an irregularly shaped red abrasion (scrape) on the left buttocks; three oval-shaped, purple contusions (bruises) on the lower quadrant of the abdomen; a faint purple contusion on the left thigh; a circular-shaped, purple contusion on the mid-shins; linear, red abrasions on the right wrist; a circular-shaped abrasion on the right first finger; and a circular-shaped, red abrasion on the left elbow.

For the internal examination, the body was entered through the standard Y-shaped incision. The vocal cords, as well as the hyoid bone and thyroid cartilage were all intact.

The cardiovascular system was normal, with only a mild amount of epicardial fat. At 260 grams, the heart weight was in the normal range, as were the two heart ventricles, the chambers that pump blood to the lungs and the rest of the body. As for the heart valves, they were thin and delicate, but the leaflets of the mitral valve, located between the left atrium and the left ventricle heart chambers, were mildly thickened.

The coronary arteries and aorta, the large artery that delivers oxygenated blood to the rest of the body, were without atheromatous plaque, making it unlikely that Savio suffered a heart attack.

The lungs were moderately edematous (filled with water) and without evidence of tumors or fibrosis, their combined weight of 900 grams consistent with the observed edema.

As for the gastrointestinal system, the esophagus was normal. The stomach, while empty of food, contained approximately two milliliters (less than half a teaspoonful) of tannish-colored fluid, suggesting that Savio died many hours after her last meal, probably in the early hours of Sunday, March 1. The duodenum, the first part of the small intestine immediately beyond the stomach, leading to the jejunum, and small and large intestines contained their normal contents; the appendix was present and unremarkable; the liver, while smooth, glistening, and of normal weight, was congested; and the kidneys were reddish-brown, smooth, and congested.

The endocrine system—pituitary, thyroid, pancreas, and adrenal glands—was normal. The spleen was of normal weight, smooth, gray, congested, and without tumor or fibrosis. The muscles were unremarkable, and the bones were white-tan and hard. The spine and pelvis were without fractures.

The scalp was intact and without hemorrhage. The brain was unremarkable, its weight of 1,160 grams within normal limits.

Of special significance for the identification of cause of death was the presence of water in the ethmoid sinuses, a hollow space in the bones around the nose, a clear indication of drowning.[14] The presence of moderately water-filled lungs was additional evidence consistent with drowning.

Cause and Manner of Death

Toxicology testing of the vitreous humor of the eye, the clear gel that fills the space between the lens and the retina of the eyeball, failed to detect alcohol, methanol, acetone, and isopropanol. In addition, no drugs of abuse, such as amphetamines, barbiturates, and opioids, were found in the liver.

Mitchell concluded that the laceration on the back of Savio's scalp "may have been due to a fall" when Savio struck her head. Two months later, a six-person Will County Coroner's jury ruled that Savio's death was an accidental drowning.

Based on my review of the circumstances surrounding Savio's death, the absence of drugs in her system, the presence of fluid in the ethmoid sinuses, and the moderately congested lungs, I agreed that the cause of death was drowning. However, in my opinion, the findings of fingerprint blanching on Savio's chest and left thigh and calf, and multiple abrasions, contusions and lacerations on her arms and legs, abdomen, and buttocks were more consistent with a struggle than an accident. I therefore concluded that the manner of death was homicide. At the very least, it was undetermined pending further investigation.

Life and Career

Savio was born in 1963 in Glendale Heights, Illinois, the youngest of four children of Mary and Henry Savio, an installer of heating and air conditioning units. Savio's parents divorced when she was just two years old. After her mother remarried, the family moved to Melrose Park, a suburb of Chicago with a large Italian American population.

Savio dropped out of high school when she reached her seventeenth birthday and moved into her own apartment. After passing the General Educational Development Test (GED), she earned an associate degree in marketing from Triton College, a public community college in River Grove, Illinois.

"It was very important for her to accomplish things," Susan Doman said of Savio. "She wanted everything right. She wanted to fall in love, like the Ozzie and Harriet family. That's why she didn't get married until she was almost thirty."

Shortly after she ended a five-year relationship with an accountant, Savio met Peterson. Sometime later, she found out that Peterson was already married; any misgivings she may have had about marrying Peterson soon vanished. "She was crazy about him," said Anna Doman, Savio's other sister.

Within six months of his first date with Savio, Peterson divorced his second wife and proposed to Savio.

Conclusions

On October 28, 2007, three years after Savio's body was discovered, Peterson's fourth wife, Cales, disappeared. At the time, Cales was nearly finished completing her nursing degree at Joliet Junior College, a public community college in Joliet, Illinois.

Peterson claimed that he awoke at eleven o'clock that morning and found Cales gone. He told investigators that Cales had told him the previous night that she was leaving him. "I believe she's with someone else, but I believe she's safe," Peterson said.

Three days after Cales vanished, James Glasgow, the Illinois State's Attorney, told reporters that his office was taking another look at the Savio case. "There are some unusual circumstances in the 2004 case," Glasgow said. Two weeks later, Savio's body was exhumed from a grave at the Queen of Heaven Catholic Cemetery in Hillside, west of Chicago and Cales's disappearance was labeled a "potential homicide."

Larry W. Blum, a forensic pathologist, conducted the autopsy on Savio's remains.[15] After reviewing photos taken at the scene where Savio died, as well as reports of the initial investigation and results of microscopic examinations and toxicological tests conducted on postmortem tissue and blood specimens, Blum concluded, like Mitchell before him, that the cause of Savio's death was drowning.[16] Unlike Mitchell, however, Blum noted, "compelling evidence exists to support the conclusions … that the manner of death was homicide." In a subsequent Fox interview, Blum stated, "I don't think there's any possibility this was an accident, and I don't think there's any indication that this was a suicide."

The Savio family retained their own expert to perform another autopsy on Savio's remains—Michael Baden, a former chief medical examiner of the city of New York.[17] Due to decomposition of the body, Baden was unable to identify the one-inch laceration on the back of Savio's scalp or the multiple bruises and abrasions described in the first autopsy report. However, Baden noted that the prominent blue-purple subcutaneous hemorrhages originally reported by Mitchell, which he presumed were due to blunt force injuries that occurred shortly before death, were still visible in the lower quadrant of the right breast, the right thigh, and the right lower quadrant of the abdomen. Baden further observed that the heart, coronary arteries, liver, brain, and gastrointestinal tract were unremarkable, but the lungs were edematous, a clear indication of drowning. Baden agreed with Blum "that the drowning of Ms. Savio, a healthy adult, in a bathtub, with multiple blunt force injuries indicative of a struggle, should be properly classified as a homicide."

It took the two autopsies by Blum and Baden for Glasgow to conclude that Savio's death was suspicious and that the manner of death most likely was homicide, a conclusion I reached after reviewing the results of the first autopsy performed by Mitchell. "[Savio's death was a] homicide staged to look like an accident," Glasgow declared after the two autopsies had been completed.

On May 7, 2009, a Will County grand jury indicted Peterson for Savio's murder. He was found guilty of first-degree murder on September 6, 2012, and was sentenced to thirty-eight years in prison. Police believed that Peterson's primary motive was money—Savio's death a month prior to completion of their divorce settlement benefited Peterson financially.

At Peterson's trial, Blum pointed to the injuries to Savio's front and the back of her head and told the jury of seven men and five women, "[A] fall to the back in the tub would produce injuries to the back, not to the front."

"I did not kill Kathleen!" Peterson shouted when his sentence was announced.[18] "Yes, you did, you liar!" Susan Doman shouted back.

To date, Cales hasn't been found, dead or alive.

On May 21, 2016, Peterson was convicted of attempting to have Glasgow, the Illinois prosecutor in his case, murdered; he was sentenced to an additional forty years behind bars.

The Savio case is an example of how police bias and missteps can ultimately affect the determination of manner of death. The lead investigator in the case, Illinois State Police Sergeant Patrick Collins, admitted that he always thought Savio's death was an accident and never considered other possibilities.[19] "Looking back now," Collins said, "everything could have been important. But at that particular moment, I was looking for things that were more obvious."

As for the Will County coroner's inquest, the jury was limited to reaching only one of three conclusions—natural, homicide or accidental. "We did not have at the time the option of … 'undetermined' status," said Walter Lee James, one of the jurors.[20] "I think if we did have the option at that time to come to an undetermined decision, I think the majority of us would have chosen that option."

Finally, Mitchell, the forensic pathologist who performed Savio's original autopsy, missed several warning signs that the manner of death was a homicide. "There were many things, many red flags that should go up in this case. They were down," said Blum, the pathologist who performed the second autopsy. In the end, "[Savio's] injuries, her circumstances, her scene, that all spoke, and spoke very loudly to that jury."

Despite the difficulty that police departments have in apprehending one of their own, by her death, Savio gained fifteen minutes of fame by finally bringing to justice one of the Chicago area's decorated "Officer of the Year" award recipients.

CHAPTER 8

Carlos Sousa

Died December 25, 2007
Blunt Force Trauma due to a Mauling by a Tiger

SOMETIME IN THE late afternoon on Tuesday, December 25, 2007, Carlos Sousa and his two friends, Kulbir and Amirtpal "Paul" Dhaliwal, twenty-three and nineteen-year-old brothers, respectively, visited the San Francisco Zoo in California. About to start a new job selling newspaper subscriptions door-to-door, Sousa was in high spirits, undoubtedly helped by smoking marijuana and having "a couple of shots of vodka" with his two friends before arriving at the zoo.[1]

At about five o'clock, Sousa and the Dhaliwal brothers visited the lion's grotto, where they stood on top of a three foot metal railing, a few feet from the edge of a thirty-three-foot moat that had no water, shouting and waving at the four-year-old, 350-pound Siberian tiger named Tatiana.[2] All of a sudden, in a surprising and unexpected move, the tiger leaped and attacked Kulbir.[3] "She had to have jumped," said San Francisco Zoo Director Manuel Molinedo. "How she was able to jump that high is amazing to me."

As the tiger clawed and bit Kulbir, Sousa and Paul tried to distract it, yelling and screaming, hoping to scare the tiger away. Instead, the tiger turned and fixed its sights on Sousa, attacking and slashing his neck, arms, and upper body. "He didn't run," Sousa's father later said. "He tried to help his friend, and it was him who ended up getting it the worst."

Kulbir and Paul dashed the three hundred yards to the zoo's Terrace Café, seeking help, but they found the door locked because it was past the closing time of five o'clock. Nonetheless, hearing their screams, a café employee called the zoo's security at 5:07 p.m. "A very agitated male is claiming he was bitten by an animal," the café worker told the security guard who answered the call.

After killing Sousa, the tiger followed the bloody trail left by Kulbir to the Terrace Café and began mauling Paul.

Four police officers arrived at the Terrace Café at about 5:25 p.m. and found the tiger sitting beside Paul; an injured Kulbir was located nearby. At first, the officers used their patrol car lights to distract the tiger, but the animal turned, ready to charge at the officers.[4] Said officer Daniel Kroos, "Fearing that the tiger was going to attack and kill Officer Scott Biggs, or that the tiger might turn around and continue to maul the victim who could not move, I fired my department issued firearm an unknown amount of times at the tiger in an attempt to stop the threat of further attack."[5] The officers continued to shoot, with one officer putting a final bullet in the tiger's head to ensure that it was dead.

Kulbir and Paul were taken to San Francisco General Hospital in critical but stable condition. Sousa was declared deceased at the scene. He was seventeen years old.

The Autopsy[6]

The autopsy was conducted by Ellen Moffatt, an assistant medical examiner, at 5:53 p.m., the same day that Sousa died. It began with an external examination.

"The body is of a well-developed, well-nourished adult man, whose appearance is consistent with the reported age of seventeen years," Moffatt wrote in the autopsy report. The body was clad in a white T-shirt, a white undershirt, black underpants, a black jersey, denim blue jeans, a pair of black-and-white athletic shoes, and a pair of white ankle socks. Multiple white hairs were present on the body and clothing.

The scalp hair was dark brownish-black, curly, measuring approximately eight inches in length. The face was covered by a dark brownish-black beard and a dark brownish-black stubble mustache.

The eyelids were intact and unremarkable; the conjunctivae, the mucous membrane that covers the front of the eye and lines the inside of the eyelids, were clear and without petechial hemorrhages, pinpoint, round spots due to capillary bleeding; the sclerae, the outer layer of the eyeball, was white. The eyes were brown, and the pupils were equally dilated at two millimeters. The nose was unremarkable; the nasal septum was intact, and the teeth were in good repair. The ears were normally formed, and the left earlobe had a single piercing.

The neck, forearms, upper arms, hands, fingers, feet, and lower extremities were all normally formed. There were no identifiable tattoos.

There was substantial evidence of blunt force injuries to various areas of the head and neck, including abrasions (scrapes), puncture lacerations (deep cuts or tears in the skin), contusions (bruises) avulsions (forcible tearing of the skin), and linear scratches of the skull. In addition, an eight-by-three-centimeter portion of the left parietal skull, two bones in the skull which, when joined at a fibrous joint, form the sides and roof of the cranium, the part of the skull that encloses the brain, was missing; the area surrounding the missing skull had comminuted fractures, bones broken into more than three separate pieces.

The brain was significantly damaged due to lacerations and hemorrhage but otherwise was free of lesions and tumors, and its weight of 1,480 grams was in the normal range. The cervical spine was fractured between the fifth and sixth cervical vertebrae.

Multiple blunt force injuries were also apparent to the chest, abdomen, back, and extremities (shoulders, arms, forearms, hands, wrists, knees, thighs, and legs). The injuries included abrasions, contusions, and puncture lacerations.

The internal examination revealed subcutaneous fat that approximated six centimeters at its maximum thickness in the midabdomen; the average midline abdominal subcutaneous fat thickness in men is 2.9 centimeters.

The pleural cavities were unremarkable and free of abnormal collection of fluid; the body cavities had no peculiar or aromatic odor; the abdominal organs had glistening surfaces and were in their usual position; and the diaphragm was intact and normally elevated.

The hyoid bone and thyroid cartilages were intact and without fractures; the larynx and trachea were unremarkable.

As for the cardiovascular system, the heart was smooth and glistening with evidence of cardiomegaly (enlarged heart), a risk factor for sudden death from an arrhythmia, an irregular heartbeat. The heart weight of 520 grams was substantially above the average weight of 233 to 383 grams for a teenage boy. The coronary arteries had no evidence of atherosclerosis (plaque deposits) or thrombi (clots); the heart ventricles, the chambers that pump blood; the aorta, the large artery that delivers oxygenated blood to the rest of the body; and the heart leaflets were all intact and unremarkable.

The surfaces of both lungs were smooth; the pulmonary vasculature was moderately congested; the lung weights of 615 and 570 grams for the right and left lung, respectively, were moderately elevated consistent with congestion; and the pulmonary vessels were without thromboemboli (clots).

The liver was smooth and unremarkable, its weight of 1,860 grams in the normal range; the gallbladder was intact, without calculi, and contained approximately 200 milliliters of yellow-brown, viscid bile; the spleen was intact and smooth, its weight of 240 grams in the normal range; and the thymus was unremarkable.

The endocrine system was unremarkable. The pituitary gland was intact, normally developed and without lacerations, hemorrhage, or lesions; the thyroid gland was firm, red-brown, without cyst, hemorrhage, fibrosis, or lesions. The adrenal glands were normally situated, and the pancreas was soft with a normal architecture.

The gastrointestinal system was as expected. The esophagus was smooth and unremarkable; the stomach contained approximately 500 milliliters of tan-brown, turbid fluid with fragments of partially digested eggs, but no identifiable tablets, capsules, or pill fragments; the duodenum, the first part of the small intestine immediately beyond the stomach, leading to the jejunum, was smooth and without ulcers; the small and large intestines were normal, unobstructed and without lesions; and the appendix was present.

The right and left kidneys were unremarkable, their weights of 150 and 140 grams, respectively, in the normal range; the urinary bladder was intact and smooth and contained approximately 120 milliliters of clear, yellow urine. The prostate was free of necrosis and not enlarged.

Besides the substantial and significant blunt force injuries to the head, neck, and extremities, the autopsy did not reveal any other anatomical changes that might have caused Sousa's death.

Harry A. Milman, PhD

Cause and Manner of Death

Police did not suspect foul play in Sousa's death.

Toxicology analysis detected 0.04 percent alcohol in the blood, equivalent to a blood alcohol concentration (BAC) of 0.04. This is substantially below 0.08, the BAC limit for drivers in the United States. In addition, cannabinoids (marijuana) were detected in the blood, including delta-9-THC (6.6 nanograms per milliliter), the pharmacologically active metabolite of marijuana; inactive metabolites of marijuana were also found in the urine. The amount of delta-9-THC measured in the blood suggested that Sousa smoked marijuana approximately one to two hours before he died.

After reviewing the circumstances surrounding the death, the autopsy and toxicology reports, as well as published lay articles and the scientific literature, I concluded that the cause of death was blunt force injuries to the head and neck due to mauling by a tiger. A contributing factor, but not a primary cause of death, was the presence of marijuana and alcohol in postmortem blood. The manner of death was accident.

Life Experiences

Sousa was born on September 26, 1990, in Berkeley, California.[7] A student at James Lick High School in San Jose, California, he enrolled in acting and music classes outside of school with the hope of becoming an actor.

According to his family and friends, Sousa was a "typical teenager," enjoying watching movies, dancing, and "hanging out."

On December 25, 2007, Sousa and two of his friends were visiting the San Francisco Zoo when a tiger escaped its exhibit and attacked Sousa, killing him; Sousa's two friends were severely injured.

Conclusions

Confusion reigned in the early moments of the mauling incident at the San Francisco Zoo. The first emergency call made by a café worker to the zoo's security office occurred at 5:08 p.m. "A very agitated male is claiming he was bitten by an animal," the café employee told the person on the other end of the line. The security guard responded by calling the 911 dispatcher.[8]

Security guard: "I'm gonna need an ambulance to come to the zoo, the south gate.... He's saying he was bitten by an animal, but there's no animal escaped so he could just be crazy.... We don't know if he's on drugs."

A woman can be heard in the background of the recording saying, "I don't know if they are on drugs or not. They are screaming about an animal that has attacked them and there isn't an animal out.... He is saying he got attacked by a lion.... Impossible! I can't possibly imagine how he could've gotten attacked by a lion."[9]

911 Operator: "Does this guy have any weapons or anything like that ... the guy that's possibly on drugs?"

The security guard eventually received word that a tiger had gotten loose and that it had attacked Sousa and the Dhaliwal brothers. By 5:20 p.m., people at the zoo were advised to leave the zoo grounds.

Sam Singer, a spokesperson for the San Francisco Zoo, announced that the zoo "shut its gates temporarily to ensure Tatiana, the tiger, would not escape and get out into the streets and possibly further harm members of the public, shutting the gates to protect the public as well as police and fire."[10] However, due to the closing of the gates, valuable time was wasted as police and paramedics were unable to enter the zoo grounds to render assistance.

As the bleeding Dhaliwal brothers waited by the Terrace Café for help to arrive, Kulbir spoke to the 911 operator, requesting an ambulance.[11] "The police have to secure the scene" before the paramedics could enter the zoo grounds so "we know it's safe," the 911 operator told Kulbir. Twenty minutes later, the paramedics still had not arrived.

"How long does it take?" Kulbir asked. "My brother's about to die out here!"

"We just have to make sure that the tiger doesn't hurt any of the emergency units. Otherwise, there's going to be no one to help you," the 911 dispatcher replied.

This was not the first time that Tatiana mauled someone. A year earlier, on December 22, 2006, the tiger attacked Lori Komejan, a zookeeper, during a routine public feeding. According to eyewitnesses, Tatiana reached through the cage and grabbed Komejan's right arm and bit it; Komejan required several surgeries and skin grafts to repair her arm.[12]

An investigation of the Sousa and Dhaliwal mauling incident determined that the wall around the tiger's pen was just 12.5 feet high, approximately four feet lower than the recommended height of 16.4 feet, and not in accordance with accreditation standards requiring that "the barriers be adequate to keep the animals and people apart from each other."[13] "Obviously something happened to cause that not to be the case in this incident," said Steven Feldman, a representative of the Association of Zoos & Aquariums (AZA).

A major source of contention in the days following Sousa's death was whether the tiger had been provoked in some way. "Nobody was there to witness it at that time of day, it was closing," said Lora LaMarca, a spokesperson for the San Francisco Zoo. "We cannot prove the animal was provoked." Nonetheless, the zoo has made several renovations since the incident to make "sure that this will never happen again," LaMarca said. The renovations included extending the height of the exterior wall to the recommended 16.4 feet, installing glass or wire mesh fencing on top of the wall to extend the height further to nineteen feet, and connecting electrified hot wire lines across the perimeters of the tiger and lion enclosures.[14]

The tragic mauling by a tiger of Sousa and the two Dhaliwal brothers highlights the danger associated with wild animals held in captivity. Since 1990, there have been 377 dangerous incidents in forty-six states and the District of Columbia involving big cats and other exotic animals, including twenty-five deaths.[15] Of these, tigers were responsible for half the incidents, with lions accounting for the next highest number of incidents.[16] Prior to Sousa's death, the last time someone died in the United States due to a mauling by a big cat was on December 30, 2018. It was then that a twenty-two-year-old intern working at the Conservators Center in Burlington, North Carolina, was attacked by a lion while he was cleaning the lion's enclosure.

Of the cases involving serious injuries due to a mauling by a tiger, the most recent occurred on March 22, 2022, when an employee of Wooten's Animal Sanctuary & Alligator Park was hospitalized after he was attacked upon entering the tiger's enclosure during feeding time. A second incident occurred on December 29, 2021, when River Rosenquist, a custodial contractor at the Naples Zoo, was seriously mauled after he jumped a barrier and stuck his arm into the tiger's enclosure.

According to the US Fish and Wildlife Service, an estimated twenty thousand big cats are kept in private ownership in the

United States. They are often purchased as cubs or are bred for photo opportunities; sometimes, their ownership results in death. For example, a four-hundred-pound tiger dragged a ten-year-old boy into its cage in North Carolina while the boy's uncle was shoveling snow; in another incident, a pet tiger bit and crushed the skull of the owner's three-year-old son. Similar incidents have been reported nationwide.

Four of fifty states have no laws on keeping any species of dangerous wild animals—Alabama, Nevada, North Carolina, and Wisconsin—while Delaware and Oklahoma do not ban or regulate keeping big cats. Twenty-one states ban all dangerous exotic pets; the remainder allow certain species of animals or require permits to keep dangerous wild animals.

On December 20, 2022, President Biden signed into law the Big Cat Public Safety Act. The act makes it illegal to privately possess or breed big cats except by qualified entities, such as AZA-accredited facilities. Hopefully, the law will help eliminate or at least reduce the number of deaths and injuries caused by exotic animals privately owned by ordinary citizens.

CHAPTER 9
Eve Carson
Died March 5, 2008
Homicide by Gunshot

EVE CARSON WAS a twenty-two-year-old student at the University of North Carolina (UNC).[1] On Tuesday afternoon, March 4, 2008, two months short of her graduation, she attended the university's Tar Heels basketball game against Florida State.[2] At 1:30 a.m. the following morning, one of Carson's roommates invited her to go out on the town, but she declined the invitation since she was working on a class paper.[3]

At about three-thirty that same morning, Demario Atwater, twenty-two years old, and his seventeen-year-old friend, Laurence Lovette, were walking along East Rosemary Street in Chapel Hill, North Carolina, looking for somebody to rob.[4] Both youths were under supervised probation, Atwater for two prior felony convictions and for engaging in unlawful conduct, and Lovette, a high school dropout, for having been convicted of two misdemeanor crimes. When they spotted Carson trying to get into her sport utility vehicle parked in front of her house on Friendly Lane, they thought they found their target.[5] "My information is she (Carson) was an extraordinarily busy woman and it wasn't unusual for her to go to the office in the middle of the night," said police chief Brian Curran.

As Carson opened the car door, Atwater and Lovette rushed and pushed her into the back seat.[6] Lovette got behind the wheel

117

while Atwater joined Carson in the back, all the while aiming his gun at Carson's head.[7]

The two abductors forced Carson to give them her ATM card, after which they withdrew seven hundred dollars from a Bank of America ATM machine at University Mall in Chapel Hill.[8] They tried to withdraw money seven more times that night, but they were unsuccessful, having reached the card's daily limit; they withdrew an additional seven hundred dollars the following day.[9]

Throughout her harrowing ordeal, Carson kept pleading with Lovette and Atwater not to kill her, telling the two young men that they didn't have to do it and that they should all pray together. Lovette and Atwater ignored Carson's pleas, and instead, drove to the intersection of Hillcrest Road and Hillcrest Circle, a densely wooded neighborhood about a half a mile from the UNC campus, where they shot Carson dead.[10] According to Lovette, Carson had to die because she saw their faces and could identify them.

At around 4:30 a.m., Carson's roommate returned to their shared apartment and found Carson gone. Also missing were her laptop computer and her 2005 Toyota Highlander. Approximately half an hour later, police responded to a 911 call from someone who had heard three or four gunshots near Hillcrest Road.[11] When the officers arrived at the Hillcrest Circle, they found Carson's body lying on the side of the road.[12] She had been shot by a small caliber weapon in the right shoulder, right upper arm, right buttock, and right cheek, but it was the fifth bullet delivered by a sawed-off 12-gauge shotgun that inflicted the fatal wound, piercing Carson's right hand and entering her right temple and brain.

Carson's SUV was recovered about a mile from where her body was discovered.

The Autopsy[13]

The body was clad in a light gray T-shirt, dark blue sweatpants, and light blue, gray, and white athletic shoes. A metal necklace with a small, yellow metal locket, possibly gold, was around the neck, and a white paper wristband printed with the words "Be True" and "Nike" encircled the left wrist. The body was identified as belonging to Carson through photographs taken prior to her death. Carson's known medical condition of scoliosis, a sideways curvature of the spine, also helped identify her.

The autopsy began with an external examination.

"The body is that of a well-developed, well-nourished adult white female appearing compatible with the stated age of twenty-two years," read the opening line of the autopsy report. The hair, fifteen inches in length, was light brown, long, and straight. The brown eyes were without petechiae, pinpoint areas of bleeding under the skin due to burst capillaries. The sclera, the white outer layer of the eyeball, was unremarkable.

Below the left eye was a small, raised brown mole. On the back of the right hand were numerous long, straight, light-colored hairs.

The body had multiple gunshot wounds caused by two different caliber weapons. The first round, perforating gunshot entrance wound, measuring 0.2 inches in diameter, was on the right shoulder. It was without soot or stippling, often caused by unburned particles of gunpowder striking the skin that unlike soot cannot be washed away. Had there been stippling, it would have meant that the muzzle of the gun was within two feet of Carson's body when it was discharged.

The direction of the wound track was right to left, front to back, as the projectile injured soft tissues, the skeletal muscle, the fourth rib, the upper and lower lobes of the right lung, the small intestine, and the right half of the diaphragm, the muscle separating the chest cavity from the abdomen and serving as the main muscle of respiration. A small-caliber, nondeformed, full yellow metal-jacketed bullet was recovered from the wound.

A second round, perforating gunshot entrance wound, measuring 0.1 inches in diameter, was on the right buttock. It was without soot or stippling. The direction of the wound track was right to left, back to front, as the bullet injured soft tissues and the skeletal muscle, exiting at the vestibule, right of the back wall of the vagina.

The third perforating gunshot entrance wound was oval, measuring 0.3 by 0.2 inches, and located on the back of the right upper arm. The wound was without soot or stippling. The direction of the wound track was back to front as the projectile injured soft tissues, exiting on the front side of the right upper arm.

The fourth perforating gunshot entrance wound was on the right cheek. It was oval, measuring 0.3 by 0.15 inches, without soot or stippling. The direction of the wound track was front to back, right to left, as the projectile injured soft tissue, the skeletal muscle, teeth numbers five and six, the alveolar ridge, the bony, raised, thickened border of the upper or lower jaw that contains the sockets of the teeth, and the palatine portion of the maxillary bone. This is a paired bone located between the maxillae and the pterygoid process of the sphenoid bone that participates in building the three cavities within the skull—the oral cavity, nasal cavity, and the orbits, and the maxillary sinus. A small-caliber, deformed, fully yellow metal-jacketed bullet was recovered from the maxillary sinuses.

The fifth and fatal irregular gunshot entrance wound measured 2.5 by 1.8 inches; it was delivered by a shotgun. The wound was on the right temporal scalp with individual birdshot pellet entry sites at the wound margin. There was no soot or stippling at the entrance wound. The direction of the wound track was right to left, front to back, as the bullet perforated the skin and soft tissues, the skeletal muscle, the right temporal bone of the skull, and several areas on the right side of the brain. Injuries to the head and scalp included fractures, hematomas, and hemorrhages.

On the back of the right hand was an irregular perforating shotgun entrance wound, measuring 3.3 inches in diameter, with a few scattered individual pellet entries at the wound margins; there was no soot or stippling. Most likely, the wound was a defensive wound that occurred when Carson raised her hand to try to shield herself from the gunshot to her scalp. The direction of the wound track was back to front as the bullet injured soft tissues, the skeletal muscle, and blood vessels and bones of the hand; it exited through the palm of the right hand, leaving an exit wound measuring 1.9 by 4.4 inches.

The internal examination revealed a right pleural cavity, the area surrounding the right lung, filled with 250 milliliters of blood.

The cardiovascular system was unremarkable, with the heart weight of 200 grams in the normal range. The coronary arteries were without significant atherosclerosis (a buildup of plaque) or thrombosis (clots); the heart chambers and heart valves were within normal limits. The aorta, the large artery that delivers oxygenated blood to the rest of the body, was intact with no evidence of infarction—an obstruction of the blood supply, typically caused by a thrombus or embolus (blood clots) leading to death of cardiac tissue—or significant atherosclerosis.

The respiratory system showed lungs filled with blood, indicating that Carson was alive and breathing after she was shot with the handgun and prior to being shot with the sawed-off shotgun. The right lung had a gunshot wound injury.

The lung weights of 190 and 260 grams for the right and left lung, respectively, were in the normal range; the pulmonary arteries were free of thrombi (blood clots) or emboli.

Besides the gunshot wound injury of the small intestine, the gastrointestinal system was intact. The stomach contained approximately 100 milliliters of partially digested food, including kidney beans. The appendix was present; a small diverticulum, an outpouching or bulge was identified in the lower part of the small intestine. The liver was unremarkable, and the gallbladder and spleen were normal.

As for the kidneys, they were of normal size, shape, and consistency. The urinary bladder was empty.

The endocrine system—thyroid, adrenal glands, and pancreas—was normal and without lesions, as was the reproductive system, except for a gunshot wound injury of the vagina at the vestibule.

The neurologic system was unremarkable, except for the shotgun wound injury to the brain.

There was no evidence that Carson had been sexually assaulted.

Cause and Manner of Death

Toxicology testing of aortic blood did not detect any alcohol or drugs of abuse. Toxicological analysis of urine was not performed since the urinary bladder was empty.

Based on a review of the circumstances surrounding the death, the autopsy and toxicology reports, as well as published lay articles and the scientific literature, I concluded that the cause of death was multiple gunshot wounds, especially to the scalp and brain. The manner of death was homicide.

Life Experiences

Carson was born on November 19, 1985, in Athens, North Carolina.[14] A graduate of Clarke Central High School, she was student body president, class valedictorian, vice president of the National Honor Society, and a member of the school's It's Academic team.[15] In addition to her academic accomplishments, Carson volunteered at the Athens Area Attention Home, a safe house for abused and runaway teenagers, served as a page in the US House of Representatives, and worked as a laboratory assistant in a stem-cell research laboratory at the University of Georgia.

After graduating from high school, Carson enrolled at UNC at Chapel Hill, having been awarded the prestigious Moorehead-Cain scholarship.[16] At UNC, she was copresident of the Honors Program Student Executive Board, a member of Phi Beta Kappa and the North Carolina Fellows leadership development program, and cochair of Nourish International, a student movement to eradicate global poverty and hunger.

A high achiever with a double major in political science and biology and a 3.9 grade-point average, Carson tutored science at Frank Porter Graham Elementary School in Chapel Hill and at Sherwood Githens Middle School in Durham. In addition, she worked with Girls on the Run, a national nonprofit organization that "designs programming to strengthen third-to-eighth grade girls' social, emotional, physical and behavioral skills to successfully navigate life experiences." In her senior year, Carson was elected student body president and served on the UNC-Chapel Hill Board of Trustees.

Upon hearing of Carson's death, one of her classmates said, "I thought I misheard or something because with a public icon like Eve, student body president—just someone everybody loves—you kind of make them invincible. You think nothing bad can happen to a person like that. And I just didn't believe it."

"Eve was just the most wonderful young woman you would ever want to know," said Maxine Easom, principal of Clarke Central High School, from which Carson had graduated. "She was brilliant. She was absolutely beautiful. Everything she did was aimed at helping other people. It's one of the greatest tragedies I've ever known. Eve was one of the young women who could change the world."

Former UNC Chancellor James Moeser summed it up best when he said, "Eve was above all an optimistic, joyful person.... These students are not morose. In fact, they're incredibly engaged, and I think, inspired by her example."

Conclusions

Based on the size of the entrance wounds—four whose diameter was 0.1 to 0.3 inches and two whose diameter was 2.5 to 3.3 inches—police concluded that Carson was shot by two different weapons—a small caliber revolver and a sawed-off shotgun. This was confirmed when parts of the .25-caliber handgun, including the barrel that Lovette had disposed of after he shot Carson, were recovered; they matched the two bullets taken from Carson's body. A similar match was made with parts of the sawed-off shotgun used by Atwater.

Atwater was arrested at 5:00 a.m. on March 12, 2008, as he left his house in Durham; he was charged with first-degree murder and related offenses and pled guilty rather than face a possible death sentence.[17] By doing so, Atwater "acknowledges that a sentence of life imprisonment will be imposed" without the possibility of parole or early release, said Anna Mills Wagoner, the United States attorney for the Middle District of North Carolina. Beside his sentence of life in prison, Atwater was ordered to pay $212,947.10 in restitution to the Carson family and to undergo treatment for substance abuse.

Lovette, who was a minor when he shot Carson, was arrested at 4:00 a.m. on March 13 and was charged with similar crimes to Atwater's; he pled not guilty in December 2011. At Lovette's trial, Orange County District Attorney Jim Woodall presented a surveillance video from a sorority house that put Lovette and Atwater about a block away from Carson's home minutes before she was abducted.[18] The jury also saw photos taken by a security camera at an ATM machine showing Lovette withdrawing money using Carson's debit card while Atwater held Carson hostage in the back seat of her SUV. Evidence of Lovette's DNA on the interior panel of the driver's side door of Carson's SUV and of footprints in the interior of the car that were consistent with Lovette's shoes was also presented at the trial.

After seven days of testimony from forty-three witnesses, the jury of seven men and five women took less than three hours to find Lovette guilty of first-degree murder. He was sentenced to life in prison without the possibility of parole.

"This was so senseless," Woodall told reporters after the verdict was read in court. "There's never been one more brutal and meaningless [crime] than this crime."

The circumstances surrounding Carson's death are reminiscent of the way Anita Cobby, a twenty-six-year-old registered nurse, died in 1986 in Blacktown, located thirty-four kilometers west of Sydney, Australia.[19] Upon her arrival by train at the Blacktown station just before 10:00 p.m., Cobby found the public phone vandalized and inoperable. Unable to call her father to pick her up, Cobby decided to walk home. As she walked, an automobile slowed down beside her and stopped. Two of the male occupants jumped out, grabbed Cobby, pulled her into the car, and robbed, bashed, raped, and tortured her before slitting her throat and leaving her naked body in a secluded cow pasture. In sentencing the five youths to "penal servitude for life," Judge Maxwell concluded, "The circumstances of ... the murder of Anita Lorraine Cobby prompt me to recommend that the official files of each prisoner should be clearly marked, 'Never to be released.'"

Carson gained much more than fifteen minutes of fame from the tragic and horrific way that she died. UNC established two merit scholarships in honor of Carson's memory—the Eve Marie Carson Memorial Junior-Year Merit Scholarship and the Eve Marie Carson "Carolina Way" Scholarship. In addition, several memorial gardens were created in Carson's name, as well as various awards and annual events, such as the annual Eve Carson Awards for students in North Carolina's Clarke County and the Eve Carson Memorial 5K Run for Education.

CHAPTER 10
Sahel Kazemi and Steve McNair
Died July 4, 2009
Murder-Suicide by Gunshot

IN MID-DECEMBER 2008, Sahel Kazemi, a nineteen-year-old native of Iran, broke up with her boyfriend, Keith Norfleet, after a four-year relationship.[1] That same month, while working as a waitress at Dave & Buster's, a family-friendly sports bar at Opry Mills, a shopping mall in Nashville, Tennessee, she met Steve McNair, a retired professional football player sixteen years her senior.[2]

"She was pretty outgoing," said Chris Truelove, restaurant manager at Dave & Buster's, speaking of Kazemi.[3] "A lot of the guests liked being around her, and she liked being around the guests."

Over the next six months, Kazemi and McNair vacationed together in Las Vegas, Nevada, and Key West, Florida.[4] In May 2009, McNair placed a down payment on a black Cadillac Escalade sport utility vehicle and gave it to Kazemi for her twentieth birthday; valuing her independence, Kazemi planned to make the loan payments herself.[5]

"[McNair] liked her so much because they would go shopping and stuff and she would want to spend her own money," said Kazemi's nephew, Farzin Abdi. "She [was] not trying to use him like other girls ... he had been with."

Although no divorce papers had ever been filed, Kazemi nonetheless introduced McNair to her family and friends, telling them that he planned to divorce his wife.[6] "She just had it made, you know, this guy taking care of everything," Abdi said. "I think she had already put her stuff up for sale on Craigslist."[7]

Kazemi's life started to unravel during the last week of June 2009. It began when her roommate, Emily Andrews, moved out of their shared apartment and went back to her home in Pittsburgh, Pennsylvania, leaving Kazemi to pay the entire cost of the monthly rent.[8] In another unexpected financial blow, Kazemi's friend Christy returned the Kia automobile that Kazemi had given her, but she had not made the remaining payments for at least two months.[9] Suddenly, Kazemi not only had to cover the nearly $1,000 per month rent on her apartment, but she also had to pay the monthly utilities, the $800 per month loan payments on the Cadillac SUV, and the installments on the Kia, all on her meager waitress salary.

"I know she was stressed out, "said Norfleet, Kazemi's former boyfriend. "I know Jenni, and she's never been stressed out like that before."

Besides her financial woes, Kazemi was horrified to find on July 1, 2009, a tampon and a used condom in the bathroom of McNair's downtown condominium apartment he rented with his friend, Wayne Neeley, a place where Kazemi and McNair had often met. Kazemi had seen McNair leaving his "bachelor pad" with twenty-five-year-old Leah Ignagni on a prior occasion, but McNair had assured Kazemi that she was "the only one."

"I know the truth about what he's doing," Kazemi confided in Norfleet. "He's been lying to me the whole time." That evening, Kazemi contacted Adrian Gilliam Jr., a man she previously met, and inquired about purchasing a gun.

Later that night, Kazemi went to the Corner Pub, a downtown sports bar, with McNair and Vent "Casper" Gordon, a chef at

Gridiron9, a restaurant co-owned by McNair; they left the bar at quarter to one in the morning. Kazemi was at the wheel of her new Cadillac Escalade, and she soon was pulled over for speeding.[10]

According to the police report, Kazemi had "bloodshot and watery" eyes, an "obvious odor of an alcoholic beverage coming from her breath, but [she] denied any consumption" and she failed sobriety tests performed at the scene.[11] Impaired and refusing a breathalyzer test, Kazemi was arrested and charged with DUI; she was released after McNair arranged bail.[12]

In the early hours of July 2, Kazemi texted McNair. "I'm gonna have all of you soon." McNair replied, "Yes, you will." At 10:00 a.m., she messaged McNair again. "Baby, I might have a breakdown, I'm so stressed." "Everything gonna be OK," McNair told Kazemi. Twenty minutes later, Kazemi sent McNair another text. "Baby, I might need to go to the hospital. Baby, what's wrong with me, I can hardly breathe." McNair texted back. "OK, please let me know. I'm here if you need me." At approximately four o'clock in the afternoon, Kazemi texted McNair for the last time. "Baby, I have to be with you tonight. I don't care where. Tell me [you're] gonna be with me." This time, McNair did not respond.

Sometime between five and six o'clock on Saturday evening, July 3, Kazemi met Gilliam in the parking lot of Dave & Buster's and paid him one hundred dollars for a nine-millimeter semiautomatic pistol. After finishing her shift later that night, she went to McNair's downtown apartment, parked her Escalade in the condominium's parking lot, and waited for McNair to arrive, the newly purchased pistol securely in her purse.[13]

McNair was out drinking with his buddies at the Blue Moon Lagoon and at Loosers in West Nashville that Saturday night. In the early hours of Sunday morning, Fowzi Ali, a driver McNair occasionally hired, drove McNair to his downtown apartment, arriving at approximately two o'clock in the morning. Kazemi's Escalade was already in the parking lot. After dropping McNair off and parking McNair's black Lincoln Navigator, Ali took a taxi back to where he had parked his own car.

Neeley arrived at the bachelor pad at about 12:40 p.m. that Sunday afternoon. When he entered the unit, he discovered McNair seated on the living room sofa with Kazemi lying on the floor beside him.[14] At first, Neeley thought that the two were sleeping, but when he saw the blood and the spent shell casings on the floor, he rushed to the parking lot and called Robert Gaddy, a longtime college friend of McNair's. Within minutes, Gaddy arrived. Seeing McNair dead on the couch, Gaddy exclaimed, "Oh, my God, it's Steve!"

Police arrived at 1:40 p.m. and discovered McNair with two bullet wounds in his head, one of which was at close range in the right temple and the other in his left temple. Two other bullet wounds were in McNair's chest, both projectiles having exited through his back. "I could recognize the male victim right away because he was on the news, on the TV, all the time," said Feng Li, a forensic pathologist in the Office of the Tennessee Medical Examiner. "I knew that was Steve McNair." As for Kazemi, she was lying at McNair's feet, a gunshot wound on the right side of her head, the bullet having exited through her left temple.

"The sun was out," former Titans running back Eddie George said, recalling the day he heard McNair had been killed. "There was not a cloud in the sky. Then all of a sudden, when the word spread of Steve's passing, it became really somber, and it started raining. It was this dark cloud just hanging over the city that whole weekend."

While it was obvious that Kazemi and McNair both died as a result of gunshot wounds, the question that hung over the police investigation was whether their deaths were a double homicide, a double suicide, or a homicide-suicide.

The Autopsy

Li conducted the two autopsies the day after the bodies were discovered—Kazemi's at 8:20 a.m. and McNair's thirty-five minutes later.

Kazemi's autopsy began with an external examination.

The body weighed 127 pounds and measured sixty-four inches long.[15] It was clothed in a pink tank top, pink shorts, and pink, black, and white panties, all of which were stained with blood.

The hair on the scalp was long and black; the eyes were brown and unremarkable; the teeth were natural and encased in braces. The mouth, ears, and nose had no abnormalities. The neck was free of palpable masses. The abdomen was flat with a tattoo of a heart in the left lower quadrant, and the arms and legs were normally developed. Of note were the three small scars—one on the belly button, another on the left buttock, and a third on the right upper arm.

Of special importance for the identification of cause of death was the single perforating gunshot wound on the right temple. That the wound was a contact wound was confirmed by a moderate amount of soot in and around the wound. It was supported by the presence of a muzzle imprint around the wound that happened when the muzzle of the gun was in direct contact with the body at the moment of discharge.

The gunshot wound track was right to left and slightly upward, causing patchy hemorrhages (bleeding) and hemoaspiration of the lungs (aspiration of blood), as well as extensive skull fractures, brain injuries, and contusions (bruises). The bullet exited through the left temple.

Other minor injuries included a few brown-colored bruises on the left forearm and a small abrasion (scrape) on the back of the left lower leg. There was no evidence of pregnancy.

Besides the injuries caused by the projectile to the scalp and brain, there was no evidence of tumor or infection in the head or brain.

The internal examination revealed a cardiovascular system that was within normal limits. The heart structure and weight were normal; the coronary arteries were without significant arteriosclerosis (plaque buildup); the heart valves were normally formed; and the heart chambers were unremarkable. The aorta, the large artery through which oxygenated blood flows from the heart to the rest of the body, was intact. As for the respiratory system, it, too, was normal, with the left and right lungs weighing 260 and 370 grams, respectively. The pulmonary arteries were free of clots.

The stomach contained approximately 200 milliliters of digested food. The esophagus, duodenum (the lower part of the small intestine immediately beyond the stomach), the small and large intestines, the appendix, the liver, and the gallbladder were all unremarkable and without lesions. The endocrine system—pituitary, thyroid, parathyroid, adrenal glands, and pancreas—was normal.

Besides the fatal gunshot injuries to the head, scalp, and brain, Kazemi had no debilitating anatomical abnormalities or infections that could have caused her death. The question remained whether she was under the influence of drugs. To find out, I turned my attention to the toxicology report.

McNair's autopsy began with an external examination.

Li described McNair's body as that of "an adult black male measuring seventy-three and a half inches and weighing 249 pounds."[16] He did not mention that McNair was the Tennessee Titans' 2003 Most Valuable Player or that he was a co-owner of a successful restaurant in Nashville.

The body was normally developed and appeared consistent with McNair's given age of thirty-six years. The outer garments included a gray shirt, short blue jeans, a brown belt, white socks, and white sneakers, while the undergarments consisted of a white undershirt and blue boxer shorts. All the clothing was stained with blood; two bullet holes were visible on the shirt and undershirt.

The hair on the scalp was black, curly, and short; the eyes were brown with no discrete petechiae (pinpoint spots of capillary bleeding). On the face was a black mustache and beard. The mouth, ears, and nose were without abnormalities. The neck had no palpable masses. The abdomen was flat, and the arms and legs were symmetrical and normally developed.

On the right upper arm was a tattoo of a star with the initials SWAC inside the star; a tattoo of the symbol for omega and a lightning bolt with the inscription "Omega Man" was on the left upper arm. Multiple scars were present on the abdomen and back, as well as on the arms and legs.

Of special significance for the determination of cause of death were the four gunshot entrance wounds—one on each temple and one on each side of the chest.

On the right temple was a penetrating gunshot entrance wound. The bullet was delivered at close range, as evidenced by the presence of soot around the wound. The wound track was right to left, backward and downward, with the projectile causing patchy hemorrhages, significant skull fractures, and extensive damage to several areas of the brain. Lodged inside the left ear canal was a distorted, copper-jacketed, and medium-caliber bullet.

A second oval-shaped perforating gunshot entrance wound was on the left temple. Marginal abrasions without soot in or around the wound indicated that the gun had been fired at least three feet away from McNair. The wound track was left to right, slightly upward and backward, the projectile causing patchy hemorrhages, several fractures in the head, destruction of the left eyeball, and injuries to the brain. The bullet exited the head through the right temple.

Of the two perforating gunshot entrance wounds to the chest, both had marginal abrasions without soot around the entrance wounds. The wound track on the right side of the chest was front to back, backward, downward, and leftward, perforating the middle lobe of the right lung and the right lobe of the liver. The bullet exited through the right side of the back, leaving approximately 750 milliliters of blood inside the right chest cavity. The wound track on the left side of the chest was front to back, passing slightly downward through the left sixth rib, as well as the left lobe of the liver, the stomach, the pancreas, and the left kidney. The bullet exited through the left side of the back, leaving approximately 50 milliliters of blood inside the abdominal cavity.

The internal examination was unremarkable. Besides the injuries to the brain, there was some congestion, but no evidence of infection or tumor in the head.

The cardiovascular system was unremarkable. The heart was not enlarged, and the heart valves were normal. The heart chambers were of the usual dimension, and the coronary arteries were without significant arteriosclerosis. As for the respiratory system, the left lung weighed approximately twice as much as the right lung due to moderate congestion—640 and 340 grams for the left and right lung, respectively.

The digestive system was unremarkable. The stomach was empty; the esophagus, duodenum, the first part of the small intestine immediately beyond the stomach, leading to the jejunum, small and large intestines, and appendix were all normal. The liver had the expected color and consistency and was without lesions; the gallbladder contained approximately eleven milliliters (about two teaspoonfuls) of bile. The spleen was normal, and the thymus was unremarkable.

The right and left kidneys weighed 150 and 170 grams, respectively, and were unremarkable. The urinary bladder contained approximately 725 milliliters of urine.

The endocrine system—pancreas, pituitary, thyroid, parathyroid, and adrenal glands—was normal.

Cause and Manner of Death

By the time police were called to McNair's bachelor pad, Kazemi and McNair had been dead for several hours. Inside the apartment, there was no sign of a struggle or forced entry.

Five bullets and five casings were recovered from the unit, as well as a 9-millimeter handgun underneath Kazemi's head. All the bullets and casings had been fired from the same 9-millimeter revolver.

Toxicology testing of postmortem blood taken from a femoral vein in Kazemi's thigh failed to detect alcohol or drugs like barbiturates, amphetamines, cocaine, opiates, or fentanyl. While delta-9-THC, the pharmacologically active metabolite of marijuana, was not detected in Kazemi's blood, low amounts (five nanograms per milliliter) of the inactive metabolite carboxy-tetrahydrocannabinol (carboxy-THC) were measured. The lack of delta-9-THC and the presence of carboxy-THC in the blood meant that Kazemi had consumed marijuana at least a week or more prior to her death.

Like Kazemi, McNair also did not have sedatives, stimulants, opioids, or other prescribed or illegal drugs in his system. However, toxicology testing measured alcohol at 150 milligrams per deciliter of blood, equivalent to a blood alcohol concentration (BAC) of 0.15 percent, an amount approximately twice the legal limit for drivers in the United States.

Two bullet holes were found in the wall above the sofa where McNair's and Kazemi's bodies were discovered; each had been caused by a bullet exiting Kazemi's and McNair's heads. A 9-millimeter bullet with remnants of Kazemi's hair and blood was recovered from the apartment next door to McNair's. Two other bullets were recovered from the couch on which Kazemi's and McNair's bodies were found; the bullets had exited through McNair's back.

Laboratory testing detected trace elements of gunshot residue on Kazemi's left hand, but not on McNair's. In addition, DNA analysis determined that blood stains on McNair's lap and shirt belonged both to McNair and to Kazemi.

Based on an analysis of the crime scene, laboratory testing, and McNair's BAC level, it appeared that McNair had fallen asleep while seated on the living room sofa, at which time Kazemi shot him first in the left side of the head, then twice more in the chest. Kazemi then placed the gun against McNair's right temple and pulled the trigger one last time before shooting herself in the head, her body falling into McNair's lap and eventually sliding down to the floor and landing at McNair's feet.

"To me, shooting [McNair] ... more than once is kind of that revenge thing," said Greg McCrary, a retired agent of the FBI. "When we have something like this, when we deal with overkill, there's more emotion. It's more affective, more rage, more getting even, whatever that idiosyncratic motive may be."

"The police department has concluded that Steve McNair was murdered by Sahel Kazemi and that, in turn, Sahel Kazemi killed herself with a single gunshot wound to her head," Nashville Police Chief Ronal Serpas announced at the conclusion of the police investigation. "The totality of the evidence clearly points to a murder-suicide."

A year after Kazemi and McNair died, a grand jury determined that there was not enough new evidence to reopen the case. "Without any doubt, I remain confident in the murder-suicide conclusion," declared Steve Anderson, the new chief of the Nashville Police Department.

After I reviewed the circumstances surrounding Kazemi's and McNair's deaths, as well as the police, autopsy, and toxicology reports, published lay articles, and the scientific literature, I concluded that McNair died from multiple gunshot wounds to the head and body; Kazemi's death was caused by a single gunshot wound to the head. The manner of McNair's death was homicide while Kazemi's was suicide.

Life and Career

Kazemi was born on May 29, 1989, in Iran. In 2000, Kazemi's mother was killed during a home invasion and robbery while visiting her daughter, Soheyla. When Iranian police arrived to investigate, they learned that the family was Baha'i, a faith not recognized by Islam. Not waiting for the punishment that often was inflicted on Baha'i worshippers, Kazemi and her sister quickly left Iran, going first to Turkey and then, on August 29, 2002, to the United States, where they settled in Jacksonville, Florida .

Kazemi attended Englewood High School and later transferred to Orange Park High School. When she was sixteen years old, she dropped out of school and moved to Nashville, Tennessee with her boyfriend, Norfleet.

"We didn't know [she was relocating] until she had her things packed and said she was leaving," said Kazemi's niece, Sepide Salmani.

According to Salmani, Kazemi was a "party girl" who liked shopping for youthful clothes at Bebe, a specialty retailer known for its line of fashionable, trendy styles geared to the twenty to midthirties age group. "She always wanted people around," said Soheyla, Kazemi's sister.

"She was always joking about something.... Even if she went out the previous night and had very little sleep, she came in with all this energy," said Courtney Carter, a friend and former coworker at Dave & Buster's.

Working at Dave & Buster's had its advantages, especially when the Tennessee Titans or other celebrities stopped by; it usually meant bigger tips. McNair was especially generous, often leaving tips that exceeded 50 percent of the food tab. One day in December 2008, McNair arrived at the restaurant and sat at one of Kazemi's tables. By the time he left, Kazemi had given him her number.

McNair was born on February 14, 1973, in Mount Olive, Mississippi.[17] His mother was a single parent who raised five sons by working the night shift at a local factory. To help pay the bills, McNair and his brothers performed odd jobs, including mowing lawns during the summers.

At Mount Olive High School, McNair ran track for the Pirates track and field team and played football, baseball, and basketball.

He earned "All State" honors in all these sports and was named "All-American" by *Super Prep* magazine.

After graduating from high school, McNair was recruited by the Seattle Mariners baseball team; however, he was determined to play football and to be a quarterback. Although pursued by many outstanding large colleges, McNair chose Alcorn State University, a public historically black university, after the school guaranteed him a shot at playing the quarterback position.

Athletic and with a strong arm, McNair was known as "Air McNair" for his passing abilities. In 1995, McNair became the third overall National Football League (NFL) draft pick when the Houston Oilers selected him for its team. Within two years, the Oilers relocated to Tennessee, changed its name to the Titans, and made McNair its starting quarterback; he remained in that position for the next eight years.

During his eleven years with the Titans, McNair played in three Pro Bowls, led his team to a heartbreaking defeat in Super Bowl XXXIV, and was named NFL's Co-Most Valuable Player in 2003.

McNair retired from professional football in April 2008 after spending his final two seasons with the Baltimore Ravens. By the time he met Kazemi, he had been married for more than ten years. Nonetheless, despite being a father of two boys from previous relationships and two more from his marriage to Mechelle, McNair was having affairs with different women and drinking, nightclubbing, and partying to all hours of the night.[18] "I think clearly ... this part of his lifestyle ... those variables, are where you would look [for McNair's] downfall," McCrary, the retired FBI agent, said when he heard that McNair had been killed.

Conclusions

"We do know that she was clearly sending a message during the last five to seven days of her life that things were going bad quickly," Police Chief Serpas said of Kazemi. Stressed out about her mounting bills, her DUI, and full of rage and jealousy knowing that McNair had been seeing another woman, Kazemi shot McNair several times in the early hours of July 4, 2009, before shooting herself in the head.

"It's the compilation, I think, of all those sorts of stressors that probably was the precipitating factor—the confluence of all that—that led to this tragedy," said McCrary, the retired FBI agent.

The tragic deaths of Kazemi and McNair have some similarity to the way Romeo and Juliet died in William Shakespeare's play of the same name. In the play, Romeo, a member of the Montague family, finds what appears to be the lifeless body of Juliet, a Capulet, whom he secretly married, in her family tomb. Believing Juliet to be dead, and filled with grief, Romeo ingests a potent, fast-acting poison and takes his own life. What Romeo does not know, however, is that Juliet had not taken poison but had ingested a powerful sedative so she could avoid being forced to marry Paris. When Juliet awakens and sees that Romeo has died, she drinks the few remaining drops of the poison, but it has no effect since the dose was too low to cause her death. Juliet then takes Romeo's dagger, stabs herself in the heart, and dies. It is a heartbreaking and tragic ending to an otherwise beautiful love story.

Like Juliet, McNair also was asleep before he died. However, in contrast to Romeo who died by poisoning and Juliet who stabbed herself to death, McNair and Kazemi both died from shotgun wounds. Thus, unlike the double suicide of Romeo and Juliet, the manner of McNair's and Kazemi's deaths was murder-suicide.

Clinical and forensic psychologist Joni E. Johnston noted that 89 percent of people who commit murder-suicide are male and about 69 percent of the victims are a current or former girlfriend or wife.[19] Perpetrators of such crimes between the age of twenty and thirty-five tend to have controlling or possessive personalities and they often perceive that a relationship they are emotionally dependent on is threatened in some way.[20] In addition, these young people may have a history of sexual jealousy or of previous incidences in which they spoke of committing suicide or homicide. Having access to a gun increases the likelihood that such individuals will commit a violent act.

Unlike the cases described by Johnston, the McNair-Kazemi murder-suicide was caused by a woman, and the victim was a boyfriend. However, like many perpetrators of these types of crimes in her age group, Kazemi also was possessive, controlling, and jealous. She thought Ignagni, McNair's other girlfriend, threatened her own relationship with McNair, even telling her shift manager at work, "My life is just shit. I should just end it." As Johnston predicted, the likelihood that Kazemi would commit murder-suicide using a firearm was substantially increased when she purchased a semiautomatic pistol.

"I couldn't mind read her totally at that point," McCrary said of Kazemi, "but that to me seems to be it. We're within hours of this thing, and she's buying the gun, and that's it. The decision's been made, probably right around then. Maybe even a little before."

One possible motive for why Kazemi killed McNair was "if I can't have him, nobody can." If so, the question we're left with is who's to blame for Kazemi's suicide? There's no doubt that much of the blame belongs to her; after all, she pulled the trigger on the revolver. However, the horrific death of her mother when Kazemi was only nine years old must have taken a heavy toll on Kazemi's psychological development and well-being; mounting financial pressures undoubtedly added additional fuel to the fire.

"What happens in these cases is they get a very constricted view of their options," McCrary said. "They just don't see any other way out, and violence seems the way to just solve everything. She won't have any more financial problems. She won't have any more relationship problems.... It resolves all those issues.... It's a release of the entire psychological trauma."

Perhaps the most likely instigating factor for Kazemi's actions, in my view, was McNair's behavior. Already married with four children, McNair began a relationship with Kazemi when she was still an impressionable teenager. It's possible that McNair considered Kazemi a "passing fling" since, according to his texting log, she was one of several women he had been seeing. On the other hand, Kazemi, naive as she was, was head-over-heels in love with McNair, even making plans for a permanent life together. When she found out that McNair had been two-timing her, it was more than she could bear, and she snapped.

Don Aaron, a police spokesperson, noted, "It may be we'll never know exactly why this happened." That may be true, but be that as it may, murder-suicide is a far cry from a fairy tale ending to what arguably was an improbable, Shakespearean love affair.

By their deaths, Kazemi and McNair achieved fifteen minutes of fame by joining close to six hundred murder-suicides that occur every year in the United States.

CHAPTER 11
Carol Daniels
Died August 23, 2009
Homicide by Stabbing

CAROL DANIELS WAS ordained into the ministry of the Christ Holy Sanctified Church in 1990 and was assigned to the Holy Temple Church in Oklahoma City, Oklahoma.[1]

In 2001, Daniels was appointed pastor of the Worthy Temple Christ Holy Sanctified Church in Anadarko, a small, economically depressed town sixty miles southwest of Oklahoma City with a population of approximately 6,500.[2]

The A-frame building in which the Worthy church was housed was located just a block from the local police station, in an area that was part business and part residential.[3] With its peeling paint and torn screen door, the church overlooked two vacant homes and an abandoned car wash, near an alley where men sometimes congregated to drink alcohol. "They sit back there [and] some of them sleep there," said Mitchell Pendarvis, who lived next door to the church.

Although Daniels resided in Oklahoma City, she made the hour-long drive to Anadarko every Sunday, even after the Worthy Temple no longer had a congregation, "[just] in case people came in to worship," her son, Alvin, said.

On Sunday, August 23, 2009, Daniels drove to Anadarko at about ten in the morning and parked her car in the church's parking lot. Less than two hours later, retired Bishop Silkey Wilson Jr. and his wife, Julia, arrived at the temple and were surprised to find the front door to the church locked. "We couldn't open it, so we began to knock on the door and knock on the windowpanes, but we couldn't get in," Wilson said. They decided to go to the police station for help.[4]

Police Officer Ashley Burris entered the Worthy Temple through an unlocked back door shortly after noon and discovered Daniels's nude body lying in a pool of blood inside the sanctuary, behind the church altar, in what some people have suggested was a "crucifix-like position." Brent Turvey, a criminal profiler and adjunct professor at Oklahoma City University, doubted there was any religious connotation in the way Daniels's body was positioned on the floor. "It's highly common to find a nude body lying on the ground with their arms outstretched like a cross," Turvey said. "In fact, it happens all the time."

Daniels, who was sixty-one years old, suffered multiple stab wounds to the chest, back, stomach, and face, but mostly to the neck and throat.[5] Her hair was burned off and her scalp was singed. Defensive lacerations were visible on her hands, undoubtedly caused when Daniels tried to fight off her attacker.

The killer had taken Daniels's clothing as they were nowhere to be found. Also, the body had been sprayed with a sort dissolving chemical solution, presumably in an effort to destroy fingerprints and DNA evidence.

"The taking of the clothes was not done for a trophy, but was rather a practical act," Turvey said. "The use of dissolving spray was also a practical act."

"I've prosecuted over fifty murders, [but] this is the most horrific crime scene I've ever witnessed," said Caddo County District Attorney Brett Burns.

The Autopsy[6]

The autopsy was conducted by the medical examiner, Chai S. Choi, at 9:53 a.m. the day after Daniels's body was discovered. It began with an external examination.

"The body is that of a well-developed, apparently obese, black female," Choi wrote in the autopsy report. "The scalp hair is black, four inches long, and shows singed hair to the scalp, likely on top of the head."

Most of the right side of the face down to the neck was smeared with blood. Blood was also dripping over the left forearm and on the back of the left hand, but there was none in the nose, mouth, or ear canals.

The conjunctivae, the mucous membrane that covers the front of the eye and lines the inside of the eyelids, was white with no petechiae, pinpoint, round spots due to capillary bleeding. A brownish birth mark and a vertical midline laparotomy scar consistent with a previous hysterectomy were on the abdomen.

Depigmented scars were identified on the legs and knees; a small red abrasion (scrape) was present over the left knee.

Of special significance for the identification of cause of death were the multiple incised (cutting) wounds on the head, including over the left eyebrow, chin, and right cheek; the front and back of the neck; the back of the right shoulder; the chest, mainly over the left breast; and on both hands. In total, there were approximately twenty-five wounds on the neck alone, seventeen on the chest, and more than twenty on the back and hands. Blood stains were all over the upper chest, the right breast, and the right shoulder, as well as on the palms, the forearms, the back of the left hand, and the sole of the left foot.

For the internal examination, the body was opened through the customary Y-shaped incision. The heart was unremarkable, its weight of 330 grams in the normal range.[7] The coronary arteries only had mild evidence of atherosclerosis (plaque buildup).

A five-centimeter horizontal cut was present across the neck, but the hyoid bone was intact. The lungs were hyperinflated; the trachea had a 2.5-centimeter horizontal cut, approximately 2.5 centimeters below the vocal cord; the endocrine system—pancreas and adrenal glands—was unremarkable.

As for the gastrointestinal system, the stomach contained approximately fifty milliliters of dark brown, partly digested food, including ground meat and cheese, but otherwise was unremarkable. The duodenum, the first part of the small intestine that connects to the stomach, was normal; the liver was yellowish and fatty; the gallbladder contained no calculi; the spleen was intact; and the thymus had no grossly identifiable lesions.

The right and left kidney weighed 130 and 150 grams, respectively, each in the normal range. The urinary bladder was empty.

The brain had no significant pathology. The ribs, pelvis, and vertebrae were all intact.

Cause and Manner of Death

It was obvious that Daniels's death involved foul play.

Toxicology testing of postmortem blood failed to detect the presence of alcohol or drugs of abuse like amphetamine, cocaine, opiates, barbiturates, and benzodiazepines. Similar toxicology analysis was not done with urine since the urinary bladder was empty.

Based on a review of the circumstances surrounding the death, the autopsy and toxicology reports, and published lay articles, I concluded that the cause of death was multiple incised wounds. The manner of death was homicide.

Life and Career

Daniels was born on October 26, 1947, and grew up in Oklahoma City.[8] She graduated from Frederick Douglass High School in 1965 and briefly attended college in Dallas, Texas.

In 1971, Daniels graduated with a Bachelor of Science in Chemistry and Biology after transferring to Central State University in Edmond, Oklahoma. Over the next several years, she lived in Spokane, Washington, but in 1978, she moved back to Oklahoma where she continued her education, earning an associate degree in health technology from Oklahoma City Community College.

In 1990, Daniels was ordained into the ministry by Christ Holy Sanctified Churches where she held several offices, the most recent of which was secretary-treasurer for the state of Oklahoma. "She just loved people," Daniels's mother said.

Kevin Cheadle of Anadarko remembered Daniels this way. "She seemed to be a real nice person. She was real quiet, but she knew how to bring the Word and give a good message. She was a very Christian lady that loved the Lord, I know that." Apparently, that wasn't enough to stop a killer from murdering Daniels.

Conclusions

The Anadarko Police Department (APD) consists of four divisions— administrative, patrol, records, and investigations. According to its website, the department is committed "to exceptional service and to enhancing the quality of life for all members and visitors of our community."[9] And yet, in 2009, the most important division to investigate Daniels's murder, the Investigations Division, was ill-equipped to handle high-profile murder investigations, such as the killing of a minister, and was woefully understaffed with only two detectives with little experience. Thankfully, the APD quickly realized its shortcomings and it called upon the Oklahoma State Bureau of Investigation (OSBI) for assistance.

Right from the beginning, police were hampered by the lack of forensic evidence—the perpetrator had taken all of Daniels's clothing, as well as her purse and briefcase, and had burned the hair on top of Daniels's head. Furthermore, in an effort to destroy fingerprints and potential incriminating DNA evidence, the killer had doused Daniels's body with a chemical solvent.

Canvassing of the neighborhood surrounding Worthy Temple failed to identify witnesses to the horrific crime. Moreover, while surveillance footage from a nearby convenience store showed Daniels arriving at the church, it failed to photograph the killer.

"We had two cameras," said Police Captain Dwaine Miller. "One showed Ms. Daniels's car. The other camera pointed in the opposite direction. Had it been angled in a slightly different direction, it would have pointed to the back of that church and right at that alley."

Robert Richardson, a homeless man who was inebriated at the time of the murder, told police, "Suddenly, I looked up and saw this man leaving the church all covered in blood, I was shocked. He was a big guy ... black, bald head, and he was carrying a knife. He turned [north along Broadway Avenue], though, so I didn't get a good look at his face. I think he was wearing some sort of overalls, but to be honest, I couldn't really tell." Police were unable to verify Richardson's statement.

In 2015, nearly six years after Daniels was murdered, a known female drug user told police that two local drug dealers had been involved in the crime. "She actually witnessed the suspect with a black blouse and a knife that had blood on it ... and it was around the time of Pastor Daniels's murder," Caddo County District Attorney Jason Hicks told reporters. "She also advised that those items were taken into the shed [behind a home in Anadarko] and burned."

Days after providing police the potentially new lead, the woman died from a drug overdose. Nonetheless, based on her account, police identified Denise Cooper, a resident of Anadarko, as a potential suspect in Daniels's murder. Cooper was on probation for distributing methamphetamine and had been previously convicted of assault and battery with a dangerous weapon. Unfortunately, Cooper died of cancer in February 2017 before she could be interrogated by police.

With no new evidence, and despite Cooper's death, prosecutors in Anadarko concluded that Cooper and at least one other unnamed suspect were involved in Daniels's death, the motive of which police theorized was burglary.

"I look at it this way," Hicks, the Caddo County district attorney, said in 2018, "[Daniels's murder] is solved. My question is, Will we ever be able to bring it to justice?"[10]

The Christ Holy Sanctified Church in Anadarko has been closed ever since the brutal slaying of Pastor Daniels. In 2010, the building was demolished. "There are too many bad memories," said pastor Ezra Randle of Elk City, Oklahoma.

Jessica Brown, a spokesperson for the OSBI, proclaimed, "[Daniels's murder] is by no means a cold case." Nevertheless, no suspect has been apprehended in this heinous crime.

CHAPTER 12
Jayne and Corinne Peters
Died July 13, 2010
Filicide-Suicide by Gunshot

THE CITY OF Coppell, a bedroom community of approximately forty-three thousand people, sits in the northwest corner of Dallas County, Texas.[1] In less than thirty minutes, residents of Coppell can reach downtown Dallas-Fort Worth, where high-end shopping, multicultural restaurants, and theatrical shows await, as well as the AT&T Stadium where the Dallas Cowboys, one of the most popular football teams in the United States, scrimmage during football season on most Sunday afternoons.

Coppell is governed by a mayor and seven council members.[2] According to the city's website, "all powers of the City, except as otherwise provided in the Home Rule Charter, are vested in the City Council, which provides for the exercise and performance of all duties and obligations imposed upon the City by law."

In May 2009, Jayne Peters, a fifty-five-year-old contract software developer, was elected mayor of Coppell after serving as a council member the previous decade and running unopposed for this unpaid job with lots of responsibilities.[3] Sharon Logan, a spokesperson for the Coppell City Council, described Peters as a "very pleasant, very professional [woman], one of the most wonderful people I had ever encountered."[4]

Peters seemed her usual, cheerful self in July 2010, balancing motherhood and fulfilling her duties as mayor.[5] "[She] was looking forward to handing out candy to people on the route" at the city's

Fourth of July parade, said Bob Mahalik, mayor pro tem of Coppell.[6]

It was during those early days of summer that Peters asked her friend and colleague, Rob Franke, the mayor of Cedar Hill, a city approximately forty miles from Coppell, if she could borrow his gun for a class she planned to attend on July 9, so she could obtain a license to carry a concealed weapon.[7] Franke was reluctant to do so, but he offered to take Peters the day prior to her class to Bullseye Range and Guns in Duncanville, about thirteen miles from Dallas, and teach her how to shoot his Glock 9-millimeter Model 17 handgun.[8] By the time they left the firing range, however, Franke acquiesced and had lent Peters his revolver, as well as magazines, ammunition, paper targets, and ear protection.[9]

At about 6:00 a.m. on July 12, neighbors saw Corinne, Peters's nineteen-year-old daughter, loading items into her brand-new 2011 silver Hyundai Sonata parked in the driveway of her two-story home in an upper-middle class neighborhood off MacArthur Boulevard.[10] Corinne had previously totaled a different Hyundai Sonata that she had received from her parents when she turned sixteen; this one was a high school graduation present she received from her mom. What Corinne didn't know, however, was that the car was a rental from Avis.[11]

Thirty minutes after Corinne went back in the house, Peters was seen unloading the items Corinne had just placed in her automobile minutes earlier.[12] When she finished removing the items, Peters returned the vehicle back to Avis.[13]

The following day, Peters didn't respond to emails or texts that city staffers sent her in preparation for the evening's meeting of the city council. She also failed to attend the work and executive sessions at 5:30 p.m. or the scheduled 7:30 p.m. regular meeting of the city council.[14]

"We started the council meeting this evening, and she's prompt as can be and if she's going to be late, she'll call you," Logan said. "You just kind of had a feeling like, *wait a minute, Jayne is just too professional and too conscientious for something like that*," said Mahalik. Concerned about Peters's whereabouts, Deputy Police Chief Steve Thomas was asked to conduct a courtesy check at the Peters home.

As the police officers approached the front door of the Peters residence shortly before 8:00 p.m., they saw an envelope labeled "First Responders" taped to the door.[15] In the envelope, the officers found a key and a note signed by Peters that read, "Here's the key for the front door. I am so very sorry for what you're about to discover. Please forgive me. Jayne." Near the entrance to the house was a bag containing Corinne's clothes.[16] "It was indicative of someone who is leaving or someone who has returned," Thomas said.

When the officers entered the house, they found animal feces and urine everywhere. Soon, they were greeted by Peters's four cats and the family's two dogs, Hope and Lucy. The July 11 edition of the *Dallas Morning News* opened to a page with a column about suicide was on a living room chair. A laptop and a BlackBerry were near the front door, as well as a handwritten note that said the items belonged to the city of Coppell.

On the kitchen island was an urn containing ashes of Peters's husband, Don, as well as two notes, one of which gave directions for the care of Peters's pets and the other containing contact information for relatives. It implored, "Please, please, please, no funeral, no memorial—just cremate us both."[17]

Peters's body was discovered in an upstairs bathroom. Next to the body were a pillow, a blanket, and a book about coping with suicide. Tucked inside the book were photos of the two most important people in Peters's life—Don, and Corinne. A handwritten note that said, "DNR. Do not resuscitate under any circumstances, Jayne Peters" was taped to the bathroom door.

Corinne's lifeless body was in the laundry room, on the ground level of the Peters home. Her head, which was wrapped in towels, had a gunshot wound. Four teddy bears and a pillow were neatly placed outside the doorway.

The Autopsy

Peters's and Corinne's autopsies were conducted on the same day, July 14, 2010.

Peters's autopsy began with an external examination.

The body weighed 118 pounds and measured sixty-three inches long.[18] It was wrapped in two blankets and clad in a white T-shirt, gray pajama bottoms, and black print panties.

The scalp hair was straight, blonde, and long; the eyes were hazel; the ears, nose, and lips were normal, and the teeth were natural. The neck was without masses, and the chest, breasts, back, abdomen, arms, and legs were unremarkable.

Two fentanyl patches, an opioid pain reliever, each at a dose of one-hundred micrograms, were on both sides of the back. The amount of opioid remaining in the patches was not measured.

Of special significance for the determination of cause of death was a "stellate gunshot entrance wound" with bony tissue underlying the injury on the midforehead. On the underlying front bone was dense soot without stippling, indicating that the gunshot was inflicted at close range.

After perforating the skin of the forehead, the bullet perforated the frontal bone, the base of the skull, and several areas of the brain, exiting at the back of the head. The direction of the projectile was downward, front to back, and slightly right to left.

A red abrasion (scrape) was identified on the upper part of the left foot as well as on the back of the right hand.

The internal examination revealed body cavities that were without an abnormal collection of fluid. The hyoid bone and laryngeal cartilage were intact, and the larynx was not obstructed.

The cardiovascular system was unremarkable. The heart had no abnormalities; the heart valves were unremarkable. The aorta, the large artery that delivers oxygenated blood to the rest of the body, was free of significant atherosclerosis (plaque buildup); the pulmonary arteries contained no emboli (blood clots); and the coronary arteries had no significant accumulation of plaque.

As for the respiratory system, the lungs were minimally congested. The upper airways were not obstructed, and the major bronchi were unremarkable.

The esophagus was gray, smooth, and unremarkable. The stomach contained approximately ten milliliters (two teaspoonfuls) of brown fluid, but no ulcers, tablets, or capsules. The small and large intestines and pancreas were unremarkable. The appendix was present; the spleen had an intact capsule, and the liver was moderately congested. The gallbladder contained about twenty milliliters (four teaspoonfuls) of dark green bile, but no calculi. The kidneys were smooth, and the urinary bladder contained about ten milliliters of clear yellow urine, but otherwise was unremarkable.

The musculoskeletal system, including the clavicles, ribs, sternum, pelvis, and vertebral column were without fractures. The diaphragm was intact.

There was no evidence of pregnancy. The uterus, fallopian tubes, and ovaries were all normal.

After reviewing the autopsy findings, I found no anatomical abnormalities to explain why Peters died besides the gunshot wound to the midforehead whose projectile entered the brain and exited through the back of the head.

Corinne's autopsy began with an external examination.

The body weighed 132 pounds and was sixty-four inches long.[19] It was clad in a gray tank top, yellow panties, denim shorts, and a tan bra. Two yellow metal flower studs, possibly gold, and two white metal studs with clear center stones were in each earlobe. A black fabric wristband encircled the left wrist; a white metal ring was on the right ring finger.

The hair on the head was black, long, and straight. The eyes were brown. The ears, nose, and lips were normal; the teeth were natural; and the neck, chest, breasts, abdomen, arms, and legs were unremarkable.

Of special significance for the determination of cause of death was the gunshot entrance wound on the upper part of the back of the neck; it had no soot or stippling, suggesting the gun had been fired from at least three feet away.

After perforating the skin and subcutaneous tissues at the back of the neck, the bullet perforated the underlying muscle, the first cervical vertebra, and various areas of the brain, exiting on the right side of the cheekbone. The direction of the projectile was upward, back to front and left to right. A spent medium caliber cartridge was found in the body bag.

Unrelated to the gunshot wound was a thin, half-inch dry, red abrasion (scrape) on the right thigh; a half-inch faint red bruise was on the right knee.

The internal examination identified the left and right pleural cavities, spaces surrounding the lungs, each filled with approximately one hundred milliliters of foul-smelling fluid due to body decomposition.

The hyoid bone and laryngeal cartilage were intact. The larynx was not obstructed.

Aside from the injuries to the brain caused by the bullet, the hemispheres were symmetrical; the cranial nerves and blood vessels were unremarkable; and no hemorrhage was present within the deep white matter or basal ganglia.

The cardiovascular system was unremarkable— the heart was without abnormalities, the heart valves were normal, the aorta was free of significant atherosclerosis, and the coronary and pulmonary arteries contained no thromboemboli.

As for the respiratory system, the lungs were moderately congested with extensive aspiration of blood, suggesting that Corinne was alive for a brief moment after she was shot. The upper airways were not obstructed; and the major bronchi were unremarkable.

The esophagus was gray and smooth. The stomach had a trace of tan fluid, but otherwise was free of ulcers, tablets, and capsules. The small and large intestines were unremarkable. The appendix was present, the liver was moderately congested, and the gallbladder contained about a teaspoonful of dark green bile, but no calculi. The pancreas and kidneys were normal, and the urinary bladder contained about twenty milliliters of clear, yellow urine. The spleen was normal, and the endocrine system—thyroid and adrenal glands—was unremarkable.

The diaphragm was intact. No fractures of the clavicles, ribs, sternum, pelvis, or vertebral column were identified.

There was no evidence of pregnancy.

After reviewing the autopsy findings, I found no anatomical abnormalities, besides the gunshot wound to the neck whose projectile entered the brain and exited through the right cheek, to explain why Corinne died.

Cause and Manner of Death

Toxicology testing did not detect alcohol, marijuana, opioids, or illicit drugs in Peters's or Corinne's postmortem blood.

According to Deputy Police Chief Thomas, there was no sign of a struggle and there was nothing to suggest that anyone other than Peters and Corinne was involved in the two deaths. "There is nothing to lead police to believe that the daughter would have been a willing participant in this act," Thomas said. "Their relationship was like most mother-daughter relationships, very loving at times and sometimes very volatile. There have been no reports of abuse, neglect, or really overt opposition to one another."

The circumstances surrounding Peters's and Corinne's deaths, as well as a review of the autopsy and toxicology reports, led me to conclude that Peters died from a gunshot wound to the head and brain and that Corinne's death was due to a gunshot wound to the neck, head, and brain. Since the gunshot entrance wound was at the back of Corinne's neck, I concluded that the manner of her death was homicide. I further concluded that Corinne was shot by Peters, since police had determined that no one besides Peters and Corinne was involved in the two deaths. Finally, I concluded that the manner of Peters's death was suicide, since her autopsy findings were consistent with a self-inflicted gunshot entrance wound to the head. Taken together, the evidence was consistent with murder-suicide.

Harry A. Milman, PhD

Life and Career

Peters was born in 1955 and was raised in Ohio.[16] She attended Miami University in Oxford, Ohio.

When she was thirty-four years old and living in Florida, Peters married Don, who worked in information technology and business development. Two years later, their only child, Corinne, was born.

In 1993, the Peters family moved to Coppell, where Peters organized neighborhood events, served as head of the PTA at Corinne's elementary school, and was a contract software developer. Five years later, Peters and Don purchased a two-story home on Greenway Drive and Peters was elected to the city council.

"[The Peters] lived a lifestyle that indicated they made good money," said Jack Stover, a close family friend who preceded Peters as mayor of Coppell. But sometime around April 2007, Don was diagnosed with colon cancer. "[He] was the picture of health, [running] four miles, three times a week," said Don's business partner, Wayne B. Hunter, Jr.

Don died on January 15, 2008; he was fifty-eight years old. Thereafter, life at the Peters household changed forever.

Corinne loved animals and was a wonderful ballet dancer, said Ashley Johnson, a close friend. "She was harder to understand than other people, but I don't think I ever met a more genuine person," said Jenny Lim, Corinne's friend since seventh grade.

In 2010, Corinne graduated from Coppell High School where she was on the Coppel Lariettes drill team. "Corinne was an outstanding student and a gifted dancer with a big heart," said Jessica Doty, a spokesperson for the Coppell school district.

Corinne planned to enroll at the University of Texas at Austin (UT-Austin) to study health science. "UT-Austin was one of the best things that happened to her for college," Lim said. "For a while, she said she wanted to go into psychiatric nursing, even though everyone would tell her what a crazy difficult job that would be."

Speaking of Corinne, Peters's neighbor, Dianne Ianni, said, "She had her whole life ahead of her and was excited about it. She was a happy, perfect senior." Tragically, Corinne's life ended much too soon.

Conclusions

"Don was the ultimate family man," said Hunter, Don's business partner. "He was the cornerstone of that family." But when Don died, Peters was left without any financial resources, said Rev. Dennis Wilkinson of Coppell's First United Methodist Church.

In July 2008, a lien was filed against Peters's home for nonpayment of the neighborhood association assessment; the bill was paid three months later. A second lien was filed against the home in August 2009, again for nonpayment of the neighborhood association assessment. As if that wasn't enough, the Peters home was up for foreclosure three times by July 2010.

Peters's financial woes didn't end there. In the three months leading up to her death, Peters charged more than $5,800 of personal expenditures on her Coppell city-issued credit card, including for rental cars, clothing, pet care, and groceries. "We began to notice some things that caught our attention in respect to the mayor's procurement card sometime in November," said City Manager Clay Phillips. Peters reimbursed the city more than $361 for some of these charges, but she failed to provide receipts for her expenditures, making it impossible for city staffers to determine which items were for personal use and which were for city use. "It had gotten to a point that we were going to have to deal with that," said Phillips.

After waiting for months to receive the requested receipts, Philips asked the city attorney to initiate an investigation into the matter. Upon Peters's death, the city attorney determined that Peters had about $6,350 remaining in personal expenses on her city-issued credit card.

Peters was still grieving for her deceased husband in early summer 2010. "Everyone grieves differently. All of us have different timeframes to handle grief," Thomas said. While she was dealing with her grief and financial pressures, Peters's fragile psychological well-being was being stressed by Corinne's imminent departure for college. "I think Corinne's mom was kind of afraid to live by herself," said Susan Wentworth, one of Corinne's classmates.

Virtually everyone who knew Corinne thought that she was planning to attend UT-Austin following her high school graduation. Corinne wore UT shirts, wrote "University of Texas—Health Science" on her high school's group wall, and posted about moving into a dorm on her Facebook page. Later, after Corinne died, UT officials reported that they had no record that Corinne had ever applied to the school. Officials at Texas Christian University, a school to which some of Corinne's friends thought she might also have applied, said the same thing. In addition, there was no evidence that Corinne had ever filed a Texas Common Application, a requirement for students applying to the state's public colleges and universities. And when police searched the Peters home, they found nothing to indicate that Corinne was about to go to college—no college brochures, catalogs, or correspondence from universities.

"Jayne was a completely organized, thorough person who would have done all the planning and preparation on Corinne's behalf" in her college application process, Stover claimed. Erin Barlow, one of Corinne's friends, agreed. "In general, [Corinne] is one of the most gullible people I've met. I can see how it wouldn't be all that hard to make her believe something that she wanted to believe so bad."

Peters must have planned the murder-suicide for some time, starting with giving Corinne a rental car on the pretext that it was a high school graduation present, and faking Corinne's acceptance to UT-Austin. "It appeared to me there had been some thought behind all of this," said Thomas. "The fact that there are notes present shows it was not a spontaneous event. There was some type of planning involved."

In recreating how the murder-suicide transpired, police concluded that on the morning of July 12, 2010, Corinne finished loading up her car sometime between six and six-thirty and then went into the laundry room. It was there that Peters shot Corinne in the back of the neck using the Glock 9-millimeter Model 17 handgun that she had borrowed from Franke. Peters then wrote a suicide note and typed three others, ensuring that the family pets were taken care of after her death and that no funeral arrangements would be made. "I can't imagine what was going through her mind and what she was thinking between the murder and the suicide," Stover said.

That night, or possibly in the early morning hours of July 13, Peters took a pillow, a blanket, and a book about coping with suicide into the upstairs bathroom, where she sat on the floor in front of the commode and shot herself in the head, using the same handgun that she had used to kill Corinne.

"Forensic tests [and] procedures performed point to Corinne being the victim in this tragedy with Mayor Peters subsequently taking her own life.... The pathologist ruled that [this] was ... a homicide-suicide," police said in a statement to reporters.

As I reviewed the records in the case, the question I was left with was what psychological factors led Peters to murder her daughter, an act known as "filicide," and to also commit suicide?

According to published scientific studies, 90 percent of filicides are committed by biological parents with the remaining 10 percent committed by stepparents.[20] The majority of women who kill their children fall into three groups—women who are severely mentally ill, young women or teenagers who kill their newborns, and immature young women who neglect and abuse their children.[21] Daniel Papapietro and Elizabeth Barbo argued that "filicide is a complex phenomenon that is the result of more than just psychosis or environmental stressors," since not all parents who are mentally ill kill their children.[22]

The strongest predictive factors for maternal child homicide include a single mother, nineteen years old or younger, who has twelve years or less of education, with late or absent prenatal care. While women tend to kill younger children, men are more likely to murder older children.[23] The men are generally unemployed, face separation from their spouse, and abuse alcohol or drugs.

Filicide can be divided into five categories, as follows: (1) "altruistic" filicide committed "out of love," rather than anger or hate, to relieve real or imagined suffering of a child; (2) "acutely psychotic" filicide committed by a psychotic parent with no comprehensible motive; (3) "unwanted child" filicide, the most common motive for killing newborns; (4) "child maltreatment" filicide, often due to a violent outburst in the application of discipline, such as after persistent crying; and (5) "spouse revenge" filicide, a deliberate attempt to make a spouse suffer, as, for example, due to spousal infidelity or in child custody disputes.

"Filicide associated with suicide" is a rare subcategory of altruistic filicide for which the most frequent method employed is a firearm. Ninety percent of mothers who commit filicide associated with suicide see their children as an extension of themselves, believing that their children suffer the same misery as they do. These mothers decide to take their own lives, but they do not want to leave their children motherless in what they perceive is a cruel world, so they also kill their children. Sometimes, there is such a "relief of tension" and an expulsion of energy after completing altruistic filicide that mothers do not perform the final act of suicide.

One of the best-known cases of altruistic filicide is that of Andrea Yates, a highly regarded nurse at the University of Texas MD Anderson Cancer Center in Houston, Texas, who had graduated valedictorian of her high school class and was described as a "wonderful mom." After her fourth son was born, Yates became overwhelmed and depressed and "felt" that Satan wanted her to kill her children. Despite the advice of her treating psychiatrist, Yates and her husband chose to have a fifth child.

In early May 2001, Yates had a delusion that television cameras were monitoring the quality of her mothering, and that Satan was within her. She believed that due to her defective mothering, she had "ruined" her children, aged six months to seven years old. She was convinced that they would "burn in hell." To "save their souls" while they were still "innocent," Yates drowned each of her five children in her bathtub on June 20, 2001. Expecting to be arrested and executed, Yates thought that Satan would be executed along with her.

In her first trial, the jury rejected Yates's insanity defense, but her sentence of life in prison was overturned by an appellate court. In a second trial, Yates was found "not guilty by reason of insanity."

Peters's and Corinne's murder-suicide is a classic example of filicide associated with suicide. It is clear, as evidenced by the unauthorized charges on Peters's city credit card and her all-consuming grief over the loss of her husband of twenty years that Peters was under extreme financial as well as personal psychological pressures. Unable to cope with her situation, she must have felt that the only way out of her predicament was suicide. As for why she committed filicide, Peters explained it this way in one of her suicide notes. "My sweet, sweet Corinne had grown completely inconsolable. The two of us were lost, alone and afraid.... We hadn't slept at all and neither one of us could stop crying when we were together."

Stover, Peters's friend, rightly pointed out that in her mind, Peters must have felt that by killing Corinne, she was relieving her daughter from suffering over the death of her father while at the same time, protecting her "from the embarrassment, shame, and humiliation of their financial ruin." This warped behavior, presumably done out of love, is precisely what defines altruistic filicide.

Sometime after Peters died, an anonymous donor gave the city of Coppell $10,000 to cover the deceased mayor's personal charges on her city credit card. An accompanying note read, "Please use these dollars to reimburse the city for any and all credit card charges of Jayne Peters, with the remainder to go to the city."

Todd Storch, who knew Peters for about a year, described Peters as "one of those rocks that was always there." Sadly, sometimes even rocks begin to crumble.

The United States has the highest rate of child murder among developed nations. The most common perpetrator of child homicide is a parent. Of all homicide arrests in the United States, about 2.5 percent are for parents who have killed their children. Tragically, Peters gained fifteen minutes of fame by becoming part of this growing statistic.

CHAPTER 13
Antonio Pettigrew
Died August 10, 2010
Suicide by a Drug Overdose

ON MONDAY MORNING, August 9, 2010, Antonio Pettigrew failed to report for work at the University of North Carolina (UNC) in Chapel Hill where he coached sprinters, hurdlers, and relay teams.[1] By midnight, Pettigrew still had not returned to his home in Apex, just outside of Raleigh, in Wake County, so his wife reported him missing to authorities.[2] At the same time, two of Pettigrew's friends began retracing his route from his home to UNC.[3]

Pettigrew's 2008 white Dodge Aspen automobile was located at about 3:15 a.m. on Tuesday morning, parked on a bridge on North Carolina's Highway 751, near Jordan Lake.[4] When deputies arrived at the scene, they found Pettigrew dead in the back seat of his locked car.[5] "[He] appeared to be sleeping, but he was unresponsive," said Major Gary Blankenship of the Chatham County Sheriff's Office.

According to the sheriff's office, Pettigrew may have taken the sleep aid Unisom. An empty bottle of the over-the-counter medication whose active ingredient is diphenhydramine, an antihistamine with sedative properties, was found in his vehicle.[6] "Obviously, we don't know if it was intentional or accidental at this point," Blankenship said when asked whether Pettigrew had overdosed. Pettigrew was forty-two years old.

Forensics

The Autopsy[7]

The autopsy was conducted at 1:30 p.m. on the same day Pettigrew's body was discovered. It began with an external examination.

The body, weighing 165 pounds and measuring seventy-four inches in length, was that "of a well-developed, well-nourished lean black man," wrote the medical examiner in the autopsy report.

The hair on the scalp was short and black; the scalp was free of lacerations (deep cuts or tears in the skin) and contusions (bruises). A beard and mustache covered the face, the eyes were brown, and the teeth were natural and in good repair. On the right lower lip was a short, linear, well-healed scar; a short, curved scar was on the right knee. No skull, rib, or long bone fractures were noticeable.

Of special significance for the identification of cause of death was the abundant presence of pink foam in the mouth, nostrils, and in the tracheobronchial tree, a sign of labored breathing. While the lungs were smooth and glistening, they showed diffuse and moderate to severe congestion and edema (fluid), but no inflammation.

On internal examination, no unusual accumulation of fluid was found in the pleural cavity (the space enclosed by a thin layer of tissue covering the lungs and lining the interior wall of the chest), pericardial cavity (a space around the heart), or peritoneal cavity (a space enclosed by a membrane lining the inside of the abdomen and pelvis and covering many of the internal organs).

The cardiovascular system was unremarkable. At 330 grams, the heart weight was in the normal range and not a risk factor for sudden death from an arrhythmia. The heart valves were normally formed; the leaflets were delicate; and the heart chambers and walls were not enlarged. The main coronary arteries were without atherosclerosis (plaque buildup), and the aorta, the large artery that carries oxygenated blood to the rest of the body, was intact and unremarkable.

An examination of the gastrointestinal system identified an esophagus that was unremarkable; a stomach that contained a small amount of thick, brown liquid; a small intestine that was normal; and a colon that had a moderate amount of brown-green stool. The liver and spleen were similarly unremarkable. The gallbladder contained a large amount of orange-green bile; the appendix was present.

The kidneys had one moderate-to-large-sized simple cyst and multiple small, simple cysts, all without inflammation. The urinary bladder contained a large amount of clear yellow urine; the prostate was slightly enlarged with scattered small, circumscribed benign nodules.

Histological examination of brain tissue revealed no abnormalities and no evidence of edema or herniation.

As for the endocrine system, the thyroid was slightly enlarged, but otherwise was free of nodules and malignancy. Both adrenal glands were unremarkable, and the pancreas was in its normal configuration and location.

Besides the severe pulmonary congestion and edema and the presence of froth throughout the tracheobronchial tree, mouth, and nose, no other abnormalities were identified in the autopsy that might be related to Pettigrew's death. I next reviewed the toxicology report, hoping that it would provide additional clues to how Pettigrew died.

Cause and Manner of Death

Toxicology analysis of postmortem blood failed to detect alcohol or drugs of abuse, such as benzodiazepines, cocaine, fentanyl, opiates, and oxymorphone.[7] Nonetheless, diphenhydramine was measured in central (heart) and peripheral (femoral vein in the leg) blood at 4.0 and 5.4 milligrams per liter, respectively, as well as in the liver (fifty-nine milligrams per kilogram), concentrations that have been reported to be lethal.[8]

After reviewing the autopsy and toxicology reports, as well as published lay articles and the scientific literature, and in the absence of other possible causes for Pettigrew's death, I agreed with the coroner's conclusion that Pettigrew died from diphenhydramine intoxication. Although the police investigation failed to find a suicide note or evidence that Pettigrew had financial problems, I nevertheless concluded that the manner of death was suicide, mainly because there was no evidence of foul play and Pettigrew's body was found alone in his locked car with a large amount of diphenhydramine in his blood.[9]

Life and Career

Pettigrew was born on November 3, 1967, in Macon, Georgia.[10] In 1993, he graduated from Saint Augustine's University in Raleigh, North Carolina, where he was a ten-time NCAA Division All-American and won four NCAA Division II championships in the 400-meter dash.[11]

After turning professional, Pettigrew won gold at the 1991 World Championships in Tokyo.[12] Then, as a member of Team USA at the 1998 Goodwill Games, he again won gold, setting an impressive team world record time of 2:54:20.14. And in 2000, Pettigrew was on the 4x400-meter relay team that won gold at the Summer Olympics in Sydney, Australia.

Prior to joining the coaching staff at UNC in 2006, Pettigrew was an assistant track coach at St. Augustine's University and then director of cross country and track and field at Cardinal Gibbons High School in Raleigh.[13] While at UNC, he coached the Tar Heels sprinters, hurdlers, and relay teams, as well as an ACC Champion and an All-America women's 4x400-meter indoor relay squad.

In August 2008, Pettigrew testified in federal court that between 1997 and 2001, he took human growth hormone and EPO, a synthetic form of erythropoietin, a hormone normally produced by the kidneys, to increase the availability of oxygen to his muscles and to improve his endurance and performance. "I was running incredible times as I was preparing for track meets and I was recovering better," Pettigrew told the court.[14] Although he had never failed a drug test, "I'm in it now and I have to face the consequences," Pettigrew testified.

The International Olympic Committee stripped Pettigrew and his teammates of their 2000 Olympic medals after Pettigrew admitted to using performance-enhancing drugs. In addition, all of Pettigrew's competitive results since January 1997 were nullified, including the world championship gold he won in the 4x100-meter relay and the part he played in setting a world record in that event in 1998.

"It takes courage to accept full responsibility for such egregious conduct," Travis Tygart, chief executive of the United States Anti-Doping Agency said at the time.[15] "Hopefully Mr. Pettigrew's case will serve as another powerful reminder to young athletes of the importance of competing clean."

Conclusions

Diphenhydramine, an antihistamine that relieves symptoms due to allergies, was discovered in 1940 by George Rieveschi, a member of the University of Cincinnati faculty in the Department of Chemical Engineering.[16] The drug was approved by the US Food and Drug Administration (FDA) in 1946; by the 1980s, it was approved for over-the-counter use. Today, diphenhydramine is found in almost every medicine cabinet to treat symptoms of allergies, including itching and hives, as well as for insomnia and motion sickness.[17]

Since diphenhydramine is inexpensive and readily available without a doctor's prescription, it is often abused for its euphoric effects, leading to acute intoxication and death, especially among teenagers and young adults.[18] One such example is of a fifteen-year-old girl from Oklahoma who died in 2020 after taking an excessive amount of diphenhydramine as part of a challenge on the social media app TikTok.[19]

"Do not underestimate how dangerous Benadryl (diphenhydramine) is just because it's available without a prescription. It doesn't mean it can't kill you if you take enough of it," said David Juurlink, head of the division of clinical pharmacology and toxicology at the University of Toronto in Canada.

Nearly 15 percent of all overdose deaths in the United States during the years 2019 to 2020 involved an antihistamine.[20] Of the antihistamine-positive deaths, "most ... included diphenhydramine," said Amanda Dinwiddie of the Centers for Disease Control and Prevention.[21]

Diphenhydramine is the third most common medicine used in suicide when only a single drug is involved.[22] As a class, antihistamines were implicated in 6 percent of the 1.7 million self-poisoning (suicide and attempted suicide) reports made to the US National Poison Data System between 2010 and 2018.[23] The incidence of antihistamine-related suicide most likely is much higher since these deaths are sometimes misclassified as accidental.[24]

Harry A. Milman, PhD

As a first generation H_1-histamine receptor antagonist, diphenhydramine has significant anticholinergic activity, blocking the action of the neurotransmitter acetylcholine at nerve endings and causing moderate to severe neurological and respiratory side effects, such as dry mouth, constipation, blurred vision, urinary retention, thick secretions, confusion, impaired memory, and seizures. The drug's sedative effects due to binding to H_1-histamine receptors in the frontal cortex, temporal cortex, hippocampus, and pons areas of the brain are exacerbated when it is combined with illicit opioid drugs to reduce opioid-related side effects, such as itchy skin.

When ingested as an overdose, diphenhydramine can have a negative effect on the cardiovascular system, prolonging and widening the QT interval on an electrocardiogram and increasing the heart rate (tachycardia) and the likelihood of death from torsades de pointes—a type of potentially fatal ventricular arrhythmia, an erratic heartbeat.[25]

That Pettigrew's death was the result of ingesting an overdose of diphenhydramine is clear. An empty bottle of Unisom whose active ingredient is diphenhydramine, fifty milligrams per tablet, was found in his locked car and the drug was detected in his system at a concentration that has been reported to cause death.[26] In addition, Pettigrew's respiratory system was thick with foamy mucous, a sign consistent with the anticholinergic effect of the drug.

Assuming that Pettigrew ingested all thirty Unisom tablets contained in a bottle of the sleep aid, he would have consumed 1.5 grams of diphenhydramine, an amount that can cause delirium, psychosis, seizures, coma, and death.[27] Since an electrocardiogram cannot be performed after death, it's impossible to determine whether Pettigrew suffered an arrhythmia; however, with no evidence of foul play and in the absence of other possible causes, it can be concluded that the most likely explanation for the manner of Pettigrew's death is that it was suicide.

Why Pettigrew committed suicide is not known. However, by his death, Pettigrew gained fifteen minutes of fame by highlighting the seriousness of ingesting large amounts of over-the-counter medications that contain antihistamines, such as diphenhydramine. Saying it another way, over the counter does not equal safety; these drugs can be as lethal as any therapeutic or illicit drug, such as heroin and fentanyl.

CHAPTER 14

Adrienne Martin

Died December 19, 2010
Accident due to a Drug Overdose

THE CITY OF Huntleigh, with its rolling hills and mature trees, is centrally located in St. Louis County, Missouri.[1] It consists of 750 acres and is completely residential with more than one hundred multimillion-dollar homes, each on at least three acres of land and several with family-owned stables.[2]

Wall Street Cheat Sheet has named Huntleigh "the wealthiest community in America." With a population of more than five hundred, 94 percent of whom are White, Huntleigh's median yearly household income is one of the highest in the state.[3] Its residents include August Busch IV, the former chief executive officer of the Anheuser-Busch Brewing Company.

By 2010, Busch had already been dating twenty-seven-year-old Adrienne Martin on and off for about a year and a half, and she often stayed at his 6,300-square-foot home set on four wooded acres.[4] On the afternoon of December 18, 2010, Martin left Busch's residence for about two hours, but when she returned, she sat down with Busch for a steak dinner.[5] Martin didn't eat much, Busch later recalled, since she wasn't feeling well and she "looked bad."

Busch called it an early night at about six o'clock and went to bed while Martin stayed up until two in the morning, watching television. Unable to sleep, Busch awoke several times during the night. At about three in the morning, he saw that Martin was still awake, looking "kind of groggy."

At approximately 11:45 a.m., Busch saw that Martin appeared to still be asleep. After getting out of bed, he went to the kitchen and made two protein shakes, one for himself and the other for Martin. But when he returned to the bedroom, he couldn't arouse Martin, so he called his housekeeper, Michael Jung, for assistance. Together they tried to revive Martin, but they were unsuccessful. Jung then called 911, telling the operator, "This girl is not waking up."[6] "Is she breathing?" the operator asked. "We don't know," Jung replied. "It's dark back there."

The police department of the city of Frontenac, which has jurisdiction over the exclusive and affluent Huntleigh neighborhood, received the phone call regarding an unresponsive person at Busch's gated mansion on South Lindbergh Boulevard sometime before 1:15 p.m.[7] Several officers were immediately dispatched to the residence, where they were met by Busch at the patio entrance.[8] "She's in the bedroom and she's not breathing," Busch told the police officers, motioning them into the house.

When they entered the residence, the officers found the master bedroom and the adjoining bathroom in complete disarray with power cords, cell phones, adapters, radios, speakers, shoes, tools, flashlights, and flat screen monitors haphazardly strewn all over the room. A nightstand on the right side of the bed had flashlights and numerous half-full or nearly full bottles of Gatorade, as well as two plastic cups filled with a chocolate protein shake and a glass of red wine.

A loaded shotgun stood behind the door of a small bathroom, next to the master bathroom. Hanging on a hook near the toilet paper roll was a loaded Glock pistol with an extended magazine.

"[The Busch family] were not unlike the Kennedy family," said the author William Knoedelseder. "I like to say they were like the Kennedys, but with guns."

On top of a wooden chest in the master bedroom were three pill bottles, each prescribed for Martin. One vial for sulfamethoxazole-trimethoprim, an antibiotic, had no pills, but it contained a trace of a white powder residue that later was identified as oxycodone, an opioid. A second prescription bottle, which was also empty, was for escitalopram, an antianxiety medication. It, too, contained a white powder residue that was identified as a "speedball," a combination of cocaine and oxycodone. The third vial had five white trazodone pills, a sedative and antidepressant drug, as well as four pieces of an unknown white tablet.

Martin was lying on the bed in the master bedroom on top of a tan, unplugged electric blanket that had two light-green colored bed sheets underneath it, one of which had six dried spots of blood. She was unresponsive and appeared lifeless; her face and hands were pale, and her lips were blue. Martin was dressed in a black zip-up sweatshirt jacket, a blue T-shirt, and gray spandex pants and had only one black sock on her left foot; a white sock lay on the floor, near the bed. On her wrist was a silver and diamond Breitling watch, the hands of which had stopped at precisely 5:38:08 a.m.

Near Martin's head were three pillows—two light green and one brown. Other items on the bed included a laptop computer, a pair of scissors, a flashlight, an electronics magazine, a clear plastic box containing an iPod remote, and a white plastic case. Attached to the footboard bedposts were two flat-screen television sets.

A white plastic straw filled with a white powdery substance identified as cocaine was tucked between the mattress and the box spring, just below Martin's head. A similar powder-filled straw was found in one of Martin's jacket pockets.

Paramedics pronounced Martin deceased at 1:26 p.m.

The Autopsy[9]

The autopsy began with an external examination.

"The body," weighing 118 pounds and measuring sixty-nine inches long, "is that of a well-developed, well-nourished Caucasian woman whose appearance is consistent with the stated age" of twenty-seven years, forensic pathologist Michael Graham wrote in the autopsy report.

The scalp hair was brown and long and the eyes were hazel gray. The contours of the chest, back, abdomen, neck, arms, and legs were unremarkable as were the conjunctivae, the mucous membrane that covers the front of the eye and lines the inside of the eyelid, and the sclerae, the white outer layer of the eyeball. Both ears were pierced; the breasts had "prominent" implants.

Of special significance was the presence of a six-millimeter round, chronic perforation in the distal nasal septum, the edges of which were lined by a soft gray-white inflamed mucosa. Nasal perforation is a telltale sign of chronic insufflation of illegal drugs, such as cocaine or opioids.

For the internal examination, the body was opened through the abdominal wall with the usual Y-shaped incision. The soft tissues of the chest and abdomen, as well as the diaphragm and the pleural cavity (the fluid-filled space that surrounds the lungs) and pericardial cavity (the space around the heart) were unremarkable. The peritoneal cavity, the space within the abdomen that contains the intestines, stomach, and the liver, was also unremarkable.

The hyoid bone, thyroid cartilage, and larynx were unremarkable, as was the thymus, a small gland in the lymphatic system that makes special white blood cells called T-cells.

As for the cardiovascular system, the heart weight of 230 grams was in the normal range and not a risk factor for sudden death from an arrhythmia.[10] The heart chambers were normal; the heart valves were thin and pliable; and the coronary arteries and aorta, the large artery that delivers oxygenated blood away from the heart to the rest of the body, were unremarkable. In addition, no significant pathologic alterations were evident in the heart when cardiac tissue was viewed under a microscope.

The lungs were congested and edematous (water filled); together, they weighed 910 grams. The liver and spleen were smooth and glistening and without lesions; the gallbladder, pancreas, esophagus, stomach, small and large intestines, adrenal glands, and urinary bladder were all unremarkable.

The kidneys, while showing mild arteriosclerosis due to plaque buildup, were otherwise normal. The scalp and skull had no intracranial hemorrhage or pathologic brain abnormalities. The ovaries, fallopian tubes, and uterus were all without significant pathologic alterations. There was no evidence of pregnancy.

After reviewing the autopsy report, I concluded that the most significant finding in the autopsy was the six-millimeter hole in the nasal septum, an indicator of long-term insufflation of illicit drugs. I was anxious to review the toxicology report to see whether it confirmed my suspicion that Martin was a chronic drug abuser.

Cause and Manner of Death

Foul play was not suspected in Martin's death since police did not find any sign of a struggle.

Busch said that the night Martin died, he had been drinking alcohol with Martin "most of the evening;" however, toxicology testing failed to detect alcohol in Martin's blood or urine.[12] Nonetheless, cocaine, fifty nanograms per milliliter (ng/ml), and two cocaine metabolites, benzoylecgonine and methylecgonine,

1.4 and 410 micrograms per milliliter, respectively, as well as the opioids oxycodone (490 ng/ml) and oxymorphone (120 ng/ml), the primary active metabolite of oxycodone, were measured in Martin's postmortem blood.

While the amount of cocaine in Martin's blood was not sufficiently elevated to be considered an overdose, the level of oxycodone was.[11] This is corroborated by two separate scientific studies, the first of which involved seventy cases of adults whose deaths were attributed primarily to oxycodone and whose blood levels of the drug averaged 408 ng/ml, and a second study of 117 fatalities in which the average blood concentration of oxycodone was 480 ng/ml.[12] Martin's oxycodone blood level of 490 ng/ml was above the level previously reported to cause fatalities.

Cocaine, cocaine metabolites, oxycodone, and oxymorphone were also found in the urine, but testing of the vitreous humor of the eye detected only cocaine and its metabolites.

That both cocaine, a stimulant, and oxycodone, a depressant, were identified in Martin's blood meant that Martin had consumed a "speedball," a combination of cocaine and an opioid. The National Institute on Drug Abuse notes that people may take speedballs to get an intense high and to amplify euphoria and minimize the negative side effects of the two drugs. Theoretically, the energizing action of cocaine, the stimulant, may counteract some of the sedating and depressant effects of the opioid, such as heroin and oxycodone. However, one of the biggest risks of using a speedball is that the effects of cocaine wear off faster than those of the opioid. Thus, if too much opioid is consumed, a person may experience an opioid overdose, the symptoms of which include respiratory failure and death as the stimulating effects of cocaine subside.

Kevin Martin, an osteopathic physician and Martin's ex-husband, claimed that in 2002, he diagnosed Martin with a heart rhythm disorder, a condition in which there is a longer than normal QT interval on an electrocardiogram (EKG).[13] "She refused to see a cardiologist about it," Kevin Martin said.[14] If true, then Martin's death could have been due to cocaine intoxication, a drug that can cause an abnormal heart rhythm, such as an arrhythmia. However, a review of Martin's medical records obtained from Audrain Medical Center, Boone Hospital Center, and Barnes-Jewish Hospital St. Peters failed to provide evidence of a prior EKG examination. Furthermore, the autopsy revealed that Martin was at a low risk for an arrhythmia as her heart was of average size with no evidence of atherosclerotic plaque that could have been a risk factor for a heart attack. In addition, Martin's mother stated that to the best of her knowledge, Martin never had an EKG performed and that she never had heart-related symptoms.

The autopsy failed to identify any anatomical changes that might have led to Martin's death or that Martin had been suffering from a fatal infection or disease. Based on the presence of a hole in her nasal septum, however, I concluded that Martin had been abusing drugs by insufflation for a long time.

After reviewing the circumstances surrounding Martin's death, as well as the autopsy and toxicology reports, published lay articles, and the scientific literature, I concluded that the cause of death was respiratory depression due to oxycodone intoxication. The manner of death was accident.

Life and Career

Martin was born on August 30, 1983, in Springfield, Missouri.[15] She attended MacMurray College, a small college in Jackson, Illinois, earning a Bachelor of Science in Psychology and Art. Thereafter, Martin completed a year of study toward a Master of

Science in Art Therapy Counseling at Southern Illinois University in Edwardsville, Illinois.

For two years, Martin worked as a waitress for Hooters and did some promotional advertising for the company.[16] She also worked as a model, did calendar photo shoots, and participated in several pageants and swimsuit competitions.[17]

In 2002, when she was nineteen years old, Martin married Kevin Martin, a forty-five-year-old physician who practiced in Cape Girardeau, Missouri; they divorced in 2009.[18] Later that year, fun-loving Martin met Busch at a local nightclub.

"I really would like to do beer advertising," Martin wrote on her home page on the website iStudio.com.[19] "Since I have only just begun, I can't wait for my exciting times ahead!" She never got the chance to fulfill her dream.

Conclusions

In 1860, prosperous soap manufacturer Eberhard Anheuser and pharmacist William D'Oench purchased the Bavarian Brewery, which was on the brink of bankruptcy. A year later, Adolphus Busch, a German immigrant, married Anheuser's daughter, Lilly. After serving in the Union Army during the American Civil War, Adolphus Busch began working as a salesman for his father-in-law's brewery, now renamed the Anheuser Brewery.

Adolphus Busch purchased D'Oench's half-interest in the Anheuser Brewery in 1868 and assumed the role of secretary of the newly formed company, E. Anheuser & Company. Seven years later, the company introduced a new, light-colored beer called Budweiser; it became one of the largest-selling beers in the United States. In 1879, Anheuser-Busch Brewing Association was incorporated. Upon Anheuser's death a year later, Adolphus

Busch became president and the driving force of the company. He introduced Michelob in 1896, and in the process, built the Anheuser-Busch brand into an American icon.

Clydesdales were introduced as the symbol of Anheuser-Busch's Budweiser beer on April 7, 1933; the Dalmatian became the official mascot of the Budweiser Clydesdales on March 30, 1950.

Busch, nicknamed "The Fourth," the eldest son of August Busch III, great-grandson of Adolphus Busch, and heir to the Anheuser-Busch fortune, was born in St. Louis, Missouri, on June 15, 1964.[20] His parents divorced when he was five years old and Busch went to live with his mother for the remainder of his childhood.[21] "I never, ever had a father-son relationship," Busch once said. "[It was] purely business," adding, "He has been extremely tough on me. Maybe you can call it tough love." Buddy Reisinger, whose family had deep roots in Anheuser-Busch, observed that Busch's father "would say to August, 'You're never going to make it. You better watch your back.' He tortured that kid. There's carrot and there's stick. 'The Fourth' got all stick."

By the time Busch was in his twenties, he developed a reputation as a playboy who "liked to party," said Knoedelseder, the author. "He always had a beautiful girl" and loved anything that went fast—cars, powerboats, motorbikes, jet planes, and women.

In 1983, Busch, then a twenty-year-old student majoring in finance at the University of Arizona, crashed his black Corvette in Tucson, resulting in the death of twenty-two-year-old Michele Frederick, a local bartender. Busch fled the scene of the accident, hitching a ride home, but police found his wallet and driver's license in his car, as well as a 44-caliber Magnum revolver. Later that morning, Pima County deputies went to Busch's town house, where they discovered bloody clothes, a semiautomatic AR-16 rifle, and a loaded sawed-off shotgun. Eight months later, the Pima County Attorney's Office declared that while Busch had been driving "in excess of the posted speed limit," it was "insufficient alone to support any homicide charges."

In a separate incident on May 31, 1985, Busch was driving home from a nearby topless bar at about one thirty in the morning when he nearly crashed his silver Mercedes into an unmarked police car in St. Louis, Missouri.[22] A high-speed chase ensued for nearly twenty minutes that ended after detectives shot out the left rear tire of Busch's car, bringing it to a stop. When police inspected Busch's Mercedes, they discovered a .38-caliber Smith & Wesson revolver on the floor behind the driver's seat. At his trial, Busch's attorney argued that Busch thought that he was being chased by kidnappers; the jury acquitted Busch of all charges.

After earning a master of business administration degree from Saint Louis University, Busch began working at Anheuser-Bush as an apprentice brewer. By the early 1990s, he was promoted to senior brand manager for Bud Dry Draft and eventually to vice president of Budweiser brand, vice president of brand management, and finally to vice president of marketing. "I'd be lying if I told you I didn't want to be CEO," Busch said in 2000. "That's an ambition I have and one I want to see become a reality. But I'm young, with time on my side."

Over the years, Anheuser-Busch went through several corporate leaders who were always members of the Busch family. In 2002, thirty-eight-year-old Busch was deemed not ready to become CEO, and he was passed over in favor of Patrick Stokes, the first and only non-Busch family member to lead the company. It wasn't until December 2006, after Busch "settled down" and married twenty-six-year-old Kathryn Thatcher, a woman sixteen years his junior, that Busch finally became CEO of Anheuser-Busch, thereby returning the leadership of the company back to the Busch family.[23]

At the time Busch took over as CEO, Anheuser-Busch owned approximately half the beer market in the United States, thanks in large part to the Budweiser and Bud Light brands. Busch wanted to explore the possibility of expanding into the international market through partnerships and acquisitions, but in almost every case, his father disapproved of everything Busch did and ensured that the board opposed all his son's moves. "It had elements of a Greek tragedy," said Trevor Stirling, an analyst at Sanford C. Bernstein. "A very controlling father and a son who probably would have been a good head of marketing but didn't have the skill set to be CEO."

Within two years, Busch's father sold Anheuser-Busch to InBev, a Belgian firm, for $52 billion, and Busch lost control of the company he had waited all his life to lead. Said Reisinger, who worked at Anheuser-Busch for twelve years, "It would appear that he saw the train wreck coming and got out of the way," referring to August Busch III, Busch's father.

With that sale, the Busch family's 150-year legacy in brewing had finally ended. "Rightly or wrongly, it will always be recalled that he was the CEO when the company was sold," Terry Ganey, a veteran journalist, said of Busch.

Randel S. Carlock of the Wendel International Centre for Family Enterprise explained how family psychology influences of ownership allowed InBev, a small European brewer in a country of ten million people, to acquire their much larger competitor.[24] "In the case of InBev ... the firm ... [was] ... more important than any individual or the controlling family," while in the case of Anheuser-Busch, "Management succession was a birthright.... In the end, even August IV, who suffered under his father's domination, could not separate his personality from the firm," Carlock said.

When Anheuser-Busch was sold, Busch struggled to find a new identity.[25] "I would have given up my life to save the company," Busch said, "but I couldn't do anything." Thatcher, Busch's now ex-wife, said the company "was his life, it was everything he knew, he loves beer."

Despite his reputation as a party boy and a "wild guy," people who knew Busch thought highly of him. According to his former mother-in-law, the press had perpetuated a misleading picture of Busch who, in her view, was a diligent, humble, and hardworking man. Even Kevin Martin, whose former wife died in Busch's home, agreed. Referring to his deceased ex-wife, Kevin Martin said, "We both think the world of August. He is a good man."

Judy Buchmiller, a former longtime girlfriend of Busch's, expressed the sentiments felt by many of Busch's supporters. "I wouldn't want anything bad to happen to him. He's a good guy. He's really misinterpreted."

Prosecutors declined to press charges against Busch after Martin died, claiming that there was "no evidence to indicate it was anything other than accidental." According to Knoedelseder, "The talk around town was he got away with it again. The rich kid got away with it again."

CHAPTER 15

Michael Faherty

Died December 22, 2010
Spontaneous Human Combustion

AT ABOUT 3:00 a.m. on Wednesday, December 22, 2010, just three days before Christmas, Tom Mannion, a neighbor of Michael Faherty in Ballybane, Galway, Ireland, was awakened by the sound of his smoke alarm.[1] When he went outside, he saw heavy smoke billowing skyward from Faherty's home at Clareview Park.[2] Mannion banged on the front door of Faherty's house but he received no reply, so he awoke some of his neighbors and called the fire brigade.[3]

When the fire was extinguished, a search of Faherty's home by firemen and forensic experts revealed that the fire had been confined to the living room while the rest of the house only sustained smoke damage.[4] In addition, the only noticeable fire damage was to the ceiling above and the floor beneath Faherty's totally cremated body, which lay on its back with the head closest to the burning fire in the fireplace.[5] No accelerant, such as gasoline or alcohol, was found on the premises.[6]

After a thorough investigation by a police crime investigator and a senior fire officer, Assistant Fire Chief Gerry O'Malley reported that he was satisfied that the fire in the fireplace was not the source of the blaze that led to Faherty's death.[7]

Faherty was seventy-six years old.[8]

The Autopsy

An autopsy or toxicology analysis were not performed since the body had been completely burned and the major organs had undergone substantial damage.[9]

"The extensive nature of the burns sustained precludes determining the precise cause of death," pathologist Grace Callagy declared.

Faherty suffered from type 2 diabetes and hypertension, but his death was not due to heart failure, Callagy said.

Cause and Manner of Death

Police did not suspect foul play in Faherty's death.[10] In addition, there was no sign that anyone other than Faherty had entered or had left his house before the body was discovered.

When West Galway coroner Ciaran McLoughlin reviewed Bernard Knight's book on forensic pathology, he noticed that a high number of alleged incidents of "spontaneous human combustion," a death in which a live person bursts into flames and is ignited without an external fire source or accelerant, had been reported to have taken place near a fireplace or a chimney.[11] This led McLoughlin to declare in September 2011, "This fire was thoroughly investigated, and I'm left with the conclusion that this fits into the category of spontaneous human combustion, for which there is no adequate explanation."[12]

After I reviewed the circumstances surrounding the death, as well as published lay articles and the scientific literature, I concluded that the cause of death was cremation. However, because of the rare and unusual circumstances of the death, I concluded that the manner of death was undetermined pending further investigation.

Life Experiences

Michael Faherty was born in 1934. Originally from Connemara, a district in western Ireland, Faherty lived in Galway at the time of his death.

Conclusions

McLoughlin's conclusion that Faherty's death was caused by spontaneous human combustion was a first for McLoughlin, who admitted that he had never encountered such a case in his twenty-five years as a coroner, nor had it ever been reported in Ireland.[13] Nonetheless, the phenomenon has been reported well over 150 to 200 times in the past.

Thomas Bartholin, a Danish physician and mathematician, was the first to describe a case of spontaneous human combustion in 1641.[14] According to Bartholin, one evening in 1470, Italian knight Polonus Vorstius, a man who enjoyed his wine before going to bed for the night, burst into flames in his home in Milan, Italy, and died.[15] In another incident in 1731, sixty-two-year-old Countess Cornelia DiBandi of Ceséna, Italy, rose from her bed one night to open a window but combusted before she could do so.[16] The next morning, DiBandi's maid found a pile of ash and everything except for DiBandi's two lower legs and three fingers burned to a crisp.[17]

Russian novelist Nikolai Gogol popularized spontaneous human combustion in his 1842 novel, *Dead Souls*, when he included an account of a blacksmith who burned to death. English writer and social critic Charles Dickens similarly described human conflagration in his 1851 novel, *Bleak House*.[18] In the book, Dickens's character, an eccentric and alcoholic scrap dealer named Mr. Krook, bursts into flames and dies.[19]

In the United States, one of the more mysterious and bizarre deaths caused by spontaneous human combustion occurred in St. Petersburg, Florida.[20] On the morning of July 2, 1951, Mary Reeser's neighbor, Pansy Carpenter, arrived at Reeser's apartment to deliver a telegram, but when she tried to open the door, she found the metal doorknob incredibly hot.[21] Police were called and upon entering the soot and smoke-filled residence, they found that all that remained of Reeser were her ashes, left foot, backbone, and skull; no flame source or accelerant was ever discovered.[22] Near Reeser's remains was a pile of newspapers that was completely untouched by the flames, as well as furniture that wasn't scorched or damaged. St. Petersburg Police Chief J.R. Reichart called Reeser's death "the most unusual case I've seen during my almost twenty-five years of police work in the City of St. Petersburg." The death was ruled an "accidental death by fire of unknown origin."

In 1982, sixty-one-year-old Jeannie Saffin burst into flames at her kitchen table in Edmonston, north London, in the United Kingdom, right in front of her family. Saffin's brother-in-law, Don Carroll, claimed that blue flames suddenly began shooting from Saffin's mouth and midriff. "She was roaring like a dragon; the kitchen wasn't damaged, but her cardigan melted," Carroll said. Three years later, on May 25, nineteen-year-old Paul Hayes, a nonsmoker, suddenly ignited as he was walking on a street in London. And on December 27, 2017, a man burst into flames on Thanet Road in Hull, England. Similar cases of spontaneous human combustion have been reported in Germany, Sweden, France, and the United States.[23]

Spontaneous human combustion appears to have three components: (1) the body is destroyed, but the immediate surroundings are left almost intact; (2) often there is no visible source of heat that might have started the fire; and (3) certain parts of the body, including the extremities, are perfectly preserved while adjacent parts, such as the abdomen, are reduced to ashes.[24] The question that has baffled scientists and laymen alike, and for which a universally acceptable explanation has not yet been provided, is whether spontaneous human combustion is real.

Stephen Cina, a forensic pathologist and a former medical examiner of Broward County in Florida, claimed that he has never seen a single case of spontaneous human combustion as a cause of thermal injury or death. "It's not well-documented that you could generate enough focal energy inside the body and burst into flame," Cina said. "It would have to start at some focus point, somewhere."

Several theories have been proposed to explain the observed phenomenon, including "phosphorus on the hand," methane gas, ammonia, luminescence, psychic energy, malignant hyperthermia, telekinesis, and bioelectricity, among others.[25] In 1853, Dr. Lindsley wrote that those who had died from spontaneous human combustion were "habitually drunken" or "frequently indulged" in alcohol, thereby suggesting that alcohol was responsible for the phenomenon. However, not all the victims, including Reeser, the so-called "Cinder Lady," drank alcohol.

German chemist Justus von Liebig rightly noted that anatomical specimens stored in 70 percent alcohol cannot be set on fire. To prove his point, von Liebig injected rats with alcohol and then tried to set them on fire, something that would not be approved of today, but the alcohol-laden rodents wouldn't burn. Years later, Brian J. Ford, a prominent scientist, television broadcaster, and lecturer in the UK marinated pig abdominal tissue in alcohol for a week and then tried to ignite the specimens. "Even when cloaked in gauze moistened with alcohol, it would not burn," Ford declared, thereby debunking the "alcohol hypothesis" of spontaneous human combustion once and for all.

Since victims of spontaneous human combustion often were found near a source of heat or a flame, as from a candle, cigarette, fireplace, or chimney, London coroner Gavin Thurston proposed in 1961 a mechanism for human conflagration he called the "wick effect."[26] Thurston theorized that since human fat combusts at temperatures above 250 degrees centigrade, when fat is melted to oil, it can burn on a wick at a room temperature of twenty-five degrees centigrade, well below normal body heat of thirty-seven degrees centigrade. To prove his theory, Thurston wrapped a roll of fat with gauze and showed that the heat of a flame could melt the fat and produce continuous combustion like a candle. In January 1986, the British Broadcasting Corporation demonstrated the wick effect on its television program *Newsnight*.

The wick effect soon became a generally accepted theory for spontaneous human combustion. "The way the body burns—the so-called wick effect—seems to me and to my colleagues to be the most scientifically credible hypothesis," said Michael Green, a pathologist. Nonetheless, some forensic scientists were still skeptical. The theory failed to account for the fact that clothing worn by people who burst into flames quickly burned away, thereby leaving no potential wick; the wick effect is slow acting, taking ten to twelve hours, compared to the rapid disintegration of the body in spontaneous human combustion, twenty-one minutes in the case of the annihilation of Helen Conway's torso in 1964. The wick effect does not reduce the corpse to ash; for the wick effect to be operative, a tear in the skin has to occur so that the melted fat reaches the charred clothing; and in wick effect experiments, the color of the flame is yellow while the color of the flame in victims of human conflagration is blue.[27] In addition, the wick effect fails to explain the absence of an initial flame or accelerant or why the extremities remain unscathed.

In 1998, the BBC television program *QED* tried to show that spontaneous human combustion can be explained by conventional means. But after six hours of heating a piece of pig bone in a small furnace at 500 degrees centigrade, as well as heating a wooden-framed armchair in an experimental chamber, the bone and chair were still intact, although parts of the back and armrest of the chair were charred.

Ford of the UK argued that a human body, composed of 60 percent water and 12 to 15 percent or 25 to 28 percent of noncombustible fat in men and women, respectively, will not burn without an external source of fuel. The mystery of spontaneous human combustion, Ford claimed, is not what initiates the burning, but how the body turns into a raging furnace. The answer Ford proposed is acetone.[28]

According to Ford, many of the victims of spontaneous human combustion had been unwell; some, including Faherty, suffered from type 2 diabetes while others were obese, which can lead to type 2 diabetes. Type 2 diabetes, excessive dieting, alcoholism, and even teething can cause a complex series of biochemical reactions that utilize fat molecules as an energy source, ultimately producing ketone bodies, such as acetone, a highly flammable gas. Acetone permeates in the body in fat deposits and can accumulate under clothing; when present in high amounts, its odor can be detected in breath. Moreover, acetone can ignite at a concentration below 14 percent and it burns with a clear-blue flame. Static electricity from synthetic fabrics or combing the hair is all that is required to set off a fierce combustion of acetone; fat can provide the fuel to keep the fire burning.

To prove his theory that acetone is responsible for spontaneous human combustion, Ford marinated pig abdominal tissue in acetone for five days and used it to make a model of a human, which he then clothed. Next, he set the clothed model on a size-appropriate wooden chair and placed it on a square of carpet in front of a room setting as a backdrop. A gas lighter was then brought close to the acetone-impregnated model, which immediately burst into flame as the acetone vaporized from the model and caught fire. Within thirty minutes, the human model was reduced to ash, burning with a blue flame and leaving protruding limbs relatively untouched, most likely because like in humans, there was little acetone impregnated on the limbs of the model. "For the very first time, a feasible mechanism of spontaneous human combustion has been experimentally demonstrated," Ford excitedly declared.

To date, there is substantial difference in opinion among forensic scientists regarding the mechanism of spontaneous human combustion. While Ford's theory involving acetone appears to be scientifically sound, the wick effect has much support among forensic fire investigators. Still others believe the phenomenon is a myth, perpetuated by the media and the public's fascination with mysterious and unexplained deaths. There is one thing we can all agree on, however. Reported cases of human conflagration have been extremely rare so that the likelihood of unexpectedly bursting into flames is very remote. Nonetheless, Faherty gained a modicum of fame from the way he died since he drew attention to the yet unexplained phenomenon of spontaneous human combustion.

CHAPTER 16
Ellen Greenberg
Died January 26, 2011
Undetermined due to Self-Stabbing

A NORTHEASTER PASSED through Philadelphia, Pennsylvania on January 26, 2011, blanketing the city with heavy snow.[1] With schools letting out early, Ellen Greenberg, a first grade teacher at Juniata Park Academy, rushed to her Venice Lofts apartment on Flat Rock Road in Manayunk, a trendy neighborhood of row houses, lofts, and Victorian homes, where she shared a two-bedroom unit with her fiancé, Sam Goldberg, a television producer.[2] On her way home, she stopped at approximately 1:30 p.m. to fill up her car with gas.[3]

Greenberg and Goldberg were in their apartment until 4:45 p.m., at which time Goldberg went to the building's gym, returning thirty to forty-five minutes later.[4] Using his key to unlock the door, he tried to enter the unit, but he was unable to do so since the door was secured from the inside with the solid safety bolt.[5] After attempting to reach Greenberg with phone calls, text messages, and emails, Goldberg forced the door open; he later claimed that the building's security guard was present when he broke down the door.[6]

Upon entering the residence, Goldberg discovered Greenberg lying dead on the kitchen floor with multiple stab wounds.[7] Her head, some of her upper body, and both of her shoulders were resting against the lower half of the white cabinets, next to the range, and a strainer filled with blueberries and a freshly sliced orange was on the kitchen counter.[8] In Greenberg's left hand was a white towel; a scrunchie was on her right wrist.[9] A pair of eyeglasses lay on the floor, to Greenberg's right.

Greenberg's head was smeared with blood, as was her hair, neck, right hand, the front side of her shirt, her pants, the front and top of both of her boots, and the facing of the cabinet behind her. One small blood spatter was on the cabinet to Greenberg's left; two others were on the granite countertop directly above Greenberg's body.

Goldberg called 911 and was instructed to start CPR, but when he saw a knife embedded almost four inches deep into the left side of Greenberg's chest through her clothing, he was told to stop.[10] The Cutco knife had a single-edged serrated blade, approximately five inches long and a half an inch wide, and its shape and size were similar to two knives in the kitchen sink and others in the knife block on the kitchen counter.

Police arrived at Greenberg's apartment and found the swing bar on the front door broken and the screws holding the swing bar to the door loose. The balcony, six stories above ground, was undisturbed with no tracks or footprints on the snow-covered patio. "Everything that happened pretty much happened right where she was," homicide Sergeant Tim Cooney said. "The rest of the apartment was pretty unremarkable."

Several medications prescribed for Greenberg by psychiatrist Ellen Berman were recovered from a nightstand in the master bedroom. They included alprazolam and clonazepam for anxiety and zolpidem for sleep.

Paramedics pronounced Greenberg deceased at 6:40 p.m.; she was twenty-seven years old.[11]

Harry A. Milman, PhD

The Autopsy[12]

The autopsy was performed at nine on the morning of January 27, 2011, by Marlon Osbourne, an assistant medical examiner. It began with an external examination.

"The body is that of a five foot seven inches, 136 pounds, white female who appears compatible with the reported age of twenty-seven years," Osbourne wrote in the autopsy report.

The scalp was covered with brown hair, and the facial bones had no palpable fractures. The eyes were brown; the conjunctivae, the mucous membrane that covers the front of the eye and lines the inside of the eyelids, had no petechiae, tiny spots of bleeding under the skin. The nasal bones and septum were intact. The oral cavity, tongue, and lips had no injuries, and the teeth were natural and in good repair. The neck, chest, and back were symmetrical, and the arms and legs had no deformities or fractures.

Of special significance for the determination of cause of death were the twenty stab wounds to the chest, abdomen, head, and neck.[13]

Of the eight stab wounds to the chest, the most severe was ten centimeters (3.9 inches) deep. It pierced the skin and muscles of the left side of the chest, the left second intercostal space, and the superior mediastinum, creating a nearly one-inch incised (cutting) defect to the aortic arch, incising the upper lobe of the left lung, and filling the pericardial sac surrounding the heart and the left and right pleural cavities, the space that surrounds the lungs, with 120, 600, and 500 milliliters of blood, respectively. Of the remaining stab wounds to the chest, five were superficial "hesitation" wounds, only 0.2 centimeters deep. One was approximately a half an inch deep, with the remaining 1.5 inches deep wound entering the liver. The pathways of the five stab wounds to the chest were left to right.

Ten stab wounds were identified at the back of the neck; their pathways were back to front. The two most severe wounds were seven and eight centimeters deep (2.7 and 3.1 inches), respectively, extending through the neck muscles and causing hemorrhage over the right cerebellar hemisphere of the brain, as well as spinal cord injury; three stab wounds to the neck appeared to be hesitation wounds, only 0.2 to 0.3 centimeters deep.

Besides the stab wounds to the chest and neck, a single, six-centimeter (2.3 inches) deep wound pierced the skin and muscles of the abdominal wall while an incised wound to the scalp extended through the skin above the right ear. In addition, multiple contusions (bruises) in various stages of resolution were on the right forearm, the right thigh, above the right knee, and in the right lower quadrant of the abdomen.

The internal examination was unremarkable. The intrathoracic and intraabdominal organs were in their normal positions; the hyoid bone and thyroid cartilage were intact; and the larynx and trachea had no foreign objects.

As for the cardiovascular system, the heart weight of 230 grams was in the normal range; the heart chambers were free of thrombi (blood clots), and the heart valves were normally formed and without calcification. The coronary arteries showed no atherosclerosis (plaque deposits); the aorta, the large artery that delivers oxygenated blood from the heart to the rest of the body, had a normal branching pattern and was without atherosclerosis. The pulmonary arteries were free of thromboemboli (clots).

The kidney weights were in the normal range. The urinary bladder contained 100 milliliters of yellow urine. The esophagus was unremarkable; the stomach was empty and free of ulcers; and the small and large intestines had no obstruction, masses, or injuries. The appendix was present. The liver was unremarkable, its weight of 1,160 grams in the normal range. The gallbladder was empty, the spleen had an intact capsule, and the pancreas had no masses or cysts.

Aside from the stabbing injury to the upper lobe of the left lung, the tracheobronchial tree was normal. At 200 and 220 grams, respectively, the left and right lung weights were in the normal range.

The endocrine system was unremarkable. The thyroid gland had no masses or cysts, the parathyroid gland was inconspicuous, and the adrenal glands were normal.

The brain was free of gross defects; its weight of 1,440 grams was in the normal range.

In summary, beside the multiple stab wounds to the chest, abdomen, and neck, the autopsy failed to reveal any other anatomical abnormalities that might have caused or contributed to Greenberg's death.

Cause and Manner of Death

Toxicology testing detected a trace amount of zolpidem and clonazepam in postmortem heart blood and urine, consistent with Greenberg's treatment for insomnia and anxiety. No benzodiazepine, fentanyl, or opiate medications were measured in the blood or urine.

It was obvious that the cause of Greenberg's death was multiple stab wounds to the chest, abdomen, and neck; however, determining the manner of death was a bit of a challenge.

The circumstances surrounding Greenberg's death suggested that it was not an accident or a homicide—Greenberg was alone in her sixth-floor apartment with no evidence of forced entry or a struggle and nothing was obviously missing or disturbed.

The furniture and other items were in their rightful places and numerous valuables, including money, keys, and three laptop computers, were present throughout the unit, suggesting that Greenberg did not die in the course of a botched robbery.[14] Furthermore, Greenberg's neighbors did not hear any loud noises or arguments, the snow-covered balcony was undisturbed and without footprints, and the security bolt on the front door of the unit was engaged from the inside, all of which were inconsistent with an intruder.[15] Finally, Greenberg did not exhibit defensive injuries on her hands, wrists, or forearms, and DNA analysis of blood stains on the knife penetrating her chest and clothing matched Greenberg's DNA.[16]

It also was not readily apparent that the manner of death was suicide; a search of Greenberg's apartment failed to locate a suicide note. Nonetheless, suicide-related internet searches were found on Greenberg's computer, as well as text messages indicating that Greenberg had been distressed. Also, a message from Greeenberg to her mom on January 8 stated, "I'm starting the med. I know you don't understand, but I can't keep living with feeling this way."[17]

Transcripts of police interviews of Goldberg were unavailable for review. However, Greenberg's parents said that they had no reservations about their daughter's engagement to Goldberg and that they would have been happy to have had him as a son-in-law.

Greenberg's behavior had changed in the weeks prior to her death, according to Alyson Stern, Greenberg's best friend since grade school and her roommate at Penn State University. "I knew something wasn't right," Stern said. "We spent that Saturday together bridesmaid dress shopping for my wedding [and] I could tell she was not herself." Debbie Schwab, another of Greenberg's friends, agreed. "[She went from being] one of the happiest people

I knew [to one] filled with anxiety. She kept saying it was because of school. She was very vague about everything."

Greenberg's parents were so concerned about their daughter's severe anxiety that they urged her to see a psychiatrist.

Based on the autopsy findings and the "unique wound pattern," Osbourne initially concluded that the manner of death was homicide and issued a death certificate reflecting his opinion accordingly.[18] But on April 4, 2011, Osbourne amended the manner of death to suicide after speaking to police and representatives of the Philadelphia District Attorney's Office, who informed him that there were no signs of an intruder in the Greenberg apartment and that the security guard corroborated Goldberg's claim that he witnessed Goldberg break down the door to enter the residence.

Osbourne's amended conclusion was supported by the autopsy's failure to identify defensive wounds on Greenberg's hands and arms, and the absence of incapacitating drugs in Greenberg's blood. Cementing his opinion was a "curbside examination" by a neurophysician who noted that the spinal cord was not severed and that at the time of her death, Greenberg was capable of inflicting the fatal stab wounds to her chest.

"[It] was important to find out if [the door] was broken, if anyone was there to see it be broken, or is it just the story we're getting from the decedent's boyfriend that it was broken by him," Osbourne said. "[It] doesn't seem like anyone else could have been in the room to inflict those injuries other than Ms. Greenberg herself, and that is how I came to the conclusion of suicide. I think the consensus initially was that it was very, very weird."

After I reviewed the circumstances surrounding Greenberg's death, the autopsy and toxicology reports, as well as published lay articles and the scientific literature, I, too, concluded that the manner of death was suicide.

Life and Career

Greenberg was born on June 23, 1983. She majored in communications at Penn State University and considered becoming a speech pathologist, but she later attended night classes at Temple University and earned her teaching credentials instead.

Greenberg met Goldberg in 2007; they became engaged three years later. Greenberg's parents described Goldberg as a "fine young man."

Erica Hamilton, Greenberg's childhood friend and Penn State classmate, declared, "Ellen was always looking for that happily-ever-after true love. She wanted to start a family; she loved kids; she was excited about getting married."[19]

Greenberg began teaching first grade at Juniata Academy Elementary School in Philadelphia in 2008; by 2011, she received her master's degree in education with certification in reading.

In January 2011, overwhelmed by her teaching responsibilities, Greenberg saw Berman, a psychiatrist, three times for "severe anxiety;" she was prescribed several medications.[20] Berman later claimed that at no time did Greenberg ever express suicidal thoughts or have anything but good things to say about Goldberg and her impending marriage.

"[She] was struggling with something," Greenberg's mother said, but she was not suicidal.

Conclusions

The likelihood that Greenberg committed suicide by stabbing herself twenty times until she died was beyond belief for Greenberg's parents and for many who knew Greenberg. "She was a vivacious, loving daughter," Greenberg's mom said.[21] "She was looking forward to getting married; she sent out her save the date cards.... The authorities trying to make us believe that our daughter committed suicide when she didn't is just reprehensible to me." Hamilton, Greenberg's close friend, agreed. "Had Ellen ever committed suicide, her using a knife would be the absolute last way that I would ever even consider her to do that.... If she wanted to kill herself, she had a whole bottle of pills she could have taken," Hamilton said. Joseph Podraza Jr., an attorney retained by the Greenberg family to help them secure justice for their daughter noted, "It makes no sense. They [just] want to know what happened."

As horrific and implausible as suicide by multiple stabbing is, the possibility that Greenberg stabbed herself to death is not as farfetched as it may seem. "I'm not going to say it couldn't happen," said Courtney Conley, a licensed clinical professional counselor, "but it would be extremely rare, and it would be extremely difficult" to achieve.

That Greenberg's stab wounds were self-inflicted can be appreciated from the observations made by Gregory McDonald, dean of the School of Health Sciences at the Philadelphia College of Osteopathic Medicine. McDonald noted that Greenberg had several superficial, shallow "hesitation" stab wounds, five to the chest and three on the neck, that tend not to occur in homicides. Referring to knife-wielding murderers, McDonald said, "They will stab you, not hesitate significantly." As for Greenberg's stab wounds, "It wouldn't have been impossible for [Greenberg] to inflict them upon herself. It's unlikely, it's unusual, but it's not impossible."

The peer reviewed scientific literature is filled with cases of suicide by multiple self-stabbings.[22] In one such case, a thirty-year-old man was found dead on the floor of his apartment with more than forty stab wounds to his neck, chest, and abdomen; some of the wounds were hesitation wounds.[23] Based on the circumstances surrounding his death, including his locked apartment from the inside and the autopsy findings, the death was ruled a suicide. In another incident, a man committed suicide by stabbing himself ninety-two times on the forehead, on both temples, the chest, the sides of his trunk, and in the front and back of his neck.[24] A third death was of a forty-one-year-old man who stabbed himself 120 times in the chest.[25]

Other reports of suicide by multiple self-cutting and self-stabbing over the chest and neck include those of a twenty-seven-year-old man found in his bedroom with multiple hesitation wounds, a thirty-six-year-old man found in a forest near his home whose T-shirt had numerous clearly visible holes in places corresponding to the nineteen wounds to his chest, and a forty-three-year-old woman found dead in her bathtub with multiple stab wounds and a knife embedded in her chest.[26]

Some people are so determined to commit suicide that they not only stab themselves multiple times, they combine self-stabbing with a second suicide method, such as drowning, hanging, or a car crash in what is known as "complex suicide."[27] Often, but not always, an underlying undiagnosed mental disorder is suspected to be responsible for their actions.[28]

While deaths caused by more than forty single stab wounds are usually attributable to homicide, the pattern of the injuries is more important than the number of stab wounds. Since most authors of medicolegal textbooks emphasize that stab wounds inflicted through the clothing indicate homicide, some people have suggested that Greenberg's stab wounds, which were through her clothing, were not self-inflicted.[29] However, a cursory look through the published scientific literature found at least four instances of suicidal stabbings to the chest or abdomen with concomitant damage to the clothing.[30]

Although published scientific articles and the manufacturer's product monograph for zolpidem, a drug detected in Greenberg's blood, report that the medication has been associated with suicides, homicides, and with "emergence of new thinking or behavior abnormalities," it's impossible to determine whether the drug played a role in Greenberg's suicide.[31] As the product monograph notes, "It can rarely be determined with certainty whether a particular instance of the abnormal behaviors ... is drug induced, spontaneous in origin, or a result of an underlying psychiatric or physical disorder."[32]

Tom Brennan, a retired Philadelphia State Police veteran and a former chief of Dauphin County who assisted the Greenberg family in trying to change the manner of death from suicide to homicide or at the least, to undetermined, declared, "Our next step is to get the cause of death changed. Then we can go about the whodunit."

Over the next eleven years, Podraza, the Greenberg family's attorney, filed judicial motions and lawsuits, held several depositions, and retained various experts, including forensic pathologist Cyril H. Wecht and blood spatter expert Henry Lee. Wecht claimed that the circumstances of Greenberg's death were "strongly suspicious of homicide.... [It] is highly unlikely" that she could have killed herself. Lee concluded, "The number and types of wounds and bloodstain patterns observed are consistent with a homicide scene."[33]

Podraza further reviewed Greenberg's medical records and declared that they showed that two of the twenty stab wounds were inflicted after Greenberg's heart had already stopped beating. In addition, he noted that photogrammetry of Greenberg's corpse, a 3D anatomical recreation methodology that was unavailable at the time Greenberg died, revealed that the wounds at the back of the neck and head could not have been self-inflicted. Finally, a signed affidavit from the doorman on duty the night Greenberg died stated that he didn't witness the door being broken by Goldberg; video surveillance footage from the building's lobby confirmed the doorman's account. Nonetheless, attorneys for the city of Philadelphia argued that it's likely that a different apartment worker had accompanied Goldberg when he broke down the door.

The Greenberg family's prayers for a change in the manner of death from suicide to undetermined were answered on June 8, 2022. In his final ruling on the matter, Judge Glynnis D. Hill wrote, "Since the current death certificate reflecting that Greenberg committed suicide would present a nearly insurmountable hurdle for the [Greenbergs] in bringing a wrongful death action, it is not unreasonable, unjust or an abuse of discretion for the Court to make a declaratory finding that Dr. Osbourne may have erroneously determined Greenberg's manner of death or abused his discretion by not even considering whether it was appropriate to amend her death certificate under the unique circumstances of this case."

While the Chester County District Attorney's office to which the case was referred reopened the Greenberg investigation in August 2022, to date, no one has been charged in Greenberg's death.

The fame that Greenberg gained due to her self-stabbing was short lived. Nonetheless, when the school district where Greenberg taught learned of her death, it issued the following statement: "Ellen Rae Greenberg made a significant positive impact in the life of students, colleagues and the entire school family. She will be greatly missed." Greenberg's coworkers echoed these sentiments entirely. "[She] was extremely dedicated to her students and an excellent teacher," said one of her fellow teachers.

CHAPTER 17
Russell Armstrong
Died August 15, 2011
Suicide by Hanging

IT'S NOT EASY being married to one of the original members of *The Real Housewives of Beverly Hills*. Just ask Russell Armstrong. Unfortunately, you can't. He's dead.

"He worked hard to get her where she was," Armstrong's attorney, Ronald Richards, said in an interview with Reuters, referring to Armstrong's wife.[1] "Who do you think paid for that lifestyle? He basically spent all their savings … to support the show."

Armstrong's wife was born Shana Lynette Hughes in Independence, Kansas, on June 10, 1971, but she changed her name to Taylor Ford when she moved to Beverly Hills, California, to become an actress.[2] In 2005, Ford met Armstrong, a venture capitalist, while waiting to be seated at a local restaurant; they were married less than a year later.[3]

The Real Housewives of Beverly Hills was launched on Bravo in 2010 with Ford in the original cast.[4] Rumors soon began circulating among the "housewives" about the difficulty the Armstrongs were having fulfilling their financial obligations. While they lived an affluent lifestyle of parties and exotic vacations, the Armstrongs had been living way beyond their means for many years.

"He wasn't rich," Richards said of Armstrong. "He was just generating enough income to not lose cover (the illusion of wealth)" so his wife could become famous on the show.

Armstrong appeared along with Ford in the first season of *The Real Housewives of Beverly Hills,* but he never wanted to be in the show. "[It] literally pushed us to the limit" by the lack of privacy, Armstrong told *People* magazine. Richards agreed. "He was constantly ridiculed by [the] other 'housewives' and by people who would make comments about the show. Stuff that would never have come up [inevitably] was exposed."

Compounding the personal pressures brought on by *The Real Housewives* were Armstrong's deep financial troubles. Armstrong had filed for Chapter 7 bankruptcy in 2005, claiming that while he had $1 million to $10 million in debts, he only had $50,000 in assets. Then, in 2011, Armstrong was sued for $1.5 million by a company that alleged he misappropriated funds for his own personal use, including to redecorate his multimillion-dollar mansion and to invest in a restaurant.[5]

As if that wasn't enough to bring a desperate Armstrong closer to the edge, Ford filed for divorce in mid-July 2011. "Unfortunately for me this year, there were a lot more tears, a lot more pain; it's been such an emotional ride this year," Ford said.[6] Accusing Armstrong of verbal and physical abuse during their five-year marriage, Ford called it a "difficult decision," but one that was in the best interest of her family. "I have a titanium mesh implant holding up my right eye right now, so I don't know what more radiographic evidence you need than that," Ford said.[7] The injury occurred when Armstrong punched Ford in the face on the night of her fortieth birthday. Some birthday present! Still in her hospital bed, Ford filed for divorce. Richards described Armstrong as "extremely 'bummed' out about the [impending] divorce."[8]

After separating from his wife, Armstrong began residing at a friend's house on Mulholland Drive in West Los Angeles, California.[9] At approximately eight o'clock on the evening of

Friday, August 12, 2011, while having dinner with his housemate, Armstrong mentioned his plans to meet his estranged wife the following evening to discuss custody arrangements for their five-year-old daughter; the meeting never took place. After finishing eating, Armstrong retired for the night.

On Sunday, August 14, Armstrong's housemate began getting phone calls asking about the whereabouts of Armstrong, since no one had seen or had heard from him. At 8:00 p.m. the following day, after receiving no answer when he knocked on Armstrong's bedroom door, Armstrong's housemate went around the side of the house and peaked through Armstrong's bedroom window only to see Armstrong, wearing a black short-sleeve T-shirt, black briefs, and black socks, hanging by an orange extension cord double-wrapped around his neck, a slip knot against the back of his head, and the other end of the cord wrapped three times around one of the wooden beams in the ceiling of his room.

As Ford later recounted, "I had gone to the house. I had been calling him all day. No answer. I just knew something had gone wrong.... I had a friend of my husband meet me there who was a world championship kick boxer, just in case things were to go awry.... I never assumed it was going to be something so catastrophic."[10]

Paramedics arrived at 8:16 p.m. and declared Armstrong deceased.[11] He was forty-seven years old and had been dead for more than twenty-four hours.

The Autopsy[12]

The autopsy was performed at 7:30 a.m. on August 17, 2011, by Yulai Wang, a deputy medical examiner of the County of Los Angeles. It began with an external examination.

The body was identified as that of an adult Caucasian male, weighing 181 pounds and measuring sixty-nine inches in length. It was "very well-built and well-nourished" and in the early stage of decomposition with green discoloration on the abdomen, undoubtedly due to sulfhemoglobin, a product of a biochemical reaction that occurs after death between hydrogen sulfide gas and hemoglobin.[13] Dark red discoloration was noticeable on the arms and legs, and most prominently on the fingertips.

The scalp, covered by two inches of long brown hair, was without bald spots. The eyes were brown with white sclerae (the "whites of the eyes"). The teeth were all present; there were no significant scars, burns, or tattoos.

Three overlapping furrows were identified around the upper neck, consistent with the ligature found wrapped around Armstrong's neck at the time his body was discovered. In addition, the hyoid bone and larynx were intact, and both were without fractures.

The internal examination began with the standard Y-shaped incision of the abdomen, exposing the body cavity and the internal organs. It revealed a pleural cavity, the space enclosed by a thin layer of tissue that covers the lungs and lines the interior wall of the chest cavity that was free of fluid.

The cardiovascular system was unremarkable. The heart weighed 400 grams, approximately 21 percent more than the average heart weight for men, but well within the normal range of 188 grams to 575 grams.[14] The heart chambers were normally developed and without thrombosis (blood clots); the heart valves were unremarkable; the heart muscle was normal; the septum, the dividing wall between the left and right sides of the heart, was without defects; and the coronary arteries had minimal evidence of plaque. While the aorta, the large artery that carries oxygenated blood to the rest of the body had mild atherosclerosis (plaque buildup), it was otherwise elastic and without aneurysm (a bulge).

Mild congestion was present in the lungs, but it was not an unexpected finding in a postmortem examination. The lung weights of 360 and 260 grams for the left and right lung, respectively, were in the normal range (the average left and right lung weights in men is 395 and 445 grams, respectively) and without thromboembolism (clots).[15]

As for the gastrointestinal system, the stomach was free of food and pill fragments, the esophagus was intact, and the small intestine and colon were unremarkable. The appendix was present, and the pancreas was normal. In addition, the liver was smooth and intact and its color and weight of 1,070 grams were as expected.

Both kidneys were smooth, normally situated, and of average weight. The urinary bladder, which contained less than a teaspoonful of urine, was unremarkable. The prostate was not enlarged or nodular; the spleen was smooth and intact; and the endocrine system—thyroid, pituitary, and adrenal glands—was unremarkable. The parathyroid glands were not identified. The scalp and brain showed no evidence of abnormality, such as hemorrhage, fracture, contusion, atherosclerosis, or aneurysm.

Cause and Manner of Death

Police did not suspect foul play in Armstrong's death. Toxicology testing of postmortem blood failed to detect alcohol or drugs of abuse, such as cocaine, fentanyl, amphetamines, opioids, or barbiturates.

It was clear that Armstrong's death was caused by asphyxiation due to hanging. Although the hyoid bone and thyroid cartilage were intact and without fracture, this was not an unusual finding as these are seen in about 25 to 33 percent of strangulations due to hanging.[16]

Fractures of the hyoid bone are most common in men over forty; Armstrong was forty-seven years old when he died.[17] However, such fractures do not always occur since fracturing of the hyoid bone and thyroid cartilage is dependent on the nature and magnitude of the force applied to the neck, the age of the victim, the type of ligature, and the intrinsic anatomical features of the hyoid bone and thyroid cartilage. A prospective study of forty cases of suicidal hanging between 1996 and 1999 found that only 15 percent of the deaths had fractures of the hyoid bone and thyroid cartilage.[18]

After reviewing the circumstances surrounding Armstrong's death, as well as the autopsy and toxicology reports and published lay articles and the scientific literature, I concluded that the cause of death was asphyxiation due to hanging. The manner of death was suicide, notwithstanding the absence of a suicide note.

Life and Career

Armstrong was born in Dallas, Texas, on December 21, 1963.[19] He graduated from Richardson High School and the University of Hawaii, after which he became a venture capitalist.

"He was the exact opposite of how he was portrayed on that show [*The Real Housewives of Beverly Hills*]," said Randy Edwards, Armstrong's close friend since the days when they played Little League together in Carrolton, Texas. "He was the most engaging, hilarious guy, always pulling pranks on his buddies. He could talk to anybody." Armstrong's sister, Laurie, echoed Edwards's sentiments entirely. "I want ... [people] ... to know that he was funny as heck and fun-loving, that he worked his butt off to take care of the people who needed him."

Armstrong had gotten into trouble for his anger management even before he married Ford. In December 1997, he was arrested in West Hollywood and was charged with misdemeanor spousal battery after an altercation with his then wife, Barbara. In March 1998, Armstrong pled "no contest" to misdemeanor battery for another fight with his wife. This time, he was sentenced to three days in the Los Angeles County jail. He was given an additional three years' probation and was ordered to perform fifty hours of community service, spend a minimum of one year in anger management therapy, attend fifty Alcohol Anonymous meetings, and donate $1,000 to a women's clinic in Venice, California.

And yet, despite their impending divorce and Armstrong's history of abusive behavior toward both of his wives, Ford was still in love with Armstrong. "Oh, my God!" she was heard sobbing on the 911 call, after discovering Armstrong hanging from a beam in his bedroom ceiling.[20] "My little girl's daddy is dead."[21]

"I feel bad because his credit cards weren't working.... He had tremendous financial problems," Richards, Armstrong's attorney, said after Armstrong's body was discovered. "As far as a will, even if he does have one, they don't have any assets, so I'm not sure what there would be left to leave. I am extremely saddened.... I had no idea he was [clinically] depressed."

"I'm not going to say he was perfect," Armstrong's sister said. "I think he got into that Hollywood lifestyle, [with] all that excitement and glamour."[18] Apparently that, as well as his financial troubles, was just too much for Armstrong to bear. He must have felt there was only one way out of his misery.

Conclusions

With sitcoms becoming more difficult to create and the number of cable channels exceeding the number of available shows, reality TV shows emerged to fill the void.[22] "It's really hard to produce something innovative anymore," said Marjorie Fox, head of the electronic-media division at the College Conservatory of Music. Reality shows, on the other hand, are cheap to produce—no writers, no professional actors, and no unions.

In the hierarchy of the television entertainment industry, "actors" in reality TV rank very low.[23] "Theater actors look down on film actors, who look down on television actors," said George Clooney, a onetime television star and now a movie superstar. "Thank God for reality TV, or we wouldn't have anybody to look down on."

The question that remains to be answered is, how real is reality TV? "I think most of the shows are fake," said Mike Fleiss, creator and executive producer of *The Bachelor*.[24] Besides *The Bachelor*, on which Fleiss spends a lot of money and time to make sure it's real, "Seventy to 80 percent of the shows on TV are ... loosely scripted," Fleiss declared. "Things are planted. Things are salted into the environment, so things seem more shocking."

Many producers note that while reality shows are not scripted, the action is definitely planned, shot over days or weeks, and then significantly edited to keep the shows entertaining. "I have never worked on a Bravo show where anything is scripted ... where we tell people what to say and what to do," one reality TV producer told Brian Moylan, author of *The Housewives: The Real Story behind the Real Housewives*.[25]

The term "reality TV is a misnomer," Fleiss said. "In many cases, there is nothing remotely real about it." Members of the cast often pretend to be more affluent than they really are. Fleiss blames the public for the success of reality TV. "They know it's somewhat fake, but they're OK with it."

On *The Real Housewives,* storylines are sometimes contrived, and conversations and "drama" are often planned prior to the shoot by the "housewives" themselves.[26] At other times, producers steer the plot and provide direction and instruction as scenes are shot multiple times. Still at other times, "spontaneous moments" are not spontaneous at all. Outbursts and physical altercation, while discouraged and rare, they are "central to a show's plotline," which *Entertainment Weekly* finds troubling.

While commercially successful, *The Real Housewives* franchise has had a significant and disturbing effect on marriages; at times, it has led to financial ruin of some of its cast.[27] According to *US* magazine, over forty divorces have occurred among members of *The Real Housewives,* at least eleven of whom had been married more than ten years to as long as twenty-six years.[28]

Besides the breakup of Ford's marriage, other cast members of *The Real Housewives* who divorced or separated include Countess LuAnn de Lesseps (*The Real Housewives of New York City*) and Tamara Barney (*The Real Housewives of Orange County*); most recently, Ashley Darby (*The Real Housewives of Potomac*) split from her husband of nearly eight years, Michael Darby.[29] As for financial ruin, the most famous cases include those of Teresa Giudice (*The Real Housewives of New Jersey*) who filed for Chapter 7 bankruptcy, claiming $11 million worth of debt, and of Sonja Morgan's (*The Real Housewives of New York*) who filed for Chapter 11 bankruptcy, claiming $19.8 million in debt and $13.5 million in assets.

Participating in reality shows has led to more than twenty suicides among the casts, however none of the "housewives" or their spouses in *The Real Housewives* franchise has taken their life beside Armstrong.[30]

"Your life is an open book to people and that makes you feel very vulnerable," said Nadine Kaslow, chief psychologist at Emory University School of Medicine.[31] "When people feel very publicly shamed and humiliated that's a risk factor for suicide."

Prior to his death, Armstrong lamented about the pressures of being on television. "[It] was pretty overwhelming. It took our manageable problems and made them worse." Jesse Csincsak, the fourth-season winner of *The Bachelorette*, agrees, saying, "[The contestants] didn't sign up to be portrayed as the bully or the slut or the drunk or whatever, but they were, because that creates ratings, and ratings equals dollars."

In a shocking twist in an already twisted tale, Armstrong's friend, Alan Schram, a managing partner of Wellcap Partners, an investment partnership, was found dead in his parked car on Mulholland Drive in Los Angeles only twenty-four hours after Armstrong's body was discovered.[32] Schram suffered a gunshot wound to the head, which the coroner determined was self-inflicted.[33] Although he did not leave a suicide note, Schram's death was labeled a suicide. Whether the two suicides—Armstrong's and Schram's—are connected has not been determined.

Armstrong already achieved fame from his involvement in *The Real Housewives of Beverly Hills*. He gained more fame from his suicidal hanging.

CHAPTER 18
Katherine Morris
Died May 6, 2012
Undetermined due to Carbon Monoxide Poisoning

ONE EVENING IN February 2011, twenty-year-old Katherine Morris, a student at the University of Maryland in College Park, Maryland, visited a local club where she met Army Specialist Isaac Goodwin.[1] Goodwin was stationed at Fort Belvoir, an army base in Virginia, so over the following months, the two dated mostly by phone calls and text messages.[2]

In June, Goodwin was transferred to Fort Bragg military base in North Carolina.[3] Unsatisfied with their long-distance relationship, Morris texted Goodwin on July 4. "I think it would be better if we just end this.... I still can't help but feel like you have somebody else and that you never took me or us seriously."

It took Goodwin nearly a month to respond but when he did, he proclaimed his love for Morris and asked her to marry him.[4] Morris said yes, and on August 3, one month prior to her senior year, Morris and Goodwin were married in a civil ceremony in Arlington, Virginia.[5] What Morris didn't know at the time was that Goodwin was deeply involved in a long-term relationship with Latoya King, an army sergeant, and that the relationship would continue throughout her marriage.[6]

Before returning to Fort Bragg, the marriage license securely in his hand, Goodwin admonished Morris to keep their marriage a secret. "She was naive, simple fact she was very naive," said Juanita Long, Morris's cousin.[7] "I think this guy had a plan, sought her out, knew what he was looking for, and he took advantage of her."

Once married, the army gave Goodwin $600 to $700 per month spousal allowance, which he allegedly kept for himself for eight months instead of forwarding it to Morris.[8] Besides the spousal allowance, Goodwin also received a $100,000 life insurance policy on Morris that lacked an exclusion clause for suicide.

"He married her, took the license back to Fort Bragg, and immediately filed for the financial benefits," said Morris's mother, Marguerite.[9] "Every month, up to December or January [2012], he pocketed that money."

According to Michelle Harper, Morris's roommate, Morris and Goodwin never lived together after they were married. "Besides Isaac not showing up, Kathy confided to me that they barely spoke," Harper said. Angry and despondent, Morris contemplated filing for divorce. On December 18, she sent Goodwin an email stating, "I still don't know why you suddenly wanted to marry me out of the blue.... It confused me then and still confuses me. Why me? Why so soon?"

Morris was convinced that Goodwin was cheating on her, so on December 21, she sent him another email. "I hope she's worth it," Morris wrote. "I've cut the screen out of my bedroom window.... Now all I have to do is take the dive, and you'll be free from having to deal with me forever." The following day, Morris sent her mother an email expressing suicidal thoughts. Upon receiving the message, Marguerite had Morris admitted to the Washington Adventist Hospital for signs of depression and suicidal ideation. It was only then that Morris's parents learned of their daughter's marriage to Goodwin. After spending six days in the hospital, Morris was discharged with a diagnosis of "major depressive disorder and recurrent, severe and adjustment disorder with mixed emotion."

On March 3, 2012, Goodwin was deployed to Afghanistan; a few days later, Morris discovered that he had been having affairs with at least five other women. Outraged, she sent an email to all of Goodwin's lady friends informing them that Goodwin was married, adding, "Don't worry. As soon as he gets back from Afghanistan, I'll be divorcing him so y'all can fight over who gets to have him then." Shocked by Morris's revelation, King, Goodwin's long-term mistress, wrote Goodwin, "To think that you would go ahead and marry someone you know likes/cares about you just for financial gain is crazy … or should I say, just plain stupid. Dumb!"

On May 2, King, using an alias, called Morris on a cell phone belonging to her best friend, Damaris Brown, a civilian working for the Army Reserve. It was then that Morris learned of Goodwin's and King's three-and-a-half year relationship and that Goodwin had told King that he was getting a divorce. Tired of her husband's lies, Morris texted Goodwin two days later, threatening to notify his army chain of command about his adulterous relationship with King and to have him dishonorably discharged, since adultery is a crime in the military.

The following day, at approximately 6:55 p.m., security cameras recorded Morris's car arriving at the overflow parking lot of a movie theater, close to the Anne Arundel Community College, near Arundel Mills Mall in Hanover, Maryland. Two hours later, a tweet originating from Morris's iPhone read, "The Lord is close to the brokenhearted and saves those who are crushed in spirit." A second tweet at 9:49 p.m. declared, "Waiting for this to be over."

On May 6, at half past five in the morning, Arundel Mills Mall Security Officer Stephen Jones observed a gold 2005 Pontiac G6 automobile parked with the lights off and the engine running at the rear of a building of the Anne Arundel County Community College, Arundel Mills Campus.[10] Inside the vehicle, Jones saw Morris lying in a contorted position across the front seats, her arm twisted past its natural range of motion, her upper body partially on the passenger seat, and her head down toward the front passenger foot well with the legs stretched out across the driver's seat. Unable to get Morris's attention, Jones opened the unlocked door, removed the key from the ignition and checked Morris for a pulse. There wasn't any.

Police arrived within fifteen minutes and detected a strong odor of charcoal and lighter fluid permeating the interior of Morris's vehicle. Inside the car, the officers discovered Morris's lifeless body. It was partially lying on top of two disposable charcoal grills in the front passenger foot well. The left side of Morris's face was in contact with the grills, as was Morris's shoulder, and a large burn mark was on Morris's back.

Nothing in the interior of the automobile was burned or melted. On the front passenger seat, police found an iPod, a charcoal lighter, a purse containing credit cards, and an open bottle of CVS Maximum Strength Nighttime Sleep Aid that was missing eight tablets, each containing 50 milligrams of diphenhydramine, an antihistamine with sedative properties. Morris's iPhone was in the center console. Packaging for the two charcoal grills, plastic shopping bags from Walmart and Dollar Tree, a McDonald's bag, a Pepsi can, and other miscellaneous items were in the back seat of the vehicle.

Paramedics pronounced Morris dead at approximately 5:37 a.m. Based on a download of a video on Morris's iPhone, the time of death was estimated at sometime between midnight and 1:00 a.m. Morris was twenty-two years old.

Harry A. Milman, PhD

The Autopsy[12]

Assistant Medical Examiner Patricia Aronica-Pollak performed a partial autopsy at 10:00 a.m. on May 6; she signed the death certificate later that day.

The autopsy began with an external examination.

"The body is that of a well-developed, well-nourished, African American female," Aronica-Pollak wrote in the autopsy report. It was clad in a floral tank top and blue jeans, weighed 119 pounds, and measured sixty-four inches in length. The earlobes were pierced, and a yellow metal ring, possibly gold, with a blue stone, was on the left ring finger.

The hair on the scalp was curly, brown, and of medium length. The brown eyes were covered with contact lenses. The ears and mouth were free of foreign material and abnormal secretions, the teeth were natural, the lips showed no injury, and the nasal orifices contained soot. There were no tattoos.

The neck revealed no evidence of injury; neither did the ribs and sternum. The chest was unremarkable. The abdomen had a half-inch linear scar on the right side, possibly from an appendectomy. The legs and arms showed no evidence of fractures, lacerations (deep cuts), or deformities; and there were no needle tracks anywhere on the body.

A nine-by-eleven-inch area of charring was identified on the back, from the neck to the midback, mostly on the left side.

For the internal examination, only the brain was examined; at 1,290 grams, its weight was in the normal range.

The most significant anatomical finding in the autopsy for the identification of cause of death was the presence of pink colored parenchyma, the functional tissue in the brain, in both cerebral hemispheres, most likely due to high levels of carboxyhemoglobin, a combination of carbon monoxide and hemoglobin indicative of carbon monoxide poisoning.

Cause and Manner of Death

While waiting for Forensics Investigator Abby Glenn to arrive on the scene, and unfamiliar with this type of death, police Sergeant Keith Clark searched the internet. Clark later said that he found several articles referencing people committing suicide by ingesting sleeping pills and igniting charcoal grills in an enclosed space, such as a vehicle. However, Sergeant Nathaniel Hollis clarified that the articles did not mention sleeping pills, only that igniting charcoal grills in an enclosed space was a common method of suicide in Asia. Nonetheless, Aronica-Pollak assured the two police officers that she had seen this type of suicide before in the Baltimore metropolitan area.

Gary Lyle, chief of police and director of public safety at Anne Arundel Community College, reviewed surveillance footage of the parking lot where Morris's vehicle was found and reported, "It does not appear that anyone ever exited or entered the deceased's vehicle" or that there was any suspicious activity in or around Morris's automobile from the moment it arrived at the parking lot until Morris's body was discovered. Hollis, who also reviewed the footage, disputed Lyle's claim, declaring that the video was of "poor quality and difficult to see anything."

In a judicial hearing in 2020, Administrative Law Judge Susan A. Sinrod noted that she, too, examined the surveillance video footage. She questioned how Lyle could affirmatively state that no one had entered or had exited Morris's vehicle the night her body was discovered, considering the great distance of the camera from the vehicle, the obstruction of the car by trees, the glare of bright lights, and the large shadows in the parking lot. "There easily could have been activity that could not be seen from that camera's location," Judge Sinrod said.

No signs of trauma were apparent on Morris's body other than burn marks from the two disposable charcoal grills. The color of her skin, however, was consistent with carbon monoxide poisoning.

Toxicology analysis detected a lethal amount (65 percent) of carbon monoxide in Morris's blood.[13] For comparison, carbon monoxide levels in the blood of nonsmokers, smokers, and heavy smokers (more than two packs a day) is less than 2 percent, 4 to 5 percent, and 6 to 8 percent, respectively.[14] Compared to oxygen, carbon monoxide has 250-fold greater affinity for heme-containing proteins, such as hemoglobin, cytochrome C, cytochrome P450, and myoglobin.[15] Death from carbon monoxide intoxication is due to asphyxiation, as the binding of carbon monoxide to hemoglobin results in an increased level of carboxyhemoglobin and a reduction in the delivery of oxygen to tissues with the highest metabolic demand, such as the brain.[16]

Diphenhydramine was measured in Morris's heart and peripheral blood at a concentration of 2 and 1.7 milligrams per liter (mg/L), respectively.[17] The drug is considered a safe medication, but when taken in large quantities, reaching a level of 5 mg/L of blood, it can cause cardiac arrest and death.[18] The product monograph for diphenhydramine cautions against ingesting more than 300 milligrams of diphenhydramine within a twenty-four hour period, which is equivalent to six CVS Maximum Strength Nighttime Sleep Aid tablets.[19] While the amount of the sedative in Morris's blood was decidedly toxic, it was not sufficient to cause death.[20]

A "suicide note" was found on Morris's iPhone that read, "I don't see myself ever being happy again ... I just see more misery."

The note implored, "Please don't let him get away with what he's done and what he's doing. I didn't deserve this." A second letter left on Morris's computer said, "I want my death to bring attention to this person and what he has done so that it can stop.... I feel the only way for justice to truly be served in this situation is for me to give my life for the cause."

That Morris's death was neither natural nor an accident was clear. Aronica-Pollak also ruled out homicide since police failed to find evidence of foul play or other suspicious activity and there was no sign of trauma on Morris's body. Pamela E. Southall, the acting chief medical examiner, claimed that the standard by which the manner of death was determined was whether it was "more likely than not" to have been a suicide, an accident, or a homicide; however, according to the Maryland Code, the standard in Maryland is a "preponderance of the evidence."[21]

Notwithstanding this discrepancy, Aronica-Pollak was confident that Morris's death was a suicide caused by carbon monoxide intoxication—Morris was alone in her vehicle along with two charcoal grills containing lit briquettes that gave off toxic fumes of carbon monoxide. Morris had been diagnosed with major depressive disorder and had threatened to commit suicide five months earlier, and two "suicide notes," presumably written by Morris, were found on Morris's iPhone and computer.[8] The possibility that Morris's death was a homicide disguised to look like suicide apparently was never seriously considered.

In her rush to judgment, Aronica-Pollak failed to review the police report before concluding on the manner of death, since the report wasn't completed until June 25, 2012. She did not interview Goodwin, King, Brown, or Morris's family and friends, as recommended in the guidelines of the *Medical Examiners' and Coroners' Handbook on Death Registration and Fetal Death*

Reporting, which state, "The medical examiner or coroner must use all information from his or her own investigation, police reports, staff investigations, and discussions with the family and friends of the decedent." Furthermore, she failed to fully explore other potential causes or contributing factors in Morris's death, since she only performed a partial autopsy—an external examination of the body and an internal assessment just of the brain.

The OCME's *Standard Operating Procedures* (SOPs) for the performance of an autopsy in neighboring District of Columbia whose autopsy procedures most likely resemble those of Maryland, note, "a complete/full autopsy examination shall be the standard of care" and "a complete autopsy examination is mandatory [in] suicides or suspicion thereof."[22] In addition, the DC SOPs declare that a partial autopsy may only be performed "when there are valid concerns of safety for autopsy personnel ... for the purpose of retrieving evidence of identification ... or when there is a religious objection." Therefore, performing a partial autopsy when suicide is suspected is contrary to DC's SOPs, for which a complete autopsy is mandatory; it most likely also is contrary to Maryland's SOPs.

Alan R. Moritz discussed the adequacy of performing a partial autopsy in *The American Journal of Forensic Medicine and Pathology*.[23] "A partial autopsy is always a mistake in a medico legal case," Moritz wrote. "Failure to perform a complete autopsy ... is a dangerous practice in any instance of clinically unexplained death, even though it appears that an acceptable cause of death has already been demonstrated." MGF Gilliland agreed, noting, "Partial autopsies provide partial answers."[24]

By coincidence, one month before Morris died, Kanae Kijima, dubbed the "Japanese Black Widow," was sentenced to death in Japan for murdering three men by poisoning them with carbon monoxide generated from the burning of charcoal briquettes after giving them sleeping pills and making the deaths look like suicide.[25] One of the deaths was in a car and the other two were in their homes.[26]

After I reviewed the circumstances surrounding Morris's death, the autopsy and toxicology reports, the two "suicide" notes allegedly written by Morris, and published lay articles and the scientific literature, I agreed that the cause of death was carbon monoxide intoxication. However, since the circumstances surrounding the death were rare and unusual, and in light of the similarity of Morris's death to the Kijima case, I concluded that the manner of death was undetermined pending further investigation.

Life Experiences

Morris was born on March 11, 1990, in Baltimore, Maryland, the sixth child of Marguerite and Willie Morris.[27] As a teenager, Morris loved dogs and easily made friends. Some of her hobbies included cooking, reading, and writing. Morris even took lessons in tap dancing, ballet, and the violin; in church, she played the drums.

Morris attended St. Mary's County and Anne Arundel County Public Schools, eventually graduating from St. Mary's Ryken High School in Leonardtown, Maryland.[28]

Following her high school graduation, Morris attended the University of Maryland, majoring in family science and posthumously earning a Bachelor of Science. Shortly prior to her death, Morris applied for admission to the Air Force Officer Training School located at Maxwell Air Force Base in Montgomery, Alabama. Sadly, her dream of attending the Air Force Officer Training School was never realized.

Conclusions

There were 45,979 suicide deaths in the United States in 2020.[29] Of these, only 0.2 percent were due to carbon monoxide intoxication from charcoal grilling, making this method of suicide particularly rare in America.[30] In Asia, death due to charcoal grilling in an enclosed space accounted for 5 to 13 percent of all suicides in 2011, making it much more common than in the United States.[31]

Suicide by breathing carbon monoxide gas generated from charcoal grilling in an enclosed space is a painless way to die. In the United States, there are on average two suicide deaths of this type per state per year, compared to an average of five to six accidental deaths per state per year due to charcoal grills used for heating purposes.[32] Aronica-Pollak claimed that in Maryland, suicide due to inhalation of carbon monoxide fumes generated by charcoal grilling accounted for 10 percent (twenty cases, or two cases per year) of the 204 cases of nonfire-related carbon monoxide deaths in the ten year period prior to Morris's death, thirteen of which were in motor homes. This is consistent with the published number of suicide deaths per state per year from charcoal grilling in an enclosed space nationwide.[33]

Considering how uncommon suicide due to inhalation of carbon monoxide gas from charcoal grilling in an enclosed space is in Maryland, especially in an automobile, it's highly unlikely that Morris, a twenty-two-year-old student of family science, was familiar with this method of suicide without somebody having told her about it or by searching the internet.[34] Unfortunately, the internet search history on Morris's computer and iPhone have never been examined by digital forensics experts.[35] Without knowing how Morris learned about this rare method of suicide, it's impossible to determine whether she willfully inhaled carbon monoxide gas generated by charcoal grills in her automobile or whether her death was contributed to or committed by someone else and made to look like suicide.

There are several puzzling aspects to Morris's death, one of which is why Morris allegedly drove nearly a half hour to the Anne Arundel Community College parking lot the night she allegedly committed suicide when she had no connection to the college. While surveillance video footage showed Morris's vehicle entering the Anne Arundel Community College parking lot, the driver of the vehicle has never been positively identified, so the possibility that somebody other than Morris had driven Morris's automobile that night has never been explored.

The suggestion that Morris willfully ingested a toxic, but nonfatal dose of diphenhydramine and also inhaled carbon monoxide fumes generated by charcoal grilling is perplexing. To commit suicide, she only had to ingest all thirty-two tablets of the sleep aid, thereby consuming 1,600 milligrams of diphenhydramine, a more than sufficient amount to cause death. Morris also could have simply inhaled the carbon monoxide fumes and not ingested any of the sleep aid. Carbon monoxide, known as "the silent killer," is colorless, odorless, tasteless, nonirritating, and has no warning properties, so death would have been painless and easy to initiate.[36]

While there have been a few reports of suicide due to the combination of carbon monoxide gas generated by burning charcoal in motor vehicles and the ingestion of sedatives or high amounts of prescription drugs, these deaths usually involved children or people of Asian descent, neither one of which describe Morris.[37]

There is substantial circumstantial evidence that somebody other than Morris may have been involved in Morris's death. No receipts or credit card transactions have been located showing that

Morris had purchased the charcoal grills, the charcoal lighter, or the sleep aid.[38] In addition, no viable fingerprints or DNA have been found in the interior of Morris's vehicle, on the charcoal lighter, on the bottle of CVS pills, or on the box and plastic packaging materials for the two disposable charcoal grills, suggesting that these items may have been wiped clean. While heat above 212 degrees Fahrenheit can degrade DNA, charcoal grilling does not produce temperatures high enough to ignite or melt materials in the interior of an automobile and no such melting was found in Morris's car. Finally, although the video surveillance camera was far from Morris's vehicle, flames produced by the lit charcoal grills should have been seen on the video footage, but they weren't.

The possibility that Morris's death was a homicide made to look like suicide cannot be discounted. Someone other than Morris could have lit the charcoal grills and placed them in Morris's car as she slept in her automobile while under the influence of the sedative effects of diphenhydramine. Alternatively, Morris could have consumed the diphenhydramine elsewhere. Then, while sedated, she could have been driven to the Anne Arundel Community College parking lot, the two lit charcoal grills placed in her car, and her body thrown into her vehicle, landing in an awkward, contorted position on top of the grills. According to Robert Hamblen, an orthopedic surgeon, the way Morris's shoulder was twisted "constituted a contortion of the thoracic region that would not have been possible if she was alive."

As for motive, Judge Sinrod observed that three people may have had a motive to want Morris dead—Goodwin, King, and Brown. Two days before she died, Morris threatened to expose Goodwin's adulterous relationship with King to his military chain of command; had she done so, it could have ruined Goodwin's, King's, and possibly Brown's careers.

Goodwin, already under significant financial pressure due to his misappropriation of government funds, admitted in an army investigation that "his marriage was a sham and solely for the [financial] benefits." As the sole beneficiary of Morris's $100,000 life insurance policy, he had a good reason to want Morris dead.

As for King, she hoped to marry Goodwin. King even went looking for an engagement ring with Goodwin. The only obstacle standing in her way to the altar was Morris.

Brown may not have been an innocent bystander either. She had a background in forensics and some knowledge about accessing electronic devices that did not belong to her. Judge Sinrod noted that this raised the question as to the validity and authenticity of Morris's tweets and typed suicide notes. Furthermore, in a strange coincidence, a white SUV similar to Brown's was seen driving suspiciously in the Anne Arundel Community College parking lot at approximately 9:30 p.m. on May 5, 2012, pulling up directly behind Morris's parked vehicle, idling for a few minutes with the headlights illuminated, and then driving away.

Finally, there is some suggestion that Brown, Brown's husband, and King may have known of Morris's death approximately twenty-four hours before her body was discovered.

In the ten years since Morris died, her mother, Marguerite, filed several legal motions in an attempt to change the manner of Morris's death from suicide to undetermined so that a complete investigation could be done to ascertain whether Goodwin, King, or Brown were involved in her daughter's death. In March 2021, Marguerite finally got the judicial ruling that she had been fighting for a decade to obtain.

After evaluating all the evidence related to Morris's death, Judge Sinrod concluded that Marguerite "gathered an abundance of evidence that weighs heavily against a determination of suicide....

While I certainly acknowledge that it is possible that the ultimate determination will be that Katherine (Morris) committed suicide, prudence and diligence would dictate allowing such an investigation to occur. For these reasons, I conclude and recommend that the OCME's determination that the manner of Katherine's death should be changed, pending further investigation, from suicide to undetermined." It was a judicial ruling with which I very much agreed.

Morris's manner of death isn't the first to be changed to undetermined. One of the most famous is that of Natalie Wood, a talented and much-loved actress whose career spanned the 1940s until she drowned under mysterious circumstances off the southern coast of California in 1981.[39] The coroner initially concluded that the death was an accident, but thirty years later, the manner of death was changed to undetermined. Despite this change, no one has yet been charged in Wood's or for that matter, in Morris's death.

CHAPTER 19
Elisa Lam
Died February 19, 2013
Accident due to Drowning

THE FOURTEEN-FLOOR, 700-ROOM, Beaux-Arts style building called the Cecil Hotel was built in 1924 on Main Street in Los Angeles, California, between Sixth and Seventh Streets.[1] Complete with stained-glass windows, a marble lobby, an opulent staircase, and palm trees, the Cecil was intended to be an exclusive destination for international travelers and the socially elite.[2] Unfortunately, the Great Depression of 1929 prevented hotelier William Banks Hanner from fully realizing his dream, so instead, he converted the building into a hostel-type, budget hotel.[3] In time, the Cecil became a home for prostitutes, people down on their luck, and squatters, but most notably, for crime and suicide.[4]

The first person to die at the Cecil Hotel was Percy Ormond Cook, a former real-estate salesman, who shot himself in the head in 1927 after he was unable to reconcile with his estranged wife and son. Three other suicides followed between 1931 and 1938, including those of WK. Norton, who died after ingesting poison capsules; Army Sergeant Louis D. Borden, who slit his throat with a razor blade; and Roy Thompson, a fireman in the United States Marine Corps who jumped off the roof, landing on a skylight of the adjacent building. Seven additional accidental or possibly intentional deaths were recorded between 1938 and 2015 as "fell from building."

In 1944, nineteen-year-old Dorothy Jean Purcell gave birth to a baby boy in the bathroom of her hotel room; she claimed she didn't know she was pregnant. Thinking the baby was stillborn, Purcell threw it out the window. The coroner determined that the infant had been alive when she did so. Purcell was tried for murder and was found not guilty by reason of insanity.

One of the most bizarre deaths at the Cecil Hotel occurred in 1962, when twenty-seven-year-old Pauline Otton jumped from the ninth floor after an argument with her husband. Otton accidentally landed on top of sixty-five-year-old George Giannini, who was standing on the sidewalk. They both died instantly.

Two notorious serial killers resided at the Cecil Hotel while they committed their heinous crimes.[5] Richard Ramirez, famously known as "The Night Stalker," had a room on the fourteenth floor of the hotel between June 1984 and August 1985, the same time he killed and sexually assaulted several women in the Los Angeles area.[6] Convicted of thirteen murders, eleven sexual assaults, and five attempted murders, Ramirez was sentenced to die in the gas chamber. However, in 2013, after spending twenty-four years on death row, Ramirez died while undergoing treatment for cancer. Austrian serial killer Jack Unterweger strangled three prostitutes with their bra straps while staying at the Cecil Hotel between 1990 and 1991.[7] Found guilty of murdering at least nine women, Unterweger served his sentence in an Austrian prison where he committed suicide in 1994.

In May 2007, the Cecil Hotel was sold to Fred Cordova, who renovated the building, reopening it in 2011 as Stay on Main, a budget hostel for young tourists on floors four through six, the Cecil Hotel on the top floors, and housing for long-term, low-income tenants on floors two and three. It is at this infamous Los Angeles hotel, the place *Esquire* magazine called "America's

Hotel Death," that Elisa Lam, a twenty-one-year-old student at the University of British Columbia in Vancouver, Canada, chose to stay on her way to Santa Cruz, California.[8]

After traveling alone by Amtrak and visiting the San Diego Zoo, Lam, who had been suffering from bipolar disorder and depression, arrived in Los Angeles on January 26, 2013.[9] Two days later, she checked into the Cecil Hotel, where she stayed in one of the hostel-type rooms on the fifth floor. But when her roommates complained about Lam's odd behavior, including locking the door to their room, requiring a password to enter, and leaving notes saying, "go home" and "go away," Lam was moved to a private room on the same floor.[10]

On Thursday, January 31, the day Lam was supposed to check out of the Cecil, Lam's parents became concerned when they failed to hear from their daughter.[11] Four days later, they reported Lam missing to the Los Angeles Police Department (LAPD).[12]

Police searched Lam's hotel room where they found Lam's belongings, including a wallet, an identification card, and a laptop. "The room was in disarray," one investigator said. Surveillance footage taken inside the hotel's elevator on February 1 showed Lam alone wearing a red hoodie, waving her hands, and acting strangely, exiting and reentering the elevator several times, and pressing buttons for nearly every floor.[13] It was the last time Lam was seen alive.

"I'm convinced that Lam was not fleeing an attacker or under imminent threat," said Michael Drane, a forensic psychotherapist who examined the elevator footage. "She isn't displaying typical fight-or-flight mechanisms, such as hands up in a defensive posture and being more guarded, and she does exhibit some vulnerable body language."

At 10:00 a.m. on the morning of February 19, Santiago Lopez, a hotel maintenance worker, was sent to the roof of the Cecil Hotel to check on the water tanks after residents complained about poor water pressure and the foul smell and taste of water coming out of their taps. Taking the elevator to the fifteenth floor, Lopez climbed up a set of stairs to the roof and, using his staff key to deactivate the alarm, unlocked the rooftop door and climbed up a ladder to reach one of the 1,000-gallon water tanks. Inside the tank, Lopez discovered Lam's naked, bloated, and decomposing body; floating beside Lam were her shoes and clothing coated with "sand-like particulate." Lam's watch and room key were also retrieved from the water tank.

By the time Lam's nude body was found, nineteen days had passed since her disappearance. Although police had searched the roof of the hotel with dogs, they had failed to look inside the water tanks.

Finding Lam's body raised several questions. How did she die and was her death a homicide, a suicide, or an accident? I hoped a review of the autopsy and toxicology reports would shed light on the likely cause and manner of Lam's mysterious death.

The Autopsy[14]

The autopsy began with an external examination.

"The body is identified by toe tags and is that of an unembalmed, refrigerated, adult female Asian who is in moderate decomposition," wrote the medical examiner in the autopsy report. "She appears the given age of twenty-one years."

Lam's body was thin, weighing 121 pounds and measuring sixty-six inches in length. It was in a state of moderate decomposition and had green discoloration on the abdomen and upper legs, undoubtedly due to sulfhemoglobin, a chemical formed after death through the oxidation of iron in hemoglobin by drugs and chemicals that contain sulfur.[15]

The scalp was covered by long, straight brown hair. The eyes were brown and bulging with no petechial hemorrhages (areas of bleeding) of the conjunctivae, the mucous membrane that covers the front of the eye and lines the inside of the eyelids, and/or sclera (the white outer layer of the eyeball). There was skin slippage on the forehead and right cheek, as well as on the chest, back, arms, and left lower leg, a common finding in decomposition. A one-inch scar was identified on the right knee and a quarter-inch abrasion (scrape) was present on the left knee. There were no tattoos, nontherapeutic punctures, or needle tracks on the arms and legs.

The anus was edematous (swelling) with pooling of blood in tissues surrounding the orifice. This condition can be caused by anal sex, but it most often is due to an acidic diet, stress, or excessive diarrhea.[16]

The external examination did not reveal any abnormalities that might have caused Lam's death, including the absence of external traumatic injury or evidence of intravenous drug use.

Since Lam's body was found in a water tank, I looked for evidence of drowning in the internal examination.

The lungs, which in about 50 percent of drowning victims are heavy and filled with water, were without fluid and voluminous (overinflated with air). In addition, their weights at 250 and 350 grams for the left and right lung, respectively, were within the normal range.[17] While most drowning victims exhibit heavy, water-filled lungs, 20 percent of victims do not, so the absence of water in the lungs alone was not sufficient to eliminate the possibility that Lam had drowned.[18]

The pleural cavities—the space between the two thin membranes that line and surround the lungs—contained about ten ounces of dark-brown fluid in the right cavity and nearly seven ounces in the left cavity, consistent with "pleural effusion." Published scientific reports note a direct link between the amount of pleural effusion and the length of time a body remains in water after a drowning.[19]

To determine whether Lam had suffered a cardiac event prior to her death, I reviewed the section in the autopsy report related to the cardiovascular system. An enlarged heart is a risk factor for an arrhythmia, an irregular heartbeat, but at 175 grams, Lam's heart was well within the normal range of 148 to 296 grams. In addition, the major coronary arteries were without atherosclerosis (deposition of plaque of fatty material on the inner walls of coronary vessels), a likely cause of a heart attack.[20] Finally, there was no thrombosis (blood clots) in the heart chambers; the heart valves were thin and leafy, and the heart septum, the dividing wall between the heart chambers, was without defects.

I next explored whether Lam was strangled or whether she had suffered a concussion. In strangulation, the hyoid bone and thyroid cartilage are sometimes, but not always, fractured; however, Lam's hyoid bone and thyroid cartilage were intact with no evidence of trauma or fracture.[21] In addition, I saw no evidence of subcutaneous hemorrhage of the scalp, fracture of the base of the skull, tears of the dura mater—one of the layers of connective tissue that make up the meninges of the brain—or any abnormality in the brain to indicate that Lam had died from a concussion or a brain injury.

The autopsy did not provide any evidence that Lam was sexually assaulted. The cervix and vagina had a normal appearance with no indication of trauma. The uterus was symmetrical; the uterine cavity was not enlarged, the fallopian tubes were unremarkable, and the ovaries were normal.

Of the remaining autopsy findings, no trauma was identified in the oral cavity, including the tongue and the larynx, and no abnormalities were detected in the musculoskeletal system. As for the gastrointestinal system, the esophagus was intact. The stomach had no pill fragments, and it was not distended. The small intestine and colon showed the typical postmortem discoloration, the pancreas and pancreatic ducts were normal, and the liver was smooth and of average size, color, and consistency. The kidneys were of the expected weight. The urinary bladder was unremarkable, the spleen was of average size, and the thyroid and adrenals were present and normal.

In view of the lack of anatomical changes that might have caused Lam's death, I next reviewed the toxicology report, hoping it would shed the necessary light on how Lam died.

Cause and Manner of Death

Police concluded that there was no foul play involved in Lam's death. This was confirmed in the autopsy by the lack of puncture wounds, a concussion, or other signs of trauma or brutality. In addition, there was no evidence of strangulation, water-filled lungs, or that Lam had suffered a cardiovascular event, a seizure, or other serious incident, such as an asthma attack.

Blood taken directly from the heart revealed the presence of venlafaxine as well as metabolites of buprion, an antidepressant. Both medications had been prescribed to Lam for her bipolar disorder. Since there wasn't enough blood available for further testing, the amount of these drugs in the blood could not be quantified, so their contribution, if any, to Lam's death could not be evaluated.

Further toxicology testing identified bupropion metabolites as well as venlafaxine, 5.3 micrograms per gram (μ/g) and lamotrigine (14μ/g), an anticonvulsant, in the liver, neither of which was in the overdose range.

Alcohol was found in the bile at twenty milligrams per deciliter. This very low level of alcohol most likely was due to putrefaction and postmortem fermentation by microflora deposits, such as bacteria and yeast.[22]

The urinary bladder was empty, so toxicology testing of urine was not performed.

The toxicology report failed to provide any indication that Lam died from alcohol intoxication, a drug overdose, or toxic levels of venlafaxine, bupropion, or lamotrigine, three medications that had been prescribed for Lam's bipolar disorder.

After reviewing the investigator's narrative report, the autopsy and toxicology reports, as well as published lay articles and the scientific literature, I concluded that in the absence of other possible causes, the most likely explanation for why Lam died, despite the absence of water in her lungs, was that she drowned. While most drowning victims exhibit heavy, water-filled lungs, 20 percent of victims do not. This is because in "dry" drowning victims, the muscles around the larynx (the voice box) spasm and block the airways, a condition known as "laryngospasm," causing the vocal folds to close, thereby reducing airflow, allowing water to enter the sinuses instead of the lungs.[23] I further concluded that the manner of death was accident. Bipolar disorder was a contributing factor.

Life Experiences

Lam was born on April 30, 1991, in Vancouver, British Columbia, Canada.[24] Her parents had immigrated from Hong Kong to Burnaby, British Columbia, where they opened Paul's Restaurant, specializing in homestyle Canadian and Chinese food.

Lam attended the University Hill Secondary School in Vancouver. She loved fashion, *The Great Gatsby*, and *Harry Potter,* and was interested in feminism, classic novels, and impressionist painters. On her social media blog, Lam expressed disappointment in her personal life and in her academic accomplishments, often claiming that she was being stalked.[25]

A self-described introvert with a witty personality, Lam spoke English and Cantonese. She enrolled at the University of British Columbia, but uncertain about her career goals, she did not register for classes in 2013, deciding instead to take a solo trip to California, an excursion about which her parents had serious misgivings. Lam's parents gave their approval, however, after Lam promised to call home every day. When she failed to do so on January 31, 2013, they became concerned and filed a missing person report with the LAPD.

Conclusions

A question I was left with after I reviewed the available records was how Lam managed to climb up to the roof of the Cecil Hotel and enter the water tank. Amy Price, the hotel manager, reported that the roof was restricted, and that the only way to access it was by climbing up one of three fire escapes running along the side of the building or through a locked door that set off an alarm when it was opened.

Using dogs, investigators tracked Lam's scent up to the fifth floor, where her room was located, and then to a window overlooking a fire escape. Based on these findings, police concluded that Lam most likely reached the roof by way of the fifth-floor fire escape. As for how she entered the water tank, Lopez, the maintenance man at the Cecil, reported that the hatch to the tank was open when he discovered Lam's body inside the tank.

"I went down to the main water tank and saw that the hatch was open, so I looked inside and discovered an Asian woman floating face-up in the water, about twelve inches from the top of the tank," Lopez said.

Another question that puzzled me was why Lam decided to climb up to the roof of the Cecil Hotel and enter the water tank in the first place, let alone take off her clothes. The answer may be found in her bipolar disorder, a mental condition characterized by extreme mood swings ranging from periods of mania that include elation and intense emotion, irritability, and energized behavior, to very low, sad, hopeless, and indifferent periods of depression.[26] People with severe episodes of mania or depression often have impaired judgment, engage in high-risk behaviors, and may experience psychotic symptoms, such as hallucinations or delusions, and have unrealistic belief that they have special powers.[27] Lam may have been in one of these psychotic states the day she disappeared.

Symptoms of bipolar disorder are treated with mood stabilizers and antipsychotic drugs for the manic phase and antidepressant medicines for the depressive episodes, both of which had been prescribed for Lam. However, based on the number of pills remaining in Lam's prescription vials, it appears that she had not been taking her medications as prescribed. Thus, in the thirty days prior to her death, Lam ingested only five days' worth of quetiapine, an antipsychotic drug, three days' worth of bupropion, an antidepressant medication, and none of her lamotrigine for bipolar disorder and seizures and venlafaxine for depression. By abruptly stopping her medications, Lam's symptoms of bipolar disorder most likely worsened.[28] This is supported by her strange interaction with her roommates, for which she was reassigned to another room, and her bizarre behavior in the hotel's elevator on February 5, 2013, six days before her body was discovered.

"She was likely in a psychotic state of some kind, which is totally possible with bipolar disorder," Drane, the forensic psychotherapist, said of Lam's strange behavior in the hotel's elevator.

Exactly what happened to Lam may never be known. What is known, however, is that she had been suffering from bipolar disorder and had not taken her medicine as prescribed. This most likely led to a more severe rebound of her symptoms of bipolar disorder. While in a delusional state, Lam probably thought she was being followed or chased and thus hid in the water tank. This is consistent with statements Lam's sister made to investigators in which she recounted that on several previous occasions, Lam believed that someone was following her. When Lam was unable to come out of the water tank, she treaded water, but after tiring, she took off her clothes to lighten the weight. Eventually, she succumbed to hypothermia, and she drowned. That is as good an explanation as any for the strange and unusual death of a Canadian student touring Southern California on winter break.

CHAPTER 20
Marco McMillian
Died February 26, 2013
Homicide by Asphyxiation

MARCO MCMILLIAN, PRESIDENT and chief executive officer of MWM & Associates, a firm in Clarksdale, Mississippi, that provided consulting services to nonprofit organizations, was a thirty-three-year-old African American Democrat running for mayor of Clarksdale.[1] Considered by many to be "a man on the rise," McMillian was often described as "the first openly gay man to be a viable candidate for public office in Mississippi."[2]

Clarksdale is an agricultural and trading center located along the Sunflower River in the Mississippi Delta. The town has a population of approximately 18,000, nearly 82 percent of whom are African American and about 40 percent who live below the poverty line.[3]

Many African American musicians developed the blues in Clarksdale, a place that calls itself the "birthplace and world capital of the blues," before taking the music to cities in the north, including Chicago.[4] The Oscar-winning actor Morgan Freeman is a co-owner of Ground Zero Blues Club adjacent to the Delta Blues Museum in the heart of historic downtown Clarksdale.[5]

Sometime around ten o'clock the evening of Monday, February 25, 2013, McMillian left his house to move cars out of his driveway.[6] By midnight, he still had not returned inside the house.[7] The following day, weather conditions deteriorated so much that the heavy rain slowed down the search for McMillian.

It took another twenty-four hours to find McMillian's unclothed body, which had been shoved under barbed wire near the Mississippi River levee on an isolated, steep embankment of pasture, about twenty miles west of town.[8] When Mark M. LeVaughn, the chief medical examiner, arrived at the scene, he noticed a small amount of semen on McMillian's penis.

The Autopsy[9]

LeVaughn performed the autopsy at the Mississippi State Medical Examiner's Office in Jackson, Mississippi. It began with an external examination.

The body was of a normally developed thirty-three-year-old adult Black male, weighing 196 pounds and measuring seventy-one inches long. The hair on the head was black, the teeth were natural, and the eyes were brown. A four-millimeter conjunctival hemorrhage was present in the right eye due to a broken blood vessel.

Multiple blunt traumatic injuries, as well as multiple areas of thermal injuries, were identified on the body. A three-centimeter vertical laceration (deep cut) was noted on the right forehead, near the right eyebrow; an abrasion (scrape) was present above the left eyebrow. A superficial abrasion was identified on the left upper arm, as well as several abrasions measuring 2.5 centimeters on both knees. Swelling, a contusion (bruise), and an eight-millimeter laceration were on the soft tissue surrounding or lining the orbit of the left eye.

Two small abrasions were present on the shin of the right leg; a five-centimeter abrasion was on the left elbow. Two other similar size abrasions were on the mid-upper back and on the right shoulder.

Two abrasions with thermal injury were found on the left side of the back. Thermal injury and blunt trauma were also evident on the neck.

Multiple areas of second- and third-degree burns with a random "splash type" pattern were noted on the chest, the right side of the face, the right side of the neck, the right arm, and the right hand, as well as on the midabdomen, the left arm, the left hand, the left upper back, both thighs, and on both calves.

The skull was without fractures; however, there was a three-by-four-centimeter contusion on the left side of the scalp. An examination of the cranial cavity, the space within the skull that accommodates the brain, showed no evidence of hemorrhage or exudate.

The brain, weighing 1,320 grams, was unremarkable with no evidence of pathologic changes, traumatic injury, swelling, or herniation.

The left side of the face had a linear superficial abrasion measuring over five centimeters long, as well as two other abrasions, one measuring five centimeters and the other, three centimeters. On the left lower lip was a 1.5-centimeter laceration. Several contusions were present on each side of the tongue and in the middle of the tongue.

The upper airways were normal. The thyroid gland was unremarkable, the hyoid bone was intact and without hemorrhage, and the thyroid cartilage had no evidence of traumatic injury.

The internal examination revealed a cardiovascular system that was unremarkable. At 410 grams, the heart weighed approximately 10 percent more than an average male heart. The two ventricle chambers of the heart were normal with no substantial thickening, and the heart valves were thin and flexible.

The lungs showed some congestion and edema, but no evidence of tumor or emboli (clots). When lung tissue was viewed under a microscope, scattered postmortem bacterial growth was noticeable. The right and left lungs weighed 600 and 540 grams, respectively.

The gastrointestinal tract had no pathologic changes or evidence of traumatic injury, nor did the liver, gallbladder, pancreas, spleen, adrenal glands, kidneys, and urinary bladder. The esophagus was normal; the stomach contained approximately one hundred milliliters of gray-brown liquid, but otherwise was free of hemorrhage or ulcer. The liver, spleen, kidneys, and pancreas weights were all within acceptable limits.

In summary, the autopsy provided clear evidence that McMillian's body had been beaten, burned, and dragged. The evidence of postmortem bacterial growth in the lungs suggested that at some point, McMillian's head had been under water.

Cause and Manner of Death

It was clear that McMillian's death involved foul play. His body was found in the woods, near the Mississippi River levee, and he had suffered multiple bruises due to beatings and burn marks.

Toxicology testing detected seventy-seven milligrams of alcohol per deciliter of blood, equivalent to a blood alcohol concentration (BAC) of 0.077, just below the acceptable limit for drivers in the United States. This BAC is usually achieved by men of average size and weight after ingesting two to three standard glasses of wine or beer. Caffeine, probably from coffee, and nicotine, possibly from smoking, were also found in the blood, the amount of which was not measured.

Duloxetine, 650 nanograms per milliliter (ng/ml), an antidepressant drug, was detected in McMillian's blood. While the average concentration in the blood for a sixty-milligram daily pill of duloxetine is twenty-seven to ninety ng/ml, multiple once-daily doses produced approximately one and a half times higher levels.[10] Thus, the amount of duloxetine in McMillian's postmortem blood was seven to twentyfold higher than what was expected from a single sixty milligram dose of the drug.

Signs and symptoms of a duloxetine overdose include somnolence (sleepiness), seizures, vomiting, and tachycardia (fast heart rate); however, no fatalities have been reported in clinical trials at doses as high as 3,000 milligrams.

Delta-9-THC, the pharmacologically psychoactive metabolite of marijuana that is responsible for impairment, was detected at ten ng/ml of blood; delta-9-carboxy-THC, the inactive metabolite of marijuana, was also measured at a concentration of 6.5 ng/ml. That both delta-9-THC and delta-9-carboxy-THC were present in McMillian's blood meant that McMillian consumed marijuana shortly before he died.

Other autopsy findings that contributed to McMillian's death included multiple areas of blunt trauma to the head, consistent with a beating. While there were thermal injuries and superficial scratches to the left side of the face and arm, most likely due to a sharp, pointed object, these did not contribute to McMillian's death. Finally, abrasions on the knees appeared to have been due to "drag type" injuries.

After reviewing the circumstances surrounding the death, as well as the autopsy and toxicology reports, published lay articles, and the scientific literature, I had no reason to dispute the medical examiner's conclusion that the cause of death was "asphyxia of undetermined etiology," as evidenced by conjunctival hemorrhage in the right eye and multiple contusions of the tongue, and that the manner of death was homicide.

Life and Career

McMillian was born in 1979 in Mississippi.[11] His parents divorced when he was six years old. "He was spoiled," McMillian's mother said of her son, as she often served him breakfast in bed.

As a young boy, McMillian liked to skate and bowl with his friends; he even sang in the church choir. Blessed with charisma, McMillian became a leader among his schoolmates. LaSonya Wilson, who knew McMillian as a child, described him as "the peacemaker."

McMillian attended Clarksdale High School, where he led the effort to integrate the senior prom and raised money for the senior trip to New York and Washington.[12] After graduating from high school in 1997, he enrolled at W.E.B. DuBois Honors College at Jackson State University, a public historically black university in Jackson, Mississippi, from which he graduated magna cum laude with a major in business.[13] McMillian next enrolled at the Saint Mary's University in Minnesota, where he earned a master's degree in development and philanthropy.

Between 2007 and 2011, McMillian served as the international executive director of Phi Beta Sigma, a historically black fraternity, and was assistant to the vice president for institutional advancement at Jackson State University, an executive assistant and chief of staff to the president of Alabama A&M University, and a recruiter for New Leaders, an organization that trains school principals.[14]

McMillian was recognized by *Ebony* magazine as one of the nation's "thirty up-and-coming African American leaders" under thirty in 2004; in 2009, he received the Thurgood Marshall Prestige Award.[15]

In 2013, McMillian became one of four Democratic candidates to run for mayor of Clarksdale. "Marco dreamed about putting Clarksdale on the map," said Wilson, McMillian's childhood friend. Brad Fair, an opponent candidate for mayor of Clarksdale, agreed. "He was definitely CEO-minded. He never took no for an answer."

According to his mother, McMillian had warned her, "If you get a call and they tell you I am missing, or that my body was found in the woods somewhere, do not be surprised. These people are out to get me out of the race. I am uncovering stuff they do not want people to know about."

When McMillian's body was discovered, his mother couldn't help wondering whether her son's prophecy had been fulfilled.

Conclusions

What McMillian's parents were not aware of the night McMillian disappeared was that after moving the cars in his driveway, McMillian went to a party in Quitman County, Mississippi, with twenty-two-year-old Lawrence Reed of Shelby, Mississippi.[15] Driving his black Chevy Tahoe sport utility vehicle, McMillian first stopped at Marks, a convenience store, then parked on a desolate rural road where he and Reed smoked marijuana and consumed alcohol.[16] This explained why toxicology testing detected elevated levels of alcohol and Delta-9-THC in McMillian's postmortem blood.

According to Reed, McMillian masturbated, which is consistent with the small amount of semen found on McMillian's penis when his body was discovered, and that McMillian made sexual advances toward Reed after he watched pornographic material on his cellphone.[17] In response, Reed used the chain on his wallet to choke McMillian until he became unresponsive and then pushed McMillian out of the driver's side door of the vehicle. Thinking that McMillian wasn't dead, Reed next pushed McMillian into a nearby ditch that had standing water.[18] "He wasn't moving. He was fidgeting a little bit," Reed told police. "He was jerking a little bit. I think, 'I need to push him into the ditch before he wakes up.'"

After making sure that McMillian was dead, Reed placed the body in the back seat of the SUV and drove toward Clarksdale where he called his girlfriend, Dampier, and told her that he had just killed McMillian.

When he returned home, Reed changed his clothes and went to a gas station to purchase gasoline. Driving a short distance, he stopped and attempted to burn McMillian's phone, but it didn't burn fast enough. Frustrated, Reed cracked the phone, took the battery out, and threw the phone against a light pole. He then drove to an isolated area near the Mississippi River levee, stripped McMillian of his clothing, lifted the body through a barbed-wire fence, and tried to set it on fire with the remaining gasoline. "He burned for like a minute, but that's when I said, 'Man, I can't do nothing with this, and so I drug him behind the back side of a tree to try and burn him," Reed said.

Failing to cremate McMillian's body, Reed left it behind by the levee. While driving away, he threw McMillian's identification and wallet out the car window. After stopping to eat, he filled up the gas tank in his vehicle, threw his own sweatshirt and McMillian's clothing into a dumpster, and drove to his girlfriend's house, staying there only for a short time.

Later that evening, Reed returned to his girlfriend's house, but when he left, he was involved in a head-on collision with another vehicle on US Highway 49 South, near the Coahoma and Tallahatchie county line, approximately thirty miles from where McMillian's body was discovered.[19] When Police Officer Milton Williams Jr. arrived on the scene of the vehicular accident, Reed told him that he had killed somebody. Williams immediately read Reed his Miranda rights before continuing the conversation.

"The guy tried to rape me," Williams recalled Reed saying.

Reed was airlifted to the Regional Medical Center in Memphis, Mississippi, with a broken collar bone and broken ribs.[20] At the hospital, he saw news reports of the accident on the television and recounted to Coahoma County Sheriff's Deputy Joseph Wide all that had happened to him over the previous two days. "I stopped him, and I advised him I would have to read him his rights if I was going to talk to him," Wide said.

For a second time, Reed confessed to killing McMillian, claiming it was in self-defense after McMillian tried to rape him; notwithstanding his explanation, Reed was arrested and charged with McMillian's murder.[21]

Quitman County District Attorney Brenda Mitchell disputed Reed's story. "This version of the story does not match the physical evidence," Mitchell said. "This case is not a case of who done it, but why he did it." Many people in Clarksdale wondered whether McMillian's death was a hate crime against an African American man or a tragic example of gay bashing, or possibly both. That McMillian's death might have been related to politics was never far from anyone's mind.

Four months after McMillian was murdered, people gathered at an NAACP-sponsored town hall meeting in the sanctuary of Chapel Hill Missionary Baptist Church. "Marco was brutally murdered," said Carter Womack, McMillian's godfather. "That much we do know. We have to raise the level of voices otherwise it's just another Black man dead in Mississippi."

"I believe it was political," one of McMillian's family members said. "Maybe some people didn't want him to run. Maybe he was a threat. They wanted Clarksdale to stay the same."

Jarod Keith, McMillian's campaign spokesperson, did not believe McMillian's death was politically motivated; neither did the Coahoma County Sheriff's office.[22] McMillian's sexuality was a detail McMillian diligently left out of his conversations. "Marco's family and friends knew," Mississippi State University Assistant Professor of Political Science Ravi K. Perry said, "but he wasn't talking about his sexuality in press releases." McMillian's godfather, Womack, declared, "If it was a passing hookup, [then] something bad happened."

"I just don't believe that Marco's death had anything to do with his lifestyle choice," said Chikita Sanders, a biologist and McMillian's first cousin and close confidant.

Police had no reason to suspect that McMillian's death was a hate crime. Nonetheless, "being gay is still an issue for many people in Mississippi," Perry said.

Sharon J. Lettman-Hicks, executive director and CEO of the National Black Justice Coalition, noted, "Here we have a young man who by all accounts was a rising star. But the minute society learns that he's gay it is almost as if we, particularly in Black America, are absolved from public outcry and support."

The National Coalition of Anti-Violence Programs, whose members include local member programs, affiliate organizations, and individual affiliates working to prevent, respond to, and end all forms of violence against and within LGBTQ communities, worried that Reed might use the "gay panic" defense as a tactic in his trial. The same legal strategy was used in 1998 to defend the killers of Matthew Shepard, a gay twenty-one-year-old University of Wyoming student who was brutally beaten and tied to a fence in a field and left to die outside Laramie, Wyoming; Shephard succumbed to his wounds in a hospital in Fort Collins, Colorado.[23]

A more inclusive phrasing of the "gay/trans panic" defense is the "LGBTQ+ panic" defense, defined by the LGBT Bar of the American Bar Association as "a legal defense strategy that asks a jury to find that a victim's sexual orientation or gender identity is to blame for the defendant's violent reaction, including murder."[24] This legal tactic is sometimes used in combination with other defense strategies to bolster the argument that the defendant is innocent of committing the crime.[25] The strategy has three variations: (1) defense of insanity or diminished capacity—that a sexual proposition by a victim triggered a nervous breakdown in the defendant, causing an LGBTQ+ panic; (2) defense of provocation—the victim's proposition was sufficiently "provocative" to induce the defendant to kill the victim; and (3) defense of self-defense—the defendant believed that because of the victim's sexual orientation or gender identity, the victim was about to cause the defendant serious bodily harm.[26] In 2009, Joseph Biedermann was acquitted of stabbing to death his neighbor, Terrance Hauser, more than sixty times, after he claimed that Hauser had threatened to rape him.[27] And in 2016, James Dixon received a "light" sentence of twelve years in prison for beating to death Islan Nettles, after discovering that Nettles was a transgender person.

The gay panic defense has been used as recently as 2018 in Austin, Texas. In that case, sixty-nine-year-old James Miller claimed that his thirty-two-year old neighbor, Daniel Spencer, tried to kiss him. According to Miller, when he rebuffed Spencer's sexual advances, Spencer went into a rage and threatened him with a glass. This prompted Miller to defend himself by stabbing Spencer with a knife. The jury convicted Miller of the lighter charge of criminally negligent homicide rather than murder or manslaughter; he received six months in jail, ten years' probation, one hundred hours of community service, and a financial restitution penalty of $11,000. Anthony Michael Kreis, a legal expert, called the Miller verdict "repugnant." Said Kreis, "[Miller] didn't claim it was just the discovery of the sexual orientation per se" that led him to stab Spencer. "It was ... this mix of the same-sex interaction and the rejection in combination. It was that the victim's stature and kind of aggressive tone that created a scenario where he felt compelled to 'defend himself.'"

While the gay panic defense is still in use today, it does not seem to be very productive. W. Carsten Andresen of St. Edwards University in Austin, Texas, analyzed ninety-nine cases between 2000 and 2019 where criminal defendants killed one hundred gay men or trans women and raised gay panic defenses in court. Of these, only six defendants were acquitted of their charges. Forty-seven of fifty-eight convicted defendants went on to file legal appeals; the courts affirmed the original verdict in forty-six of the forty-seven appeal submissions.

In 1990, President George H.W. Bush signed into law the Hate Crime Statistics Act that required the US Attorney General to track and report annually on "crimes that manifest evidence of prejudice based on race, religion, sexual orientation, or ethnicity."[28] In 2009, President Barack H. Obama expanded protection granted in the 1990 Act by signing the Matthew Shepard and James Byrd, Jr. Hate Crimes Prevention Act. To date, fifteen states have prohibited the use of legal defenses claiming that the victim's sexual orientation or gender identity contributed to the defendant's actions.[29]

As it turned out, despite all the speculation about Reed's possible motive for killing McMillian, the McMillian murder case was just another "common" homicide in a town rife with violence.

"I didn't know what he would do if I ran," Reed said in court. "I choked him because he grabbed me, and I didn't know what his intentions were."

After all the evidence was presented, the jury deliberated for less than two hours; on March 12, 2015, it found Reed guilty of murdering McMillian.

Reed was sentenced to life in prison without the possibility of parole on April 2, 2015. This time, justice prevailed in Mississippi, the state where in 1964, three young college students—Michael Schwerner, James Chaney, and Andrew Goodman—were murdered by members of the Ku Klux Klan (KKK) simply because they volunteered to work on voter registration, education, and Civil Rights as part of the Congress of Racial Equality (CORE) Mississippi Summer Project.[30] "The slaying of a Negro [Chaney] in Mississippi is not news," Schwerner's wife, Rita, said at the time. "It is only because my husband and Andrew Goodman were White that the national alarm has been sounded."

In that case, the charges were dismissed in the majority of the eighteen defendants, seven of whom were found guilty but none of whom served more than six years behind bars. Edgar Ray Killen, a leader of the local KKK and a Baptist minister, walked free because one of the jurors refused to convict a minister. Mississippi has come a long way since the 1960s, but it still has a long way to go.

CHAPTER 21

George Floyd

Died May 25, 2020
Homicide due to Police Brutality

Operator: "911, how can I help you?"

Caller: "Um, someone came to our store and gave us fake bills and we realize it before he left the store, and we ran back outside; they was sitting on their car. We tell them to give us their phone, put their (inaudible) thing back and everything and he was also drunk and everything and return to give us our cigarettes back and so he can, so he can go home, but he doesn't want to do that, and he's sitting in his car 'cause he is awfully drunk and he's not in control of himself."[1]

SOMETIME BETWEEN SEVEN and eight o'clock in the evening on May 25, 2020, George Floyd, a forty-six-year-old African American man, entered Cup Foods in Minneapolis, Minnesota, and purchased a pack of cigarettes, paying with a twenty-dollar bill.[2] It was Memorial Day, and the owner of the store, Mike Abumayyaleh, was not at work that day.[3] Nonetheless, Abumayyaleh later said that Floyd was a regular "pleasant customer" with a "friendly face" who had never caused trouble.

Christopher Martin, the teenage clerk who sold Floyd the cigarettes, noticed the unusual blue color of the bill and thought that it was counterfeit.[4] When he told his boss of his suspicion, Martin was instructed to ask Floyd to come back inside so he could be questioned.[5] It was only after Floyd refused to enter the store for the second time that another employee made the 911 call and reported the incident to police.[6] Thereafter, all hell broke loose!

At 8:08 p.m., two rookie Minneapolis Police Department (MPD) officers, J. Alexander Kueng and Thomas Lane, arrived at the 3700 block of Chicago Avenue South and immediately located the blue Mercedes Benz sport utility vehicle that had been described in the 911 call.[7] Floyd was seated behind the wheel with Maurice Hall in the passenger seat and Shawanda Hill, whom Floyd had offered to drive home, seated in the back.[8] Courtenay Ross, Floyd's girlfriend, later told investigators that Floyd was addicted to drugs and that she and Floyd had occasionally purchased opioids from Hall and heroin from Hill.[9]

Lane approached the driver's side of the SUV and tapped on the window with his flashlight; his partner, Keung, stood by the passenger side door.[10]

"Stay in the car and let me see your hands," Lane commanded.[11]

Startled, Floyd exclaimed, "Hey man, I'm sorry! I didn't do nothing."

Without an explanation, Lane pulled out his weapon and, pointing it at Floyd's open window, asked Floyd at least ten times to put both hands on the wheel. Upon seeing the gun, Floyd begged Lane not to shoot him. He had reason to worry. He had been shot "the same way" once before.

"I'm not going to shoot you," Lane told Floyd, trying to put him at ease.

It was only after Floyd followed the police officer's instructions and put both hands on the wheel that Lane put away his gun.

"Hands on top of your head.... Step out of the vehicle and step away from me, all right?" Lane commanded.

At first, Floyd hesitated, telling Lane several times that he was sorry and that he didn't do anything wrong, but eventually he got out of the car, put his hands behind his back, and was handcuffed.

"Are you on something right now?" Lane asked Floyd. Because you're acting "a little erratic?"

"No, nothing.... I'm scared, man," Floyd replied.

Lane led Floyd toward the squad car and motioned him to get in the back seat. "I'm claustrophobic, man, please man, please," Floyd said, trying to explain why he didn't want to sit in the back of the police car. Lane was not sympathetic. "Well, you're still going in the car," he said.

While Floyd stood next to the police cruiser, Kueng searched Floyd's pockets. "[You're] under arrest right now for forgery," Kueng told Floyd.

"Forgery? For what?" Floyd asked, bewildered, but he received no reply. Later, Martin, the clerk at Cup Foods, told investigators that he suspected Floyd was unaware that the twenty-dollar bill he used to pay for the cigarettes was fake. Christopher Harris, Floyd's lifelong friend since their time together at James D. Ryan Middle School, agreed, saying, "I've never known him to do anything like that."

"Grab a seat," Lane urged Floyd, pointing to the back seat, "I'll roll the windows down if you put your legs in, all right?"

Floyd was reluctant to do so and again said that he was claustrophobic. "Can I get in the front, please?" Floyd begged the two officers, to which they both responded in unison, "No, you're not getting in the front."

Trying a different approach, Floyd repeated, "I want to lie on the ground. I want to lie on the ground, I want to lie on the ground." Lane had other ideas. "You're getting in the squad car," Lane said.

Bending his knees and trying to reach the pavement, Floyd told the officers, "I'm going down, I'm going down, I'm going down."

Frustrated that Floyd would not get into the police car voluntarily, Lane, Kueng, and MPD officer Derek Chauvin, who by now had appeared on the scene, were determined to get Floyd into the back seat of the police car by force, if necessary. As they wrestled with Floyd, one of the officers suggested that they "just lay him on the ground." Once down, Floyd complained twenty-seven times, "I can't breathe. I can't breathe. I can't breathe."

"Stop moving," Kueng demanded as he knelt on Floyd's lower body and held his wrist while Lane held his legs.[12] Chauvin, who is White and a senior police officer with nineteen years in the MPD, placed his left knee on Floyd's neck, by some estimates for as long as nine and a half minutes, although some have suggested it was closer to eight.

"It makes no difference how many minutes Chauvin had his knee on Floyd's neck," said Jamar Nelson, who works with families of crime victims in Minneapolis. "The bottom line is, it was long enough to kill him, long enough to execute him."

"Mama, mama, mama," Floyd cried out several times as the three police officers hit him with their batons and Chauvin pinned his face to the ground. "Tell my kids I love them. I'm dead."

Throughout the unimaginable and excruciating ordeal, Floyd kept pleading with the officers, "I can't breathe. I can't breathe, I can't breathe," and gasping, "You're going to kill me, man."

A large crowd had gathered on the sidewalk; seeing Floyd being manhandled by the three police officers, spectators began filming the incident with their smartphones.

"He's not even resisting arrest right now, bro," one bystander told Chauvin.[13] "You could have fucking put him in the car by now, bro. He's not even breathing right now, bro, you think that's cool?"

Within six minutes of being placed on the ground, Floyd became unresponsive. Kueng checked Floyd for a pulse, but he didn't find one. Nonetheless, despite Floyd having lost consciousness, Kueng continued to maintain his knee on Floyd's lower body while Chauvin kept his knee on Floyd's neck.

By the time the ambulance arrived, it was too late. Floyd was rushed to Hennepin Medical Center where he was pronounced deceased.

The Autopsy[14]

The autopsy was conducted by Andrew M. Baker, the chief medical examiner of Hennepin County, at 9:25 a.m. the morning after Floyd died. The body was identified by comparing fingerprints obtained at the autopsy with those on file with the Federal Bureau of Investigation (FBI).

The autopsy began with an external examination.

The body weighed 223 pounds and was six feet four inches long. It was normally developed, muscular, and with evidence of medical intervention. The scalp was covered with closely cropped black hair that was thinning in some areas. The face had a short black mustache and beard stubble; below the lower lip was a small patch of slightly longer black beard. Near the left jawline was a faint, two-centimeter V-shaped scar.

The teeth were in good repair. The eyes were brown, and the pupils were round and of equal diameter. The ears were unremarkable, except for the lobe of the left ear, which was pierced once.

The body had many small healing or healed scars, including on the left clavicle, the right forearm, both hands and wrists, the right hip, both knees, the left thigh, and the right shin.

Tattoos included an eagle holding a rifle across the upper chest; a pair of praying hands on the abdomen; the names "Laura" and "Cissy" on the upper right and left abdomen, respectively; the name "Floyd" across the abdomen; and a gravestone with unidentified letters and numbers, the letters "R.I.P," and an unidentified blue tattoo on the left forearm.

The wrists showed evidence consistent with restraints using handcuffs.

Numerous blunt force injuries included contusions (bruises), abrasions (scrapes), and an avulsion (a tear) on the left eyebrow, forehead, face, left cheek, lips, shoulders, elbows, wrists, legs, right shin, left calf, right index and middle fingers, and both hands.

The scalp was free of injury; the skull had no fractures; and the brain was without hemorrhage or abnormalities.

The hyoid bone and thyroid cartilage were intact, and the larynx was unremarkable. The tongue was without bite marks, hemorrhage, or other injuries; the spinal column was stable and free of hemorrhage; and the ribs, sternum, and vertebra were without fractures.

The internal examination found no excess fluid in any of the body cavities—pleural (the cavity that surrounds the lungs), pericardial (the area surrounding the heart and major blood vessels), or peritoneal (a space defined by the diaphragm, the walls of the abdominal and pelvic cavities, and the abdominal organs).

A firm, four-centimeter, thinly encapsulated mass consisting of red-brown and fleshy white-gray areas, admixed with scarred and calcified areas, was identified adjacent to the left external iliac vessels that supply blood to the legs and feet, and near the left psoas muscle, one of the muscles that overlies the vertebral column. When viewed under a microscope, the tumor had neuroendocrine features with a carcinoid-like pattern, suggestive of an "extraadrenal paraganglioma," the majority of which are benign.

The cardiovascular system showed evidence of severe heart disease. At 540 grams, the heart weight was substantially above the normal range and a significant risk factor for sudden death from an arrhythmia. In addition, there was 75 and 90 percent narrowing of the left and right descending coronary arteries, respectively, due to atherosclerosis (plaque buildup), a significant risk factor for a heart attack.

The tracheobronchial tree of the respiratory system had no masses or lesions and was free of blood, fluid, and foreign material; the pulmonary vascular system was without clots; and the pulmonary parenchyma, that portion of the lungs involved in gas exchange, was congested and edematous (fluid filled). At 1,085 and 1,015 grams, respectively, the weights of the right and left lungs were substantially above the maximum average normal weight of 720 and 675 grams, respectively.

The right and left kidneys weighed 205 and 225 grams, respectively. The urinary bladder contained approximately eighty milliliters of yellow urine; the prostate was normal in size; the testes were free of lesions, masses, contusions, or other abnormalities; and the seminal vesicles were unremarkable.

As for the gastrointestinal tract, the esophagus was intact and lined by smooth, gray-white mucosa (a soft inner lining);

the stomach contained approximately 450 milliliters of dark-brown fluid and fragments of food particles resembling bread; the duodenum, the first part of the small intestine immediately beyond the stomach, leading to the jejunum, as well as the small intestine, and colon, were unremarkable. The liver had no masses, lesions or other abnormalities; the gallbladder was without stones and contained a moderate amount of green-black bile; the spleen was smooth and intact; and the appendix was present.

The adrenal glands were symmetrical and without masses or areas of hemorrhage. The thyroid was not cystic or nodular, and the pancreas was firm and without masses, lesions, or other abnormalities.

In summary, the autopsy did not reveal any facial, oral, or conjunctival petechiae, often a sign of possible mechanical compression of the neck and jugular veins; and no injuries to the scalp, skull, brain, neck, larynx, chest, spinal column, or rib fractures from causes unrelated to CPR. In addition, there was no evidence of a recent heart attack, such as dead cardiac tissue.

Cause and Manner of Death

At the time of his arrest, Floyd told police that he had been infected with COVID-19 and that it was confirmed by a positive PCR viral test on April 3, 2020. A postmortem PCR test also was positive for COVID-19. Since PCR positivity for COVID-19 can persist for weeks after the onset and resolution of clinical disease, the postmortem positive result most likely reflected asymptomatic but persistent PCR positivity from the earlier infection.

Toxicology testing of postmortem blood detected the presence of caffeine, probably from coffee, and cotinine, a metabolite of nicotine, most likely from smoking cigarettes. Also detected were fentanyl, eleven nanograms per milliliter (ng/ml), an opioid that is eighty to 200 times more potent than morphine; despropionylfentanyl, (0.65 ng/ml), a pharmacologically weak metabolite and precursor of fentanyl; norfentanyl, (5.6 ng/ml), the primary inactive metabolite of fentanyl; delta-9-THC, (2.9 ng/ml), the active metabolite of marijuana and a hallucinogen; delta-9-carboxy-THC, (42 ng/ml), an inactive metabolite of marijuana; 11-hydroxy delta-9-THC, (1.2 ng/ml), an active intermediate metabolite of marijuana; and methamphetamine, (19 ng/ml), a potent stimulant.[1] Since both fentanyl and amphetamine were present in Floyd's blood, it's likely that Floyd ingested a "speedball," a combination of a depressant and a stimulant.[15]

The concentration of methamphetamine in Floyd's postmortem blood was 90 percent lower than the amount reported in people who exhibited violent and irrational behavior, so it's unlikely the drug contributed to Floyd's behavior the night he died. The level of fentanyl in his system, however, was approximately 3.7 times more than the lowest level (3 ng/ml) reported to cause respiratory depression and fatalities in some people. In addition, the autopsy showed that Floyd had been suffering from heart disease; he had an enlarged heart and substantial occlusion of two coronary arteries. The question that remained was, did a fentanyl overdose or a heart-related event play a role in Floyd's death?

Since Floyd was a chronic abuser of opioids, he undoubtedly had developed a tolerance to fentanyl and its side effects. Although Floyd complained that he couldn't breathe when he was being restrained by law enforcement, death from respiratory depression due to a fentanyl overdose is a slow process, which was not the way Floyd died.[16] In addition, Floyd's clinical signs, behavior, breathing, and energy prior to being restrained by law enforcement were not consistent with a fentanyl overdose.[17] As for whether

Floyd had a heart attack, the autopsy did not reveal any cardiac muscle death, an indication of myocardial infarction. Furthermore, there was no evidence that Floyd experienced an arrhythmia, an irregular heart rhythm, since an arrhythmia can only be detected on an electrocardiogram, which cannot be performed after death. After I reviewed the relevant records and the scientific literature, I concluded that high blood levels of fentanyl and heart disease contributed to but were not the primary cause of Floyd's death.

Baker, the chief medical examiner, explained that because of the enlarged heart and narrowing of the coronary arteries, Floyd needed more oxygen than a healthy man to efficiently function, especially during periods of high oxygen demand.[18] "In my opinion," Baker declared, "the law enforcement subdual restraint, and the neck compression was just more than Mr. Floyd could take by virtue of those heart conditions. The way law enforcement held Floyd down and compressed his neck complicated his ability to breathe."

Having reviewed the circumstances surrounding Floyd's death, the autopsy and toxicology reports, as well as published lay articles and the scientific literature, I agreed with Baker that Floyd died from cardiopulmonary arrest—the complete cessation of adequate heart function and respiration—due to law enforcement's subdual restraint and neck compression. As for the manner of death, clearly it was not natural since heart disease was not the primary cause of Floyd's death; it also wasn't suicide. Despite detecting a large amount of fentanyl in Floyd's postmortem blood, Floyd's death wasn't an accident due to fentanyl intoxication. As Baker said, "Mr. Floyd's use of fentanyl did not cause the subdual or neck restraint; his heart disease did not cause the subdual or neck restraint."

That the manner of death was homicide can be appreciated from the fact that but for the physical restraint and neck compression by law enforcement, Floyd would not have died on the evening of May 25, 2020. According to Martin Tobin, a pulmonologist and critical care specialist at the Edward Hines Jr. VA Hospital and the Loyola University's medical school, Chauvin placed more than ninety pounds of pressure on Floyd's neck so that 85 percent of Floyd's airways were restricted. "[Any] healthy person subjected to what Mr. Floyd was subjected to would have died."

Life and Career

Floyd was born in Fayetteville, North Carolina, on October 4, 1973.[19] His parents separated when he was two years old, after which Floyd's mother moved with her four children to the Cuney Homes, a complex of 500 public housing apartments known as "The Bricks" located in Houston, Texas's Third Ward, a historically African American neighborhood south of downtown.[20]

When he was in second grade, Floyd dreamed of becoming a U.S. Supreme Court Justice. His mother, who worked at a neighborhood fast-food restaurant, "thought that [Floyd] would be the one that would bring them out of poverty and struggle," said Travis Cains, Floyd's boyhood friend.

Jonathan Veal, Floyd's childhood classmate, recalled that even in middle school, Floyd was already six feet, two inches tall. "I was just blown away because I had never seen a twelve-year-old that tall," Veal said.[21]

Athletic with an interest in football and basketball, "Big Floyd," as he was affectionately known, became a star tight end for the Yates Lions, the varsity football team at Jack Yates High

School, playing in the 1992 state championship game at Texas Memorial Stadium in Austin against the Temple Wildcats.[22]

According to Donnell Cooper, Floyd had "a quiet personality, but a gentle spirit." Said Maurice McGowan, Floyd's former football coach, "[He] just wasn't going to ball up and act like he wanted to fight you."

Floyd's performance on the basketball court was noticed by George Walker, a former assistant coach at the University of Houston who became head coach at South Florida Community College in Avon Park, a small town in Florida. Floyd's mother urged Floyd to follow Walker to Avon Park. "They wanted George to really get out of the neighborhood, to do something, be somebody," Walker said.

After graduating from Yates in 1993, Floyd spent two years at South Florida Community College and then a year at Texas A&M University in Kingsville, Texas, before returning to Houston. "[He] was like a superhero" to the children in the neighborhood, said Cal Wayne, a well-known rapper who credits Floyd for encouraging him to pursue music.

Living in the projects, Floyd was unable to escape being pulled into crime. Arrested several times between 1997 and 2005 for drug possession and robbery, Floyd spent time in jail. In 2009, Floyd pled guilty to aggravated robbery with a deadly weapon; he was sentenced to five years in prison. After he was paroled in January 2013, Floyd seemed to turn his life around. "He came home with his head on right," said Cains.

Floyd's "rebirth" began after he attended a Christian rap concert where he met rapper Ronnie Lillard, a.k.a. Reconcile, and Pastor Patrick Ngwolo. "He had made some mistakes that cost him some years of his life," Lillard said of Floyd, "and when he got out of that, I think the Lord greatly impacted his heart."

Ngwolo had been looking for ways to reach residents at Cuney Homes, so Floyd volunteered to introduce him to potential worshippers in the neighborhood. Floyd began by assisting in baptisms, participating in basketball tournaments and barbecues organized by the outreach ministry, and in identifying candidate residents for grocery deliveries and Bible study.[23] He also became a mentor to students and teachers alike, offering advice based on his own experiences about living in the projects and the effect it has on young people's behavior and development.

Philonise, Floyd's younger brother, recalled that Floyd "was like a person that everybody loved around the community. He just knew how to make people feel better." In a homemade video, Floyd revealed, "I've got my shortcoming and my flaws and I ain't better than nobody else, but man, the shootings that's going on, I don't care what 'hood you're from, where you're at, man. I love you and God loves you. Put them guns down."

In 2014, Floyd "was looking to start over fresh, a new beginning," said Christopher Harris, who preceded Floyd to Minneapolis. "He was happy with the change he was making." After moving to Minnesota, Floyd found a job as a security guard at the Salvation Army's Harbor Light Center in downtown Minneapolis.

Speaking of Floyd, Brian Molohon, director of development for the Salvation Army's Minnesota office, said, "[He was] just a big strong guy, but with a very tender side ... [who] ... would regularly walk a couple of the female coworkers out ... at night and make sure they got to their cars safely and securely."

Floyd left the Salvation Army after a year to train as a truck driver, while at the same time, working as a bouncer at Conga Latin Bistro, a local club. "Always, cheerful; he had a good attitude," said Jovanni Tunstrom, owner of the bistro.[15] When the Conga was forced to close in 2020 after Minnesota governor Tim Walz issued a stay-at-home order due to the COVID-19 pandemic, Floyd became unemployed.

Sometime around eight o'clock the evening of Memorial Day 2020, Floyd went to Cup Foods to buy a pack of cigarettes. It was the last time anybody saw him alive.

Conclusions

"The sanctity of life and the protection of the public shall be the cornerstones of the MPD's use of force," prosecuting attorney Jerry Blackwell reminded the jury in his opening statement in the trial of Chauvin and his three codefendants on March 29, 2021. Police officers take an oath to "enforce the law courteously and appropriately ... [and to] ... never employ unnecessary force or violence.... [Chauvin] betrayed his oath when he used excessive and unreasonable force upon the body of Mr. George Floyd." It was a strong opening statement that set the tone for the rest of the trial.

After a week of damning testimony, the jury, composed of six White jurors, four Black, and two who identified themselves as multiracial, convicted Chauvin of murdering Floyd; he was sentenced to twenty-two and a half years in prison.[24] Three other police officers—Lane, Kueng, and Tou Thao—were each found guilty of depriving Floyd of his constitutional rights and of willfully failing to provide Floyd medical care that resulted in bodily harm and death; they were each sentenced to several years in prison.

Apparently, when the law enforcement officers confronted Floyd, they were intent that he performed four specific tasks: (1) put both hands on the wheel; (2) get out of the car; (3) be handcuffed and walk to the squad car; and (4) sit in the back seat of the police car. Floyd completed three of the tasks, but he failed to get into the back seat of the squad car because he was claustrophobic. Unsympathetic, the officers were determined that Floyd completed the fourth task as well. As Floyd continued to resist, the situation escalated, and emotions rather than training overtook the officers, ultimately leading to a tragic and shocking outcome and Floyd's death.

"The way he died was senseless," said Harris. "He begged for his life. He pleaded for his life. When you try so hard to put faith in this system, a system that you know isn't designed for you, when you constantly seek justice by lawful means and you can't get it, you begin to take the law into your own hands."

Police brutality is not a new phenomenon in the United States. "A person gets killed by the police, on average, every eight hours," said Rashawn Ray, a senior fellow at the Brookings Institute.[25] "That's a normal thing.... We've been dealing with it ever since slave patrols." While Floyd's death was a well-publicized case of police brutality against African American men, it wasn't the only one. On March 3, 1991, Rodney King was shot twice with a Taser by Los Angeles Police Department officers and was struck as many as fifty-six times by their batons, causing King to suffer a fractured leg, multiple facial fractures, and numerous bruises and contusions.[26] Then, on July 17, 2014, while New York Police Department officer Daniel Pantaleo locked him in an illegal chokehold, Eric Garner repeatedly cried out, "I can't breathe, I can't breathe" before losing consciousness; he was pronounced dead an hour later.[27] As if that wasn't enough to raise the public's consciousness to police brutality, one month later, an unarmed eighteen-year-old Michael Brown was shot to death at least six times by police officer Darren Wilson during an altercation in Ferguson, Missouri.[28] And just two months prior to Floyd's death, Breonna Taylor, a twenty-six-year-old African American emergency medical technician, was shot and killed by police in her Louisville, Kentucky, apartment after officers busted through her door, looking for signs of drug trafficking.[29]

African American citizens make up 13 percent of the US population, but they accounted for approximately 26 to 27 percent of all people killed by police in 2022.[30] According to one report, 65 percent of Black adults feel that they have been targeted by police because of their race; 84 percent believe that police treat White people better than Black people; and 87 percent think that the US criminal justice system is more unjust toward Blacks than Whites.[31]

By some estimates, a Black person is five times more likely to be stopped by police without just cause and two to three times more likely to be killed by police than a White person. And yet, despite clear evidence that African American men, especially young men, are more likely to be harmed by police than White men, there are no definitive estimates of the prevalence of police-involved deaths.[32] A recent study estimated that the US National Vital Statistics System underreported 55.5 percent of deaths due to police violence, the largest proportion of which was among Black people.[33] This was corroborated in an investigation conducted by the *Washington Post* that found that fatal police shootings were underreported to the FBI by more than 50 percent.[34]

"It's bad and it's sad, but it's not shocking that we're still being killed at a higher rate" than White people, said Karundi Williams, executive director of re:power, an organization that builds leaders for social justice.

"Being Black in America should not be a death sentence," Minneapolis Mayor Jacob Frey said after the horrific and graphic video of Floyd's killing went viral. Jacob Blake Sr., who runs

Families United, a group that assists people whose loved ones have been killed by police, agreed. "Police's ability to be judge, jury, and executioner has been taken to another level," said Blake.

Despite the intense interest and the public outcry that followed Floyd's death, the number of people killed by law enforcement since 2013 has increased annually to 1,176 in 2022. Of these, 8 percent involved traffic violations, 11 percent were cases where no offense was alleged, and in 32 percent, a person was killed after fleeing from police. "These are routine police encounters that escalate to a killing," said Samuel Sinyangwe a data scientist and policy analyst.

Efforts by local Minneapolis officials to curb police brutality following Floyd's death were short lived. Not only did the overall number of killings by police stay high, but the death rate of Black residents remained twenty-eight times more than that of White residents. "Change moves at the speed of an ocean liner and not a speedboat," said Carl Douglas, a Los Angeles civil rights lawyer. "Even in California, which is supposed to be the bastion of liberalism, we were only able to pass a watered-down version of a police reform bill in the wake of George Floyd."

Said Williams of re:power, "The system wasn't built to protect Black people. When we have moments of racial injustice that is thrust in the national spotlight, there is an uptick of outrage.... But then the media tends to move on to other things, and that consciousness decreases.... Until we get to the root cause of policing and police brutality and the differences in the way police treat Black folks versus White folks, we're not going to get to change." Douglas agreed. "There has to be a cultural shift from the warrior versus them mentality to more of a guardian mentality."

Leslie Mac, a New York organizer and activist, went even further. "There's nothing that actually addresses the root issues ...

whether that's under-accountability ... the amount of weaponry that [police] have at their disposal or ... who they're accountable to."

Despite the national increase in racially related killings, there are some proposed solutions and very small signs of progress made to reduce the number of police-related shootings. Denver, Colorado, initiated a program where clinicians and medics respond to mental health calls instead of police; some cities have restricted traffic stops by police for minor offenses; and California has decriminalized jaywalking.

Recently, there has been a noticeable cry to defund police departments, but defunding the police is not the answer, said Elizabeth Jordie Davies, an expert on social movements. Interestingly, while some cities have cut police funding after Floyd's killing, many have restored or even increased these budgets by 2021. "I don't know any other instance where an apparatus can be so bad at its job and continue to get increased funding," said Mac, the New York activist. "It really flies in the face of conventional wisdom. It's just putting bad money on top of bad money."

Instead of defunding the police, money should be redirected toward other resources. "I don't see a way out of this until we look beyond policing for safety for our communities. It's also about where we put those resources," Mac said. Funds should go to addressing root problems of racial discrimination and police brutality—safe housing, sufficient clothing, food, and mental health and drug addiction services.

"One of my greatest desires as a result of this (Floyd's killing) taking place is that there be a heightened level of accountability within law enforcement; second, that human life would be valued at a high level and we would treat each other in such a way that this wouldn't happen to anyone else," said Veal, Floyd's friend since sixth grade. I can't think of a better outcome for such a tragic and heinous act.

On June 16, 2023, the US Department of Justice (DOJ) announced the results of its investigation of the MPD in the aftermath of Floyd's killing.[35] The DOJ concluded that the MPD uses excessive force, including unjustified deadly force and unreasonable use of Tasers; unlawfully discriminates against Black and Native American people; violates the rights of people engaged in protected speech; and discriminates against people with behavioral health disabilities. "Every American deserves policing that is fair, equitable, and nondiscriminatory," said Assistant Attorney General Kristen Clarke of the DOJ's Civil Rights Division.

Following the release of the DOJ investigative report, First Assistant US Attorney Ann Bildtsen for the District of Minnesota declared, "These findings present a sobering picture of a flawed system—but today we turn toward change through justice." Unfortunately, that change is slow in coming.

In the aftermath of George Floyd's tragic death, Floyd gained much more than fifteen minutes of fame. Mass protests for racial equality and justice, the largest since the civil rights movement, erupted across the country and the world. Legislatively, more than thirty states have passed 140 oversight and reform laws on local police since Floyd died in an attempt to hold police more accountable, especially when people are killed while in police custody. In addition, several books have been written about George Floyd, including the 2023 Pulitzer Prize Winner in general nonfiction, *His Name Is George Floyd: One Man's Life and the Struggle for Racial Justice* by Robert Samuels and Toluse Olorunnipa. Finally, Floyd's now famous last words, "I can't breathe," have become a rallying cry against police brutality.

CHAPTER 22

Thomas Mansfield

Died January 5, 2021
Accident due to Caffeine Intoxication

COLWYN BAY, A seaside resort on the north coast of Wales, overlooks the Irish Sea. Established in 1844 with just a small number of homes and farms, the town has expanded to become the second-largest community and business center in north Wales with a population exceeding thirty-five thousand inhabitants. Colwyn Bay boasts that it "supports a healthier community by creating direct fitness activities such as running and cycling routes along the waterfront to encourage exercise."[1]

In early January 2021, Thomas Mansfield, a twenty-nine-year-old self-employed personal trainer, ordered a one-hundred gram packet of pure caffeine powder from Blackburn Distributions, a United Kingdom supplier of sports supplements and health-care products; the drug is used by many athletes to increase endurance.[2] On the morning of January 5, shortly after the supplement arrived at his home in Colwyn Bay, Mansfield began preparing the preworkout drink by mixing the caffeine powder with water.[3]

At first, Mansfield sipped the mixture but then, he rapidly finished the remainder.[4] Soon, he began clutching his chest and frothing at the mouth.[5] As he lay down on the sofa, Mansfield's wife, Suzy, contacted emergency medical services.[6]

It took paramedics only a few minutes to arrive. Finding Mansfield with a "grossly abnormal" heart rhythm, they used a defibrillator before transporting Mansfield in cardiac arrest to Glad Clwyd Hospital.[7]

All attempts at the hospital at resuscitation were unsuccessful.[8] Mansfield was pronounced dead at 4:00 p.m.

The Autopsy

The autopsy report was not available for review.

Cause and Manner of Death

Foul play was not suspected in Mansfield's death.

Information obtained from published lay articles indicated that Mansfield had a lethal amount of caffeine in his blood—392 milligrams per liter (mg/L). Caffeine toxicity begins at a plasma concentration of 15 mg/L; the level of caffeine in Mansfield's blood was nearly five times more than the minimum level, 80 mg/L, considered lethal.[9]

A study of fifty-one reported deaths in which caffeine intoxication was implicated determined that the median caffeine blood concentration in males was 182 mg/L; Mansfield's caffeine blood level was more than twice as much.[10]

After I reviewed the circumstances surrounding the death, as well as several published lay articles and the scientific literature, I agreed with John Gittins, senior coroner of North Wales east and central, that Mansfield died from caffeine intoxication and that the manner of death was "misadventure," equivalent to accidental in the United States.

Harry A. Milman, PhD

Life and Career

Mansfield was born sometime around 1992. Married and the father of two, a boy and a girl, Mansfield lived with his family on Lawson Road in Colwyn Bay. Besides being a personal trainer and holding fitness classes, Mansfield occasionally worked as a security guard.

Mansfield was "really healthy," and he normally would not drink more than two cups of coffee a day, Suzy said. "He was my whole life. I'll never get over this.... My world has been ripped apart, and my kids have lost their daddy."

Conclusions

Evidence was presented at the inquest that followed Mansfield's death that Mansfield had used a digital kitchen scale with a starting weight of two grams, ten times the typically recommended starting weight to measure the powdered caffeine.[11] Said Gittins, the senior coroner, Mansfield was "likely aiming for a mid-range serving," but he weighed out too much caffeine. By his miscalculation, Mansfield accidentally ingested enough caffeine to equal almost two hundred cups of coffee, a decidedly lethal amount of the drug.

Mansfield isn't the only person to have miscalculated the dose of pure caffeine powder. On March 23, 2015, six years prior to Mansfield's death, two twenty-year-old students of sports science at Northumbria University in Newcastle upon Tyne in the UK nearly died after they miscalculated the dose of caffeine powder for a class experiment.[12] Ingesting one hundred times the correct amount of caffeine dissolved in orange juice, the boys consumed enough caffeine to equal three hundred cups of coffee. Within minutes, they suffered a rapid heart rate, dizziness, blurred vision, shaking, and vomiting. Rushed to intensive care, the boys underwent dialysis to remove the excess caffeine from their systems and made a full physical recovery. In a hearing held at Newcastle Crown Court after the incident, prosecutor Adam Farrer, said, "The resulting overdoses could easily have been fatal."

Caffeine is found at low concentrations in energy drinks, appetite suppressants, and exercise supplements.[13] While the drug is the most widely consumed over-the-counter stimulant, it is not on the list of banned performance enhancing substances of the World Anti-Doping Agency.[14] "Of all the legal supplements an athlete could take, [caffeine] has the biggest effect on performance," said Mark Glaister, an exercise physiologist at St. Mary's University in Twickenham in the UK.[15]

Many people habitually ingest caffeine on a daily basis, with an average cup of brewed coffee containing ninety-five milligrams of caffeine. Symptoms of caffeine toxicity are rarely seen after drinking two to three cups of coffee or tea; however, after five to six cups, "people start to feel agitated and jittery and may feel nausea," said Robert Glatter, an assistant professor of emergency medicine at Northwell Health and Lenox Hill Hospital in New York.[16]

When taken in large, overdose quantities, symptoms of caffeine intoxication include heart-related events, such as an arrhythmia, an erratic heartbeat, as well as seizures, cardiac arrest, and death. Vomiting, diarrhea, stupor, and disorientation can also occur.[17] "You stimulate the heart and cause a rhythm problem, and generally the heart is going to go into ventricular tachycardia (fast heart rate) or ventricular fibrillation (erratic heart beat). It shoots up to 180 beats per minute," said Thomas A. Sweeney, associate chair of the department of emergency medicine at Christiana Care Health System in Wilmington, Delaware.

While energy drinks have become increasingly popular, ingesting several cans a day can cause the onset of caffeine toxicity due to their high caffeine content; a twenty-ounce can of Red Bull contains 190 milligrams of caffeine, nearly twice the amount in a cup of coffee, while a sixteen-ounce can of Monster has 160 milligrams. "It's recommended by physicians across the country and around the world that 400 milligrams [of caffeine] a day is considered a safe dose that is pretty clearly not associated with the onset of any illness," said Michael Broman of OSF Heart of Mary Medical Center in Urbana, Illinois.[18]

In 2018, David Cripe, a sixteen-year-old from South Carolina, consumed three heavily caffeinated energy drinks within two hours and died.[19] "Parents, please, talk to your kids about the dangers of these energy drinks. And teenagers and students, please stop buying them," Cripe's father, Sean, said after his son died from a caffeine-related arrhythmia and cardiac arrest.[20] In 2023, Matthew Mayer, a forward on the University of Illinois basketball team, admitted to drinking one Monster energy drink before the game against Ohio State on Sunday, February 26, and five more cans after the game had ended.[21] "I've been sick the last few days," Mayer told reporters three days later. "I had caffeine poisoning … because I like a caffeine-induced euphoria to play video games. I could barely get out of bed the next day. It was basically like a caffeine hangover." It is estimated that Mayer ingested 960 milligrams of caffeine, more than twice the recommended daily dose of the drug.

According to the US Food and Drug Administration (FDA), pure and highly concentrated caffeine products, such as caffeine powder, present an even greater public health threat than energy drinks. This is because each teaspoonful of pure caffeine powder can contain as much caffeine as twenty-eight cups of coffee, enough to kill a child; one tablespoon can kill an adult. In 2010, twenty-three-year-old Michael Bedford died at a party in Nottingham, England, after ignoring the product's recommended dose of no more than one-sixteenth of a teaspoon of the pure caffeine powder that his friend bought on the internet; instead, he ingested two teaspoonfuls and washed it down with an energy drink.[22] "Caffeine is freely available on the internet, but it's so lethal if taken in the wrong dose and here we see the consequence," said coroner Nigel Chapman.

In 2014, another young man—Logan Stiner, an eighteen-year-old senior at Keystone High School in LaGrange, Ohio—died of a caffeine overdose after ingesting pure caffeine powder that was purchased on Amazon.com. "He was a young, healthy guy," Lorain County Coroner Steven Evans said.[23] "People don't realize [that caffeine] could potentially kill you." The following month, James Sweatt, a twenty-four-year-old, newly married electrical engineer living in Alpharetta, Georgia, died after consuming pure caffeine powder that also was purchased on Amazon. Finally, in the early hours of New Year's Day 2018, after returning from a New Year's Eve party, twenty-one-year-old Lachlan Foote made himself a protein shake mixed with pure caffeine powder before retiring for the night at his home in Blackheath, a town on the east coast of Australia.[24] Foote "innocently added too much pure caffeine powder" to his shake, his father, Nigel, said. In the morning, Foote's parents found their son dead on the bathroom floor, a day before his twenty-second birthday. "It's just insane that something so dangerous is so readily available" on the internet, Nigel said.[25]

The difference between a safe dose and a toxic or life-threatening dose of pure caffeine powder is very small. Common kitchen scales and utensils, such as teaspoons, are not precise enough to measure safe quantities; a measuring spoon sized to one-sixteenth of a teaspoon is needed. Knowing that she didn't have such a measuring spoon, Stiner's mother in Ohio summed it up best when she said that her son "had no clue what he was doing.... Since it was a powder, he probably didn't know how much he was taking."

The Stiner family sued Amazon, claiming that the giant internet retailer was responsible for their son's death, but the judge in Ohio concluded that the company was not liable.[26] Under current product liability laws, Amazon did not meet Ohio's definition of a supplier because it did not "participate in placing [the] product in the stream of commerce" and never had possession or control of the pure caffeine powder.

In a separate report, Justice Michael Donnelly wrote, "Applying the 1980s retail-sales paradigm to modern e-commerce produces results that strike me as inequitable." Donnelly suggested that state lawmakers should update and replace the archaic law that was enacted "when brick-and-mortar retail was the norm and even mail-order retailers facilitated their own sales and fulfilled their own orders."

By all accounts, the FDA has been paying attention. On September 1, 2015, the agency issued warning letters to five distributors of pure powdered caffeine products; it issued two additional warning letters in March 2016 and in June 2018. On April 13, 2018, the FDA released a guidance document for companies that manufacture, market, or distribute dietary supplements containing pure or highly concentrated caffeine, or are considering doing so, in order to help them determine when a product is considered adulterated and illegal.

"Please warn your friends, talk to your children ... and perhaps check your kitchen cupboards ... pure caffeine powder looks just like any other white powder ... but a heaped teaspoon of it will kill you," Nigel Foote warned.

CHAPTER 23
Lori McClintock
Died December 15, 2021
Accident due to Dietary Supplements

LORI MCCLINTOCK, WIFE of Tom McClintock, a Republican US congressman from California, had been trying to lose weight.[1] Taking white mulberry leaf, a Chinese herbal dietary supplement, McClintock had "just joined a gym and was counting down the days to Christmas," her husband said, adding that when he spoke to his wife on December 14, 2021, she was fine and "carefully dieting."[2] Nonetheless, sometime that day, McClintock complained of an upset stomach.[3]

On December 15, after having voted in Congress the previous night, Tom McClintock returned to his home in Elk Grove, California.[4] When he entered his residence, he found McClintock unresponsive.[4] She was sixty-one years old.

The Autopsy[5]

Chief Forensic Pathologist Jason P. Tovar performed the autopsy the morning after McClintock's body was discovered. The body was identified by a Sacramento County Coroner's identification tag.

The autopsy began with an external examination.

"The body is that of an unembalmed, refrigerated, adult woman who appears consistent with the reported age of sixty-one years," Tovar wrote in the autopsy report. The body weighed 190 pounds, measured seventy inches in length, and was well nourished.

No abrasions (scrapes), bruises, lacerations (deep cuts or tears in the skin), burns, scars on the wrists, or tattoos were identified. The head was covered by long, wavy gray hair; the eyes were green and without petechial hemorrhages, areas of pericapillary bleeding. The oronasal passages were unobstructed, the teeth were natural and in good repair, the earlobes were unremarkable, and the auditory canals were without hemorrhage or discharge. The neck was unremarkable, the chest had no deformity, and the abdomen was flat. The extremities showed no needle tracks, edema, joint deformity, or abnormal mobility, and the feet were unremarkable.

Cyanosis of the fingernail beds, which occurs when the blood doesn't have enough oxygen, was evident, but the cause of it was not determined. In addition, a three-quarter-inch abrasion was identified on the right knee.

For the internal examination, the body cavity was entered through the standard Y-incision. The breasts had no abnormalities. The organs of the abdominal cavity were present and in their normal position, and there was no evidence of peritonitis (inflammation) in the peritoneal cavity, the space defined by the diaphragm, the walls of the abdominal and pelvic cavities, and the abdominal organs.

The skull had no fractures. The brain was anatomically normal, its weight of 1,350 grams in the normal range.

The mouth, upper airways, and trachea were free of foreign material. The hyoid bone and larynx were intact and without fractures.

As for the cardiovascular system, the heart, weighing 330 grams, was mildly enlarged; the heart chambers were normally developed and without thrombosis (clots); the heart valves were thin and pliable; the left anterior coronary descending artery had 50 percent narrowing due to atherosclerosis and plaque buildup.

The aorta, the large artery that carries oxygenated blood to the rest of the body, was unremarkable.

There was some congestion in the respiratory system, but the right and left lung weights of 280 and 250 grams, respectively, were well within the normal range.

The stomach contained a partial plant leaf, later identified as a white mulberry leaf, as well as fifty milliliters of a tan fluid. The esophagus was intact, the small intestine was unremarkable, the appendix was present, and the liver was tan-brown in color, of normal size and with mild fatty deposits. The gallbladder contained four milliliters of bile, about a teaspoonful, but was without stones, and the pancreas showed no necrosis or calcification.

The kidneys were normal with the right and left kidney weights of 110 and 120 grams, respectively, in the normal range. The urinary bladder had no urine and was not distended.

The thymus was inconspicuous; the spleen was normal in size and weight; the adrenal and pituitary glands were unremarkable; and the thyroid gland was red-tan in color with a firm right lobe. While microscopic examination of the thyroid showed mild nodularity, there was no dominant nodule.

The most significant finding in the autopsy for the determination of cause of death was the presence of a partially intact white mulberry leaf in the stomach.

Cause and Manner of Death

Toxicology analysis detected the presence of caffeine in postmortem blood taken from the femoral vein, a large blood vessel located in the thigh, the amount of which was not reported.[5] Most likely, the caffeine had originated from coffee, tea, soft drinks, chocolate, or possibly from an over-the-counter medication.

Harry A. Milman, PhD

Testing of the vitreous fluid, also called vitreous humor, a clear gel-like substance that is located in the space between the lens and retina of the eye, measured substantially elevated levels of creatinine, urea nitrogen, and sodium at 1.72, 44, and 154 milligrams per deciliter, respectively, abnormalities that are indicative of dehydration.[6]

Based on the circumstances surrounding the death, the presence of an upset stomach the evening before McClintock died, and the identification of a white mulberry leaf in the stomach that according to Alison Colwell, curator of the University of California-Davis Center for Plant Diversity, "was likely ingested when fresh," Tovar concluded that the cause of death was dehydration due to gastroenteritis, an inflammation of the stomach and small intestine, resulting from the adverse effects of ingesting white mulberry leaves.

While I agreed with Tovar that McClintock's death was due to dehydration, I was unable to determine to a reasonable degree of scientific certainty that the dehydration was caused by the ingestion of white mulberry. The manner of death was accident.

Life and Career

McClintock was born on Mother's Day, May 8, 1960, in Grand Haven, Michigan. The daughter of a Baptist pastor, she grew up in Spring Lake, Traverse City, and Webberville, Michigan.

In 1977, McClintock moved with her family to Thousand Oaks, California, where she attended Morrpark College and earned a real estate license. As a young woman, McClintock toured with the Continental Singers for three years.

On November 7, 1987, McClintock married Tom McClintock, a popular California politician.[7] After her marriage to the congressman, she worked at the First Baptist Church in Elk Grove and was a homemaker.[8] In 2015, McClintock returned to real estate; by 2020, she became an agent recruiting coordinator at Lyon Real Estate in Sacramento, California.

Conclusions

The white mulberry tree is found worldwide but it originated in Asia, in countries such as China, Japan, Korea, and India.[9] By some accounts, the leaves, fruit, and bark have been used as an herbal remedy to treat cancer, inflammation, diabetes, and various bacterial infections at least since 3,000 BC.[10] In many countries, white mulberry leaves are used as food for animals and humans.[11] The leaf extract is often used in patients with diabetes type 2 to help control glucose levels in the blood and as a dietary supplement, an antioxidant, and as an ingredient in cosmetic products.

Dietary supplements containing white mulberry are regulated by the US Food and Drug Administration (FDA) under the Dietary Supplement Health and Education Act of 1994.[12] Under the act, FDA prohibits manufacturers and distributors of dietary supplements and dietary ingredients to market products that are adulterated or misbranded. However, the act does not provide FDA the authority to require manufacturers to show that the dietary supplements are safe and effective before they are marketed.[13] As a result, dietary products with white mulberry may contain contaminants that can cause unexpected adverse side effects. In addition, the amount of white mulberry can vary between different batches and preparations of the same supplement. Nonetheless, "There's really been very few, if any, serious side effects seen with this," said Melinda Ring, director of the Osher Center for Integrative Health at Northwestern University, referring to white mulberry leaves. Since 2004, only two cases of people sickened by mulberry supplements have been reported to the FDA Adverse Event Reporting System; of these, only one required medical follow-up.

Bill Gurley, principal scientist at the University of Mississippi's National Center for Natural Products Research, claimed, "It would take literally bushel baskets of white mulberry leaves to cause some type of untoward effect and even then, you don't see anything lethal." White mulberry leaves are "probably one of the safest leaves in the world," Gurley added. "Its track record for safety is unsurpassed."

The day prior to her death, McClintock experienced an upset stomach, possibly due to ingestion of white mulberry leaves; at the autopsy, a partial mulberry leaf was found in her stomach. According to Brent Bauer, director of the Mayo Clinic Complementary and Integrative Medicine Program, some people who ingest more than one gram per day of white mulberry leaves may develop mild gastrointestinal distress including nausea, abdominal bloating, and discomfort. An upset stomach, in turn, can lead to diarrhea, vomiting, and dehydration, noted Ring.

D'Michelle DuPre, a retired forensic pathologist and a former medical examiner in South Carolina, observed, "[White mulberry leaves] do tend to cause dehydration, and part of the uses for that can be to help someone lose weight, mostly through fluid loss, which in this case was just kind of excessive."

James Gill, chair of the College of American Pathologists' Forensic Pathology Committee and chief medical examiner of Connecticut claimed, "It takes at least a week or so for someone to die from dehydration.... There are some things that really don't fit" in the McClintock cause of death determination.

Besides diarrhea and vomiting, dehydration can be caused by fever, excessive sweating, increased urination, and some medications.[14] Complications of dehydration include heatstroke, urinary tract infections, kidney stones and kidney failure, seizures due to electrolyte imbalance, and hypovolemic shock, which can be life-threatening. Since McClintock died from dehydration after ingesting white mulberry leaves, in the absence of other known causes, her dehydration may have been due to consumption of more than the recommended amount of the herbal supplement.

The incidence of adverse effects from long-term use of alternative medicine, such as so-called "natural" products, including hypericum, valerian, ginseng, gingko, and herbal medicines, has been increasing worldwide.[15] In March 2017, a man and a woman fell critically ill and were hospitalized after consuming herbal tea purchased from the same herbalist in San Francisco's Chinatown.[16] Within an hour, "each … developed weakness, and then life-threatening abnormal heart rhythms, requiring resuscitation and intensive hospital care," said Tomas Aragon, a health officer with the San Francisco Department of Public Health.[17] The man recovered, but the thirty-year old woman died six days later. It was determined that the tea the two victims drank contained aconite, a plant-based fast-acting poison that causes severe side effects, such as nausea, vomiting, breathing problems, heart problems, and death.

In a separate March 2017 incident, thirty-year-old Jade Erick's eczema was treated by a California naturopathic practitioner with an intravenous "turmeric emulsion," a common spice in Indian food. After 2 percent of the turmeric emulsion was administered, Erick became unresponsive. Six days later, she died from "severe anoxic brain injury secondary to cardiopulmonary arrest, most likely due to turmeric infusion." The FDA investigated Erick's death and discovered that the intravenous turmeric emulsion that was administered contained less than 2 percent of the curcumin concentration represented on the label.[18] Moreover, the emulsion was prepared with laboratory grade polyethylene glycol 40 castor oil (PEG-40 castor oil) containing diethylene glycol, an impurity that was not suitable for humans or for therapeutic use. Drug products containing PEG-40 castor oil have been associated with severe and sometimes fatal hypersensitivity reactions. Such products include warnings about these reactions on their labels, but the label for the turmeric product that was administered to Erick had no such warnings. In addition, there are few, if any, toxicological or clinical studies regarding the safety of intravenous curcumin or its effectiveness in the treatment of eczema.

In 2020, the global dietary supplements market size in the US was $61.2 billion.[19] McClintock's tragic death, as well as those related to turmeric, highlight the deficiencies in FDA's regulatory authority over dietary supplements and alternative medicine. "There's no guarantee that a supplement is effective or safe," said Ring of Northwestern University.

As with any over-the-counter supplement, "some things that are purportedly sold as botanical supplements are not what they appear to be," said Pieter Cohen of Cambridge Health Alliance.[20] "They can contain the wrong plant and they can also contain untested and unproved drugs. And those substances, especially in combination, can be powerful enough and dangerous enough to kill people."

Obtaining fifteen minutes of fame by virtue of the circumstances surrounding a death is not the best way of becoming famous, especially when there are other options readily available. Nonetheless, McClintock's death due to ingestion of white mulberry highlighted the safety concerns and lack of regulatory controls over the sale of dietary supplements and herbal medicines.

CHAPTER 24

Mary Jane Thomas

Died March 22, 2022
Accident due to Cosmetic Surgery

MARY JANE THOMAS was the third wife of musician Hank Williams Jr., son of country music legend Hank Williams.[1] On March 21, 2022, after being cleared for elective surgery by her primary care physician in Nashville, Tennessee, Thomas traveled to the Bafitis Plastic Surgery in Jupiter, Florida, for cosmetic surgery that included liposuction and for removal of her breast implants and replacing them with a breast lift, a surgical procedure that changes the shape of the breasts by removing excess skin and reshaping breast tissue to raise the breasts.[2]

Harold Bafitis, an osteopathic physician and a cosmetic, plastic, and reconstructive surgery specialist and head of the plastic surgery bearing his name, performed the procedures on Thomas.[3] Bafitis was well qualified to perform these elective surgeries. Before opening his surgical practice, Bafitis did a five-year general surgery residency at Grandview Medical Center in Dayton, Ohio, two additional years of training in plastic and reconstructive surgery at the Plastic Surgery Institute and affiliated hospitals in Des Moines, Iowa, and a one-year fellowship in cosmetic surgery, breast surgery, and breast reconstruction with the Cincinnati Plastic Surgery Associates and affiliated hospitals in Cincinnati, Ohio.[4] According to his website, "Dr. Bafitis … gives advice on how to avoid the pitfalls of a non-board certified plastic surgeon …

and how to tell if the plastic surgeon you have chosen is practicing safe medicine."

Thomas was released from Bafitis Plastic Surgery at about seven o'clock in the evening on March 21, after the surgical reconstructive procedures had been completed; she was then transferred to the nearby Jupiter Beach Resort & Spa for her recovery.[5] The following day, Thomas was sitting up in bed and speaking normally when, at about five o'clock in the afternoon, she suddenly became unresponsive.[6] Immediately rushed to the Jupiter Medical Center by the Palm Beach County Fire Rescue squad, Thomas was pronounced deceased in the emergency room. She was fifty-eight years old.[7]

The Autopsy[8]

The autopsy was conducted at ten in the morning on March 23 by associate medical examiner Heidi Reinhard. It began with an external examination.

"The body is that of a well-developed, well-nourished, five foot, eight inches, 172-pound female that appears the reported age of fifty-eight years," Reinhard wrote in the autopsy report.

The head was normally formed; the hair on the scalp was brown, as were the eyes. The corneas of the eyes were clear; the sclerae (the white outer layer of the eyeball) was white-tan; and the conjunctivae, the thin, clear membrane that protects the eye, had no petechiae (small red or purple spots caused by bleeding into the skin). The ears were unremarkable; the nasal septum and nasal bones were intact.

The lips were symmetrical, and the mouth was free of foreign material. The teeth were natural and in good condition. The neck, chest, and abdomen were symmetrical, and the breasts had no palpable masses. The arms and legs had no deformities, palpable fractures, or track marks, and the wrists were free of scars.

The scalp had no fractures. When it was reflected, marked congestion was evident below the scalp.

The brain had mild swelling but was without discoloration, hemorrhage, masses, or injury; at 1,392 grams, its weight was in the normal range.

The internal examination revealed a cardiovascular system that was unremarkable. The heart weight at 402 grams was slightly enlarged; the left anterior descending coronary artery had 10 percent stenosis due to atherosclerosis (plaque buildup). The myocardium (heart muscle) had no fibrosis, necrosis, or hemorrhage; the right and left heart ventricles (the heart chambers that pump blood) were of normal thickness; and the thin, elastic aorta, the large artery that carries oxygenated blood to the rest of the body, was free of atherosclerosis.

The digestive system was normal. The esophagus had a smooth mucosa and was not dilated or exhibited any evidence of stenosis; the stomach was of normal size and shape, containing approximately fifty milliliters of dark brown fluid and partially digested food particles. The small intestine was of normal length, configuration, and diameter; the large intestine was smooth, pink-tan, with no palpable masses or obstructions. The liver had some fatty metamorphosis but otherwise was intact, smooth, of the usual tan to tan-yellow color, and without masses or lesions. Its weight of 1,633 grams was in the normal range. The appendix was unremarkable.

The kidney weights were in the normal range—119 and 126 grams for the right and left kidney, respectively. The bladder contained a thin film of opaque, white-yellow urine.

The musculoskeletal system was well developed and unremarkable.

As for the endocrine system, the pituitary and thyroid glands were unremarkable. The adrenal glands were normal, and the pancreas had the expected color and consistency.

An examination of the respiratory system gave the first clue what might have led to Thomas's death. The right lung was collapsed; at 247 grams, it weighed approximately 62 percent less than the left lung. The upper airways, trachea, bronchi, and distal bronchioles contained a tan, mucoid fluid. With such a large decrease in lung capacity, it is understandable why Thomas had substantial difficulty with respiration.

Cause and Manner of Death

The toxicology report of postmortem iliac blood taken from a pelvic vein revealed the presence of low levels of several drugs, some of which were administered to Thomas during surgery. These included ephedrine (for hypotension); phenylpropanolamine (a decongestant and appetite suppressant); ibuprofen (for pain); lidocaine (an anesthetic); trazodone (an antidepressant and sedative); o-desmethyl venlafaxine (a metabolite of Venlafaxine, an antidepressant); diphenhydramine (an antihistamine); promethazine (an antihistamine); fentanyl (an opioid); cyclobenzaprine (a muscle relaxant); hydromorphone (an opioid); and cotinine (a byproduct of nicotine).[6,3,4] None of these medications contributed to Thomas's death.

After reviewing the circumstances surrounding the death, as well as the autopsy and toxicology reports, published lay articles, and the scientific literature, I agreed with the coroner's conclusion that the cause of death was a "pneumothorax"—the presence of air in the space between the lungs and the chest wall, causing collapse of the lung—"due to perforated parietal pleura," a membrane that is connected to the inner surface of the chest wall, "during liposuction with autologous fat reinjection treatment." Simply put, Thomas died from a collapsed lung resulting from a puncture of the parietal pleura during the fat transfer procedure. The manner of death was accidental due to therapeutic complications from elective cosmetic surgery.

Life and Career

Thomas was born in Tennessee in 1964. Throughout her childhood, she competed in baton events and in cheerleading.

Thomas attended college before pursuing a modeling career. She worked with several renowned companies and talent agencies, participated in several beauty pageant competitions, and became one of the top models for Hawaiian Tropic, a maker of "skin-loving, island-inspired sun care products."

In 1985, Thomas met Hank Williams Jr., a well-known musician, songwriter, and vocalist, at one of his concerts; they were married in 1990.

Conclusions

According to the American Society of Plastic Surgeons, 1.8 million cosmetic surgical procedures were performed by board-certified plastic surgeons in the United States in 2018.[9] Liposuction, one of the top five surgical procedures, had a 1.3:50,000 mortality rate; the mortality rate of breast augmentation has not been recorded.

Pneumothorax is a well-known complication following breast augmentation surgery and is more common than most plastic surgeons realize.[10] A 2001 survey of 363 members of the California Society of Plastic Surgeons revealed that one in three plastic surgeons in the study had at least one patient who experienced a pneumothorax; one in ten surgeons had two or more patients who experienced a pneumothorax while undergoing breast augmentation.[11]

Pneumothorax can be caused by surgical damage to the pleura (43 percent), needle injury during local anesthetic injection (37 percent), ruptured pulmonary blebs, a small collection of air between the lung and usually the outer surface of the upper lobe of the lung, during or after the breast augmentation procedure (16 percent), or lung injury from mechanical ventilation (3 percent).[12] Symptoms of pneumothorax include shortness of breath, tachypnea (abnormally rapid breathing), chest pain, and hypoxia (low levels of oxygen reaching the tissues); it can be life-threatening if left untreated.[13]

In one case in Bondi, Australia, thirty-three-year-old Krystle Morgan complained that her back was aching and that she was short of breath after waking up from cosmetic surgery for breast augmentation.[14] Told that sometimes it's normal for tall, thin girls to have lungs collapse for no apparent reason, Morgan was sent to the emergency room. "I arrived at emergency and was given X-rays, where I was told that I had a large hole in my right lung where the needle had gone through and completely deflated my lung," Morgan said.

Pneumothorax is a rare occurrence in liposuction, a cosmetic surgical procedure that was introduced in the United States in the 1980s and is considered one of the safest and most common cosmetic surgeries performed worldwide.[15] A 2020 retrospective study over a sixteen-year period of eight surgeons in the same practice identified 16,215 liposuction procedures, in which only seven cases of pneumothorax (0.0432 percent) had been reported.

Cosmetic tourism—a process by which patients travel from their home country to another country to receive cosmetic surgery—has been on the rise, in part due to rising cosmetic surgical costs and the COVID-19 pandemic.[16] In one retrospective review of two cohorts of patients over a thirteen-month period, the most popular destination for such surgeries was Turkey, and the most common postoperative complaint following these cosmetic surgeries was wound infection.

Another popular destination for cosmetic surgery is the Dominican Republic, where in 2018, more than 18,000 foreigners had liposuction, breast augmentation, or a tummy tuck done; some patients died and never returned to their home country.[17]

"Are you calling me to say that my sister is dead?" Kendra Cedeño asked when she answered a WhatsApp video call from Tiffany Concha, a friend of Sharilene Cedeño, Kendra's sister, in the Dominican Republic. "[Tell me] you're not calling me to tell me that." That was exactly what Concha had called to say. At twenty-three, Kendra Cedeño became one of twelve known New Yorkers to die from a plastic surgery procedure performed in the Dominican Republic between 2013 and 2019.

The cosmetic surgery industry has received greater scrutiny in the recent past following several high-profile deaths after these elective medical procedures.[18] In 2021, thirty-three-year-old Xiaoran, a web celebrity with more than 130,000 followers who lived in East China, died of a serious infection after spending more than five hours in the operating room undergoing three different cosmetic surgeries—waist and abdomen liposuction, upper arm liposuction, and breast augmentation surgery.[19] Then, in 2023, Saint Von Colucci, a twenty-two-year-old Canadian actor, passed away from an infection at a South Korea hospital following surgery to remove jaw implants.[20] And in late April 2023, Christina Ashten Gourkani, a thirty-four-year-old Kim Kardashian lookalike, died after suffering cardiac arrest while recovering from cosmetic surgery.[21]

While all surgeries, including cosmetic surgery, carry some risk, state health officials encourage patients contemplating these procedures to verify that a licensed surgeon with substantial experience performs their cosmetic surgery and that the operation takes place in an accredited facility that is equipped to handle emergencies.[22] "Patients need to ask a lot of questions," agreed one plastic surgeon.

CHAPTER 25

Angela Craig

Died March 18, 2023
Suspected Homicide by Cyanide Poisoning

ANGELA CRAIG, A forty-three-year-old mother of six, and her husband, James, a dentist and co-owner of Summerbrook Dental Group, had been married for twenty-three years, having tied the knot when they were both in their twenties.[1] Originally from Kansas, they resided in Aurora, Colorado, with their eldest boy and five girls, ages eight to twenty years.[2] Said Craig's sister, Toni Kofoed, "Angela's and James's marriage had always been tumultuous. James had multiple affairs with several women."[3]

On March 6, 2023, James made Craig a protein shake before her daily workout as was his usual custom. After consuming the preworkout drink, Craig became faint and dizzy, so she went to Centura Parker Adventist Hospital in Parker, Colorado complaining of "global heaviness" and vertigo; she was treated and released the same day.[4] Three days later, Craig returned to the hospital with symptoms of fatigue, vomiting, headache, lightheadedness, and confusion.[5] This time, she was kept in the hospital for five days.

At approximately 11:08 a.m. on March 15, only one day after she was discharged from Centura Parker hospital, Craig was admitted to UC Health University of Colorado Hospital in Aurora with severe headache and dizziness; at about 2:00 p.m., she had a seizure.[6] Suffering from hypoxia, a lack of oxygen, an increase in intracranial pressure, and with no pupil reaction, Craig was admitted to the intensive care unit.[7] With her medical condition rapidly deteriorating, she was placed on a ventilator.

On March 18, 2023, Craig was declared brain dead at 4:29 p.m.; she was taken off life support and died on March 21.

The Autopsy

James would not allow hospital staff to conduct an autopsy on his wife; nonetheless, it being a suspicious death, the autopsy was conducted on March 22 by Arapahoe County Coroner and forensic pathologist Kelly Lear.

The autopsy report was not available for review; however, based on published lay articles, there was no evidence of significant traumatic injury.

Cause and Manner of Death

Toxicology testing detected a lethal amount of cyanide in Craig's postmortem blood and more than four hundred times the therapeutic dose of tetrahydrozoline, an ingredient commonly found in over-the-counter eyedrops.[8] A toxic but not lethal blood level of arsenic was an additional contributing factor in Craig's death.

At a preliminary hearing, Lear, the forensic pathologist who conducted Craig's autopsy, testified that the level of cyanide in Craig's blood had increased on March 15 between noon and 8:00 p.m. "That increase is consistent with her receiving additional cyanide exposure in that time period," Lear said.

Lear concluded that the cause of Craig's death was acute cyanide and tetrahydrozoline poisoning. The manner of death was homicide. After reviewing published lay articles and the scientific literature, I had no reason to dispute Lear's conclusions.

Harry A. Milman, PhD

Life and Career

Craig, the youngest of ten children, was born on April 15, 1979, in Dodge City, Kansas.[9] She "got out of Dodge" by marrying James on December 18, 1999, and moving to Aurora, a suburb of Denver, Colorado.[10]

Intelligent, energetic, quick witted, and with a keen sense of humor, Craig was a member of the Church of Jesus Christ of Latter-day Saints, where she served in various capacities, including as choir director, teacher, and youth organization leader.

Although allergic to animals, Craig loved her bird, Ember.[11] An avid reader of books, Craig was a passionate student of interior design, but above all, she was a dedicated mother to her six children. As her eldest son, Toliver, said, Craig loved a lot of things, but she didn't have time for all of them, so "she had six children instead."

Conclusions

Craig's sister, Kofoed, told investigators that about five to six years prior to Craig's death, James drugged Craig with an unknown medication because "he planned to commit suicide and didn't want her to stop him."[12] Said Gail Saltz, a clinical associate professor of psychiatry at the New York Presbyterian Hospital in New York, "It is a little mystifying that she would stay with him, and I would say it is a good bit of denial to stay with a man who has drugged you."

James was not only addicted to pornography since he was a teenager, as well as a philanderer, he was also a risk taker, said his business partner Ryan Redfearn. As a result, his dental practice had been struggling financially for at least two years and he was on the verge of filing for bankruptcy for the second time. Adding to James's financial woes was his new relationship with

Forensics

an orthodontist from Marble Falls, Texas, whom he met at a dental conference in February 2023. "If I had known what was true, I would not have been with this person," said Karin Cain, James's new flame.[13] "I didn't willingly have a relationship with somebody who was in a marriage."[14]

Money troubles and sexual fantasies sometimes can lead married men to do things that they wouldn't otherwise do, possibly even criminal things; apparently, James was no exception. On February 27, 2023, James surreptitiously conducted a computer search in a backroom office of his dental practice for "the top five undetectable poisons that show no signs of foul play." Later that afternoon, he performed a second internet search for "How many grams of pure arsenic will kill a human?" The following morning, James googled "How to make murder look like a heart attack." And that same afternoon he conducted a fourth internet search for "Is arsenic detectable in an autopsy?" Armed with new information about poisoning, James ordered arsenic from Amazon.com; it was delivered to his home on March 4.

On March 6, two days after the arsenic was delivered, Craig went to Centura Parker Adventist Hospital with symptoms consistent with arsenic poisoning. While there, she texted James complaining of dizziness and feeling "drugged" to which he replied, "Given our history, I know that must be triggering. Just for the record, I didn't drug you." Said Saltz, "It is a good bit of denial when you are hospitalized and not feeling well after drinking a strange-tasting smoothie that your husband gave you to then go back home and live with him … it is just unusual given the prior situation."

Craig's doctors couldn't determine what was causing her illness, so Craig was released from the hospital the same day she was admitted. That night, James sat in the dark in exam room number nine of his dental practice and again used the computer. This time, he ordered oleandrin, a highly cardiotoxic substance found in the poisonous plant oleander that when ingested, can cause an arrhythmia, an irregular heart rhythm and death. When police learned of the order, they contacted FedEx, which intercepted the package; it was never delivered.

Craig was readmitted to Centura Parker hospital on March 9. A blood test showed that she had a toxic, but not lethal level of arsenic in her blood. That same day, James placed an online order with Midland Scientific and told a coworker at his dental practice that a personal package would soon arrive and that it shouldn't be opened. When asked what was in the package, James said that it was a ring, a surprise present for his wife.

James's package was delivered on March 13, a day prior to Craig's discharge from Centura Park, but it was mistakenly opened by one of the dental office employees. Inside was a circular biohazard container labeled "potassium cyanide," a highly lethal chemical that prevents cells in the body from utilizing oxygen and thereby causing respiratory arrest and death. According to one of the Summerbrook Dental Group employees, there was no medical reason for the use of potassium cyanide in their dental practice.

Two days after the cyanide was delivered, Craig was admitted to UC Health University of Colorado Hospital where she died. I was convinced that the timing of Craig's hospitalizations and James's ordering of two different poisons—arsenic and potassium cyanide—was more than coincidental.

By March 20, 2023, police felt that they had enough evidence to charge James with first-degree murder in his wife's death. James had conducted multiple computer searches on poisoning and had ordered arsenic and potassium cyanide, two lethal chemicals, shortly after which Craig was admitted to the hospital with clinical signs consistent with arsenic or cyanide poisoning. In addition, James had lied when he said that the personal package he was expecting contained a ring, when in fact, it contained potassium cyanide. Finally, police uncovered sexually explicit email correspondence between James and Cain, who had visited James while Craig was being treated in the hospital.

Since James was known to regularly make protein shakes for Craig, police theorized that he administered the arsenic and cyanide to Craig in her preworkout drinks. Said Aurora Police Division Chief Mark Hildebrand, "When the suspicious details of this case came to light, our team of officers and homicide detectives tirelessly worked to uncover the truth behind the victim's sudden illness and death. It was quickly discovered this was in fact a heinous, complex, and calculated murder."[15]

James pled not guilty to murdering Craig in March 2023; he has yet to go to trial.[16]

Poisoning is an extremely rare method of murder in modern times, mainly because current forensic techniques can identify all toxic agents. While arsenic has been used to poison rivals and emperors as early as in Roman days, cyanide, which has been involved in mass murders, has been famously used in the 1980s to contaminate Tylenol, thereby causing the deaths of several people in the Chicago area.

An ideal poison is odorless, tasteless, difficult to detect, and causes symptoms that are similar to naturally occurring diseases.[17] It is not surprising, then, that arsenic and cyanide comprise two of the top five chemicals used to commit murder, the three others being atropine, strychnine and thallium.[18]

One of the most famous homicide cases due to arsenic poisoning involves Judy Buenoano, a former nurse and manicurist, also known as the "Black Widow."[19] In 1971, just three months after returning from Vietnam, her husband, Air Force Sergeant James E. Goodyear, began experiencing weakness, nausea, vomiting, and diarrhea.[20] Goodyear died on September 16 after medical efforts to stabilize him failed. Toxicology testing was not part of the autopsy protocol at the time, so the cause of death was determined to be cardiovascular collapse and renal failure. Thirteen years later, however, Goodyear's body was exhumed, and toxicology testing detected high levels of arsenic in his remains. The cause of death was changed to "chronic and acute arsenic exposure."

In 1984, Buenoano was convicted of murdering Goodyear by poisoning him with arsenic, as well as of drowning her paralyzed nineteen-year-old son, Michael, in the East River in Milton, Florida. The motive for the two killings was the $200,000 of life insurance money. At her trial, evidence was presented that Buenoano had also poisoned her subsequent live-in boyfriends, Bobby Joe Morris and later, John Gentry. Morris died, but Gentry survived, so Buenoano again tried to kill Gentry, this time by bombing his car. Gentry survived the second attempt as well.

Buenoano was sentenced to death in 1985; she was executed in the electric chair in 1998.

Unlike Buenoano, Cynthia Sommer, a mother of four working at a Subway restaurant, was wrongly convicted on January 30, 2007 of poisoning her husband, Marine Sergeant Todd Sommer, to death with arsenic.[21] It all started in February 2002, ten days before he died, when Todd Sommer began showing symptoms of arsenic poisoning at his home at Marine Corps Air Station Miramar in San Diego, California.[22] His death initially was ruled due to a heart attack, but subsequent toxicology testing found high levels of arsenic, more than 250 and 1,000 times normal levels in his kidneys and liver, respectively.[23] After a lengthy investigation, the San Diego County Medical Examiner concluded that Todd Sommer died from acute arsenic poisoning.

After her husband died, Sommer received more than $250,000 from his life insurance policy. She began hosting boisterous parties, had breast augmentation surgery, and within two months, had a new boyfriend. In charging Sommer with Todd Sommer's death, military investigators claimed that she allegedly poisoned him with arsenic to "get the kind of life that she always wanted, but until then, she could not achieve."

"There was not one cent of evidence that she had arsenic in her house, that she had ever purchased arsenic," said Sommer's attorney, Allen Bloom, after the jury reached its guilty verdict. "They made all sorts of guesses and speculations as to how she had gotten him to eat it. He would've had to ingest twelve pounds of ant bait in order to reach those levels in his system. It was no way that she had done it."

A judge granted Sommer a new trial in May 2008 after the laboratory that conducted the toxicology testing suggested that the kidney and liver samples might have been contaminated. In the second trial, Sommer's attorney presented toxicology testing results on previously untested samples of Todd Sommer's liver and kidneys that showed no arsenic. Based on the new findings, prosecutors dropped all charges against Sommer. "Our prosecutors reviewed the evidence, and based on the evidence that they had at the time, there was proof beyond a reasonable doubt," said District Attorney Bonnie Dumanis. Sommer's attorney disagreed. "She only spent more than two years in jail, lost her kids, lost her house. No matter what happens, and no matter how innocent she is, somebody is always going to say, 'Well, your husband is dead, and you had a boob job.' It was a Scarlett Letter type of prosecution," Sommer's attorney said.

One of the most interesting recent cases involving cyanide poisoning is that of Robert Ferrante, a professor of neurology at the University of Pittsburgh Medical School and codirector of the Center for Amyotrophic Lateral Sclerosis (ALS) Research.[24] Ferrante was convicted of murdering his wife, Autumn Klein, by spiking her creatine supplement drink with cyanide.[25]

Klein, who was twenty-three years younger than Ferrante, collapsed at her home on April 17, 2013, fifteen minutes after returning late from her shift at the University of Pittsburgh Medical Center Presbyterian in Pennsylvania, a medical-surgical referral hospital where she was an assistant professor of neurology, obstetrics, and gynecology and chief of the division of women's neurology.[26] Struggling to breathe, Klein was rushed to the hospital, and she was placed on a ventilator. Tragically, she was pronounced deceased three days later.[27] A blood test conducted at the hospital found lethal levels of cyanide in Klein's blood, which was bright red, a sign consistent with cyanide poisoning. "Autumn was not just a rising star, she was a shooting star," said Karen Rouse, a colleague. "She was nationally recognized as a leader in her field at a very young age."

It seems that Ferrante had been giving Klein the dietary supplement creatine to help her with her fertility problems for several weeks. Two days before Klein died, Ferrante placed an order for a 250-gram bottle of potassium cyanide, a highly toxic poison. When the cyanide container was later examined by police, Ferrante's fingerprints were found all over it, and 8.3 grams of the potassium cyanide was missing. Police theorized that Ferrante had mixed the cyanide with the creatine in a drink and had given it to Klein shortly after she arrived home from work on April 17, 2013.

The Ferrante case had its share of controversy, the most important of which was the discrepancy in the forensic toxicology testing results. Sonia Obcemea, a medical technician at Quest laboratories, measured 2.2 milligrams of cyanide per liter (mg/L) of Klein's blood, a decidedly fatal amount, but her supervisor, Ryan Bartolotti, recalculated the finding and changed it to 3.4 mg/L; both levels are lethal. Subsequently, however, Bartolotti claimed a mathematical error and changed the value back to the original.[28] A later test of Klein's blood conducted by National Medical Services (NMS) laboratories found only 0.3 milligrams of cyanide per liter of blood, an amount that is within the normal range. A third test done by Alicia Smith of the Allegheny County Medical Examiner's office identified but did not quantify cyanide in Klein's blood.

Defense attorney William Difenderfer put three forensic experts on the stand to dispute the toxicology findings. The experts claimed that the results of the toxicology tests were inconclusive and at best, were a "false positive" due to an impurity present in the creatine.

There's no doubt that inferior starting materials and inadequate purification procedures in the commercial synthesis of creatine can result in an increased amount of impurities, such as creatinine and dicyandiamide, a substance that can be converted in the body to the less toxic thiocyanate. Moreover, dicyandiamide can also be converted to the more toxic hydrogen cyanide in the stomach's acid environment, thereby giving a false positive result for cyanide in a toxicology test.[29] Carol Gebert, a Massachusetts scientist, noted that dimethylamine, a predicted metabolite of creatine, can react with reagents used by Quest laboratories, thereby leading to a false positive result for cyanide.[30] Cyril Wecht, a forensic pathologist, agreed, saying, "In some instances, creatine can break down to produce cyanogens, cyanide-like products." However, Wecht said,

"I don't think that just talking about it more would have made a difference [in the case]."[31]

It seems unlikely that the cyanide Ferrante purchased contained a substantial amount of impurities, if any. According to the complaint, Ferrante bought "the best and purest cyanide he could get." The jury apparently agreed because despite the differences between the three toxicology testing results, the jurors concluded that the lethal levels of cyanide measured by Quest laboratories were the most reliable.

Ferrante was found guilty of poisoning Klein with cyanide, thereby causing her death. He is now serving a life prison sentence without parole at the State Correctional Institution at Houtzdale, Pennsylvania. "The motivation," said former reporter Alan Jennings, was "jealousy" of Klein's professional accomplishments and her "meteoric" career, as well as Ferrante's unsubstantiated belief that his wife was having an affair. Several judicial appeals did not change the verdict nor result in a new trial.

Interestingly, Klein's and Craig's cyanide poisoning deaths have several similarities. Both perpetrators, Ferrante (convicted) and James (charged), were medical professionals—Ferrante, a neurologist, and James, a dentist. Both assailants ordered cyanide two days before their victims (spouses) became ill, claiming they needed it for their work. Both refused to give permission for autopsies to be done on their victims, and both administered the cyanide in a drink that they prepared for their respective victims (James's case has yet to be tried).

In a separate case, thirty-six-year-old Sararat "Am" Rangsiwuthporn, dubbed "Am Cyanide," was accused of murdering fourteen people between 2015 and 2023 by poisoning them with cyanide; a fifteenth victim survived. Described as "the worst serial killer in Thailand's history," Am Cyanide was arrested in April 2023.[32] According to police, all the victims were people to whom Rangsiwuthporn owed large sums of money or from whom she had stolen to fund her online gambling addiction.[33] "She is a psychopath who has no conscience or guilt," said Thailand's Deputy Police Chief General Surachate Hakparn.

The case against Rangsiwuthporn gained momentum after her friend, Siriporn "Koy" Khanwong, unexpectedly died when she went on a fishing trip with Rangsiwuthporn. Told Koy died from heart failure, her mother cried, "She was healthy, she was very healthy, and she left [home] in good shape.... I said right away, it was murder." An autopsy found traces of cyanide in Koy's body. Soon, other families began raising questions about the deaths of their loved ones. "[The families] wondered why the victims were healthy and then had heart failure like that," said Hakparn. Further investigations detected the presence of cyanide in seven of the fourteen suspicious deaths; in the remaining victims, "the nails, hands, and lips had turned black in color from being poisoned, and the poison that made the bodies look like this was cyanide," said Hakparn.

When it comes to poisoning as a method of homicide, ingenuity often comes to play. This is exemplified by the arrests in August 2023 of twenty-nine-year-old Veronica Cline, who allegedly spiked a man's drink with Raid cockroach spray after the pair met at a local bar in Florida.[34] And in November of the same year, Ina Kenoyer of Minot, North Dakota, allegedly poisoned her partner, Steven Riley Jr., to death with ethylene glycol, an ingredient present in antifreeze, after he inherited $30 million.[35] Together, these homicides give credence to the notion that "where there's a will (for murder), there's a way."

CHAPTER 26
Conclusions

IN *FORENSICS III: They Got Fifteen Minutes of Fame from the Way They Died*, I reviewed twenty-eight ordinary people who were thrust into the spotlight, gaining fame not for their talents or accomplishments while living, but for the way they died. Newspaper and magazine articles ensured that stories of the circumstances surrounding their deaths remained in the public eye, so as Andy Warhol had predicted, their fame would last at least fifteen minutes. In some cases, it lasted much longer. While these individuals may have been "ordinary" before they died, they became extraordinary after death.

Of the twenty-eight people I reviewed, two were young children—Joseph Zarelli, also known as the "Boy in the Box," four to six years old when he died, but whose remains took sixty-five years to be identified, and Azaria Chamberlain, a nine-week-old baby who was whisked away from her family's tent and was devoured by a dingo, a wild dog, at Ayers Rock, Australia. Both Zarelli and Azaria earned more than their fair share of fame.

Zarelli obtained eternal fame by boosting the use of forensic genetic genealogy, a new and unique subdiscipline of forensic science that not only successfully identified his remains but helped solve crimes. As for Azaria, her mother, Lindy, wrongly accused of murdering her daughter, spent three years in prison before she was exonerated. Books, a successful movie starring Meryl Streep, and monetary numeration ensured that any fame Lindy gained from Azaria's death remained long lasting.

Two murders I reviewed in *Forensics III* that have remarkable similarities include the brutal bludgeoning of Marilyn Sheppard, wife of osteopathic physician Dr. Sam Sheppard, and the vicious stabbing of Ron Goldman and Nicole Brown Simpson, ex-wife of football star O.J. Simpson. In all three cases, the main suspect was a husband (Sheppard) or an ex-husband (Simpson). Blood spatter was the primary forensic evidence in both trials. In addition, both Simpson and Sheppard (in his second trial) retained the same defense attorney, F. Lee Bailey; both were found not guilty of murder; and both spent nearly ten years in prison, Sheppard after his first trial and Simpson, after he was found guilty in an unrelated case of robbery and kidnapping.

Great public interest, the spectacle of the corresponding trials, and the unsatisfying verdicts, ensured that the public would forever talk about the murders of Marilyn Sheppard, Ron Goldman, and Nicole Brown Simpson. Sheppard's first trial was so uncontrolled and the media circus so intense that Chief Judge Carl A. Weinman of the US District Court for the Southern District of Ohio called it a "mockery of justice." As for Simpson's trial, Judge Lance Ito mismanaged the trial to such a degree that under his direction, the Simpson trial was the longest jury trial in California history, the verdict of which was televised and viewed by more than 150 million people, approximately 57 percent of the country.

Sheppard professed his innocence until he died, claiming that a "bushy-haired" figure was the real murderer; however, no other suspect has ever been apprehended. As for Simpson, while he insisted that he was "absolutely 100 percent not guilty," the country remains racially divided about his guilt—83 percent of White Americans say they are "definitely" or "probably" sure that he is guilty, but only 57 percent of Black Americans agree. Like in the Sheppard case, no other suspect has ever been arrested for Goldman's and Brown Simpson's murders.

Two other murders I reviewed for *Forensics III* were committed by police officers—Sherri Rasmussen's by Stephanie Lazarus, a decorated police officer on "the fast track" in the Los Angeles Police Department, and George Floyd's by Derek Chauvin, a senior police officer with nineteen years of experience in the Minneapolis Police Department. Unwilling to believe that one of their own was responsible for Rasmussen's death, LAPD detectives failed to pursue Lazarus as a possible suspect; she remained free for twenty-three years before DNA evidence led to her arrest and murder conviction. Unlike Lazarus, Chauvin, who held Floyd on the ground and kept his knee on Floyd's neck until he died, by some estimates for as long as nine and a half minutes, was brought to justice within fourteen months.

Rasmussen gained only fifteen minutes of fame since her name quickly disappeared from the headlines, only to reappear twenty-three years later when Lazarus was finally apprehended and convicted. On the other hand, Floyd's fame was much longer lasting; his death led to mass protests across the United States and around the world against police brutality and for racial equality and justice, as well as to several books, and the enactment of 140 oversight and reform laws to hold police more accountable. Floyd's now famous last words, "I can't breathe," became a rallying cry against police brutality.

Of the five remaining murders or suspected murders I reviewed for this book, Kathleen Savio's was due to drowning by a philandering ex-husband; Eve Carson's was caused by a gunshot delivered by two young men, seventeen and twenty-two years old, who were out looking for someone to rob; Carol Daniels's was from stabbing committed by an unknown assailant in the sanctuary of her ministry; Marco McMillian's was from asphyxiation by his so-called "friend;" and Angela Craig's was due to poisoning with cyanide and tetrahydrozoline, a common ingredient in eye drops, allegedly committed by her husband. All the victims gained short-lived fame by virtue of published newspaper articles that described the unusual circumstances of their deaths, the capture of their assailants, and the eventual trials.

That anyone could gain any level of fame by committing murder-suicide is unthinkable and yet, I identified two such cases—the murder-suicide of Sahel Kazemi and Steve McNair and the filicide-suicide of Jayne and Corinne Peters.

The motive for McNair's killing by his girlfriend, Kazemi, was jealousy and financial stress; Corinne's altruistic filicide by her mother, Jayne Peters, presumably was done out of misguided love brought on by grief over the recent death of Corinne's father from cancer, overwhelming financial stresses, and Peters's desire to alleviate real or imagined suffering in her daughter. In murdering Corinne, Peters gained a modicum of fame by joining a small group of parents who murder on average 450 children each year in the United States.

Five accidental deaths were reviewed in *Forensics III*, including those of Adrienne Martin, the twenty-seven-year-old girlfriend of August Busch IV, former chief executive officer of the Anheuser-Busch Brewing Company, who died from a drug overdose; Lori McClintock, wife of Tom McClintock, a Republican US Congressman from California, who died after ingesting the dietary supplement white mulberry; Elisa Lam, a twenty-one-year-old student at the University of British Columbia who was on her way to Santa Cruz, California, and died by drowning in her hotel's rooftop water tank; Thomas Mansfield, a twenty-nine-year-old personal trainer who died by ingesting an overdose of caffeine powder; and Mary Jane Thomas, wife of musician Hank Williams Jr., who died from therapeutic complications following liposuction and breast augmentation cosmetic surgery. All these deaths presumably could have been avoided.

Of the accidental deaths, those of McClintock, Mansfield, and Thomas are especially concerning as they highlight the potential dangers associated with dietary supplements, caffeine powder, and elective cosmetic surgery. While dietary supplements containing white mulberry are regulated by the US Food and Drug Administration, the agency does not have the authority to require manufacturers to prove that the supplements are safe and effective. As a result, the amount of white mulberry can vary between different products and batches of the same preparation, all of which may contain contaminants that can cause unexpected adverse side effects. As for caffeine powder, which is freely available on the internet, special measuring spoons are required for optimum accuracy in dosing; otherwise, the drug can be lethal. Finally, pneumothorax, the presence of air in the cavity between the lungs and the chest wall causing collapse of the lung, is a well-known complication of breast augmentation surgery.

Three people I reviewed in *Forensics III* gained fifteen minutes of fame by committing suicide—Admiral Mike Boorda by gunshot; Andrew Pettigrew by ingesting an overdose of the over-the-counter antihistamine and sedative diphenhydramine; and Russell Armstrong by hanging. Two others—Ellen Greenberg and Katherine Morris—had their manner of death changed from suicide to undetermined. The practical implication of such a change can sometimes include the ability to collect life insurance proceeds; however, this was not the reason the Greenberg and

Morris families pursued this change for over a decade. A more compelling reason was the inability of the families to bear the thought that their daughters committed suicide in what arguably was an unusual manner—Greenberg's from twenty self-stabbings in the chest, abdomen, head, and neck, and Morris's from carbon monoxide poisoning due to charcoal grilling in her automobile. Thus, while suicide was a final and definitive determination of the manner of death, changing the manner of death to "undetermined" left the door open for further investigation and gave the families hope that an alternative explanation may be found, even though none has yet been provided.

Of the remaining deaths I reviewed in *Forensics III*, two were unusual—Michael Faherty's, whose death in Ireland was concluded to have been due to spontaneous human combustion, and Carlos Sousa, who was mauled by a tiger at the San Francisco Zoo.

Despite having been reported well over 150 to 200 times in the past, spontaneous human combustion is extremely rare, so that the likelihood of unexpectedly bursting into flames is very remote. As for mauling by an exotic animal, such as a tiger or a lion, there have been 25 deaths and 377 dangerous incidents in forty-six states and the District of Columbia involving big cats and other exotic animals since 1990. Of these, tigers were responsible for half of the incidents with lions coming in second.

The actor Harrison Ford called fame and the loss of privacy a "burden."[1] Others say that fame brings loneliness because a famous person stops having a "normal" life. Richard Burton, the Welsh actor whose baritone voice captivated audiences in the mid-twentieth century may have said it best. "Fame doesn't change who you are. It changes others. It is a sweet poison you drink of first in eager gulps and then you come to loathe it."[2]

Harry A. Milman, PhD

With few exceptions, fame is a fleeting phenomenon—here today and forgotten tomorrow. When fame is based on the circumstances surrounding a death, it may last only fifteen minutes, or it could be everlasting. One thing is certain, however; fame won't be a burden to the recipient since he or she will already be dead.

NOTES

Introduction

1. E.D. Ramirez and S.J. Hagen, "The quantitative measure and statistical distribution of fame," *PLoS One* 13(7) (2016): e0200196, https://www.ncbi.nlm.nih.gov/pmc/articles/PMC6034871/.
2. B. Carey, "The Fame Motive," *The New York Times*, August 22, 2006, https://www.nytimes.com/2006/08/22/health/psychology/22/fame.html.
3. J. Maltby, "An interest in fame: confirming the measurement and empirical conceptualization of fame interest," *Br. J Psychol* 191(Pt. 3) (2010): 411–432.
4. R. Nuvwer, "Andy Warhol Probably Never Said His Celebrated 'Fifteen Minutes of Fame' Line," *Smithsonian*, April 8, 2014, https://www.smithsonianmag.com/smart-news/andy-warhol-probably-never-said-his-celebrated-fame-line-180950456/.
5. "Physicians' Handbook on Medical Certification of Death," US Centers for Disease Control and Prevention, US Department of Health and Human Services, 2003 revision, https://www.cdc.gov/nchs/data/misc/hb_cod.pdf.
6. H.A. Milman, "Introduction," (*Forensics: The Science Behind the Deaths of Famous People*, pp. xi-xx, Xlibris, 2020).

1. Marilyn Sheppard

1. "Dr. Sam Sheppard Trials: An Account," https://www.famous-trials.com/sam-sheppard/2-sheppard.
2. G. Glaub, "Murder in Bay Village: The Marilyn Sheppard Story," Midwest Crime Files, original published date February 8, 2023, last updated February 14, 2023, https://www.themidwestcrimefiles.com/post/murder-in-bay-village-the-marilyn-sheppard-story.

3. "Sheppard v. Maxwell, 384 U.S 333," JUSTIA, U.S. Supreme Court, argued February 28, 1966, decided June 6, 1966, https://supreme.justia.com/cases/federal/us/384/333/.
4. S.R. Gerber, "Verdict from Coroner on death of Marilyn Reese Sheppard," https://engagedscholarship.csuohio.edu/coroer¬_docs_1954/6.
5. R.F. Schottke and D. Kerr, "Report of the Cleveland Police Department," July 6, 1954, https://engagedscholarship.csuohio.edu/police_reports_1954/54.
6. "Autopsy Report—Marilyn Sheppard," July 4, 1954, https://engagedscholarship.csuohio.edu/coroner_docs_1954/4.
7. S.R. Gerber, "Autopsy Protocol of Marilyn Reese Sheppard," July 4, 1954, https://engagedscholarship.csuohio.edu/coroer¬_docs_1954/7.
8. "Marilyn Reese Sheppard," https://www.findagrave.com/memorial/6876/marilyn-sheppard.
9. "Sam and Marilyn Sheppard," https://www.famous-trials.com/sam-sheppard/18-sammarilynsheppard.
10. "Crime Investigation Report – The Initial Police Report," July 16, 1954, http://law2.umkc.edu/faculty/projects/ftrials/sheppard/sheppardreports.html.
11. P.A. Gareau, "Cleveland Police Department Report, Detectives Gareau and Schottke arrive at the murder scene at 8:05 a.m.," July 4, 1954, https://engagedscholarship.csuohio.edu/police_reports_1954/44.
12. "Sheriff's Office Summary of Marilyn Sheppard Homicide," July 4, 1954, https://engagedscholarship.csuohio.edu/police_reports_1954/21.
13. "Coroner Inquest Transcript—Parts 1 and 2," https://engagedscholarship.csuohio.edu/inquest_transcript/.
14. "Selected Testimony of Susan Hayes in Sam Sheppard's 1954 Murder Trial," https://www.famous-trials.com/sam-sheppard/12-excerpts-from-the-trial-transcripts/23-hayestestimony.
15. "Selected Testimony of Mary Cowan in Sam Sheppard's 1966 Murder Trial," https://www.famous-trials.com/

sam-sheppard/12-excerpts-from-the-trial-transcripts/20-cowantestimony.
16. "Selected Testimony of Doctor Paul Kirk in Sam Sheppard's 1966 Murder Trial," https://www.famous-trials.com/sam-sheppard/12-excerpts-from-the-trial-transcripts/24-kirktestimony.
17. "Affidavit of Dr. Roger W. Marsters," April 30, 1955, https://engagedscholarship.csuohio.edu/sheppard_eight_disdtrict_1950s/13.
18. "Samuel Sheppard," The National Registry of Exonerations, https://www.law.umich.edu/special/exoneration/Pages/casedetailpre1989.aspx?caseid=300.
19. "Selected Testimony of Coroner Sam Gerber in Sam Sheppard's 1966 Murder Trial," https://www.famous-trials.com/sam-sheppard/12-excerpts-from-the-trial-transcripts/22-gerbertestimony.
20. "Did Sam Do It?" https://www.famous-trials.com/sam-sheppard/5-didsamdoit.
21. "Plaintiff vs Samuel H. Sheppard Defendant, Petition for Declaration of Innocence as a Wrongfully Imprisoned Individual," October 19, 1995, https://www.famous-trials.com/sam-sheppard/12-petition.
22. "Who Killed Marilyn? Evidence Concerning Richard Eberling – Was He 'the Bushy-Haired Man'?" https://www.famous-trials.com/sam-sheppard/10-evidence.

2. *Joseph Zarelli*

1. P. Duke, "Cold Case #2: 'The Boy in the Box,'" https://theknighttimes.net.
2. "The Boy in the Box: The Tragic Story of an American Unsolved Mystery," American Hauntings, https://www.americanhauntingsink.com/the-boy-in-the-box.
3. J. Jiménez, "After 65 Years, the 'Boy in the Box' Has a Name," *The New York Times*, original published date December 6, 2022, last updated December 9, 2022, "https://www.nytimes.com/2022/12/08/us/boy-in-the-box-philadelphia-homicide-html.

4. L. Pennock, "Inside the 65-year hunt to identify the 'Boy in the Box': How a DNA test taken after a 2017 break-up and technique used on mummies finally helped name cold case murder victim and reveal parents -- which investigators kept secret for A YEAR. So, who killed him?" the *Daily Mail*, February 11, 2023, https://www.dailymail.co.uk/news/article-11696709/Inside-65-year-hunt-identify-Philadelphias-Boy-Box-cold-case-murder-victim.html.
5. K. Fraga, "How the Creepy Case of 'The Boy in the Box' Was Finally Solved After 65 Years," original published date December 8, 2022, last updated December 10, 2022, https://allthatsinteresting.com/boy-in-the-box.
6. "The location where Joseph Augustus Zarelli's body was found," https://oddstops.com/location.php?id=302.
7. P. Somasundaram, "'The Boy in the Box' now has a name, police reveal 65 years later," *The Washington Post*, December 8, 2022, https://www.washingtonpost.com/nation/2022/12/08/boy-in-the-box-name/.
8. "'Boy in a box' identified almost 66 years after gruesome discovery," 9News, December 9, 2022, https://www.9news.com.au/world/boy-in-a-box-mystery-killing-name-revealed-usa/1870039a-6645-40e1-8f45-787c1aaa793a.
9. M. Morales and D. Andone, "Philadelphia police reveal identity of child found dead inside a box 65 years ago," CNN, December 9, 2022, https://www.cnn.com/2022/12/08/us/philadelphia-boy-in-box-thursday/index.html.
10. N. Acosta, "Philadelphia's 'Boy in the Box' Identified After 65Years in One of City's Oldest Unsolved Murders," *People*, December 8, 2022, https://people.com/crime/philadelphias-boy-in-the-box-identified-after-65-years/.
11. C.L. Glynn, "Bridging Disciplines to Form a New One: The Emergence of Forensic Genetic Genealogy," *Genes* (Basel) 13(8): (2022) 1381-1402.

12. D. Kling, C. Phillips, D. Kennett, and A. Tillmar, "Investigative genetic genealogy: Current methods, knowledge and practice," *Forensic Sci Int: Genetics* 52, (May 2021).
13. J.W. Hazel and E.W. Clayton, "Law Enforcement and Genetic Data," The Hastings Center, January 20, 2021, https://www.thehastingscenter.org/briefingbook/law-enforcement-and-genetic-data/?gclid=Cj0KCQjw756lBhDMARIsAEI0AgmEflxUXLsGaFezrvxHiqRwwlJBu6VbjLStYdhC3GznL2bcaA-EPdEaAmu2EALw_wcB.
14. R.A. Wickenheiser, "Forensic genealogy, bioethics and the Golden State Killer case," *Forensic Sci Int Synerg* 1: 114-125 (2019).
15. J.V. Chamary, "How Genetic Genealogy Helped Catch The Golden State Killer," *Forbes*, June 30, 2020, https://www.forbes.com/sites/jvchamary/2020/06/30/genetic-genealogy-golden-state-killer/?sh=306b276c5a6d.
16. "BCA uses family DNA to identify victims in cold cases, bring answers to loved ones," January 19, 2023, https://dps.mn.gov/blog/Pages/20230119-bca-family-dna-cold-cases.aspx.
17. Z. Sylla, "Woman known as 'Nation River Lady' is identified nearly 5 decades after she was found floating in river, Canadian police say," CNN, July 6, 2023, https://www.cnn.com/2023/07/06/americas/nation-river-lady-missing-woman-identified-canada/index.html.
18. J. Kaiser, "We will find you: DNA search used to nab Golden State Killer can home in on about 60% of white Americans," *Science*, October 11, 2018, https://www.science.org/content/article/we-will-find-you-dna-search-used-nab-golden-state-killer-can-home-about-60-white.
19. "Interim Policy for Forensic Genetic Genealogical DNA Analysis and Searching," US Department of Justice, September 2, 2019, https://www.justice.gov/olp/page/file/1204386/.

3. Azaria Chamberlain

1. D.O. Linder, "The Trial of Lindy and Michael Chamberlain ('The Dingo Trial')," November 17, 2007, https://papeers.ssrn.com/so13/papers.cfm?abstract_id=1030557.
2. "The Death of Azaria Chamberlain (Dingo Ate My Baby)," September 4, 2021, https://www.killerqueenspodcaset.com/the-death-of-azaria-chamberlain-dingo-ate-my-baby/.
3. "Report of Inspector Michael Gilroy of the Northern Territory Police," August 30, 1980, https://www.famous-trials.com/dingo/466-gilroyreport.
4. "Finding of coroner Elizabeth Morris following the third coroner's inquest into the death of Azaria Chamberlain," June 12, 2012, https://justice.nt.gov.au/-_data/assets/pdf_file/0006/205377/azaria-chantel-chamberlain.pdf.
5. "Appendix A of the Report of the Royal Commission of Inquiry into Chamberlain Convictions," Commonwealth Parliamentary Papers 15, 192 (1987), https://justice.nt.gov.au/__data/assets/pdf_file/0005/209057/azaria-hamberlain-appendix-av-web.pdf.
6. C. Cunneen, "Azaria Chantel Chamberlain," https://adb.anu.edu.au/biography/chamberlain-azaria-chantel-9719.
7. K.J.A. Asche, J.A. Nader, and W. Kearney, "Chamberlain, re: Conviction of," September 15, 1988, https://www.famous-trials.com/dingo/469-reconviction.
8. "Finding of Coroner John Lowndes following the third coroner's inquest into the death of Azaria Chamberlain," December 13, 1995, https://www.famous-trials.com/dingo/467-lowndesreport.
9. A. Brumm, "Before Azaria: A Historical Perspective on Dingo Attacks," *Animals* (Basel) 12(12): (2022) 1592.
10. "Report of Les Harris, Expert on Dingo Behavior, on the Propensity of Dingoes to Attack Humans," December 1980, https://www.famous-trials.com/dingo/464-dingoreport.

11. "Coroner Gerry P. Galvin's Findings in the Second Inquest into the Death of Azaria Chamberlain," February 1982, https://www.famous-trials.com/dingo/465-galvinfindings.
12. R. Cavanagh, "The Shameful Tale of What Happened to Lindy Chamberlain," July 5, 2021, https://www.injustice.law/2021/07/05/the-shameful-tale-of-what-happened-to-lindy-chamberlain/.
13. M. Brown, "After 32 years of speculation, it's finally official: a dingo took Azaria," the *Sydney Morning Herald*, June 12, 2012, https://www.smh.com.au/national/after-32-years-of-speculation-its-finally-official-a-dingo-took-azaria-20120612-20711.html.
14. "Lindy Chamberlain-Creighton Biography," https://lindychamberlain.com/biography/.
15. "Michael Chamberlain Biography," https://web.archive.org/web/20160305001349/http://www.michaelchamberlain.com.au/biography.html.
16. "Everlasting nightmare," the *Sydney Morning Herald*, September 13, 2008, https://www.smh.com.au/national/everlasting-nightmare-20080913-gdsusa.html?page=fullpage.
17. "Lindy Chamberlain: The true story of what happened to baby Azaria," September 28, 2020, https://www.news.com.au/entertainment/tv/current-affairs/lindy-chamberlain-the-true-story-of-what-happened-to-baby-azaria/news-story/4a2be10c10f41fd2818b1912ace0c3ff.
18. "The Morling Report," May 22, 1987, https://www.famous-trials.com/dingo/468-morlingreport.
19. J. Waterford, "No safety from legal lynching," *Canberra Times*, original published date June 12, 2012, last updated April 18, 2018, https://www.canberratimes.com.au/story/6169200/no-safety-from-legal-lynching/.
20. "New Forensic Evidence in Support of an Inquiry into the Convictions of M. and L. Chamberlain," The Chamberlain Innocence Committee, https://murderpedia.org/female.C/images/chamberlain_lindy/blue-book.pdf/.

21. "Risk Assessment: Risk to humans posed by the dingo population on Fraser Island," Environmental Protection Agency, May 2001, https://web.archive.org/web/20130419204457/http://www.nprsr.qld.gov.au/register/p00560aa.pdf.
22. L. Brown, "Family rescues 6-year-old girl after dingo attacks her and drags her underwater," *The New York Post*, April 4, 2023, https://nypost.com/2023/04/04/family-rescues-6-year-old-girl-after-dingo-attacks-her-and-drags-her-underwater/.

4. Sherri Rasmussen

1. "Sherri Rae Rasmussen," https://wickedness.net/murders/sherri-rasmussen/.
2. P. Thornton, "How the Ice-Cold Case of Sherri Rasmussen's Murder was finally solved," December 22, 2021, https://www.ranker.com/list/sherri-rasmussen-case/patrick-thornton.
3. "People v. Lazarus," Court of Appeal, Second District, Division 4, California, https://caselaw.findlaw.com/ca-court-of-appeal/1707766.html.
4. M. Martinez and S. Wilson, "Retired L.A. detective sentenced to 27 years to life for 1986 murder," CNN, May 11, 2012, https://www.cnn.com/2012/05/11/justice/califronia-cop-cold-case/index.html.
5. M. Bowden, "A Case So Cold it was Blue," *Vanity Fair*, June 14, 2012, https://vanityfair.com/culture/2012/07/lapd-lazarus-murder-mystery-killer.
6. "Stephanie Ilene Lazarus," https://murderpedia.org/female.L/I/lazarus-Stephanie.htm.
7. C. Pelisek, "L.A. Policewoman on Trial for Murdering Her Ex's Wife," *The Daily Beast*, original published date March 8, 2012, last updated July 13, 2017, https://www.thedailybeast.com/la-policewoman-on-trial-for-murdering-her-exs-wife?re+scroll.
8. M. McGough, "The Lazarus File," the *Atlantic*, June 2011, https://www.theatlantic.com/magazine/archive/2011/06/the-lazarus-file/308499/.

9. "Murder victim's husband tearfully describes affair with woman accused of killing her," the *Mercury News*, February 15, 2012, https://www.mercurynews.com/2012/02/15/murder-victims-husband-tearfully-describes-affair-with-woman-accused-of-killing-her/.
10. "Autopsy report—Sherri Rasmussen," http://www.autopsyfiles.org/reports/Other/rasmussen,%20sherri_report.pdf.
11. "Where is John Ruetten Now?" December 19, 2020, https://thecinemaholic.com/where-is-john-ruetten-now/.
12. "Stephanie Lazarus," https://deadlywomen.fandom.com/wiki/Stephanie_Lazarus.
13. "Weeping widower of woman murdered 26 years ago tells of regret over love triangle that led his former cop lover to kill his wife," the *Daily Mail*, February 15, 2012, https://www.dailymail.co.uk/news/article-2101816/Weeping-widower-woman-murdered-26-years-ago-tells-regret-love-triangle-led-lover--LAPD-detective-Stephanie-Lazarus--kill-wife.html.
14. H. Breuer and C. Keating, "Scorned LAPD Detective Murdered Her Ex-Boyfriend's Wife -- and Got Away With It for Decades," *People*, December 4, 2017, https://people.com/crime/how-lapd-detective-stephanie-lazarus-murdered-sherri-rasmussen/.
15. "Jennifer Francis v The City of Los Angeles (LAPD)," Trials & Tribulations, March 28, 2019, https://sprocket-trials.blogspot.com/2019/03/jennifer-francis-v-city-of-los angeles_28.html.
16. W. Congreve, "The Mourning Bride: A Tragedy," July 30, 2019, https://www.amazon.com/Mourning-Bride-Tragedy-William-Congreve/dp/1011124866/ref=tmm_hrd_swatch_0?_encoding=UTF8&qid=1657641073&sr=8-1.

5. Ron Goldman and Nicole Brown Simpson

1. D. Kiner, "From dance recital and dinner to dead -- The murder of Nicole Brown Simpson and Ron Goldman in 1994," June 12, 2021, https://www.pennlive.com/crime/2021/06/

from-dance-recital-and-dinner-to-dead-the-murder-of-nicole-brown-simpson-and-ron-goldman-in-1994.html.

2. N. Henderson, "Goldman was trapped, coroner says," *The Washington Post*, June 10, 1995, https://www.washingtonpost.com/archive/politics/1995/06/10/goldman-was-trapped-coroner-says/029cf8b3-4f65-42d8-b691-bdf075040293/.

3. Vermeulen, "O.J. placed series of anxious calls," UPI, June 21, 1995, https://www.upi.com/Archives/1995/06/21/OJ-placed-series-of-anxious-calls/4675803707200/.

4. A. Beeman, "Disturbing details discovered in Nicole Brown Simpson's autopsy report," *Grunge*, May 19, 2022, https://www.grunge.com/644849/disturbing-details-in-nicole-brown-simpsons-autopsy-report/.

5. "The Trial of Orenthal James Simpson: An Account," https://famous-trials.com/simpson/1862-home.

6. "Nicole Brown Simpson," https://www.crimemuseum.org/crime-library/famous-murders/nicole-brown-simpson/.

7. "Testimony of Philip Vannatter," https://famous-trials.com/simpson/1889-vannattertestimony.

8. "Autopsy Report—Ron Goldman," https://pdf4pro.com/amp/view/autopsyfiles-org-ronald-goldman-autopsy-report-3f0854.html.

9. "Autopsy Report—Nicole Brown Simpson," https://www.autopsyfiles.org/reports/Other/simpson,%20nicole%20brown_report.pdt.

10. "Ron Goldman Biography, Life, Interesting Facts," https://www.sunsigns.org/famousbirthdays/d/profile/ron-goldman/.

11. "Ron Goldman," A&E Television Networks, original published date December 28, 2015, last updated April 16, 2019, https://www.biography.com/crime/ron-goldman.

12. "Ron Goldman Biography," https://www.imdb.com/name/nm2466635/bio/?ref_=nm_ov_bio_sm.

13. S.S. Brown, "Merchant Pays Price for 'Cutthroat' Ad: Retailing: Although the flyers were printed in May, customers are fuming over what they believe is a tasteless attempt to capitalize on slayings

of Simpson and Goldman," the *Los Angeles Times*, July 21, 1994, https://www.latimes.com/archives/la-xpm-1994-07-21-we-18306-story.html.

14. S.L. Erdman, "The Truth about Nicole Brown Simpson and Ron Goldman's Relationship," *Grunge*, November 16, 2021, https://www.grunge.com/662636/the-truth-about-nicole-brown-simpson-and-ron-goldmans-relationship/.

15. S. Nolasco, "Ron Goldman's sister, Kim Goldman, shuts down 'mistruths' about horrifying murders: 'I see all the comments,'" Fox News, August 7, 2022, https://www.foxnews.com/us/ron-goldman-sister-kim-goldman-shuts-down-mistruths-horrifying-murders.

16. H. Freeman, "The Goldmans on their pursuit of OJ Simpson: 'We were called racist for not agreeing with the verdict,'" *The Guardian*, July 24, 2017, https://www.theguardian.com/us-news/2017/jul/24/ron-goldman-pursuit-oj-simpson.

17. J.E. Reich, "Inside Nicole Brown Simpson and Ron Goldman's Relationship," May 27, 2022, https://www.nickiswift.com/478981/inside-nicole-brown-simpson-and-ron-goldmans-relationship/.

18. "Nicole Brown Simpson Biography," A&E Television Networks, original published date April 2, 2014, last updated June 7, 2021, https://www.biography.com/crime/nicole-brown-simpson.

19. N. Finn, 'Inside the Short, Tragic Life of Nicole Brown Simpson and Her Hopeful Final Days," June 12, 2019, https://www.eonline.com/news/1048564/inside-the-short-tragic-life-of-nicole-brown-simpson-and-her-hopeful-final-days.

20. "Nicole Brown Simpson," https://www.thefamouspeople.com/profiles/nicole-brown-simpson-10404.php.

21. "Philip Vannatter," https://famous-trials.com/simpson/1850-vannatter.

22. N. Henderson, "Driver says he didn't see Simpson's bronco, but saw person enter the house," *The Washington Post*, March 29, 1995, https://www.washingtonpost.com/archive/politics/1995/03/29/driver-says-he-didnt-see-simpsons-bronco-but-saw-person-enter-house/c1ff2854-c3ac-4e69-b137-9794bfda0604/.

23. D. Linder, "The Trial of Orenthal James Simpson," http://law2.umkc.edu/faculty/projects/ftrials/Simpson/Simpsonaccount.htm.
24. "O.J. Simpson trial: Houseguest Kato Kaelin testifies," CNN, https://www.cnn.com/2007/US/law/12/11/court.archive.simpson3/.
25. "O.J. Simpson trial," Encyclopedia Britannica, Inc., July 24, 2023, https://www.britannica.com/print/article/1982560.
26. N. Henderson, "Simpson Depicted as Looking Bizarre," *The Washington Post*, February 7, 1995, https://www.washingtonpost.com/archive/politics/1995/02/07/simpson-depicted-as-looking-bizarre/17b4b2a2-dffc-4958-952f-3a88ce52ade8/.
27. C. Spolar and W. Hamilton, "Review of records shows Simpson abused wife," *The Washington Post*, June 16, 1994, https://www.washingtonpost.com/archive/politics/1994/06/16/review-of-records-shows-simpson-abused-wife/7638e2c9-b24f-4d11-8b81-af5caa401efa/.
28. "Excerpts of prosecution's opening statements in the O.J. Simpson Trial," *The Washington Post*, https://www.washingtonpost.com/archive/politics/1995/01/25/excerpts-of-prosecutions-opening-statements-in-the-oj-simpson-trial/52cb3b7b-14a4-4e3b-9370-41d332c00214/.
29. N. Finn, "Inside the Short, Tragic Life of Nicole Brown Simpson and Her Hopeful Final Days," June 12, 2019, https://www.online.com/news/1048564/inside-the-short-tragic-life-of-nicole-brown-simpson-and-her-hopeful-final-days.
30. K.B. Noble, "Prosecution Says Simpson Abused Wife for 17 Years," *The New York Times*, January 12, 1995, https://www.nytimes.com/1995/01/12/us/prosecution-says-simpson-abused-wife-for-17-years.html.
31. "Nicole Brown Simpson and Ron Goldman murdered," History, https://www.history.com/this-day-in-history/nicole-brown-simpson-and-ron-goldman-murdered.
32. M. Harris, "Star reporter looks back at covering the O.J. Simpson murder trial," *Ventura County Star*, January 23, 2015, https://archive.vcstar.com/news/courts/

star-reporter-looks-back-at-covering-the-oj-simpson-murder-trial-ep-894773571-349167411.html/.

33. "1995: OJ Simpson verdict: 'Not guilty,'" BBC, http://news.bbc.co.uk/onthisday/hi/dates/stories/october/3/newsid_2486000/2486673.stm.

34. "The Trial of O.J. Simpson: The Incriminating Evidence," https://web.archive.org/web/20080618074624/http://www.law.umkc.edu/faculty/projects/trials/Simpson/Evidence.html.

35. D. Margolick, "Limousine Driver Deals a Blow to Simpson," *The New York Times*, March 29, 1995, https://www.nytimes.com/1995/03/29/us/limousine-driver-deals-a-blow-to-simpson.html.

36. "O.J. Simpson: Week-by-week, week 9," *Court TV News*, March 20-24, 1995, https://web.archive.org/web/20080123094707/http://www.courttv.com/trials/ojsimpson/weekly/09.html.

37. "Final Jury Composition," https://web.archive.org/web/20110209115654/http://www.law.umkc.edu/faculty/projects/ftrials/Simpson/Jurypage.html#Final%20Jury.

38. "Nicole Brown Simpson's letter to O.J. Simpson," https://famous-trials.com/simpson/1833-brownletter.

39. Simpson Civil Trial Explainer," CNN, http://www.cnn.com/US/9609/16/simpson.case/.

40. "New Testimony about Simpson Brings Surprise," *The New York Times*, December 16, 1995, https://www.nytimes.com/1995/12/16/us/new-testimony-about-simpson-brings-surprise.html.

41. M. Fleeman, "Paula Barbieri Says She Dumped Simpson Hours before Slayings She Left 'Dear John' Message On O.J.'s Answering Machine," *The Spokesman-Review*, December 16, 1995, https://www.spokesman.com/stories/1995/dec/16/paula-barbieri-says-she-dumped-simpson-hours/.

42. T. Vermeulen, "O.J. placed series of anxious calls," UPI, June 21, 1995, https://www.upi.com/Archives/1995/06/21/OJ-placed-series-of-anxious-calls/4675803707200/#.

43. "O.J. Simpson: Week-by-week, week 22," *Court TV News*, June 19-23, 1995, https://web.archive.org/web/20071211050819/http://www.courttv.com/trials/ojsimpson/weekly/22.html.

44. "O.J. Simpson: Week-by-week, week 1," *Court TV News*, January 23-27, 1995, https://web.archive.org/web/20080209202303/http://www.courttv.com/trials/ojsimpson/weekly/01.html.
45. "O.J. Simpson trial: The prosecution rests," CNN, December 11, 2007, https://www.cnn.com/2007/US/law/12/11/court.archive.simpson7/index.html.
46. N. Henderson and L. Adams, "Ito to bar Simpson team's attempt to link drug dealers to killings," *The Washington Post*, July 14, 1995, https://www.washingtonpost.com/archive/politics/1995/07/14/ito-bars-simpson-teams-attempt-to-link-drug-dealers-to-killings/6b80d0d8-504b-406f-812d-1eb5ef3e1047/.
47. "Forensic chemist testifies in O.J. Simpson trial on blood drops found at crime scene," https://web.archive.org/web/20200507235605/https://www.nbclearn.com/portal/site/k-12/flatview?cuecard=5465.
48. "O.J. Simpson: Week-by-week, week 34," *Court TV News*, September 11-15, 1995, https://web.archive.org/web/20080209202508/http://www.courttv.com/trials/ojsimpson/weekly/34.html.
49. "O.J. Simpson: Week-by-week, week 11," *Court TV News*, April 3-7, 1995, https://web.archive.org/web/20071211050739/http://www.courttv.com/trials/ojsimpson/weekly/11.html.
50. "O.J. Simpson: Week-by-week, week 12," *Court TV News*, April 10-14, 1995, https://web.archive.org/web/20071211050744/http://www.courttv.com/trials/ojsimpson/weekly/12.html.
51. "Case File: The OJ Simpson Trial," https://forensicsciencesociety.com/thedrip/case-file-the-oj-simpson-trial.
52. "O.J. Simpson: Week-by-week, week 16," *Court TV News*, May 8-12, 1995, https://web.archive.org/web/20080202233509/http://www.courttv.com/trials/ojsimpson/weekly/16.html.
53. "O.J. Simpson: Week-by-week, week 17," *Court TV News*, May 15-18, 1995, https://web.archive.org/web/20071211050804/http://www.courttv.com/trials/ojsimpson/weekly/17.html.
54. "O.J. Simpson: Week-by-week, week 23," *Court TV News*, June 26-30, 1995, https://web.archive.org/web/20080209202410/http://www.courttv.com/trials/ojsimpson/weekly/23.html.

55. "O.J. Simpson: Week-by-week, week 29," *Court TV News*, August 7-11, 1995, https://web.archive.org/web/20071211050854/http://www.courttv.com/trials/ojsimpson/weekly/29.html.
56. "Excerpts from the Ruling on the Fuhrman Tapes," *The New York Times*, September 1, 1995, https://www.nytimes.com/1995/09/01/us/excerpts-from-the-ruling-on-the-fuhrman-tapes.html.
57. N. Henderson, "Expert: Hair like Simpson's found on victim's shirt," *The Washington Post*, July 1, 1995, https://www.washingtonpost.com/archive/politics/1995/07/01/expert-hair-like-simpsons-found-on-victims-shirt/15fa8dc0-a7c4-4d35-a47b-b5a07769ec8f/.
58. "Mark Fuhrman," https://famous-trials.com/simpson/1840-fuhrman.
59. R. Chang, "O.J. Simpson's Freeway Chase: What Happened to the White Ford Bronco," Biography, June 4, 2020, https://www.biography.com/crime/oj-simpson-bronco-chase-car-museum.
60. "O.J. Simpson: Week-by-week, week 24," *Court TV News*, July 5-7, 1995, https://web.archive.org/web/20080209202412/http://www.courttv.com/trials/ojsimpson/weekly/24.html.
61. "O.J. Simpson: Week-by-week, week 14," *Court TV News*, April 24-28, 1995, https://web.archive.org/web/20071211050754/http://www.courttv.com/trials/ojsimpson/weekly/14.html.
62. W. Avila, "Timeline: OJ Simpson Murder, Civil Trials," NBC Los Angeles, original published date June 9, 2014, last updated July 18, 2017, https://www.nbclosangeles.com/.
63. "The O.J. Simpson Trial: The Jury," http://law2.umkc.edu/faculty/projects/ftrials/Simpson/Jurypage.html#Final%20Jury.
64. J. McManus, "Marcia Clark Explains Domestic Violence Bias in OJ Simpson Trial," ABC News, June 14, 2016, https://abcnews.go.com/Sports/marcia-clark-explains-domestic-violence-bias-oj-simpson/story?id=39852403.
65. "Gloves May Have Shrunk, Expert Says at O.J. Trial," https://web.archive.org/web/202000427191119/https://www.questia.com/newspaper/1P2-32943569/gloves-may-have-shrunk-expert-says-at-o-j-trial.

66. "O.J. Simpson: Week-by-week, week 21," *Court TV News*, June 12-16, 1995, https://web.archive.org/web/20080209181334/http://www.courttv.com/trials/ojsimpson/weekly/21.html.
67. "More Photos Show Simpson Wearing Bruno Magli Shoes," *The Washington Post*, January 2, 1997, https://www.washingtonpost.com/archive/politics/1997/01/02/more-photos-show-simpson-wearing-bruno-magli-shoes/8d1fe383-449a-480a-9a14-45d2e554289c/.
68. "Ronald Goldman," https://famous-trials.com/simpson/1842-goldman.

6. Admiral Mike Boorda

1. E. Thomas, "A Matter of Honor," *Newsweek*, May 26, 1996, https://www.newsweek.com/matter-honor-178450.
2. P. Shenon, "His Medals Questioned, Top Admiral Kills Himself," *The New York Times*, May 17, 1996, https://www.nytimes.com/1996/05/17/us/his-medals-questioned-top-admiral-kills-himself.html?sec=$spon=$pagewanted=all.
3. P. Shenon, "Admiral, in Suicide Note, Apologized to 'My Sailors,'" *The New York Times*, May 18, 1996, https://www.nytimes.com/1996/05/18/us/admiral-in-suicide-note-apologized-to-my-sailors.html.
4. D. Eisman and J. Dorsey, "Navy's Top Admiral is Dead Notes Found in Adm. Mike Boorda's Home; President Mourns 'Great Loss' He Shot Himself 25 Minutes Before Interview on Medals," *The Virginian-Pilot*, May 17, 1997, https://scholar.lib.vt.edu/VA-news/VA-Pilot/issues/1996/vp960517/05170652.htm.
5. N. Kotz, "Breaking Point," *Washingtonian*, December 1996, https://charleswarner.us/articles/BreakingPoint.htm.
6. "Beneath The Waves," *Newsweek*, May 29, 1996, https://www.newsweek.com/beneath-waves-178388.
7. D. Morgan and G. Lardiner, "The Enigma of an Admiral's Death," *The Washington Post*, May 20, 1996, https://www.washingtonpost.com/archive/politics/1996/05/20/the-enigma-of-an-admirals-death/7e8da409-7f49-47d8-a1b9-75b54f0bd08d/.

8. P. Frazer, "Obituary: Admiral Jeremy Boorda," *Independent*, May 17, 1996, https://www.independent.co.uk/news/people/obituary-admiral-jeremy-boorda-1347903.html.
9. "Navy agrees admiral was entitled to wear combat decorations," Associated Press, June 25, 1998, https://freerepublic.com/focus/news/847886/posts.
10. T. Weiner, "Jeremy M. Boorda, 57; Rose through Ranks," *The New York Times*, May 17, 1996, https://www.nytimes.com/1996/05/17/us/jeremy-m-boorda-57-rose-through-ranks.html.
11. "Admiral Jeremy M. Boorda," Naval History and Heritage Command, History, https://www.history.navy.mil/content/history/nhhc/browse-by-topic/people/chiefs-of-naval-operations/admiral-jeremy-m--boorda.html.
12. B.E. Trainor, "Suicide over a Medal? An Ex-General's View," *The New York Times*, May 20, 1996, https://www.nytimes.com/1996/05/20/us/suicide-over-a-medal-an-ex-general-s-view.html.
13. T. Weiner, "Military Combat Insignia Are Key to Officers' Image," *The New York Times*, May 18, 1996, https://www.nytimes.com/1996/05/18/us/military-combat-insignia-are-key-to-officers-image.html.
14. Letter dated June 18, 1998 from Chairman, Board for Correction of Naval Records, to the Secretary of the Navy, regarding an independent review of the naval records of Mike Boorda.
15. C. Hauser, "Ex-Marine Can Wear Medals He Didn't Earn. A Court Calls It Free Speech," *The New York Times*, January 13, 2016, https://www.nytimes.com/2016/01/14/us/ex-marine-can-wear-medals-he-diddnt-earn-a-court-calls-it-free-speech.html.
16. P. Elias, "U.S. court: Wearing unearned military medals is free speech," *Military Times*, January 12, 2016, https://www.militarytimes.com/veterans/2016/01/12/u-s-court-wearing-unearned-military-medals-is-free-speech/.

17. "Facts and Case Summary -- U.S. v. Alvarez," https://www.uscourts.gov/educational-resources/educational-activities/facts-and-case-summary-us-v-alvarez.
18. V. Rose, "Summary of United States v. Alvarez," July 25, 2012, https://www.cga.ct.gov/2012/rpt/2012-R-0313.htm.
19. "Stolen Valor Act of 2013," https://www.govinfo.gov/content/pkg/COMPS-10517/pdf/COMPS-10517.pdf.
20. A. Wooley, "The Fall of James Forrestal," *The Washington Post*, May 34, 1999, https://www.washingtonpost.com/archive/lifestyle/1999/05/23/the-fall-of-james-forrestal/60c653b3-c537-462f-b523-5fdc5cd934aa/.
21. "Chester W. Nimitz, Jr.," Woods Hole Oceanographic Institution, https://www.whoi.edu/who-we-are/about-us/people/obituary/chester-w-nimitz-jr/.
22. L.M. Cohen, "Deaths with Dignity," *Slate*, June 6, 2013, https://slate.com/technology/2013/06/death-with-dignity-joint-suicide-of-rear-adm-chester-nimitz-jr-and-joan-nimitz.html.
23. T.V. Brook, "General is most senior Army officer to kill self," *USA Today*, October 28, 2016, https://www.usatoday.com/story/news/politics/2016/10/28/army-generals-death-ruled-suicide/92880986/.
24. "Army: Two-star general committed suicide on Alabama military base," CBS News, October 28, 2016, https://www.cbsnews.com/news/army-two-star-general-committed-suicide-alabama-military-base/.
25. M. Myers, "Army report: Self-doubt and sleep deprivation led to 2-star's suicide," *Army Times*, January 11, 2017, https://www.armytimes.com/news/your-army/2017/01/11/army-report-self-doubt-and-sleep-deprivation-led-to-2-star-s-suicide/.
26. G. Ziezulewicz, "The Navy's investigation into Vice Adm. Scott Stearney's suicide," *Navy Times*, February 25, 2020, https://www.navytimes/news/your-navy/2020/02/25/the-navys-investigation-into-vice-adm-scott-stearneys-suicide/.
27. A. France-Presse, "Scott Stearney, US navy chief in Middle East, found dead in Bahrain," *The Guardian*, December 2, 2018,

https://www.theguardian.com/us-news-2018/dec/02/scott-stearney-us-navy-head-in-middle-easet-found-dead.

28. "Suicide in the Military," https://deploymentpsych.org/disorders/suicide-main.
29. J.A. Smith, M. Doidge, R. Hanoa, and B.C. Frueh, "A historical comparison of U.S. Army & U.S. civilian suicide rates, 1900-2020," *Psychiatry Research* 323 (2023).
30. "Military Suicide," Association for Behavioral and Cognitive Therapies, https://www.abct.org/fact-sheets/military-suicide/.
31. C. Dickstein, "Pentagon 'cautiously encouraged' by 15% drop in military suicides last year," *Stars and Stripes*, October 20, 2022, https://www.stripes.com/theaters/us/2022-10-20/military-suicides-decrease-annual-report-7756629.html.
32. A. Novotney, "Stopping suicide in the military," *Monitor on Psychology*, January/February, (2020) 33-36.
33. Z. Perez, "Military suicide stats released, Army saw highest increase of deaths," *Military Times*, July 3, 2023, https://www.militarytimes.com/news/your-military/2023/07/03/military-suicide-stats-released-army-saw-highest-increase-of-deaths/.
34. "Suicide statistics," https://afsp.org/suicide-statistics/.
35. Department of Defense Releases the Annual Report on Suicide in the Military: Calendar Year 2021," October 20, 2022, https://www.defense.gov/News/Releases/Release/Article/3193806/department-of-defense-releases-the-annual-report-on-suicide-in-the-military-cal/.
36. "Preventing Suicide in the U.S. Military: Recommendations from the Suicide Prevention and Response Independent Review Committee," December 2022, https://media.defense.gov/2023/Feb/24/2003167430/-1/-1/0/SPRIRC-FINAL-REPORT.PDF.

7. Kathleen Savio

1. G. Glaub, "The Police Officer's Wives: Kathleen Savio & Stacy Peterson," February 23, https://themidwestcrimefiles.com/post/the-police-officer-s-wives-kathleen-savio-stacy-peterson.
2. "Biography—Kathleen Savio," https://www.imdb.com/name/nm11717416/bio.
3. "Drew Peterson," https://peoplepill.com/people/drew-peterson.
4. K. Fraga, "Drew Peterson: The Chicago Cop Who Killed His Third Wife -- And Whose Fourth Wife Went Missing," original published date May 30, 2022, last updated May 31, 2022, https://allthatsinteresting.com/drew-peterson.
5. "Drew Peterson," https://crimemuseum.org/crime-library/famous-murders/drew-peterson/.
6. D. Murray, "Unanswered Cries: Drew Peterson Ex-Wife Kathleen Savio's Death," *Chicago*, May 6, 2008, https://www.chiagomag.com/Chicago-Magazine/May-2008/UnansweredCries/.
7. M. McPadden, "Meet the 4 Wives of Convicted Killer Drew Peterson," April 6, 2018, https://www.investigationdiscovery.com/crimefeed/murder/meet-the-4-wives-of-convicted-killer-drew-peterson.
8. "Body of Illinois Cop's 3rd Wife Exhumed," CBS News, November 13, 2007, https://www.cbsnews.com/news/body-of-illinois-cops-3rd-wife-exhumed/.
9. "Third Autopsy Report—Kathleen Savio," https://s3.documentcloud.org/documents/332983/baden-autopsy-report.pdf.
10. Drew Peterson guilty: Peterson convicted of killing Kathleen Savio," WJLA, September 6, 2012, https://wjla.com/news/crime/drew-peterson-convicted-of-killing-kathleen-savio-79601.
11. D. Grigas, "Expert calls Savio autopsy items 'a bit suspicious,'" *The Evening Tribune*, original published date November 13, 2007, last updated November 14, 2007, https://www.eveningtribune.com/story/news/2007/11/14/expert-calls-savio-autopsy-items/46599011007/.

12. "First Autopsy Report—Kathleen Savio," including the Death Certificate, http://www.autopsyfiles.org/reports/Other/savio,%20kathleen_report.pdf.
13. S.H. Lee and K. W. Ryu, "The significance of fluid in the sphenoid sinuses in death by drowning," *Korean J Leg Med* 37(3): (2013) 129-133.
14. "Doctor Who Ruled Savio's Death a Homicide Speaks out about Peterson Trial," CBS News, September 25, 2012, https://www.cbsnews.com/chicago/news/doctor-who-ruled-savios-death-a-homicide-speaks-out-about-peterson-trial/.
15. "Pathologist declares Kathleen Savio's death a homicide," Will County State's Attorney, February 21, 2008, https://willcountysao.com/2019/01/pathologist-declares-kathleen-savios-death-a-homicide/.
16. "Pathologist: Savio death was homicide," ABC7 NY, February 21, 2008, https://abc7ny.com/archive/5971961/.
17. "Dr. Michael Baden Performed New Autopsy on Kathleen Savio," Fox News, January 13, 2015, https://www.foxnews.com/story/dr-michael-baden-performed-new-autopsy-on-kathleen-savio.
18. "Drew Peterson Screams, Then Gets 38 Years for Wife's Murder," NBC Chicago, original published date February 21, 2013, last updated March 7, 2013, https://www.nbcchicago.com/news/loca/drew-peterson-sentence-kathleen-savio/1945921/.
19. "Former Cop Admits Mistakes in Savio Death Investigation," NBC Chicago, January 22, 2010, https://www.nbcchicago.com/news/local/peterson-hearsay-hearing-4/1899263/.
20. "Coroner's Juror on Kathleen Savio's Death," Fox News, January 25, 2017, https://www.foxnews.com/transcript/coroners-juror-on-kathleen-savios-death.

8. Carlos Sousa

1. "Victims 'taunted tiger' before it killed zoo visitor," *The Guardian*, January 18, 2008, https://www.theguardian.com/world/2008/jan/18/animalwelfare.usa.

2. "Teen killed by tiger saved friend," NBC News, December 28, 2007, https://www.nbcnews.com/id/wbna22419664.
3. C. Pillar and T. Reiterman, "New details of tiger attack released," the *Los Angeles Times*, December 29, 2007, https://www.latimes.com/local/la-me-tiger29dec29-story.html.
4. "Zoo probes deadly tiger mauling," GMA, February 9, 2009, https://www.goodmorningamerica.com/.
5. J. Dearen and M. Wohlsen, "Feds release San Francisco tiger attack documents," the *San Diego Union-Tribune*, February 12, 2011, https://www.sandiegouniontribune.com/sdut-feds-release-san-francisco-tiger-attack-documents-2011feb12-story.html.
6. "Autopsy Report—Carlos Sousa," https://www.autopsyfiles.org/reports/Other/sousa,%20carlos_report%20.pdf.
7. "Carlos Eduardo Sousa Jr.," https://www.findagrave.com/memorial/23573207/carlos-eduardo-sousa.
8. "Transcript of tiger 911 tapes: Confusion about whether a tiger is loose and victim is 'crazy' or bitten," *Mercury News*, January 15, 2008, https://www.mercurynews.com/2008/01/15/transcript-of-tiger-911-tapes-confusion-about-whether-a-tiger-is-loose-and-victim-is-crazy-or-bitten/.
9. "Tiger attack victim's desperate phone call from zoo: 'My brother's about to die,'" the *Daily Mail*, January 17, 2008, https://www.dailymail.co.uk/news/article-508778/Tiger-attack-victims-desperate-phone-zoo-My-brothers-die.html.
10. L. Goldston, L Griffy and S. Webby, "Police tapes reveal chilling details about tiger attack," *East Bay Times*, original published date January 16, 2008, last updated August 17, 2016, https://www.eastbaytimes.com/2008/01/16/tapes-reveal-chilling-details-in-tiger-attack/.
11. 'Transcript of Tiger 9-1-1 Tape Released," JEMS, January 14, 2008, https://www.jems.com/news/transcript-tiger-9-1-1-tape-re/.
12. P. Yollin, "Horrified zoogoer recalls tiger attack / Keeper's mauling a reminder wild animals can turn vicious at any time, experts say," January 1, 2007, https://www.sfgate.com/news/article/Horrified-zoogoer-recalls-tiger-attack-Keeper-s-2626456.php.

13. "Teen died saving friend from tiger," the *Denver Post*, original published date December 28, 2007, last updated May 7, 2016, https://www.denverpost.com/2007/12/28/teen-died-saving-friend-from-tiger/.
14. P. Yollin, "S.F. Zoo's big cats meet people again," February 22, 2008, https://www.sfgate.com/bayarea/article/s-f-zoo-s-big-cats-meet-people-again-3225833.php.
15. "Big-Cat Incidents in the U.S.," PETA, https://www.peta.org/wp-content/uploads/2021/06/BigCatIncidentList.pdf.
16. K. Block, "North Carolina, where a lion just killed a woman, is one of only four states with no law against private ownership of dangerous wild animals," The Humane Society of the United States, January 2, 2019, https://www.humanesociety.org/blog/north-carolina-where-lion-just-killed-woman-one-only-four-states-no-law-against-private#.

9. Eve Carson

1. S. Harker, "The Heinous and Unforgiving U.N.C. Murder of Eve Carson," April 23, 2020, https://talkmurder.com/eve-carson-murder/.
2. "Eve Marie Carson Obituary," http://www.legacy.com/ns/eve-carson-obituary/105220419.
3. "State v. Lovette," February 5, 2013, https://caselaw.findlaw.com/nc-court-ofappeals/1622595.html.
4. "Prosecutors paint chilling picture of Eve Carson's last moments," WRAL, original published date December 19, 2011, last updated December 21, 2011, https://www.wral.com/news/local/story/10514000/.
5. C. Glynn, "Eve Carson, slain UNC student president, wanted to pray before murder, says witness," CBS News, December 14, 2011, https://www.cbsnews.com/news/eve-carson-slain-unc-student-president-wanted-to-pray-before-murder-says-witness/.
6. T. Durante, "'Let's pray together': The heart-breaking plea by kidnapped college student to her captors -- just minutes before they executed her," the *Daily Mail*, January 12, 2012, https://

www.dailymail.co.uk/news/article-2074232/Eve-Carson-trial-Kindapped-UNC-student-president-wanted-pray-murder.html.

7. "Laurence Lovette—Killer of Eve Carson," National Organization of Victims of Juvenile Murderers, https://teenkillers.org/juvenile-lifers/offenders-cases-state/north-carolinaoffenders/laurence-lovette-killer-of-eve-carson/.

8. E. Martinez, "Eve Carson's Killer Sentenced to Life in Federal Prison, Says 'Sorry' for Murdering Her with Shotgun," CBS News, September 24, 2010, https://www.cbsnews.com/news/eve-carsons-killer-sentenced-to-life-in-federal-prison-says-sorry-for-murdering-her-with-shotgun/.

9. L. Loflin, "Eve Marie Carson Murder," https://sullivancounty.com/wcva/lilley_dec_1009.htm.

10. "Report of Investigation by Medical Examiner—Eve Carson," WRAL, https://wwwcache.wral.com/asset/news/state/2008/06/30/3125964/investigation.pdf.

11. "Two Charged in Eve Carson's Death; Second Charged in Killing of Duke Student," March 6, 2008, https://alumni.unc.edu/news/two-men-charged-in-eve-carsons-shooting/.

12. "Multiple gunshots killed Eve Carson," WRAL, original published date June 30, 2008, last updated July 15, 2008, https://www.wral.com/multiple-gunshots-killed-eve-carson/3125964/.

13. "Autopsy Report—Eve Carson," http://www.autopsyfiles.org/reports/Other/carson,%20eve_report.pdf.

14. "Eve Marie Carson," the *Daily Tar Heel*, https://www.dailytarheel.com/section/eve_carson.

15. A. Thompson, "Eve Carson: A promising life taken in a brutal crime," *Athens Banner-Herald*, January 4, 2009, https://web.archive.org/web/20090923112628/http://www.onlineathens.com/stories/010409/new_373740949.shtml.

16. "Eve Carson's Biography from UNC's Chancellor," March 6, 2008, WSFA, https://www.wsfa.com/story/6977116/eve-carson-biography-from-uncs-chancellor/.

17. "Guilty Plea in Eve Carson Case," FBI, May 5, 2010, https://archives.fbi.gov/archives/charlotte/press-releases-2010/ce050510.htm.
18. "Lovette found guilty in Eve Carson's 2008 shooting death," WRAL, original published date December 20, 2011, last updated December 21, 2011.
19. B. Hosking, "Anita Cobby murder: 'Everyone in the car that dreadful night had a passport to doom,'" *The Guardian*, March 19, 2017, https://www.theguardian.com/australia-news/2017/mar/20/anita-cobby-everyone-in-the-car-that-dreadful-night-had-a-passport-to-doom.

10. *Sahel Kazemi and Steve McNair*

1. M. Thomas, "The Tragic Death of Steve McNair Still Causing Heartache for Family," June 24, 2020, https://www.sportscasting.com/the-tragic-death-of-steve-mcnair-still-causing-heartache-for-family/.
2. "Sahel 'Jenni' Kazemi," https://www.findagrave.com/memorial/39119194/sahel-kazemi.
3. D. Nasaw, "Former NFL star Steve McNair was killed by jealous girlfriend, police, say," *The Guardian*, July 9, 2009, https://www.theguardian.com/sport/2009/jul/09/steve-mcnair-murder-girlfriend.
4. T. Loller and J. Edwards, "Sahel Kazemi's nephew reveals she expected Steve McNair to divorce wife," the *Seattle Times*, July 7, 2009, https://www.seattletimes.com/sports/seahawks/sahel-kazemis-nephew-reveals-she-expected-steve-mcnair-to-divorce-wife/.
5. "Police: Retired QB McNair murdered by girlfriend, who then killed herself," NFL, July 8, 2009, https://www.nfl.com/news/police-retired-qb-mcnair-murdered-by-girlfriend-who-then-killed-09000d5d8113375c.
6. C. Hine, "Steve McNair's Death Is Declared a Homicide," *The New York Times*, July 5, 2009, https://www.nytimes.com/2009/07/06/sports/football/06mcnair.html.

7. "Steve McNair's case ruled murder, suicide," the *Seattle Times*, July 9, 2009, https://www.seattletimes.com/sports/seahawks/nfl-steve-mcnairs-case-ruled-murder-suicide/.
8. M. O'Keeffe, "Cops: Steve McNair shot dead by girlfriend Sahel Kazemi while he slept in murder-suicide," the *New York Daily News*, https://www.nydailynews.com/sports/football/cops-steve-mcnair-shot-dead-girlfriend-sahel-kazemi-slept-murder-suicide-article-1.427035.
9. "Sahel Kazemi, 20-Year-Old Killed with Steve McNair," the *Huffington Post* original published date June 9, 2010, last updated December 6, 2017, https://www.huffpost.com/entry/sahel-kazemi-20-year-old_n_225854.
10. E. Merrill, "The Woman Forever Tied to Steve McNair," ESPN, July 1, 2010, https://www.espn.com/espn/otl/news/story?id=5347315.
11. L.V. Hooser, "Sister: Former Clay woman in love with McNair," the *Florida Times-Union*, https://www.jacksonville.com/story/news/crime/2009/07/06/stub-1101/15980428007/.
12. E. Bacharach and M. Timms, "Tracing a tragedy: Reconstructing the final days of Steve McNair and Sahel 'Jenni' Kazemi," the *Tennessean*, original published date July 3, 2019, last updated January 14, 2020, https://www.tennessean.com/story/sports/nfl/titans/2019/07/03/steve-mcnair-sahel-jenni-kazemi-death/1553404001/.
13. T. Deas, "Steve McNair's death: Sahel 'Jenni'Kazemi's behavior leaves clues to motive," the *Tennessean*, original published date July 3, 2019, last updated January 19 2020, https://www.tennessean.com/story/sports/nfl/titans/2019/07/03/steve-mcnair-death-sahel-jenni-kazemi-anniversary/1601318001/.
14. "Police Report" and supporting documents, http://www.autopsyfiles.org/reports/policereport/mcnair,%20steve_police%20report.pdf.
15. "Autopsy Report—Steve McNair," and supporting documents, http://www.autopsyfiles.org/reports/Celebs/mcnair_steve_report.pdf.
16. "Autopsy Report—Sahel Kazemi," and supporting documents, http://www.autopsyfiles.org/reports/Other/kazemi_sahel_report.pdf.

17. E. Bacharach, "10 years after the death of Steve McNair, the former NFL QB who seemingly led a double life," *Greenville News*, July 5, 2019, https://www.greenvilleonline.com/story/news/2019/07/05/steve-mcnair-death-former-nfl-tennessee-titans-qb-who-seemingly-led-double-life/1657872001/.
18. "Steve McNair Biography," https://americanfootball.fandom.com/wiki/Steve_McNair.
19. J.E. Johnston, "The Tragedy of Murder-Suicides," *Psychology Today*, March 29, 2020, https://www.psychologytoday.com/us/blog/teh-human-equation/202003/the-tragedy-murder-suicides.
20. K. Galta, WL. Olsen, and G. Wik, "Murder followed by suicide: Norwegian data and international literature," *Nord J Psychiatry* 64(6): (2010) 397-401.

11. Carol Daniels

1. "Rev. Carol Daniels," https://unresolved.me/rev-carol-daniels.
2. K. Dillingham, "God's Razor of Judgment," December 19, 2016, https://www.theodysseyonline.com/gods-razor-of-judgment.
3. M. Evans, "Mother: Slain Okla. Pastor 'just loved people,'" the *San Diego Union-Tribune*, August 24, 2009, https://www.sandiegouniontribune.com/sdut-us-pastor-killed-082409aug24-story.html.
4. R. Jackson, "Slaying details of Oklahoma City pastor shocking," the *Oklahoman*, August 30, 2009, https://www.oklahoman.com/story/news/technology/2009/08/30/slaying-details-of-oklahoma-city-pastor-shocking/61365464007/.
5. J. Pittman, "Anadarko church where pastor slain is torn down; memorial planned," the *Oklahoman*, July 13, 2010, https://www.oklahoman.com/story/news/religion/2010/07/13/anadarko-church-where-pastor-slain-is-torn-down-memorial-planned/61227500007/.
6. "Autopsy Report—Carol Daniels," including toxicology report, http://www.autopsyfiles.org/reports/Other/daniels,%20carol_report.pdf.

7. D.K. Molina and V.J.M DiMaio, "Normal Organ Weights in Women: Part I-The Heart," *Am J Forensic Med Pathol* 36(3): (2015) 176-181.
8. "Carol Faye Dunlap Daniels," https://www.findagrave.com/meorial/41245868/carol-faye-daniels.
9. "Anadarko Police Department," http://www.cityofanadarko.org/departments/police/index.php.
10. "Nine Years Later, Evidence Revealed in the Murder of Pastor Carol Daniels," News9, August 23, 2018, https://www.news9.com/story/5e3349b71290151d52141e1a/9-years-later-evidence-revealed-in-the-murder-of-pastor-carol-daniels.

12. *Jayne and Corinne Peters*

1. T. Collington, "Texas mayor & daughter's deaths ruled murder-suicide," WTSP, July 14, 2010, https://www.wtsp.com/article/home/texas-mayor-daughters-deaths-ruled-murder-suicide/67-390548478.
2. "Mayor & City Council," The City of Coppell, https://www.coppelltx.gov/569/City-Council.
3. E.S. Perez, "Dallas-area mayor reportedly shoots, kills teen daughter, then self," July 15, 2010, https://www.cleveland.com/nation/2010/07/dallas-area_mayor_reportedly_s.html.
4. "Death of Texas mayor ruled suicide, daughter's death homicide," CNN, July 14, 2010, http://www.cnn.com/2010/CRIME/07/14/texas.mayor.death/index.html.
5. J. Stengle, "Police: Daughter Killed Well before Mayor Shot Herself," NBC Dallas-Fort Worth, September 16, 2010, https://www.nbcdfw.com/news/local/police-daughter-killed-well-before-mayor-shot-herself/1852728/.
6. "Jayne Peters," https://www.findagrave.com/memorial/549256/jayne-peters.
7. "Coppell suicide notes released, new details emerge on gun," July 16, 2010, https://www.wfaa.com/article/news/coppell-suicide-notes-released-new-details-emerge-on-gun/287-411160277.

8. M. Stinton, "Deputy Police chief, mayor pro tem address mayor's death," July 26, 2010, https://starlocalmedia.com/coppellgazette/news/deputy-police-chief-mayor-pro-tem-address-mayors-death/article_08184baa-d51e-5580-bd4f-5167f2c8db78.html.

9. "Corinne Peters," https://www.findagrave.com/memorial/54925632/corinne-peters.

10. N. Jabali-Nash, "Mayor of Coppell, Texas, Killed Daughter a Day Before Shooting Herself, Says Report," CBS News, September 17, 2010, https://www.cbsnews.com/news/mayor-of-coppell-texas-killed-daughter-a-day-before-shooting-herself-says-report/.

11. "Missing keychain offers clue into murder-suicide of Texas mayor, daughter," July 21, 2010, https://www.khou.com/article/news/missing-keychain-offers-clue-into-murder-suicide-of-texas-mayor-daughter/285-342066091#.

12. "Police report: Motive remains mystery in Coppell murder-suicide," WFAA, September 17, 2010, https://www.wfaa.com/article/news/crime/police-report-motive-remains-mystery-in-coppell-murder-suicide/287-338218717.

13. L. Reese, "In a Town of Pretenders, Two Deaths Outed Them All," June 1, 2021, https://lylareese.medium.com/in-a-town-of-pretenders-two-deaths-outed-them-all-1e94798690f9.

14. E.S. Perez, "Murder-Suicide Ruled in Mayor, Daughter's Deaths," NBC Dallas-Fort Worth, July 14, 2010, https://www.nbcdfw.com/news/local/coppell-mayor-daughter-found-dead/2118239/.

15. "UPDATE: Coppell mayor's note explains grief for late husband," July 16, 2010, https://www.beaumontenterprise.com/news/article/UPDATE-Coppell-mayor-s-note-explains-grief-for-729756.php.

16. "Police details reveal final acts of Coppell Mayor Jayne Peters after killing daughter," the *Dallas Morning News*, September 17, 2010, https://www.dallasnews.com/news/2010/09/17/police-details-reveal-final-acts-of-coppell-mayor-jayne-peters-after-killing-daughter/.

17. "Texas Mayor Shot Daughter From Behind, Then Killed Herself, Autopsy Shows," Fox News, November 21, 2015, https://www.foxnews.com/us/

texas-mayor-shot-daughter-from-behind-then-killed-herself-autopsy-shows.
18. "Autopsy Report—Jayne Peters," http://www.autopsyfiles.org/reports/Other/peters,%20jayne_report.pdf.
19. "Autopsy Report—Corinne Peters," http://www.autopsyfiles.org/reports/Other/peters,%20corinne_report.pdf.
20. P.J. Resnick, "Filicide in the United States," *Indian J Psychiatry* 58(Suppl 2): (2016) S203-S209.
21. C. Paradis, "Did Jayne Peters kill her daughter?" *Psychology Today*, August 17, 2010, https://www.psychologytoday.com/us/blog/the-measure-madness/201008/did-jayne-peters-kill-her-daughter.
22. D.J. Papapietro and E. Barbo, "Commentary: toward a psychodynamic understanding of filicide—beyond psychosis and into the heart of darkness," *J Am Acad Psychiatry Law* 33(4): (2005) 505-508.
23. S.H. Friedman, D.R. Hrouda, and C.E. Holden, et al., "Filicide-suicide: common factors in parents who kill their children and themselves," *J Am Acad Psychiatry Law* 33(4): (2005) 496-504.

13. *Antonio Pettigrew*

1. "St. Aug's grad, gold-medal sprinter Antonio Pettigrew dies," WRAL, original published date August 10, 2010, last updated August 11, 2010, https://www.wralsportsfan.com/olympics/story/8111537/.
2. R. Goldstein, "Antonio Pettigrew, Sprinter Who Doped, Dies at 42," *The New York Times*, August 11, 2010, https://www.nytimes.com/2010/08/12/sports/12pettigrew.html.
3. A. Beard, "College Track Coach and Former Olympian Antonio Pettigrew Found Dead," August 10, 2010, https://www.diverseeducation.com/sports/article/15089824/college-track-coach-and-former-olympian-antonio-pettigrew-found-dead.
4. "Autopsy: Antonio Pettigrew overdosed," ESPN, October 13, 2010, https://www.espn.com/olympics/trackandfield/news/story?id=5682180.

5. "Pettigrew autopsy reveals suicide," October 13, 2010, https://www.theglobeandmail.com/sports/more-sports/pettigrew-autopsy-reveals-suicide/article1214833/.
6. G. Cherry, "Former world champ Pettigrew died of overdose-autopsy," *Reuters*, October 13, 2010, https://www.reuters.com/article/idINIndia-52170920101013.
7. "Autopsy Report—Antonio Pettigrew," http://www.autopsyfiles.org/reports/Other/pettigrew,%20antonio_report.pdf.
8. R.C. Baselt, "Diphenhydramine," in Disposition of Toxic Drugs and Chemicals in Man, 10th ed., (Seal Beach, California: Biomedical Publications, pp 684-687 (2014).
9. "Pettigrew autopsy reveals suicide," The Globe and Mail, October 13, 2010, https://www.theglobeandmail.com/sports/more-sports/pettigrew-autopsy-reveals-suicide/article1214833/.
10. "Antonio Pettigrew: Sprinter who was stripped of his 1999 World Championship and 2000 Olympic relay gold medals," the *Independent*, August 12, 2010, https://www.independent.co.uk/news/obituaries/antonio-pettigrew-sprinter-who-was-stripped-of-his-1999-world-championship-and-2000-olympic-relay-gold-medals-2049986.html.
11. "Antonio Pettigrew found dead," ESPN, August 10, 2010, https://www.espn.com/olympics/trackandfield/news/story?id=5452124.
12. E. Denman, "Remembering Antonio Pettigrew," National Scholastic, August 16, 2010, https://www.nationalscholastic.org/article/900.
13. "Antonio Pettigrew," https://goheels.com/sports/track-and-field/roster/coaches/antonio-pettigrew/596.
14. J. Rawling, "Antonio Pettigrew obituary," August 11, 2010, *The Guardian*, https://www.theguardian.com/sport/2010/aug/11/antonio-pettigrew-obituary.
15. D. Mackay, "Drugs cheat Antonio Pettigrew found dead in car," August 10, 2010, https://www.insidethegames.biz/articles/10271/antonio-pettigrew-found-dead-in-car.
16. "Benadryl," Ohio History Central, https://ohiohistorycentral.org/w/Benadryl#.

17. "Benadryl Overdose Treatment," Missouri Poison Center, March 7, 2016, https://missouripoisoncenter.org/diphenhydramine/.
18. D.A. Huynh, M. Abbas, and A. Dabaja, "Diphenhydramine Toxicity," May 8, 2022, https://www.ncbi.nlm.nih.gov/books/NBK558578/.
19. V. Forster, "Teen Dies after Doing TikTok 'Benadryl Challenge' As Doctors Warn Of Dangers," *Forbes*, September 2, 2020, https://www.forbes.com/sites/victoriaforster/2020/09/02/teen-dies-after-doing--tiktok-benadryl-challengeas-doctors-warn-of-dangers/?sh=20a72395f0db.
20. "Morbidity and Mortality Weekly Report," Centers for Disease Control and Prevention, 71(41): (October 14, 2022) 1308-1310.
21. "Allergy meds in street opioids make overdoses more deadly," October 13, 2022, https://medicalxpress.com/news/2022-10-allergy-meds-street-opioids-overdoses.html.
22. A.M. Kang, "Substances involved in suicidal poisonings in the United States," *Suicide Life Threat Behav* 49(5): (2019) 1307-1317.
23. H.A. Spiller, J.P. Ackerman, G.A. Smith, et al., "Suicide attempts by self-poisoning in the United States among 10-25 year olds from 2000 to 2018: substances used, temporal changes and demographics," *Clin Toxicol (Phila)* 58(7): (2020) 676-687.
24. P.J. Oyekan, H.C. Gordon and C.S. Copeland, "Antihistamine-related deaths in England: Are the high safety profiles of antihistamines leading to their unsafe use?" *Br J Clin Pharmacol* 87(10): (2021) 3978-3987.
25. T. Nishino, S. Wakai, H. Aoki, et al., "Cardiac arrest caused by diphenhydramine overdose," *Acute Med Surg* 5(4): (2018) 380-383.
26. "Diphenhydramine toxicity," University of Utah, November 15, 2021, https://poisoncontrol.utah.edu/news/2021/11/diphenhydramine-toxicity.
27. L. Eckes, M. Tsokos, S. Herre, R. Gapert, et al., "Toxicological identification of diphenhydramine (DPH) in suicide," *Forensic Sci Med Pathol* 9: (2013) 145-153.

14. Adrienne Martin

1. "City of Huntleigh," https://www.huntleigh.org/index.html.
2. "Huntleigh Village Homes for Sale," https://www.janetmcafee.com/huntleigh-village-real-estate#.
3. "Ten Wealthiest Neighborhoods in Missouri," https://www.thefinancialword.com/10-wealthiest-neighborhoods-in-missouri/.
4. K. Stoller, "For This Anheuser-Busch Heir, Trouble Followed," *Forbes*, June 21, 2019, https://www.forbes.com/sites/kristinstoller/2019/06/21/for-this-anheuser-busch-heir-trouble-flollowed/?sh=699c4cbb9645.
5. S. Berfield, "Fall of the House of Busch," https://eaee301e-e4f2-4aa6-9749-b2564fc1a00a.filesusr.com/ugd/fa0024_1189ddb3edd74f748e7933c0d847160f.pdf?index=true.
6. "Medical examiner: Woman's death at Busch home accidental," CNN, February 10, 2011, http://www.cnn.com/2011/CRIME/02/09/missouri.death.busch/index.html.
7. "Adrienne Nicole Martin Death Investigation Prompts Controversy," https://news.lalate.com/2010/12/24/adrienne-nicole-martin-death-investigation-prompts-controversy/.
8. "Model, 27, found dead at Missouri home of Busch beer heir," CNN, December 25, 2010, https://www.cnn.com/2010/CRIME/12/23/missouri.busch.death/index.html.
9. "Autopsy Report—Adrienne Martin," and supporting documents, http://www.autopsyfiles.org/reports/Other/martin,%20adrienne_report.pdf.
10. D.K. Molina and V.J.M. DiMaio, "Normal Organ Weights in Women: Part I-The Heart," *Am J Forensic Med Pathol* 36(3): (2015) 176-181.
11. R.C. Baselt, "Cocaine," (*Disposition of Toxic Drugs and Chemicals in Man*, Biomedical Publications, Seal Beach, California, 10th ed., pp 511-515, 2014).
12. R.C. Baselt, "Oxycodone," (*Disposition of Toxic Drugs and Chemicals in Man*, Biomedical Publications, Sa Beach, CA, Tenth Ed., pp 1528-1531, 2014).

13. "Aspiring Model Found Dead in Ex-Busch CEO's Home," CBS News, December 24, 2010, https://www.cbsnews.com/news/aspiring-model-found-dead-in-ex-busch-ceos-home/.
14. "911 Call released after model dies at Busch home," NBC News, December 27, 2010, htttps://www.nbcnews.com/id/wbna40816270.
15. "Adrienne Martin Obituary," https://www.legacy.com/us/obituaries/news-leader-name/adrienne-martin-obituary?id=26902048.
16. "Adrienne Nicole Martin," https://www.onemodelpiece.com/models/adrienne-nicole-martin.
17. J. Salter, "Beer heir is in the headlines after woman dies," the *San Diego Union Tribune*, December 24, 2010, https://www.sandiegouniontribune.com/sdut-beer-heir-is-in-the-headlines-after-woman-dies-2010dec24-story.html.
18. C. Carter, "The 2010 Busch IV Scandal: More on Adrienne Martin's Possible Heart Condition," St. Louis, December 30, 2010, https://www.stlmag.com/news/The-2010-Busch-IV-Scandal-More-on-Adrienne-Martin-039s-Possible-Heart-Condition/.
19. M. Roper, "Budweiser's final heir and the mystery death of his model lover," *The Mirror*, original published date January 4, 2011, last updated January 26, 2012, https://www.mirror.co.uk/news/uk-news/budweisers-final-heir-and-the-mystery-death-102047.
20. August Busch IV," https://kidadl.com/famous-people-facts/august-busch-iv.
21. "Busch, August IV," https://beerandbrewing.com/dictionary/Cd92zGLNQp/.
22. M.D. Sorkin and L. Gayle, "May 31, 1985: August Busch IV leads cops on a wild chase through the Central West End," *St. Louis Today*, May 31, 2022, https://www.stltoday.com/news/archives/may-31-1985-august-busch-iv-leads-cops-on-a-wild-chase-through-the-central/article_1ecd55b6-3c62-515a-9d11-5dda18f010e8.html.
23. F. Britney, "Adrienne N. Martin Dead: August Busch IV Girlfriend," *The Hollywood Gossip*, February 12, 2015, https://www.thehollywoodgossip.com/bittenandbound/adrienne-n-martin-dead-august-busch-iv-girlfriend-photos/.

24. R.S. Carlock, "Family psychology and competitive advantage," Campden FB, July 21, 2008, https://www.campdenfb.com/article/family-psychology-and-competitive-advantage.
25. "C. Leonard, "A bitter brew to swallow," the *Courier Mail*, January 14, 2011, https://www.couriermail.com.au/ipad/a-bitter-brew/news-story/a3a2722347d3fdce1107395fc2a5d648.

15. Michael Faherty

1. "Death of Michael Faherty: Spontaneous Human Combustion Victim," June 28, 2019, https://www.soulask.com/death-of-michael-faherty-spontaneous-human-combustion-victim/.
2. "Death of Michael Faherty," https://en-academic.com/dic.ns/enwiki/11625749.
3. B. McDonald, "Man dies from spontaneous human combustion, inquest finds," the *Independent*, September 23, 2011, https://www.independent.ie/irish-news/man-died-from-spontaneous-human-combustion-inquest-finds/26774631.html.
4. M. Blake, "Spontaneous combustion killed pensioner, rules coroner," the *Independent*, September 24, 2011, https://www.independent.co.uk/news/uk/home-news/spontaneous-combustion-killed-pensioner-rules-coroner-2360082.html.
5. J. Housden, "Michael Faherty, Irish Pensioner, Dies Of Spontaneous Combustion," the *Huffington Post*, original published date September 23, 2011, last updated November 23, 2011, https://www.huffingtonpost.co.uk/2011/09/23/michael-faherty-irish-pen_n_977436.html.
6. "Solving the mystery of human spontaneous combustion," Lab News, November 8, 2011, https://www.labnews.co.uk/article/2027958/solving_the_mystery_of_human_spontaneous_combustion.
7. E. Barclay, "To Die or Not to Die from Spontaneous Combustion," National Public Radio, September 23, 2011, https://www.npr.org/sections/health-shots/2011/09/23/140738719/to-die-or-not-to-die-from-spontaneous-combustion.

8. J. Fallon, "Court finds pensioner's death in fire caused by spontaneous combustion," the *Irish Times*, September 23, 2011, https://www.irishtimes.com/news/court-finds-pensioner-s-death-in-fire-caused-by-spontaneous-combustion-1.606542.
9. H. McDonald, "Man died by spontaneous combustion: coroner," the *Sydney Morning Herald*, September 26, 2011, https://www.smh.com.au/world/man-died-by-spontaneous-combustion-coroner-20110926-1ksm4.html.
10. "'First Irish case' of death by spontaneous combustion," BBC, September 23, 2011, https://www.bbc.com/news/world-europe-15032614.
11. "OAP dies of 'spontaneous human combustion' in his sitting room," the *Daily Mail*, September 23, 2011, https://www.dailymail.co.uk/news/article-2041099/Spontaneous-human-combustion-Galway-OAP-killed-Irelands-recordded-case.html.
12. K. Gander, "Spontaneous Human Combustion: Five apparent instances that no one can explain," the *Independent*, November 5, 2015, https://www.independent.co.uk/life-style/health-and-families/features/spontaneous-human-combustion-woman-who-suffered-burns-in-germany-spurs-debate-about-controversial-phenomenon-a6722166.html.
13. B.J. Ford, "Solving the mystery of human spontaneous combustion," Lab News, November 8, 2011, https://www.labnews.co.uk/article/2027958/solving_the_mystery_of_human_spontaneous_combustion.
14. "Is spontaneous human combustion real?" History, original published date February 6, 2013, last updated May 23, 2023, https://www.history.com/news/is-spontaneous-human-combustion-real.
15. G. Calise, "Spontaneous combustion in St. Petersburg? The curious case of Mary Reeser," the *Tampa Bay Times*, original published date October 17, 2019, last updated October 27, 2019, https://www.tampabay.com/news/florida/2019/10/17/spontaneous-combustion-in-st-petersburg-the-curious-case-of-mary-reeser/.

16. "Spontaneous Human Combustion: Has The Mystery Been Solved?" August 23, 2012, https://www.ghosttheory.com/2012/08/23/spontaneous-human-combustion-has-the-mystery-been-solved.
17. D.M. West, "Up in Flames: Spontaneous Human Combustion," June 15, 2015, http://halloweenforevermore.com/up-in-flames-spontaneous-human-combustion-2/.
18. B. Radford, "Coroner Concludes Irishman Died of Spontaneous Human Combustion," *Live Science*, December 7, 2021, https://www.livescience.com/16215-spontaneous-human-combustion-real.html.
19. T.W. Levi-Faict and G. Quatrehomme, "So-called spontaneous human combustion," *J Forensic Sci* 56(5): (2011) 1334-1339.
20. "Does spontaneous human combustion exist?" BBC News, November 21, 2005, https://www.news.bbc.co.uk/2/hi/uk_news/magazine/4456428.stm.
21. "Spontaneous Human Combustion Strikes Again," January 6, 2018, https://thehauntedlibrarian.com/tag/michael-faherty/.
22. B.J. Ford, "The big burn theory," *New Scientist*, (2012) 30-31.
23. "Burn baby burn: human spontaneous combustion explained," https://cartesianproduct.wordpress.com/2012/08/17/burn-baby-burn-human-spontaneous-combustion-explained.
24. V. Kolijonen and N. Kluger, "Spontaneous human combustion in the light of the 21st century," *J Burn Care Res* 33(3): (2012) e101-e107.
25. L. Adelson, "Spontaneous Human Combustion and Preternatural Combustibility," *J Criminal Law and Criminology* 42(6): March-April (1952).
26. G. Thurston, "Preternatural combustibility of the human body," *Med Leg J* 29: (1961) 100-103.
27. B.J. Ford, "Solving the Mystery of Spontaneous Human Combustion," *The Microscope*, 60(2): (2012) 63-72.
28. "Brian J. Ford Biography," https://www.brianjford.com/wcvgen.htm.

16. Ellen Greenberg

1. "'It was very, very weird': A civil suit reveals new details in the case of Ellen Greenberg, whose death by 20 stab wounds was ruled suicide," the *Philadelphia Inquirer*, https://www.inquirer.com/news/philadelphia/ellen-greenberg-suicide-homicide-lawsuit-philadelphia-20220324.html.
2. "Juniata Park Academy," https://juniatapark.philasd.org/.
3. "Manayunk teacher death ruled 'suspicious,'" 6ABC, January 30, 2011, https://6abc.com/archive/7926882/.
4. J. Lipscomb, "A woman with 20 stab wounds died of suicide, an autopsy found. Her parents are unconvinced: 'It makes no sense.'" *The Washington Post*, October 27, 2021, https://www.washingtonpost.com/nation/2021/10/27/ellen-greenberg-suicide-stabbing/.
5. "Investigation Report," Office of the Medical Examiner, City of Philadelphia, https://s.3.documentcloud.org/documents/575959550/Me-Inv-RPT.pdf.
6. "Marlon Osbourne, M.D., and Philadelphia County Medical Examiner's Office, Appellants, vs. Joshua M. Greenberg, DMD, and Sandra Greenberg, as the Administrators of the Estate of Ellen R. Greenberg, deceased, Appellees, Trial Court Docket No. 191001241," https://media.nbcphiladelphia.com/2022/06/Philadelphia-Court-of-Common-Pleas-Ellen-Greenberg-Case.pdf.
7. J. Sederstrom, "Death of Ellen Greenberg, Which Was Ruled a Suicide after She Was Found with 20 Stab Wounds, To Get New Look," Oxygen, September 2, 2022, https://www.oxygen.com/crime-news/ellen-greenbergs-2011-death-to-be-re-examined-by-chester-county-da.
8. A. Cavallier, "Parents of Ellen Greenberg believe new evidence submitted to the Philadelphia Attorney General's Office will prove their daughter's 2011 death was murder, not suicide," NBC News, December 26, 2021, https://www.nbcnews.com/dateline/cold-case-spotlight/parents-ellen-greenberg-believe-new-evidence-submitted-philadelphia-attorney-general-n1286606.

9. S. Farr, "A locked-room mystery," *The Philadelphia Inquirer*, May 25, 2019, the *Philadelphia Inquirer*, https://www.inquirer.com/crime/a/ellen-greenberg-death-suicide-homicide-philadelphia-mystery-20190316.html
10. A. Kippert, "Ellen Greenberg's Mysterious Death: Could Someone Be Capable of Stabbing Themselves 20 Times?" original published date January 18, 2022, last updated November 17, 2022, https://www.aetv.com/real-crime/ellen-greenberg-death
11. Ichchha, "Was Ellen Greenberg Death a Murder or Suicide? Case Update," December 12, 2022, https://geniuscelebs.com/ellen-greenberg-death-murder-or-suicide/.
12. "Autopsy report—Ellen Greenberg," https://s3.documentcloud.org/documents/5759528/Autopsy-RPT.pdf.
13. C.H. Hecht, "Expert Report," January 11, 2012.
14. C. Morgan, "Ellen Greenberg 'suicide': Pennsylvania court hears arguments in family's motion to override coroner," *US Today*, November 16, 2022, https://ustodaynews/ellen-greenberg-suicide-pennsylvania-court-hears-arguments-in-familys-motion-to-override-coroner/.
15. M. Jankowicz, "Parents sue officials over ruling that their daughter's death by more than 20 stab wounds was a suicide," the *Insider*, October 27, 2021, https://www.insider.com/parents-challenge-suicide-ruling-woman-who-died-20-stab-wounds-2021-10.
16. R. Raven, "DA Reopens Case of Teacher Found with 20 Stab Wounds Whose Death Was Ruled a Suicide," September 9, 2022, https://www.investigationdiscovery.com/crime/feed/news/da-reopens-case-of-teacher-found-with-20-stab-wounds-whose-death-was-ruled-a-suicide.
17. Email, J. Grace to S. Farr, March 8, 2019. "Re: Media request - Ellen Greenberg case."
18. M. Ruiz, "Ellen Greenberg 'suicide': Pennsylvania court hears arguments in family's bid to overrule medical examiner," Fox News, November 16, 2022, https://www.foxnews.com/us/

ellen-greenberg-suicide-pennsylvania-court-hears-arguments-familys-bid-overrule-medical-examiner.

19. "Ellen Greenberg 'suicide': Philadelphia teacher 'excited' about life, never spoke of self-harm, friend says," September 2, 2022, https://www.wgmd.com/ellen-greenberg-suicide-philadelphia-teacher-excited-about-life-never-spoke-of-self-harm-friend-says/.

20. V. Serna, "Friend of Philadelphia teacher, 27, whose 2011 'suicide' death is now being reinvestigated as a murder reveals she missed a call from her before she was stabbed 20 times," the *Daily Mail*, September 2, 2022, https://www.dailymail.co.uk/news/article-11173629/Friend-woman-suicide-reinvestigated-missed-call-died.html.

21. R. Eldredge, "Suicide or homicide? Ellen Greenberg's death remains controversial as case heads to court," Local 21 News, October 14, 2021, https://local21news.com/news/local/suicide-or-homicide-case-heads-to-court#

22. F. Ventura, A. Bonsignore, M. Gallo, and F. Portunato, "A fatal case of suicidal stabbing and cutting," *J Forensic Leg Med* 17(3): (2010) 120-122.

23. M. Kaliszan, G. Kernbach-Wighton, R. Bouhaidar, "Multiple self-inflicted stab wounds to neck, chest and abdomen as a unique manner of suicide," *J Forensic Sci.* 55(3): (2010) 822-825.

24. B. Karger and B. Vennemann, "Suicide by more than 90 stab wounds including perforation of the skull," *Int J Legal Med* 115(3): (2001) 167-169.

25. K. Lieske, K. Puschel, and E. Bussmann, "Suicide by 120 stab wounds of the chest," *Arch Kriminol* 180(5-6): (1987) 143-149.

26. S. Srisont, A.V.M. Vichan Peonim, and T. Chirachariyavej, "An autopsy case report of suicide by multiple self-cutting and self-stabbing over the chest and neck," *J Med Assoc Thai* 92(6): (2009) 861-864.

27. M. Kaliszan, K. Karnecki, E. Tomczak, T. Gos, et al., "Complex suicide by self-stabbing with subsequent drowning in the sea," *J Forensic Sci* 58(5): (2013) 1370-1373.

28. P-A. Peyron, T. Casper, O. Mathieu, Y. Musizzano, et al., "Complex suicide by self-stabbing and drowning: A case report and a review of literature," *J Forensic Sci* 63(2): (2018) 598-601.
29. M. Bohnert, D. Ropohl, and S. Pollak, "Suicidal stab wounds through clothing," *Arch Kriminol* 200(1-2): (1997) 31-38.
30. G. Viel, G. Cecchetto, and M. Montisci, "An unusual case of suicide by sharp force," *Forensic Sci Int* 184(1-3): (2009) e-12-15.
31. "Highland Park man who stabbed himself to death had taken sleep aid," Dallas News, August 24, 2012, https://www.dallasnews.com/news/2012/08/25/highland-park-man-who-stabbed-himself-to-death-had-taken-sleep-aid/.
32. "Zolpidem" product monograph, https://www.accessdata.fda.gov/drugsatfda_docs/label/2008/019908s027lbl.pdf.
33. H.C. Lee and E.M. Pagliaro, "Expert Report," January 29, 2018.

17. Russell Armstrong

1. T. Molloy, "Russell Armstrong's attorney: 'He wasn't rich,'" *Reuters*, August 17, 2011, https://www.reuters.com/article/us-russellarmstrong/russell-armstrongs-attorney-he-wasnt-rich-idUSTRE77H03B20110818.
2. A. Hawks, "RHOBH Taylor's husband Russell Armstrong's criminal past," January 27, 2011, https://starcasm.net/rhobh-taylors-husband-russell-armstrongs-criminal-past/.
3. "American Television Personality Taylor Armstrong," https://peoplepill.com/people/taylor-armstrong.
4. S. Dawson, "What Happened to Taylor Armstrong —what's the Real Housewives Star Doing Now?" *Gazette Review*, https://gazettereview.com/2017/09/happened-taylor-armstrong-whats-real-housewifes-star-now/.
5. N. Finn and C. Rosenbaum, "Timeline of a Tragedy: Real Housewives' Russell Armstrong Was 'Always Depressed,'" August 16, 2015, https://www.eonline.com/news/258422/timeline-of-a-tragedy-real-housewives-russell-armstrong-was-always-depressed.

6. G. Serpe, "Real Housewives of Beverly Hills' Russell Armstrong Found Dead of Apparent Suicide," August 16, 2011, https://www.eonline.com/news/258331/real-housewives-of-beverly-hills-russell-armstrong-found-dead-of-apparent-suicide.
7. "Taylor Armstrong Denies Russell's Sister's Claims That Abuse Never Happened On 'Watch What Happens Live'," the *Huff Post*, February 8, 2012, https://www.huffpost.com/entry/watch-what-happens-live-taylor-armstrong-video_n_1262009.
8. A. Hawks, "Real Housewives of Beverly Hills' Russell Armstrong commits suicide by hanging," August 16, 2011, https://starcasm.net/real-housewives-of-beverly-hills-russell-armstrong-commits-suicide-by-hanging/.
9. M. Garvey and S. Drury, "Coroner: Russell Armstrong Dead for More than a Day Before Body Found," https://www.eonline.com/news/258899/coroner_russell_armstrong_dead_more_day
10. N. Stone, "RHOBH's Taylor Armstrong Reveals What Her Daughter Thinks of Dad Russell 8 Years after Suicide," *People*, March 18, 2019, https://people.com/tv/rhobh-taylor-armstrong-ex-husband-russell-suicide-daughter-memory/.
11. "'Real Housewives' husband dead in probable suicide," *Times News*, August 15, 2011, https://www.timesnews.net/living/arts-entertainment/real-housewives-husband-dead-in-probable-suicide/article_0b9dc1aa-4be4-5c12-b1d3-42e43b34d670.html.
12. "Autopsy report—Russell Armstrong," http://www.autopsyfiles.org/reports/Other/armstrong,%20russell_report.pdf.
13. M. Cohut, "What happens to the body after death?" *Medical News Today*, May 11, 2018, https://www.medicalnewstoday.com/articles/321792.
14. D.K. Molina and V.J.M. DiMaio, "Normal organ weight sin men: part I—the heart," *Am J Forensic Med Pathol* 33(4): (2012) 362-367.
15. D.K. Molina and V.J.M. DiMaio, "Normal organ weights in men: part II—the brain, lungs, liver, spleen, and kidneys," *Am J Forensic Med Pathol* 33(4): (2012) 368-372.

16. N. Charoonnate, P. Narongchai, and S. Vongvaivet, "Fractures of the hyoid bone and thyroid cartilage in suicidal hanging," *J Med Assoc Thai* 93(10): (2010) 1211-1216.
17. H. K. Afridi, M. Yousaf, et al., "In Strangulation Deaths: Forensic Significance of Hyoid Bone Fracture," *Pakistan J Med Health Sci* 8(2) (2014): 376–78.
18. H. Green, R. A. James, et al., "Fractures of the hyoid bone and laryngeal cartilages in suicidal hanging," *J Clin Forensic Med* 7(3) (2000): 123–26.
19. "Obituary—Russell Lynn Armstrong," the *Dallas Morning News*, September 1, 2011, https://obits.dallasnews.com/us/obituaries/dallasmorningnews/name/russell-armstrong-obituary?id=22048562.
20. "911 Call from Real Housewives Husband Russell Armstrong's Suicide Released," *Inside Edition*, original published date August 29, 2011, last updated August 30, 2011, https://www.insideedition.com/2964-911-call-from-real-housewives-husband-russell-armstrongs-suicide-released.
21. J. Ortiz, "TMZ Released Heartbreaking 911 Call Reporting 'Real Housewives' Star Russell Armstrong Suicide," *Business Insider*, August 30, 2011, https://www.businessinsider.com/russell-armstrong-suicide-911-call-tmz-2011-8.
22. D. Rieselman, "Reality TV: Is it for real?" *UC* magazine, https://magazine.uc.edu/issues/1210/reality-tv.html.
23. T. DeVolld, "Five myths about reality television," *The Washington Post*, April 19, 2019, https://www.washingtonpost.com/outlook/five-myths/five-myths-about-reality-television/2019/04/19/fdab858c-6125-11e9-9ff2-abc984dc9eec_story.html.
24. R. Hines, "'Bachelor' creator claims '70 to 80 percent' of reality TV is fake," Today, June 15, 2012, https://www.today.com/popculture/bachelor-creator-claims-70-80-percent-reality-tv-fake-829943.
25. C. Blair, "Bravo Producers Reveal How Staged the 'Real Housewives' is," June 1, 2021, https://heavy.com/entertainment/real-housewives/real-housewives-staged-scripted-is/.

26. L. Nas, "10 Things on The Real Housewives that are Totally Fake (And 10 Real)," January 14, 2020, https://www.thethings.com/real-housewives-totally-fake/.
27. T. Kenneally, "The 'Real Housewives' Legacy of Marital Destruction and Financial Ruin," *Reuters*, August 16, 2011, https://www.reuters.com/article/dUS190241744620110816.
28. S. Hearson, "Reality TV Curse: Every 'Real Housewives' Couple Who Filed for Divorce after Appearing on TV," *US*, May 17, 2022, https://www.usmagazine.com/entertainment/pictures/every-real-housewives-couple-who-filed-for-divorce/.
29. J. Nolfi, "The Real Housewives of Potomac star Ashley Darby splits from husband Michael Darby over 'different goals,'" *Entertainment Weekly*, April 20, 2022, https://ew.com/tv/real-housewives-potomac-ashley-darby-splits-husband-michael-darby/.
30. D. Schuster, "Dying for fame: 21 reality stars committed suicide in a decade," the *New York Post*, February 28, 2016, https://nypost.com/2016/02/28/dying-for-fame-21-reality-stars-commit-suicide-in-past-decade/.
31. L. Fisher and D. Praetorius, "Breakdowns, Suicides: The Dark Side of Reality TV," ABC News, June 2, 2009, https://abcnews.go.com/Entertainment/Television/story?id=7739393.
32. A. Bennett, "Russell Armstrong's business associate commits suicide just 24 hours after Real Housewives star found dead," the *Daily Mail*, August 27, 2011, https://www.dailymail.co.uk/tvshowbiz/article-2030818/Russell-Armstrong-dead-Business-associate-Alan-Schram-commits-suicide.html.
33. J. La Roche, "Hedge Fund Manager Commits Suicide Day after His Friend, Late 'Real Housewives' Husband," the *Business Insider*, August 30, 2011, https://www.businessinsider.com/alan-schram-suicide-russell-armstrong-2011-8.

18. Katherine Morris

1. D. Andersen, "Police re-open 'suicide' case of wife who was heartbroken after she discovered 'soldier husband only wed her for Army benefits and was sleeping with other women,'" the *Daily Mail*, November 27, 2013, https://www.dailymail.co.uk/news/article-2510760/Police-open-suicide-woman-heartbroken-cheating-soldier-husband-wed-Army-benefits.html.
2. "Army Specialist Isaac Goodwin allegedly marries for money, and his wife commits suicide," https://lovefraud.com/true-lovefraud-stories/isaac-goodwin/.
3. "Army Spouse Katherine Morris Found Dead in Car Near Mall; Cause of Death Initially Ruled Suicide But Further Investigation Suggests Homicide Motivated by Insurance Fraud, May 6, 2012, https://militaryjusticeforall.com/tag/isaac-goodwin/.
4. D. Belson, "Questions linger for Anne Arundel Pastor after Judge's Ruling to Overturn Cause of Daughter's 2012 Death," the *Capital Gazette*, October 2, 2022, https://www.capitalgazette.com/news/ac-cn-morris-death-folo-20221002-iyvpwycyqvdfnevjiqoe6e4crm-story.html.
5. "Proposed Decision, Statement of the Case, Issues, Summary of the Evidence, Findings of Fact, Discussion, Conclusions of Law, Proposed Order," Marguerite Morris, Appellant, v. Office of the Chief Medical Examiner, Maryland Department of Health, https://drive.google.com/file/d/1CTxqWmRY89p3oON0habebjSydN-XgoqF/view.
6. Anne Arundel County Police Department Investigative Report dated June 25, 2012 and supporting documents, https://uploads.documents.cimpress.io/v1/uploads/aefbf4b3-a55f-4c0f-96ec-2b0c104eef19~110/original?tenant=vbu-digital.
7. S. Tschida, "Only on 7: Army investigates allegation soldier drove UMd student to suicide," WJLA, May 24, 2012, https://wjla.com/news/local/only-on-7-army-ivestigates-allegation-soldier-drove-student-to-suicide-76321.

8. Letter dated June 7, 2009 from Dr. Lee Ann Grossberg, Forensic Pathology Consultation Services, P.A. to Dr. David R. Fowler, Chief Medical Examiner and Patricia Aronica-Pollak, Assistant Medical Examiner, State of Maryland Office of the Chief Medical Examiner.
9. "Fort Bragg soldier accused of fraud after wife's suicide," WRAL, May 23, 2012, https://www.wral.com/news/local/story/11134297/.
10. Anne Arundel County Police Crime Laboratory Report and Crime Scene Unit Supplemental Report, https://uploads.documents.cimpress.io/v1/uploads/0f5a2c33-2177-43c7-a902-706ab1778f4d~110/original?tenant=vbu-digital.
11. "A Mother's Quest When Your Child's dying," https://forkathyssake.com/a-mother-s-journey-for -justice.
12. "Autopsy Report—Katherine Sarah Morris" and Toxicology Report, https://uploads.documents.cimpress.io/v1/uploads/215a62c2-b750-48ec-871a-cbe809ab6014~110/original?tenant=vbu-digital.
13. C. Winder, "Carbon monoxide-induced death and toxicity from charcoal briquettes," *Med J Aust* 197(6): (2012) 349-350.
14. "Carbon Monoxide (Blood)," the University Of Rochester Medical Center, https://www.urmc.rochester.edu/encyclopedia/content.aspx?contenttypeid=167&contentid=carbon_monoxide_blood.
15. C. Velasques, T. Patchana, B. McParland, J. Lovy, et al., "Carbon Monoxide Poisoning: The Great Imitator," *Spartan Med Res* J 2(1): (2017) 6343.
16. Y. Nouma, "Carbon monoxide suicide by charcoal-burning: a case report and review of the literature," *Pan Afr Med J* 40: (2021) 190.
17. R.C. Baselt, "Diphenhydramine," (*Disposition of Toxic Drugs and Chemicals in Man*, Biomedical Publications, Seal Beach, California, 10th Ed., pp 684-687, 2014).
18. T. Nishino, S. Wakai, H. Aoki, and S. Inokuchi, "Cardiac arrest caused by diphenhydramine overdose," *Acute Med. Surg* 5(4): (2018) 380-383.
19. "Diphenhydramine" product monograph, https://www.drugs.com/monograph/diphenhydramine.html#dosage.

20. L. Eckes, M. Tsokos, S. Herre, R. Gapert, et al., "Toxicological identification of diphenhydramine (DPH) in suicide," *Forensic Sci Med Pathol* 9: (2013) 145-153.
21. "Medical Examiners' and Coroners' Handbook on Death Registration and Fetal Death Reporting," US Centers for Disease Control and Prevention, 2003 Revision, https://www.cdc.gov/nchs/data/misc/hb_me.pdf.
22. "Postmortem Examination Types," DC Office of the Chief Medical Examiner, Standard Operation Procedures, January 5, 2015, https://ocme.dc.gov/sites/default/files/dc/sites/ocme/service_content/attachments/Postmortem%20Examination%20Types.PDF.
23. A.R. Moritz, "Classical mistakes in forensic pathology," *Am J of Forensic Med and Pathol* 2(4): (1981) 299-308.
24. M.G.F. Gilliland, "What Good are Partial Autopsies?" *Sage Journals* 5(3), September 1, 2015.
25. "Kanae Kijima," Japan Innocence & Death Penalty Information Center, April 13, 2012, https://www.jiadep.org/Kijima_Kanae.html.
26. "Kanae Kijima," https://murderpedia.org/female.K/k/kijima-kanae.htm.
27. "Katherine Sarah Morris," https://www.legacy.com/us/obituaries/capitalgazette/name/katherine-morris-obituary?id=17774852.
28. "Katherine Sarah Morris," https://somd.com/announcements/obits/name/6155-Katherine-Sarah-Morris.html.
29. "Suicide," The National Institute of Mental Health, https://www.nimh.nih.gov/health/statistics/suicide.
30. N. Cobb and R.A. Etzel, "Unintentional carbon monoxide-related deaths in the United States, 1979 through 1988," *JAMA* 266(5): (1991) 659-633.
31. S-S. Chang, Y-Y Chen, P.S.F. Yip, W.J. Lee, et al., "Regional changes in charcoal-burning suicide rates in East/Southeast Asia from 1995 to 2011: a time trend analysis," *PLoS Med* 11(4): (2014) e1001622.
32. "Non-Fire Carbon Monoxide Deaths Associated with the Use of Consumer Products, 2016 Annual Estimates," US Consumer Product Safety Commission, September 2019, https://www.cpsc.

gov/s3fs-public/Non-Fire%20Carbon%20Monoxide%20Deaths%20 Associated%20with%20the%20Use%20of%20Consumer%20 Prod ... pdf.

33. N.B. Hampson, "U.S. Mortality Due to Carbon Monoxide Poisoning, 1999-2014, Accidental and Intentional Deaths," *Ann Am Thorac Soc* 13(10): (2016) 1768-1774.

34. L. Biddle, J. Donovan, K. Hawton, N. Kapur, et al., "Suicide and the Internet," *BMJ* 336(7648): (2008) 800-802.

35. P.J. Laberke, H. Bock, V. Dittmann, and R. Hausmann, "Forensic and psychiatric aspects of joint suicide with carbon monoxide," *Forensic Sci Med Pathol* 7(4): (2011) 341-343.

36. "Carbon Monoxide Poisoning," https://www.hopkinsmedicine.org/health/conditions-and-diseases/carbon-monoxide-poisoning.

37. L.M. Przepyszny and A.J. Jenkins, "The prevalence of drugs in carbon monoxide-related deaths: a retrospective study, 2000-2003," *Am J Forensic Med Pathol* 28(3): (2007) 242-248.

38. "Anne Arundel County Police Department Inter-Office Correspondence from Sergeant J. Poole to Chief Kevin Davis," February 7, 2014.

39. H.A. Milman, "Natalie Wood," (*Forensics: The Science Behind the Deaths of Famous People*, pp 73-84, Xlibris, 2020).

19. Elisa Lam

1. V. Montalti, "The infamous Cecil Hotel, where at least 16 people have died, recently reopened—here's it's history and what it's like today," the *Insider*, March 9, 2022, https://www.insider.com/cecil-hotel-history-what-its-like-today-photos-2022-3.

2. K. Serena, "The Chilling History of Murder and Hauntings inside Los Angeles' Cecil Hotel," original published date December 11, 2021, last updated December 16, 2021, https://allthatsinteresting.com/cecil-hotel-los-angeles.

3. "Elisa Lam: The Full Story of her Mysterious Death, Complete Info!" December 25, 2021, https://www.techstry.net/elisa-lam/.

4. C. Ponti, "Murder, Suicide or Accident? The Chilling Mystery of Elisa Lam's Death," original published date February 10, 2021, last updated January 7, 2022, https://www.aetv.com/real-crime/death-of-elisa-lam.
5. N. Ishak, "The Unsolved Mystery behind the Disturbing Death of Elisa Lam," original published date June 5, 2021, last updated July 10, 2021, https://www.allthatsinteresting.com/elisa-lam-death.
6. R. Fletcher, "Crime Scene: The Vanishing at the Cecil Hotel—the Elisa Lam Case Explained," February 10, 2021, https://www.denofgeek.com/culture/crime-scene-thevanishing-at-the-cecil-hotel-elisa-lam-explained/.
7. "Biography—Elisa Lam," A&E Television Networks, original published date February 9, 2021, last updated February 9, 2021, https://www.biography.com/crime-figure/elisa-lam.
8. "Elisa Lam Biography," https://www.imdb.com/name/nm1546922/bio.
9. L. Veliz, "Tragic Details Found in Elisa Lam's Autopsy Report," March 10, 2022, https://www.grunge.com/706604/tragic-details-found-in-elisa-lams-autopsy-report/.
10. "The Mysterious Death of Elisa Lam," https://museumfacts.co.uk/elisa-lam-death/.
11. B. Verhoeven, "The Vanishing at the Cecil Hotel: 8 Most Shocking Details About the Elisa Lam Case," *The Wrap*, February 10, 2021, https://www.thewrap.com/crime-scene-vanishing-cecil-hotel-elisa-lam-most-shocking-details/.
12. "The Peculiar Death of Elisa Lam," March 25, 2021, https://sites.psu/edu/passionknightly2/2021/03/25/the-peculiar-death-of-elisa-lam/.
13. J. Swann, "Elisa Lam Drowned in a Water Tank Three Years Ago, but the Obsession with Her Death Lives On," October 27, 2015, https://www.vice.com/en/article/3bkmg3/elisa-lam-drowned-in-a-water-tank-two-years-ago-but-the-obsession-with-her-death-lives-on-511.
14. "Autopsy report—Elisa Lam," http://www.autopsyfiles.org/reports/Other/lam,%20elisa_report.pdf.

15. M. Cohut, "What happens to the body after death?" *Medical News Today*, May 11, 2018, https://www.medicalnewstoday.com/articles/321792.

16. "What Causes Anal Swelling and How Can I Treat It?" https://www.healthline.com/health/swollen-anus.

17. D.K. Molina and V.J.M. DiMaio, "Normal Organ Weights in Women: Part II—the Brain, Lungs, Liver, Spleen, and Kidneys," *Am J Forensic Med Pathol* 36(3): (2015) 182-187.

18. J. Huizen and B. Weber, "What is dry drowning and what are the symptoms?" *Medical News Today*, April 29, 2022, https://www.medicalnewstoday.com/articles/323520.

19. C. Yorulmaz, N. Arican, I. Afacan, et al., "Pleural effusion in bodies recovered from water," *Forensic Sci Int* 136(1-3): (2003) 16-21.

20. D.K. Molina and V.J.M. DiMaio, "Normal Organ Weights in Women: Part I—the Heart," *Am J Forensic Med Pathol* 36(3): (2015) 176-181.

21. D.H. Ubelaker, "Hyoid Fracture and Strangulation," *J Forensic Sci* 37(5): (1992) 1216-1222,

22. M.G. Gilliland and R.O. Bost, "Alcohol in decomposed bodies: postmortem synthesis and distribution," *J Forensic Sci* 38(6): (1993) 1266-1274.

23. C. Weiss, "Mayo Clinic Q and A: What is "dry drowning?" the Mayo Clinic, June 23, 2020, https://newsnetwork.mayoclinic.org/discussion/mayo-clinic-q-and-a-what-is-dry-drowning/.

24. "Who is Elisa Lam?" https://elisalampodcast.wordpress.com/tag/pauls-restaurant/.

25. "Ether Fields," etherfields.blogspot.com/2012/01/youre-always-haunted-by-idea-youre.html.

26. A. Romero, "The Vanishing at The Cecil Hotel Ending Reveals What Happened to Elisa Lam—And Another Insidious Twist," February 10, 2021, https://www.refinery29.com/en-us/2021/02/10301000/who-killed-elisa-lam-cecil-hotel-death-drowning.

27. "Bipolar Disorder," The US National Institute of Mental Health, US National Institutes of Health, https://www.nimh.nih.gov/health/topics/bipolar-disorder.
28. T.R. Berigan and J.S. Harazin, "Bupropion-associated Withdrawal Symptoms: A Case Report," *Prim Care Companion J Clin Psychiatry* 1(2): (1999) 50-51.

20. Marco McMillian

1. H. Mohr, "Mississippi town stunned by slaying of openly gay mayoral candidate Marco McMillian," February 28, 2013, https://www.masslive.com/politics/2013/02/mississippi_town_stunned_by_sl.html.
2. "Murder in the Mississippi Delta," *Ebony*, March 4, 2013, https://www.ebony.com/news/murder-in-the-mississippi-delta-459/.
3. C. Robertson and R. Brown, "Coroner Disputes Family's Account of Mississippi Mayoral Candidate's Death," *The New York Times*, March 5, 2013, https://www.nytimes.com/2013/03/06/us/coroner-disputes-familys-account-of-candidates-death.html.
4. "Mississippi mayoral candidate Marco McMillian found dead," March 1, 2013, https://www.news.com/au/world/mississippi-mayoral-candidate-marco-mcmillian-found-dead/news-story/57d5f0dd50fdf83fe23848b36d3d71cf.
5. W.M. Welch, "Man charged in gay mayoral candidate's Miss. Murder," *USA Today*, February 28, 2013, https://www.usatoday.com/story/news/nation/2013/02/28/gay-murder-mississippi-politics/1953187/.
6. M. Basu, "Mysterious Mississippi murder stokes suspicions bred by an ugly past," CNN, July 22, 2013, https://www.cnn.com/2013/07/20/us/mississippi-murder-mystery.
7. A. Hull, "In Mississippi, death of politician Marco McMillian stirs old civil-rights fears," *The Washington Post*, March 8, 2013, https://www.washingtonpost.com/national/in-mississippi-death-of-politician-marco-mcmillian-stirs-old-civil-rights-fears/2013/03/08/5c75cfa4-8762-11e2-9d71-f0feafdd1394_story.html,

8. K. Davies, L. Boyle, and H. Pow, "Mississippi's first gay mayoral candidate, 34, 'was beaten and burned' before his body was found dumped on a riverbank," the *Daily Mail*, March 4, 2013, https://www.dailymail.co.uk/news/article-2288047/Marco-McMillian-Mississippis-gay-mayoral-candidate-34-burned-beaten-dumped-riverbank.html.
9. "Autopsy report—Marco McMillian," https://www.documentcloud.org/documents/698321-autopsy-report-marco-mcmillian.html.
10. "Cymbalta," https://pi.lilly.com/ca/cymbalta-ca-pm.pdf.
11. "Marco McMillian Biography," https://peoplepill.com/people/marco-mcmillian.
12. J. Ross, "Marco McMillian's Life and Death a Test for Civil Rights in the Mississippi Delta," the *Huffington Post*, original published date April 2, 2013, last updated April 8, 2013, https://www.huffpost.com/entry/marco-mcmillian-death-mississippi_n_2962914.
13. "Marco McMillian (1979-2013)," https://www.blackpast.org/african-american-history/mcmillian-marco-1979-2013/.
14. P. Bump, "Murder of Openly Gay, Black Mississippi Candidate Hinges on Riverbank Clues," the *Atlantic*, February 28, 2013, https://www.theatlantic.com/national/archive/2013/02/marco-mcmillian-murder/317858/.
15. "Lawrence Reed Appellant v. State of Mississippi Appellee," Court of Appeals of Mississippi, November 29, 2016, https://caselaw.findlaw.com/ms-court-of-appeals/1755780.html.
16. "Deputy says man confessed to killing Clarksdale mayoral candidate," the *Clarion Ledger*, March 11, 2015, https://www.clarionledger.com/story/news/2015/03/11/clarksdale-mayoral-candidate-murder-trial/70138738/.
17. "Lawrence Reed found guilty in Marco McMillian case," https://wreg.com/news/guilty-verdict-in-marco-mcmillian-case/.
18. "Reed guilty of murder, sentenced to life, in Clarksdale case," the *Dispatch*, March 13, 2015, https://cdispatch.com/news/2015-03-13/reed-guilty-of-murder-sentenced-to-life-in-clarksdale-case/.

19. B. Waldron and A. Castellano, "22-Year-old Charged with Murdering Miss. Politician," ABC News, February 27, 2013, https://abcnews.go.com/US/miss-mayor-candidate-marco-mcmillian-found-dead-/story?id=18614617.

20. R. Brown and T. Williams, "Mississippi Mayoral Candidate Found Dead," *The New York Times*, February 28, 2013, https://www.nytimes.com/2013/03/01/us/marco-mcmillian-mississippi-mayoral-cnadidate-found-dead.html/.

21. J. Ross and L. Shapiro, "Marco McMillian's Death Highlights Mississippi's Slow and Inconsistent Evolution," the *Huff Post*, original published date March 1, 2013, last updated February 2, 2016, https://www.huffpost.com/entry/marco-mcmillian-death-_n_2787438.

22. A. Ohlheiser, "Gay, Black Mayoral Candidate in Mississippi Found Dead, Homicide Suspected," *Slate*, February 28, 2013, https://www.slate.com/news-and-politics/2013/02/marco-mcmillian-death-lgbt-mayoral-candidate-in-darksdale-mississippi-found-dead-after-disappearing.html.

23. "The Matthew Shepard Foundation," https://www.matthewshepard.org/about-us/our-story/.

24. A. Holden, "The Gay/Trains Panic Defense: What It Is, and How to End It," https://www.americanbar.org/groups/crs/publications/member-features/gay-trans-panic-defense/.

25. "LGBTQ+ 'Panic' Defense," https://lgbtqbar.org/programs/advocacy/gay-trans-panic-defense/.

26. W.C. Andersen, "Research Note: Comparing the Gay and Trans Panic Defenses," *Women & Criminal Justice* 32(1-2): (2022) 219-241.

27. J. Compton, "Alleged 'gay panic defense' in Texas murder trial stuns advocates," NBC News, May 2, 2018, https://nbcnews.com/feature/nbc-out-alleged-gay-panic-defense-texas-murder-tria-stuns-advocates-n870571.

28. "Man accused of murdering mayoral candidate: 'I didn't know what his intentions were,'" original published date March 11, 2015, last updated March 12, 2015, https://www.actionnews5.com/

story/28398254/man-accused-of-murdering-mayoral-candidate-i-didnt-know-what-his-intentions-were/.
29. "Murder in Mississippi," PBS, https://www.pbs.org/wgbh/americanexperience/features/freedomsummer-murder/.
30. "Gay/Trans Panic Defense Bans," https://www.lgbtmap.org/equality-maps/panic_defense_bans.

21. George Floyd

1. "911 transcript of call that brought police to George Floyd released," Fox9, May 28, 3030, https://www.fox9.com/news/911-caller-said-man-tried-to-pay-with-fake-bills-appeared-drunk-before-george-floyds-death.
2. "How George Floyd Died and What Happened Next," *The New York Times*, July 29, 2022, https://www.nytimes.com/article/george-floyd.html.
3. "George Floyd: What happened in the final moments of his life," BBC, July 16, 2020, https://www.bbc.com/news/world-us-canada-52861726.
4. E. Hill, A. Tiefenthäler, C. Triebert, D. Jordan, et al., "How George Floyd Was Killed in Police Custody," *The New York Times*, original published date May 31, 2020, last updated January 24, 2022, https://www.nytimes.com/2020/05/31/us/george-floyd-investigation.html.
5. N. Bogel-Burroughs and W. Wright, "Little has been said about the $20 bill that brought officers to the scene," *The New York Times*, April 19, 2021, https://www.nytimes.com/2021/04/19/us/george-floyd-bill-counterfeit.html.
6. T. Richmond, "Who was George Floyd? Unemployed due to coronavirus, he'd moved to Minneapolis for a fresh start," the *Chicago Tribune*, May 28, 2020, https://www.chicagotribune.com/nation-world/ct-nw-george-floyd-biography-20200528-y3l67rrmfnb3dh4x3i5iipneq4-story.html.
7. "Opening Arguments in the George Floyd Murder (Chauvin) Trial," https://www.famous-trials.com/

george-floyd/2718-opening-arguments-in-the-george-floyd-murder-chauvin-trial.

8. "Timeline of the Arrest of George Floyd," https://www.famous-trials.com/george-floyd/2647-timeline-of-the-arrest-of-george-floyd.

9. P. Rizzo, "Testimony: Who is Shawanda Hill and how is she connected to George Floyd," *The Sun*, April 13, 2021, https://www.the-sun.com/news/2693882/who-shawanda-hill-connected-george-floyd/.

10. "Amended Complaint, State of Minnesota vs. Derek Michael Chauvin," https://mncourts.gov/media/High-Profile-Cases/27-CR-20-12646/AmendedComplaint06032020.pdf.

11. "Transcript of Floyd's Arrest (from police bodycam)," https://www.famous-trials.com/george-floyd/12671-transcript-of-floyd-s-arrest-from-police-video-cam.

12. "Three Former Minneapolis Police Officers Convicted of Federal Civil Rights Violations for Death of George Floyd," Office of Public Affairs, US Justice Department, February 24, 2022, https://www.justice.gov/opa/pr/three-former-minneapolis-police-officers-convicted-federal-civil-rights-violations-death.

13. "'I Can't Breath!': Video Of Fatal Arrest Shows Minneapolis Officer Kneeling On George Floyd's Neck For Several Minutes," CBS News, May 26, 2020, https://www.cbsnews.com/minnesota/news/george-floyd-man-dies-after-being-arrested-by-minneapolis-police-fbi-called-to-investigate/.

14. "Autopsy report—George Floyd," https://www.hennepin.us/media/hennepinus/residents/public-safety/medical-examiner/floyd-autopsy-6-3-20.pdf.

15. "What Caused Floyd's Death?" https://www.famous-trials.com/george-floyd/2717-what-caused-george-floyd-s-death-q-a.

16. D. Andone and A. Cooper, "Heart disease, fentanyl contributed to George Floyd's death but were not main cause, medical examiner says," CNN, April 9, 2021, https://www.cnn.com/2021/04/09/us/derek-chauvin-trial-george-floyd-day-10/index.html.

17. R. Ramirez and F. Cineas, "The controversial autopsy at the heart of the Chauvin trial, explained," April 9 2021, https://www.vox.com/22373351/george-floyd-autopsy-medical-examiner-report.

18. J. Griffith, "Medical examiner who ruled George Floyd's death a homicide blames police pressure for his death," NBC News, April 9, 2021, https://www.nbcnews.com/news/us-news/medical-examiner-who-ruled-george-floyd-s-death-homicide-blames-n1263670.

19. E. Mee, "Who was George Floyd? The 'gentle giant' who was trying to turn his life around," Sky News, June 7, 2020, https://news.sky.com/story/who-was-george-floyd-the-gentle-giant-who-loved-his-hugs-11997206.

20. A. Geller, LA. Henao, N. Merchant, and J. Lozano, "For George Floyd, a complicated life and consequential death," AP News, April 20, 2021, https://apnews.com/article/george-floyd-profile-66163bbd94239afa16d706bd6479c613.

21. R. Shaw, "George Floyd's former teammate wants him remembered as more than a news story," May 30, 2020, https://www.kwtx.com/content/news/George-Floyds-former-teammate-wants-him-remembered-as-more-than-a-news-story-570889511.html.

22. "George Floyd Obituary," Buie's Funeral Home, https://www.buiesfuneralhome.com/obituary/George-FloydJr.

23. J. Walters, "The life of George Floyd: 'He knew how to make people feel better,'" *The Guardian*, April 20, 2021, https://www.theguardian.com/us-news/2021/1pr/20/george-floyd-life-biography.

24. A. Florido, "Half of the Jury in the Chauvin Trial Is Nonwhite. That's Only Part of the Story," National Public Radio, March 25, 2021, https://www.npr.org/2021/03/25/980646634/half-of-the-jury-in-the-chauvin-trial-is-non-white-thats-only-part-of-the-story.

25. C. Bunn, "Report: Black people are still killed by police at a higher rate than other groups," NBC News, March 3, 2022, https://www.nbcnews.com/news/nbcblk/report-black-people-are-still-killed-higher-rate-groups-rcna117169.

26. "LAPD officers beat Rodney King on camera," History, https://www.history.com/this-day-in-history/police-brutality-caught-on-camera.

27. "Eric Garner dies in NYPD chokehold," History, https://www.history.com/this-day-in-history/eric-garner-dies-nypd-chokehold.
28. "Michael Brown is killed by a police officer in Ferguson, Missouri," History, https://www.history.com/this-day-in-history/michael-brown-killed-by-police-ferguson-mo.
29. "Breonna Taylor is killed by police in botched raid," History, https://history.com/this-day-in-history/breonna-taylor-is-killed-by-police.
30. S. Levin, "'It never stops': killings by US police reach record high in 2022," *The Guardian*, January 6, 2023, https://www.theguardian.com/us-news/2023/jan/06/us-police-killings-record-number-2022.
31. "Criminal Justice Fact Sheet," NAACP, https://naacp.org/resources/criminal-justice-fact-sheet.
32. F. Edwards, H. Lee, and M. Esposito, "Risk of being killed by police use of force in the United States by age, race—ethnicity, and sex," *PNAS* 116(34): (2019) 16793-16798.
33. "A Comprehensive Analysis of Fatal Police Violence in the United States from 1980 to 2019," National Institute on Minority Health and Health Disparities, National Institutes of Health, https://www.nimhd.nih.gov/news-events/research-spotlights/fatal-police-violence-in-the-us.html.
34. "1,020 People have been shot and killed by police in the past 12 months," the *Washington Post*, July 22, 2023, https://www.washingtonpost.com/graphics/investigations/police-shootings-database/.
35. "Justice Department Finds Civil Rights Violations by the Minneapolis Police Department and the City of Minneapolis," US Justice Department Office of Public Affairs, June 16, 2023, https://www.justice.gov/opa/pr/justice-department-finds-civil-rights-violations-minneapolis-police-department-and-city.

22. *Thomas Mansfield*

1. "Colwyn Bay Waterfront: Fitness for the Community," https://hardscape.co.uk/colwyn-bay-waterfront-fitness/.

2. A. Wells, "Personal trainer died after drinking caffeine powder as strong as 200 cups of coffee," March 2, 2022, https://news.yahoo.com/personal-trainer-dies-caffeine-powder-strong-200-cups-coffee-085823838.html.
3. "Man died after drinking equivalent of hundreds of cups of coffee in caffeine powder," March 3, 2022, https://www.itv.com/news/wales/2022-03-03/man-died-after-drinking-equivalent-of-hundreds-of-cups-of-coffee.
4. M. Mathers, "Personal trainer, 29, died after making caffeine drink equivalent to 200 cups of coffee," the *Independent*, March 2, 2022, https://www.independent.co.uk/news/uk/home-news/personal-trainer-dead-caffeine-drink-b2026650.html.
5. H. Evans and N. Shaw, "Trainer died after accidentally drinking caffeine equivalent to 200 coffees," Wales Online, March 1, 2022, https://www.walesonline.co.uk/news/uk-news/trainer-died-after-accidentally-drinking-23250953.
6. R. Lea, "'Health Man Dies after Mistakenly Drinking Equivalent of 100s of Coffees," *Newsweek*, March 2, 2022, https://www.newsweek.com/healthy-man-dies-mistakenly-drinking-equivalent-100s-coffees-thomas-anthony-mansfield-1684163.
7. K. Isgin, "Dad died after accidentally drinking equivalent of hundreds of cups of coffee at once," the *Manchester Evening News*, March 1, 2022, https://www.manchestereveningnews.co.uk/news-uk-news/dad-died-after-accidentally-drinking-23252639.
8. A. Nicholson and R. Fahey, "Heartbroken widow's 'world ripped apart' by dad's tragic caffeine overdose death," *The Mirror*, March 3, 2022, https://www.mirror.co.uk/news/uk-news/heartbroken-widows-world-ripped-apart-26373713.
9. S. Cappelletti, D. Piacentino, V. Fineschi, P. Frati, et al., "Caffeine-Related Deaths: Manner of Deaths and Categories at Risk," *Nutrients* 19(5): (2018) 611.
10. A.W. Jones, "Review of Caffeine-Related Fatalities along with Postmortem Blood Concentrations in 51 Poisoning Deaths," *J Anal Toxicol* 41(3): (2017) 167-172.

11. S. Sorscher, "Caffeine That Kills," https://www.citizen.org/news/caffeine-that-kills/.
12. R. Kennedy, "Northumbria University fined £400,000 after botched experiment leaves students fighting for life," the *Chronicle*, January 25, 2017, https://www.chroniclelive.co.uk/news/north-east-news/students-left-fighting-life-after-12506326.
13. A. Murray and J. Traylor, "Caffeine Toxicity," August 14, 2022, https://www.ncbi.nlm.nih.gov/books/NBK532910/.
14. P. Banerjee, Z. Ali, B. Levine, and D.R. Fowler, "Fatal caffeine intoxication: a series of eight cases from 1999 to 2009," *J Forensic Sci* 59(3): (2014) 865-868.
15. K. Hobson, "Caffeine Gives Athletes an Edge, But Don't Overdo It," National Public Radio, August 1, 2014, https://www.npr.org/sections/health-shots/2014/08/01/336889286/caffeine-gives-athletes-an-edge-but-dont-overdo-it.
16. T. Haelle, "What's The Likelihood of Dying from Too Much Caffeine?" *Forbes*, May 16, 2017, https://www.forbes.com/sites/tarahaelle/2017/05/16/how-likely-is-it-to-die-from-too-much-caffeine-anyway?sh=63312a524ad5.
17. "Pure and Highly Concentrated Caffeine," US Food and Drug Administration, https://www.fda.gov/food/dietary-supplement-ingredient-directory/pure-and-highly-concentrated-caffeine.
18. C. Sticklen, "Cardiologist warns about caffeine overdose after Illini basketball player's comments," March 3, 2023, https://www.wcia.com/news/cardiologist-warns-about-caffeine-overdose-after-illini-basketball-players-comments/.
19. G. Houston, "Death by Caffeine Overdose Isn't as Uncommon as you'd Think," *Vice*, May 17, 2017, https://www.vice.com/en/article/mgm4wa/death-by-caffeine-overdose-isnt-as-uncommon-as-youd-think.
20. A. Fernández, "South Carolina Teen Dies After Drinking Latte, Mountain Dew and an Energy Drink Within Two Hours," *People*, May 15, 2017, https://www.people.com/human-interest/teen-dies-excessive-caffeine/.

21. T. Lauletta and G. Landsverk, "A college basketball player drank 6 Monster energy drinks while chasing 'caffeine-induced euphoria.' A dietitian explains why that's a bad idea," the *Insider*, March 2, 2023, https://www.insider.com/matthew-mayer-he-suffered-caffeine-poisoning-after-drinking-6-monsters-2023-3.
22. "British man dies of caffeine overdose: report," the *New York Post*, October 29, 2010, https://nypost.com/2010/10/29/british-man-dies-of-caffeine-overdose-report/.
23. I. Horswill, "Eighteen year old Logan Stiner dies from taking too much caffeine powder," July 1, 2014, https://www.news.com.au/lifestyle/health/eighteenyearold-logan-stiner-dies-from-taking-too-much-caffeine-powder/news-story/ee98547d0d284904264d8c108be8fb97.
24. N. Chrysanthos, "'A teaspoon will kill you': Grieving father warns of caffeine powder," the *Sydney Morning Herald*, July 9, 2019, https://www.smh.com.au/national/nsw/a-teaspoon-will-kill-you-grieving-father-warns-of-caffeine-powder-20190709-p525oy.html.
25. S. Molloy, "Man's freak death from caffeine toxicity sparks urgent warning from his devastated family," the *New Zealand Herald*, July 7, 2019, https://www.nzherald.co.nz/lifestyle/mans-freak-death-from-caffeine-toxicity-sparks-urgent-warning-from-his-devastated-family/J7GHXYWMIK2REVHJQYUY4JDC3A/.
26. K.A. Uniss, "Amazon Off the hook for Ohio Teen's Caffeine Overdose Death," *Courthouse News*, October 1, 2020, https://www.courthousenews.com/amazon-off-the-hook-for-ohio-teens-caffeine-overdose-death/.

23. Lori McClintock

1. S. Young, "Congressman's Wife Died after Taking Herbal Remedy Marketed for Diabetes and Weight Loss," August 24, 2021, https://kffhealthnews.org/news/article/tom-mcclintock-death-herbal-remedy-diabetes-weight-loss-white-mulberry/.

2. J. Smith and T. Brown, "Killed by herbal remedy: California Rep Tom McClintock's realtor wife Lori, 61, died after taking Chinese herbal weight loss treatment white mulberry leaf, autopsy finds," the *Daily Mail*, original published date August 25, 2022, last updated August 29, 2022, https://www.dailymail.co.uk/news/article-11144735/California-Rep-Tom-McClintocks-realtor-wife-Lori-died-taking-herbal-weight-loss-treatment.html.

3. S. Young, "Experts question the role of white mulberry in the death of congressman's wife," CBS News, September 14, 2022, https://www.cbsnews.com/news/experts-question-white-mulberry-death-of-lori-mcclintock-congressmans-wife/.

4. "Obituary—Lori McClintock, wife of Congressman Tom McClintock," Congressman Tom McClintock's Facebook page, December 31, 2021.

5. "Autopsy report—Lori McClintock," https://www.documentcloud.org/documents/22267120-lorinmcclintockrecords.

6. "The BUN: Creatinine ratio: Understanding Biomarkers of Hydration and Kidney Function," https://ddrinkmagnak.com/the-bun-creatinine-ratio-understanding-biomarkers-of-hydration-and-kidney-function/.

7. "Tom McClintock," C-SPAN, https://www.c-span.org/person/?30359/TomMcClintock.

8. "Lori McClintock," https://www.linkedin.com/in/lori-mcclintock-0630271b7/.

9. "Is White Mulberry Poisonous?" https://www.poison.org/articles/is-white-mulberry-poisonous.

10. D. Blum, "What to Know about White Mulberry Leaf," *The New York Times*, original published date August 26, 2022, last updated August 27, 2022, https://www.nytimes.com/2022/08/26/well/live/white-mulberry-leaf.html.

11. T. Thaipitakwong, S. Numhom, and P. Aramwit, "Mulberry leaves and their potential effects against cardiometabolic risks: a review of chemical compositions, biological properties and clinical efficacy," *Pharm Biol* 56(1): (2018) 109-118.

12. "Dietary Supplements," US Food and Drug Administration, https://www.fda.gov/food/dietary-supplements.
13. "Information for Consumers on Using Dietary Supplements," US Food and Drug Administration, https://www.fda.gov/food/dietary-supplements/information-consumers-using-dietary-supplements.
14. "Dehydration," the Mayo Clinic, https://www.mayoclinic.org/diseases-conditions/dehydration/symptoms-causes/syc-20354086.
15. T. Boniel and P. Dannon, "The safety of herbal medicines in the psychiatric practice," *Harefuah* 140(8): (2001) 780-783.
16. S. Luke, O. Fleming and R. Stickney, "Woman Dies after Turmeric IV: County Medical Examiner," NBC San Diego, original published date March 22, 2017, last updated April 6, 2017, https://www.nbcsandiego.com/news/local/woman-dies-after-turmeric-iv/36378/.
17. R. Bhattacharjee, "Woman Dies after Drinking Herbal Tea from SF Chinatown Store," NBC Bay Area, original published date March 20, 2017, last updated March 23, 2017, https://www.nbcbayarea.com/news/local/two-people-poisoned-after-drinking-herbal-tea-from-chinatown-store-in-san-francisco/47130/.
18. "FDA investigates two serious adverse events associated with ImprimisRx's compounded curcumin emulsion product for injection," US Food and Drug Administration, August 4, 2017, https://www.fda.gov/drugs/human-drug-compounding/fda-investigates-two-serious-adverse-events-associated-imprimisrxs-compounded-curcumin-emulsion.
19. "Dietary Supplements Market Size, Share & Covid-19 Impact Analysis, By Type (Vitamins, Minerals, Enzymes, Fatty Acids, Proteins, and Others), Form (Tablets, Capsules, Liquids, and Powders), and Regional Forecasts, 2021-2028," *Fortune Business Insights*, https://www.fortunebusinessinsights.com/dietary-supplements-market-102082.
20. S. Putka, "Here's What's Known about White Mulberry," original published date August 25, 2022, last updated August 26, 2022, https://www.medpagetoday.com/special-reports/features/100398.

24. Mary Jane Thomas

1. A. Haneline, "Hank Williams Jr.'s wife, Mary Jane Thomas, died after cosmetic surgery, autopsy reveals," *USA Today*, original published date July 26, 2022, updated July 28, 2022, https://www.usatoday.com/story/entertainment/celebrities/2022/07/26/hank-williams-jr-wife-mary-jane-thomas-cause-death/10152209002/.
2. R. DeSantis and C. White, "Hank Williams Jr.'s Wife Mary Jane Thomas' Cause of Death Confirmed by Coroner 4 Months after Death," *People*, July 25, 2022, https://www.people.com/country/hank-williams-jr-s-wife-mary-jane-thomas-cause-of-death-revealed/.
3. "Mary Jane Thomas, wife of Hank Williams Jr., died of collapsed lung after cosmetic surgery, autopsy reveals," WPTV, https://www.wptv.com/entertainment/mary-jane-thomas-wife-of-hank-williams-jr-died-of-collapsed-lung-after-cosmetic-surgery-autopsy-reveals.
4. "Dr. Harold Bafitis," https://www.drbafitis.com/.
5. Kavi, "How did Mary Jane Thomas die? Hank Williams Jr.'s wife cause of death," July 27, 2022, https://medicotopics.com/how-did-mary-jane-thomas-die-hank-williams-jr-s-wife-cause-of-death/.
6. D. Avila and S. Michaud, "Hank Williams Jr.'s wife Mary Jane Thomas has died: 'A Beautiful Soul,'" *People*, March 23, 2022, https://people.com/hank-williams-jr-wife-mary-jane-dead/.
7. J. Taylor, "Who is Mary Jane Thomas, Third Wife of Hank Williams?" https://entrepreneurmindz.com/mary-jane-thomas-hank-williams-third-wife/.
8. "Autopsy report—Mary Jane Thomas," https://www.wptv.com/entertainment/mary-jane-thomas-wife-of-hank-williams-jr-died-of-collapsed-lung-after-cosmetic-surgery-autopsy-reveals.
9. R.J. Rohrich, I.L. Savetsky and Y.J. Avashia, "Assessing Cosmetic Surgery Safety: The Evolving Data," *Plast Reconstr Surg Glob Open* 8(5): (2020) e2643.

10. D.N. Flynn, J. Eskildsen, J.L. Levene, J.D. Allan, et al., "Pneumothorax Following Breast Surgery at an Ambulatory Surgery Center," *Cureus* 14(5): (2022) e24924.
11. J.M. Osborn and T.R. Stevenson, "Pneumothorax as a complication of breast augmentation," *Plast Reconstr Surg* 116(4): (2005) 1122-1126.
12. J.A. Mentz, H.A. Mentz, and S. Nemir, "Pneumothorax as a Complication of Liposuction," *Anesthetic Surg J* 40(7): (2020) 753-758.
13. J. Tran, W. Haussner, and K. Shah, "Traumatic Pneumothorax: A Review of Current Diagnostic Practices and Evolving Management," *J Emerg Med* 61(5): (2021) 517-528.
14. A. Patty, "The Cosmetic Institute: lung punctured during routine cosmetic surgery," the *Sydney Morning Herald*, original published date September 29, 2015, last updated September 30, 2015, https://www.smh.com.au/national/nsw/the-cosmetic-institute-lung-punctured-during-routine-cosmetic-surgery-20150929-gjx02h.html.
15. A.A. Taha and H. Tahseen, "Pneumothorax with Liposuction: Spreading Awareness," *Plast Reconstr Surg Glob Open* 8(3): (2020) e2711.
16. P. Varma, J. Kiely and A.V. Giblin, "Cosmetic tourism during the COVID-19 pandemic: Dealing with the aftermath," *J Plast Reconstr Aesthet Surg* 75(1): (2022) 506-508.
17. M. Krumholtz and N. Ciriaco, "Dying for a new body: why so many deaths from plastic surgery tourism?" *The Guardian*, August 23, 3029, https://www.theguardian.com/society/2019/aug/23/americans-plastic-surgery-dominican-republic.
18. L. Norris, "Canadian actor 'dies from complications' after spending $220,000 on surgery to look like BTS star," https://metro.co/uk/2023/04/25/canadian-actor-dies-from-surgery-complications-to-look-like-bts-star-18667550/.

19. "Chinese web celebrity, 33, dies of serious infection after cosmetic surgery," the *Global Times*, July 15, 2021, https://www.globaltimes.cn/page/202107/1228782.shtml.
20. B. Zilio, "Actor allegedly dies after undergoing 12 surgeries to look like BTS singer Jimin," April 24, 2023, https://pagesix.com/2023/04/24/actor-dies-after-undergoing-12-surgeries-to-look-like-bts-singer-jimin/.
21. J. Biggs, "Christina Ashten Gourkani: Kim Kardashian lookalike dies after undergoing plastic surgery," *Cosmopolitan*, April 27, 2023, https://www.cosmopolitan.com/uk/body/a43719599/christina-ashten-gourkani-dead/.
22. S. Dance, "After death, Maryland to limit where cosmetic surgeries are performed," the *Baltimore Sun*, April 27, 2013, https://www.baltimoresun.com/health/bs-xpm-2013-04-27-bs-hs-edspa-regulation-20130427-story.html.

25. Angela Craig

1. E. James, "'Killer' Colorado dentist 'believed he was too smart to be caught,' psychologist sys – and 'wife' he poisoned to death' was 'in denial' after first time he drugged her," the *Daily Mail*, March 21, 2023, https://www.dailymail.co.uk/news/article-11886969/Killer-Colorado-dentist-believed-smart-caught-psychologist-says.html-three.
2. C. McKinley, "Toxicology results coming soon in death of Colorado dentist's wife," *Gazette*, April 8, 2023, https://gazette.com/news/crime/toxicology-results-coming-soon-in-death-of-colorado-dentists-wife/article_33fc54c5-33ca-5937-97be-34e7744ff127.html.
3. A. Gionet, "Arrest report: Investigators gather evidence they say points to dentist James Craig planning to kill his wife," CBS News, March 21, 2023, https://www.cbsnews.com/colorado/news/aurora-denetist-james-angela-craig-poison-potassium-cyanide-death-murder-investigation/.

4. J. Oravetz, "Wife of Aurora dentist had lethal dose of cyanide, Visine ingredient in her system, autopsy shows," 9News, July 12, 2023, https://www.9news.com/article/news/crime/angela-craig-autopsy-aurora-colorado-dentist-case/73-fd9f30da-4126-4805-9ca0-d7e22cc92d28.
5. C. McKinley, "Wife of Aurora dentist died of cyanide and chemical found in Visine," the *Denver Gazette*, original published date July 12, 2023, last updated July 13, 2023, https://denvergazette.com/news/crime/james-craig-dentist-aurora-arapahoe-county-mark-pray-murder-trial/article_26c37bcc-20e0-11ee-91f9-6fbc64505af6.html.
6. S. Butzer, "Affidavit: Aurora dentist researched 'undetectable poisons,' purchased arsenic and cyanide before wife's death," original published date March 20, 2023, last updated March 27, 2023, https://www.denver7.com/news/local-news/affidavit-aurora-dentist-researched-undetectable-poisons-purchased-arsenic-and-cyanide-before-wifes-death.
7. "Affidavit of Probable Cause for Arrest Warrant," Aurora Police Department, https://www.documentcloud.org/documents/23718101-23cr664-craig-james-toliver_redacted.
8. S. Bradbury, "Aurora dentist's wife fatally poisoned with cyanide and decongestant found in Visine, coroner testifies," the *Denver Post*, July 12, 2023, https://www.denverpost.com/2023/07/12/james-craig-dentist-poison-wife-murder-case-preliminary-hearing/.
9. "The Murder of Angela Craig" podcast, April 5, 2023, https://www.youtube.com/watch?v=-4kKtlGTg9c.
10. "Angela Dawn Pray Craig Obituary," https://www.horancares.com/obituaries/AngelaDawnPray-Craig.
11. H. Kelly, "Who was Colorado dentist James Craig's wife Angela and how many children did they have?" the *Daily Mail*, March 23, 2023, https://www.dailymail.co.uk/news/article-11895139/Who-Colorado-dentist-James-Craigs-wife-Angela-children-did-have.html.

12. "Prosecutors set to present evidence against Colorado dentist accused of poisoning his wife's shakes," Associated Press, July 12, 2023, https://kdvr.com/news/local/prosecutors-set-to-present-evidence-against-colorado-dentist-accused-of-poisoning-his-wifes-shakes/.
13. E. Shapiro and I. Pereira, "Woman who dated the dentist who was accused of killing his wife speaks out," ABC News, July 12, 2023, https://abcnews.go.com/US/wooman-dated-dentist-accused-killing-wife-speaks/story?id=101164137.
14. M.L. Simpson, "Dentist James Craig, Accused of Poisoning Wife, Googled 'How to Make Murder Look Like a Heart Attack': Cops," *People*, July 13, 2023, https://people.com/dentist-accused-of-poisoning-wife-googled-how-to-make-murder-look-like-a-heart-attack-7560574.
15. "Chilling details emerge about how Colorado dentist allegedly killed his wife with poison: 'I feel drugged,'" CBS News, March 21, 2023, https://www.cbsnews.com/news/james-craig-killed-wife-poison-protein-shakes-arsenic-cyanide-court-documents/.
16. R. Razek and A. Babineau, "Colorado dentist accused of poisoning his wife with arsenic pleads not guilty," CNN, October 10, 2023, https://www.cnn.com/2023/10/09/us/colorado-dentist-wife-poisoning-plea/index.html.
17. K. Steck-Flynn, "Just a Pinch of Cyanide: The Basics of Homicidal Poisoning Investigations," *Law Enforcement Technology* 34(10): (2007) 117, 120, 126.
18. J. Emsley, "The Five Top Poisons," PBS, April 25, 2023, https://www.pbs.org/wnet/secrets/executed-in-error-the-five-top-poisons/7200/.
19. A. Rasmussen, "'Black Widow' Judy Buenoano Convicted of Murdering Her Son, Husband with Arsenic," https://www.investigationdiscovery.com/crimefeed/serial-killer/black-widow-judias-buenoano-convicted-of-murdering-her-son-husband-with-arsenic.

20. "Buenoano v. Singletary," United States Court of Appeals, Eleventh Circuit, January 25, 1996, https://casetext.com/case/buenoano-v-singletary-2.
21. K. Morrissey, "Marine wife wrongfully convicted of poisoning husband, partying," the *San Diego Union-Tribune*, May 13, 2016, https://www.sandiegouniontribune.com/news/data-watch/sdut-exoneree-sommer-2016may13-htmlstory.html.
22. "Marine wife accused of poisoning husband," NBC News, December 15, 2005, https://www.nbcnews.com/id/wbna10479896.
23. S. Denzel, "Cynthia Sommer," The National Registry of Exonerations, original published date June 2002, last updated January 24, 2014, https://www.law.umich.edu/special/exoneration/Pages/casedetail.aspx?caseid=3652k.
24. "The Dr. Robert Ferrante Poison Murder Case," November 8, 2022, https://jimfishertruecrime.blogspot.com/2013/08/did-dr-robert-ferrante-poison-his.html.
25. P. Reed Ward, "Ferrante loses appeal in 2013 poisoning death of his wife," July 1, 2022, https://triblive.com/local/ferrante-loses-appeal-in-2013-poisoning-death-of-his-wife/.
26. "Pittsburgh Husband Charged in Cyanide-Poisoning Death Waives Extradition," ABC News, July 29, 2013, https://abcnews.go.com/US/pittsburgh-husband-charged-cyanide-poisoning-death-waives-extradition/story?id=1979984.
27. J. Sederstrom, "What Unusual Method Did A Respected Medical Researcher Use To Kill His 'Rising Star' Doctor Wife?" Oxygen, April 8, 2021, https://www.oxygen.com/dateline-secrets-uncovered/true-crime-buzz/how-did-robert-ferrante-kill-wife-dr-autumn-klein.
28. "Testimony Centers around Testing of Victim's Blood in Cyanide Poisoning Trial," CBS News, October 29, 214, https://www.cbsnews.com/pittsubrgh/news/testimony-ceneters-around-testing-of-victims-blood-in-cyanide-poisoning-trial/.

29. S. Moaret, A. Prevarin, and F. Tubaro, "Levels of creatine, organic contaminants and heavy metals in creatine dietary supplements," *Food Chemistry* 126: (2011) 1232-1238.
30. C. Gebert, "Thin White Line," https://wronglyconvictedgroup.files.wordpress.com/2015/08/thin-white-line.pdf.
31. "Scientist Trying to Raise New Doubts about Researcher Convicted of Poisoning Wife," CBS News, September 10, 2015, https://www.cbsnews.com/pittsburgh/news/robert-ferrante-new-findings-in-cyanide-case/.
32. M. DePacina, "Thai woman accused of killing 14 with cyanide faces 80 criminal charges," June 30, 2023, https://news.yahoo.com/thai-woman-accused-killing-14-215857230.html.
33. L. Day and S. Vimonsuknopparat, "Thailand's worst suspected serial killer 'Am Cyanide' is accused of luring her victims to a meal and poisoning them," ABC, September 29, 2023, https://www.abc.net.au/news/2023-09-30/am-cyanide-thailand-s-worst-suspected-serial-killer/102869490.
34. L. Casiano, "Florida woman spiked man's drink with cockroach spray after they met at a bar, authorities say," August 18, 2023, https://www.yahoo.com/news/florida-woman-spiked-mans-drink-191158471.html.
35. M. DeVries and N. Jachim, "North Dakota woman accused of fatally poisoning boyfriend over $30 million inheritance," November 1, 2023, https://www.wjtv.com/news/north-dakota-woman-accused-of-fatally-poisoning-boyfriend-over-30-million-inheritance/

26. Conclusions

1. K. Harris, "13 Celebrities Who Have Regrets about Becoming Famous," *Buzz Feed*, May 27, 2021, https://www.buzzfeed.com/kristenharris1/celebrities-who-regret-becoming-famous.
2. G. Byrne, "'Fame is a sweet poison you drink of first in eager gulps. Then you come to loathe it.' Richard Burton's warning to a young

Gabriel Byrne before he fell into vortex of drink and depression," the *Daily Mail*, October 31, 2020, https://www.dailymail.co.uk/news/article-89010309/Richard-Burton-told-Gabriel-Byrne-fame-sweet-poison-fell-drink-depression.html.

Milton Keynes UK
Ingram Content Group UK Ltd.
UKHW022137290424
441966UK00010B/179/J